The City and the Coin in the Ancient and Early Medieval Worlds

Edited by

Fernando López Sánchez

BAR International Series 2402
2012

Published in 2016 by
BAR Publishing, Oxford

BAR International Series 2402

The City and the Coin in the Ancient and Early Medieval Worlds

ISBN 978 1 4073 0997 2

COVER IMAGE
RPC1 172, Obv: AVGVSTVS DIVI F, bare head, r.; Rev: C LAETILIVS APALVS II V Q, diadem (with crescent and lotus above) enclosing REX PTOL. The Trustess of the British Museum.

BAR Publishing is the trading name of British Archaeological Reports (Oxford) Ltd. British Archaeological Reports was first incorporated in 1974 to publish the BAR Series, International and British. In 1992 Hadrian Books Ltd became part of the BAR group. This volume was originally published by Archaeopress in conjunction with British Archaeological Reports (Oxford) Ltd / Hadrian Books Ltd, the Series principal publisher, in 2012. This present volume is published by BAR Publishing, 2016.

Printed in England

BAR
PUBLISHING

BAR titles are available from:

BAR Publishing
122 Banbury Rd, Oxford, OX2 7BP, UK
EMAIL info@barpublishing.com
PHONE +44 (0)1865 310431
FAX +44 (0)1865 316916
www.barpublishing.com

A Felipe, Amparo y Mercedes, mi familia.

"Ya caballeros, dezir vos he la verdad:
Qui en un logar mora siempre, lo suyo puede menguar"
(Cantar de Mio Cid, vv. 947-948)

"Ha! All my knights, unto you the truth will I confess:
Who still in one place tarries, his fortune will grow less."
(The Lay of the Cid, vv.947-948)

Contents

Preface

The City and the Coin in the Ancient and Early Medieval Worlds is a book containing eleven articles, all of which revolve around the relationship between cities and coinage during the extended period beginning in the third century BC and continuing up to the tenth century AD. Cities have tended throughout history to be the preferred location for the minting and circulation of coins and coinage has in turn generally reflected the importance of many of these cities. It is true that there have been more than a few coin series that have not been dependent on a city, but it has on the other hand been unusual for a royal, military or other authority to ignore the importance of cities in their coinage projects. The fairly recent publication on paper of Volumes I (1992), II (1999) and VII (2006) of *RPC* (Roman Provincial Coinage) has since been accompanied by other worthy projects, such as that of the Ashmolean Museum on Roman Provincial Coinage in the Antonine Period (a project based in the Herberden Coin Room of the Ashmolean Museum, University of Oxford, http://rpc.ashmus.ox.ac.uk/project/), as well as numerous publications on local and regional coinage in the ancient, medieval and modern worlds. This book is indeed another addition to the burgeoning study of local and regional currency in recent decades.

It would have been quite impossible for the pages that follow to provide a truly global overview of a phenomenon as wide-ranging as the subject of the city and the coin and the selection, both geographical and temporal, of the topics covered in this book does not aim to be all-inclusive. All of the contributors to this book are linked to universities and museums in France, the UK, Italy and Spain and the choice of the topics to be found in this volume is of course not unconnected to their institutional and geographical affiliations. There has been no attempt to harmonise the subject matter of the eleven articles contained in this book and therefore not only are there studies of classic topics such as the "identity" of cities and their real and mythical origins, but also there are articles that cover topics such as dialogue and cooperation between local, national and international authorities. There is also some exploration of the role of the city in specific coin series, as well as of the role of military mints and garrisons in certain issues. The majority of the papers in this book centre on the Hellenistic world and its Iberian, Punic, and Roman variants, but the Kushan Empire of Central Asia and the Germanic world (Frankish, Anglo-Saxon and Scandinavian) is also covered.

The article by Bartolomé Mora Serrano and Gonzalo Cruz Andreotti *Ethnic, cultural and civic identities in the Ancient Coinage of the Southern Iberian Peninsula (3rd C. BC - 1st C. AD)* provides a modern study of the iconography, epigraphy and manufacturing techniques used for a variety of series in southern Spain. The aim is to throw light on ethnocultural and civic identities in this area, which is why the focus is primarily on the mythical imagery used on the coins of the Far West around the Straits of Gibraltar, following a similar pattern to earlier numismatic work on many coin issues from the Eastern Mediterranean. Another approach to Spain, in some ways similar and in others quite different from that of Mora and Cruz, is demonstrated by Manuel Gozalbes in *Cities, drachmae, denarii and the Roman conquest of Hispania*, in which the author examines coinage produced in roughly the same period as that covered in the preceding section (from the third to the first centuries BC). The coin issues studied by Gozalbes do, however, display a much more homogeneous character than the issues from the south of Spain, as they are all silver coins with similar iconographic types. In this case it is the Levant and the centre of the Iberian Peninsula that are the objects of investigation. The questions Gozalbes asks as regards these coin series, namely "When?", "For whom?", and "How much?" are the ones that any numismatist worth his or her salt will formulate and in the answers that the author attempts to elucidate the reader will find a mixture of prudence and forceful argument. Borja Antela-Bernárdez, meanwhile, in *The Coinage of C. Annius Luscus*, seeks to explore how a series of silver coins minted somewhere in connection with Hispania by two Roman magistrates may constitute a topic for historical discussion in the context of the Sertorian wars (82-73/72 BC). These same close links between literary and monetary information are studied in depth by Toni Ñaco del Hoyo in his article on *Garrisons, coins and war stress (89-63 BCE) in Late Hellenistic towns*. For Ñaco del Hoyo, coinage is the element that allows us to fully understand tactical operations about which the literary sources do not provide complex information, focusing as they do usually on the major military strategies of the period. The method used by this author suggests that coinage does not have to be considered just as an auxiliary instrument in the study of military history and the article shows instead that in-depth study of the numismatic material at our disposal can be just as useful for historical study as epigraphic or literary sources.

C. J. Howgego rightly claims that Greek and Greco-Roman provincial coins "were the most deliberate of all public symbols of communal identities in the Roman provinces" (C. J Howgego, V. Heuchert, A. Burnett eds., *Coinage and identity in the Roman Provinces*, Oxford University Press, 2005, Preface). It is generally considered, on the other hand, that the composition of Roman imperial coin series contained a more significant narrative element than Greek or Greco-Roman provincial series. The coin series of the city of Rome, for example, provide entirely unambiguous evidence of the importance of Agrippina the Younger during the reign of Caligula and particularly during the first months of Nero's reign. In her article *Agrippine la Jeune et la monnaie: de la princesse à la «régente»*, Virginie Girod shows how literary sources concur precisely with numismatic ones as regards the major political events that took place in Rome during the year 55 AD. In accordance with Girod, in *The Coinage of Carthago Nova and the Roman fleet of Missenum: Imperial triumphs and local deductiones* I myself argue in favour of the narrative character of the Roman coin, in this case in reference to some provincial coin issues from Hispania. It is true that the autonomous cities of the Mediterranean each had their own history, but also that the municipalities and Roman colonies mirrored, at the same time and very closely, the political and military developments of the ruling house in Rome. In this sense, the precisely-timed release (every five years) of coinage in the colony of Carthago Nova tells us that the dynasty of the Julii paid particular attention to this city between the years 31 BC and 41 AD and the reason behind this interest seems to have been based on that fact that during this seventy-year period this major port was used continuously by the imperial fleet of Missenum. As in music, where the silences can be just as important as the notes themselves, in Roman narratives it is also necessary to explain the silences. This article therefore argues that the coin series minted in bronze at Carthago Nova were entirely dependent on the city's links with the imperial Julian (and not Claudian) dynasty and its military campaigns in the Spanish Mediterranean and Atlantic. It is also suggested that these coinings did not take place with a view to either the financing of imperial enterprises or the celebration of purely local festivities.

The cities of the Roman Mediterranean did not, of course, exist only in connection with the imperial family and their undertakings.The colonies and municipalities also possessed a rich local life, almost as much as the autonomous cities of the empire. In his *Monuments, myth and small change in Buthrotum (Butrint) during the Early Empire*, Richard Abdy examines the coinage of a Balkan port city which enjoyed excellent maritime links with Italy. The author is concerned with the representations in the coinage of the city of its civic monuments (and above all the aqueduct) and local mythology from the first century AD. Very near Butrint, the Balkan city of Nicopolis also enjoyed excellent connections with Italy. Founded by Octavian in commemoration of the victory over Mark Antony at Actium, Nicopolis, or Actia Nicopolis as it is also known, possesses much wider-ranging coin series than those of Carthago Nova and Butrint. Dario Calomino, who in 2011 published his monograph Nicopolis d'Epiro: nuovi studi sulla produzione monetale zecca in the collection BAR IS (no. 2214), combines in his article *Actia Nicopolis. Coinage, currency and civic identity (27 BC-AD 268)* the largely international perspective of the study of Carthago Nova with the more local viewpoint taken in Abdy's work on Butrint. Actia Nicopolis was a city that enjoyed imperial concessions throughout its history and also acquired *civitas libera* and probably *foederata* status, possessing as it did a pre-eminent political position in the Delphic Amphictiony and a leading ethnocultural role in Epirus. This Balkan city not only lived off local resources such as trade, fishing and agriculture but also for centuries played an important economic and military role in imperial foreign policy. Thus, and as the author rightly notes, "the coinage (of Actia Nicopolis) is still probably the best archaeological evidence of the city's economic and cultural life, spanning from Augustus to Gallien, with a large production of bronze issues and exceptional silver series under the Antonines".

Numismatists normally associate coin mintings with cities and therefore there is a general tendency to equate specific cities with specific coin series, even when there is a lack of firm evidence for this. In Robert Bracey's article, *The mint cities of the Kushan Empire*, an empire which covered large areas of central Asia and northern India, evidence for the mint locations of Kushan coins is explored. This evidence is illustrated by using as examples a number of cities which can be connected to a greater or lesser degree with particular coin issues. In a very different geographical and temporal context, but one in which there are similar issues concerning attribution, the article by Philippe Schiesser, *Les derniers monnayages d'argent de l'antiquité tardive en Gaule du nord: les argentei au type à la Rome assise de moins de 0.9 g*, will be of much interest. The final article in the book, *Towns and minting in northern Europe in the early Middle Ages*, written by Gareth Williams, considers links between towns and minting in northern Europe in the period from the fifth to the eleventh centuries AD. The Frankish kingdom(s) which succeeded directly to the later Roman Empire, Anglo-Saxon England and Scandinavia are analysed by the author. In all three cases, the association between coins and towns appears to relate in part to the economic role of towns as centres of production and exchange, and in part to the role of towns as local/regional centres for royal authority and administration.

Every historian keen to investigate new and relatively unexplored fields knows that numismatics is one of the disciplines most likely to bear fruit in the future. This book is the product of numismatists and historians who view currency as historical documentation and it is aimed too at numismatists and historians who are interested in the use of coinage in historical discourse. I should like to thank all of these individuals for their work and their patience during the preparation of this volume, and above all to thank Toni Ñaco del Hoyo as the source of the initial encouragement that was behind the creation of this book. The efforts of Mark Temple, Teresa Erice and Denny Collie have also played a key role - their in-depth knowledge of the English language has been invaluable in the editing process. Guilhem Pépin has been also of great help concerning the analysis of the two articles written in French. The layout of the book, on the other hand, is the work of Ana I. Navajas Jiménez, and it is to her that I owe most in the making of this book, as she also worked with me in the final stages. The responsibility for any error that still remains in the pages that follow is, however, solely mine.

Oxford, 3 July 2012

List of Contributors

Bartolomé Mora Serrano (barmora@uma.es) is Associate Professor of Archaeology at the University of Málaga. He is a specialist on the Spanish southern Ulterior-Baetica region and he is particularly interested in the Spanish historiography on Archaeology and Numismatics of the 18th and 19th centuries. He is also interested in the circulation and collection of coins in ancient and modern times He has collaborated in the making of the *Tabula Imperii Romani* in Spain and is author, among other books and publications, of *Las monedas de Malaca* (with M. Campo) Madrid, 1995; *Historia de la provincia de Málaga. De la Roma Republicana a la Antigüedad Tardía* (with P. Corrales) Málaga, 2005; *Producción y comercio en los territorios malacitanos durante la Antigüedad. Garum, aceite y vino*, Catálogo de la exposición, (with P. Corrales Aguilar, L.E. Fernández Rodríguez, C. Peral Bejarano and E. Serrano Ramos) Málaga, 2007 and T*erritorios marítimos, comunicaciones, espacios naturales y humanos en la Bética costera*, Mainake 30, Málaga, 2008.

Gonzalo Cruz Andreotti (gca6655@gmail.com) is an Associate Professor at the University of Málaga since 1995. He is a specialist on the Ancient History and the Modern Historiography of Southern Spain, a subject covered in his PhD (1990). He has continued his researches in different Universities in Spain (Universidad del País Vasco) and Italy (Tor Vergata-Roma II, Perugia) and he currently works on the views of Ancient authors regarding the geography of the Iberian Peninsula. He is author of *Estrabón, Geografía de Iberia* (with M.V. García Quintela and F.J. Gómez Espelosín), Madrid, 2007. He has also edited many different books, such as I*dentidades étnicas - identidades políticas en el mundo prerromano hispano*, Málaga, 2004 and *La invención de una geografía de la Península Ibérica. II. La época imperial* (with P. Le Roux and P. Moret), Málaga-Madrid, 2007.

Manuel Gozalbes Fernández de Palencia (manuel.gozalbes@dival.es) is Curator of Coins in the Museu de Prehistória de València. He began his work at the Museum in 2000. He is responsible for the new room of Money History opened to the public in 2009 and he is the author of its catalogue. His research interest is focused on Pre-Augustean coinages of the Iberian Peninsula (hacksilber, hoards, circulation, religion, economics, metallographical analysis), and also on Roman Numismatics (hoards, coin use, archaeological contexts). He is the author of *Los Hallazgos monetarios del Grau Vell - Sagunt, Valencia*, 1999 and of *La ceca de Turiazu*. Monedas celtibéricas en la Hispania republicana, Valencia, 2010. He is editor of *Romanos y visigodos en tierras valencianas* (with H. Bonet and R. Albiach), Valencia, 2003.

Borja Antela-Bernárdez (borja.antela@uab.cat) is a Full Lecturer in Ancient History at the Universitat Autònoma de Barcelona (UAB). He has focused his research mainly on different approaches to Alexander the Great. His PhD thesis (Universidade de Santiago de Compostela), titled *Alexandre Magno e Atenas*, was published in 2005, Santiago de Compostela. He is also interested in the period of the Late Roman Republic and the impact of Roman Imperialism on a large scale within the Mediterranean Sea from East to West and especially on the links between the Ist Mithridatic War and the Sertorian Wars. He has been a *Member of the Waterloo Institute and the Society for the Exploration of Eurasia* since 2005 and he actively takes part in many national and international research projects and institutions. He is editor of *Transforming Historical Landscapes in the Ancient Empires* (with T. Ñaco), Oxford, 2009; *La Guerra en la Antigüedad desde el presente* (with J. Vidal), Zaragoza, 2011 and *La Polis en Crisis* (with J. Pascual and D. Gómez), forthcoming.

Virginie Girod (vgirod@hotmail.fr) is an historian and numismatist. She is a specialist on the history and coins of Women during the Roman Empire, particularly at the time of the Julians and the Flavians. She is interested in the power aristocratic and imperial women had inside and outside the court. She has also studied the impact of these times on the essential femininity of women. Her PhD *L'érotisme féminin à Rome dans le Latium et en Campanie sous les Julio-Claudiens et les Flaviens : recherches d'histoire sociale*, was defended at Paris on the 4th of November 2011 before Michel Amandry, Danielle Gourevitch, Yann Le Bohec, Philippe Moreau and Gilles Sauron and her research deservedly achieved wide attention in the French academic milieu. She is author of several articles on Roman women and Roman numismatics in different French journals.

Toni Ñaco del Hoyo (toni.naco@icrea.cat) is an ICREA Research Professor (Catalan Institute for Research and Advanced Studies) at the Universitat Autònoma de Barcelona. He is a specialist in Roman Republican history (PhD 1996, UAB), working on Republican finances, warfare and post-war strategies. He is a former Fulbright Scholar (UC Berkeley, 2004), having held several postdoctoral fellowships (1998-2002) at Oxford University (Wolfson College), where he remains a member of the Common Room. In 2004 he returned to UAB in order to hold a five year Ramón y Cajal Research Fellowship until September 2009, when he joined ICREA. After being awarded a research grant by the Harry Frank Guggenheim Foundation (NY) on the collateral damage during the Mithridatic Wars (2007), he is currently Principal Investigator of two research projects: 1) the political management of humanitarian crises in classical antiquity-project funded by the Spanish government; 2) The 'empire by invitation' as a political tool in ancient peace building-project funded by the Catalan International Institute for Peace.

Fernando López Sánchez (flopezsanchez@hotmail.com) holds a five year Ramón y Cajal Research Fellowship at the University Jaume I (Castellón, Spain) and he is also a member of the Common Room of Wolfson College (Oxford). Since the conclusion of his university studies at the University of Zaragoza in 1997, historical numismatics has remained at the forefront of his research. He is especially interested in the role that coinage played in Ancient times, particularly coinage associated with allied troops belonging to the Roman army. Since 2006 he has collaborated in different projects within the Cabinet of Coins and Medals of the British Museum, all related to Late Roman and Early Medieval numismatics. He has published *Coin Hoards from Roman Britain XIII* (with Richard Abdy and E. Besly) (eds.), Wetteren, 2010. He is also preparing *Le Chrisme et le Phenix: l'iconographie monétaire, entre paganisme et christianisme sous la dynastie constantinienne* (with Dominique Hollard).

Richard Abdy (RABDY@thebritishmuseum.ac.uk) is Curator of Roman Coins and Coinage of the Roman Empire in the Department of Coins and Medals of the British Museum. He covers the middle imperial period of the second century AD through to Late Antiquity (late Roman and early Byzantine as well as the emerging 'barbarian' kingdoms). He is also responsible for the recording and reporting of the many Roman coin hoards discovered in England and Wales under the Treasure Act (1996). He is interested in the world of the Roman Emperors in general and is particularly concerned with the way such information can be gathered from Roman coins and medals. He has published, among other books, *Coin Hoards from Roman Britain XIII* (with E. Besly, and F. Lopez-Sanchez) (eds.), Wetteren, 2010; *Coin Hoards from Roman Britain XII*, (with E. Ghey, C. Hughes and I. Leins) (eds.), Wetteren, 2009 and *Romano-British Coin Hoards* , Princes Risborough, 2002. He is currently creating a new, updated and revised edition of Roman Imperial Coinage (RIC) vol. II.2, which will cover coinage minted for the Emperor Hadrian. He has given post-excavation numismatic support to the work of the Butrint Foundation.

Dario Calomino (dcalomino@thebritishmuseum.ac.uk) is currently a Researcher in the Department of Coins and Medals of the British Museum, holding a two-year Newton International Fellowship (2012-2014) on the Roman Provincial Coinage (*RPC*) VI project (from Elagabalus to Maximinus Thrax). He previously studied and worked in Italy. He obtained a BA/MA and a Post Lauream Specialisation Degree in Classical Archaeology at Padua University and a PhD in Ancient History at Verona University; he worked in the Numismatic Departments of Civic and State Museums in Verona, Venice, Piacenza, Brescia, Rovereto (TN) and he currently collaborates with the Museo Nazionale Romano in Rome. His main fields of research in Numismatics are Coin Finds of Roman Age in Italy (Veneto, Trentino and Basilicata) and Roman Provincial Coinage, especially in Greece and the East. With specific regard to this topic he published articles and a book about the coinage of Nicopolis in Epirus (*Nicopolis d'Epiro. Nuovi studi sulla zecca e sulla produzione monetale*, BAR S 2214, Oxford, 2011) and he is currently publishing the first of a series of volumes on the collection of Roman Provincial coins at the Medagliere del Museo Nazionale Romano in the monographs of the *Bollettino di Numismatica.*

Robert Bracey (rbracey@thebritishmuseum.ac.uk) is Project curator of Kushan coins and Ancients coins of South and Central Asia in the Department of Coins and Medals of the British Museum. He is currently engaged in the Kushan coins project and the production of a new catalogue of the coins of the Kushan dynasty, the principle dynasty of Northwest India in the first to third centuries AD. Beyond political history and coins this period involves major social changes and the movement of ideas: Greek art, literature and language penetration into India; Buddhism reaching China; the development of Sanskrit as a national language; and a transformation in the role of women in Indian Society. He is also Secretary of the Royal Numismatic Society and Assistant Editor of the Journal Numismatic Society.

Philippe Schiesser (numismate@yahoo.fr) is a prolific Researcher on Early Medieval French Numismatics. He has been president of the Société d'Etudes Numismatiques et Archéologiques (SÉNA) and he is member of the Société Française de Numismatique (SFN). He is particularly interested in the Coinage of the Merovingians and the Carolingians and especially on the *denarii* and the oboles bracteates of the VIII century AD. His main publications on this subject are *Oboles mérovingiennes, Revue Numismatique* 2007, pp. 283-313 and Pl. LXII-LXIII (with M. Dhénin) and *Les oboles unifaces de Charlemagne de Melle*, Numismatique et Archéologie en Poitou-Charentes, actes du colloque de Niort, 7-8 décembre 2007, Musée Bernard d'Agesci, Recherches et travaux de la Société d'Études Numismatiques et Archéologiques n°2, 2009, pp. 49-62 and pl. VI.

Gareth Williams (gwilliams@thebritishmuseum.ac.uk) is Curator of Early Medieval Coinage and Coinage of Early Medieval Britain and Europe in the Department of Coins and Medals of the British Museum. He has been a curator at the Museum since 1996, with responsibility for British and European coinage, c. AD 500 to c.1180. Within this area, he specialises in Anglo-Saxon and Viking coinage. Much of his work focuses on the use of coinage as evidence within broader historical and archaeological studies. He is the author, among other books and publications, of *Early Anglo-Saxon Coins*, Oxford, 2008). He has also edited *Sagas, Saints and Settlements* (with P. Bibire), Leiden, 2004, and *Coinage and History in the North*

Sea World, c. 500-1250 (with B. Cook), Leiden, 2006.

Ethnic, cultural and civic identities in Ancient Coinage of the Southern Iberian Peninsula (3rd C. BC – 1st C. AD)

Bartolomé Mora Serrano
Gonzalo Cruz Andreotti*

ABSTRACT

Behind the complex systematisation of the coinage from Ulterior lie relevant contributions to the ethnocultural mapping of the region. This paper explores the possibility, as in the case of Phoenician-Punic coinage, of using numismatic evidence from Turdetani, Turduli, Oretanos, and Bastetano cities to identify distinct cultural realities – enhanced or not by Roman presence in the region. It further questions whether these realities correspond with maps based on previous studies on place names, archaeological remains and ancient geographical references.

One of the most important, and hence one of the most exploited aspects in Ancient coinage since early antiquarian studies, is iconography, although perhaps it would be better to say 'imagery', so as to also include writing, in its double role as a complement to the designs and as an official document issued by the authorities.[1] Without intending to sound categorical, coinage does differentiate itself from other archaeological documents, because it is a 'thinking source', in as much as it combines writing and images, which transmit ideas full of meaning, in a similar way to literary sources. Following this idea, and leaving any economic or intrinsic-symbolical value aside, we would like to propose the possibility of finding certain identity markers belonging to the communities that issued these coins -or to be more precise, of those who ordered them to be issued. Identity is understood here as a marker, signalling differences, which were not necessarily exclusive or caused by resistance.[2]

Previous studies: ethnicity in Spanish numismatic literature of the 19th C

Not surprisingly, such avant-garde concepts in numismatics, ethnicity and identity,[3] actually trace their roots to the 19th C, when iconography and coin legends were widely used as direct testimonies of Ancient peoples, the 'essence' and singularity of which were reinterpreted in national histories of several European countries (Alföldi 1989, pp. 19-21). While still differentiated, Spanish numismatics did not escape this 19th C trend, and attempted, in tune with the historiographical interests of the time, to recognise the genuine 'Spanish character' as far back in time as possible (Wulff 2003, pp. 116-124).

Perhaps the best example for this use of Ancient Spanish coinage, together with other literary, geographical and archaeological sources, is found in the work of Antonio Delgado y Hernández.[4] He asserts that the symbols found on medals explain the origin of communities "... *los símbolos contenidos en las medallas, explican el origen de los pueblos* ..." (Delgado, 1871, i), and attributes ethnical identities to certain coin types, which he considers 'racial emblems' ("*emblemas de raza*") (Delgado, 1871, clxii). The ethnicity that according to this author may be identified in Ancient coin types of the Iberian Peninsula supports his claim to the Celtic origin of the inhabitants of *Ostur* and Celti, which he deduces from the depiction of wild boars (Delgado, 1871, clxiii, 113-115) (Fig. 1). As much may be said for the interest in documenting Phoenician presence in southern Iberia through coinage, which was not limited to the study of the well-known Phoenician Punic coinage of *Gadir*, *Bailo*, or *Asido* among others, but also included other coastal cities, such as *Lacipo* (Fig. 2) and especially others from the *Baetic* interior, such as *Bora* and *Carmo*. Despite using Latin writing and imprinting a Classical style to the iconography,

* This paper is part of the HUM 03482 Excellence Project of the Council for Innovation, Science and Entrepreneurship of the Government of Andalusia.

(1) The contribution of coin iconographies to current research is manifest (Caccamo Caltabiano 1998, pp. 57-62); also for Hispano-Roman coinage, *vid.* García-Bellido 1992, p. 240); Beltrán Lloris 2004; Chaves Tristán 2008.

(2) This interdisciplinary approach was first put forth in a Colloquium of the University of Malaga in May 2003, on ethnic identities and political identities in Pre-Roman Spain, which was subsequently published (Cruz Andretotti, Mora Serrano 2004).

(3) Also attempted for Roman Republican (Farney 2007, pp. 82-87) and provincial (Burnett 2005) coinage.

(4) (Antonio Delgado and Hernández 1871-1876), at least the writing of his general comments, inserted in his *Prolegómenos* (Delgado 1871, pp. i-clxxxvii) may be traced back to the mid 19th C. Current interest in these studies, from a historiographical perspective, is more than evident (Mora Serrano 2000a, Mora 2000, pp. 176-178).

they were still presented as evidence for the antiquity and strong Phoenician influence in a large part of Turdetania, which today is completely accepted.[5]

The work of A. Delgado constitutes an early example of the exploitation of coin iconography for the study of ethno-cultural identities in southern Iberia,[6] but it also addresses the need to overcome the rigid criteria that still today restrains explanations and studies of Ancient coinage of the Peninsula, subject to the type of writing used (García-Bellido 2001, pp. 138-141; Untermann 1992, pp. 29-33). This observation is especially relevant in relation to the important Phoenician Punic presence in the region, recorded by Strabo (3.2.13), Mela (2.94 ss.) or the known passage of Agrippa, reproduced in Pliny (*Nat. Hist.*, 3.7-8). Hence, the revision or discovery of new examples, belonging to well-known 'Latin' coinages of *Ulterior-Baetica*, such as *Nabrissa* and especially *Sacili*,[7] bearing Neo-Punic inscriptions, only confirms the evidence recorded by Ancient texts and archaeological field work.[8]

Prior considerations: limits and possibilities in the study of coin types from southern Iberia

Specific studies, particular to numismatics, such as seriation, chronology, production volumes, metrology, etc., should not cloud over the fact that, whether an object or a document, the coin is unable to explain itself on its own. In order to fully understand Ancient coin imagery, in part complemented by legends, it is necessary to first understand the culture, politics, etc., of the people who used them; and above all, the mentalities and identities they promote, which are not only or specifically ethnic in nature.

A mint demanded technical means, but it also needed a specialist able to fabricate the dies,[9] and authorities to choose the types and legends that would reflect the essence of the city's political community (Ripollès 2005, pp. 82-83). Origin, choice, and formal adaptation of coin types are complex issues, linked to the propagandistic and self-affirmation needs of each city, and may be directly associated, through iconographic and iconological analyses, to the world of images, which circulated throughout the Mediterranean ecumene in the Late Classical and Hellenistic periods.

As of the mid fifth century BC, and especially in the following two centuries, different cities in Iberia launched their own coinages. Coins were already at this time one of the main iconographic sources for new designs, not only present on prestigious issues –such as *Emporion* and *Arse*,[10] -but also on others, less technically demanding, which made adaptations a more comfortable task for the less experienced engravers. On the other hand, the limited space available on the die favoured simple designs, the meaning of which are difficult to interpret, resulting, sometimes intentionally, in multiple, and frequently complementary, readings, all well embedded in the cultural and ethnic diversity of many Ancient populations (Mora Serrano 2000b, p. 164; Chaves Tristán 2008, p. 357, 371). A good example may be found in the clearly Hellenised type of *Gadir*'s Melqart (Fig. 3). It has been interpreted as a further piece of evidence for the Hellenisation of Punic Iberia,[11] but this is actually a misleading – inexact at least- image of the archaic nature of its cult, which is gleaned from literary sources and archaeology.[12]

Much has been written on the meanings of coin types and of the different motives behind their choice, as well as on the limits and scope of the messages they attempt to transmit.[13] Coins were official documents, and as such, the authorities that designed and issued them locally during the last two centuries of the Republic, did so following established models of the Greek-Hellenistic period, which tended to portray civic identities as clearly as possible.

The degree to which these messages were understood by the local, largely illiterate, population is unknown to us, and therefore a logical limitation we must bear in mind. As has been discussed for other areas (Butcher 2005, pp. 143-145; Burnett 2005), the complex and educated constructions depicted on Ancient coinage, may have been paradoxically intended for their own creators. This exercise of self-affirmation and legitimation was as little democratic as the election of the coin types themselves,[14] and contributed towards the confirmation of certain aristocratic elites and the identity and civic model they aimed to transmit.

There are clear limitations in the communication of such messages, which we sense in the pre-Imperial coinage of southern *Hispania*. They become clearer when examining

(5) Keay 2003, p. 154, 163-166, addresses this numismatic issue; other works also explore it from an interesting and pioneering point of view, that of culture and identity (Domínguez Monedero 2000).

(6) An approach which has led to the publication of interesting studies in the last years, paying special attention to Phoenician Punic presence and influences (López Castro 2004; Chaves Tristán, García Fernández, Ferrer Albelda 2006, pp. 820-824).

(7) First published by Villaronga 2000, and shortly later by Blanco, Sáez 2002.

(8) The sanctuary of Torreparedones (Baena, Cordoba) is a good example, famous for its heterogeneous assemblage of sculpture (Marín Ceballos, Belén Deamos 2002).

(9) Gozalbes, Ripollès 2003, pp. 15-17. Naturally, there are also other factors involved, such as metal resources and the political and economic applicability of the planned issues, etc.

(10) Under the influence of Massalia for the Greek coinage (Campo 2003, pp. 25-26) and of different mints from Magna Graecia and Sicily for *Arse*'s first issues (Llorens, Ripollès 2002, pp. 65-66, 110).

(11) Among its numerous characteristics (Bendala Galán 1994, pp. 63-65), the military architecture stands out (Bendala Galán, Blánquez Pérez 2002-2003).

(12) Marín Ceballos 2001, p. 327. Recent revisions (Mierse 2004) also address the archaic features that may be gleaned from Ancient descriptions of the temple of Melqart in *Gadir*, which were already noted in the well-known syntheses of García y Bellido and J. M. Blázquez.

(13) Including the possibility of recognizing 'territorial images' in coin types (García-Bellido 1995, pp. 131-134).

(14) Mora Serrano 2003, pp. 60-61 for Hispano-Punic coinage. A similar development has recently been suggested for the coin assemblage of *Ulterior* (Chaves Tristán 2008, p. 361).

later coinage, such as Tiberius' issues from the city of *Abdera*, which have from an early stage been interpreted as a model for the gradual Romanisation of Hispano-Punic coinage (Woods 1964). When analysed in the new political, cultural and economic context of *Hispania* after Caesar and especially Augustus,[15] interesting conclusions may be made about the civic images that these southern coin types portray as a group. The mechanisms displayed in the gradual incorporation of municipalities and peregrine cities to Roman parameters made use of the cities' ancient signs of identity, such as coinage, although these new types have no ethno-cultural affiliations, as may be argued for previous periods (Beltrán Lloris 2002, p. 165, 168-171; Ripollès 2005, p. 87).

After an hiatus of inactivity,[16] *Abdera* reopened its mint with Tiberius and used previous civic depictions in its reverses. Two tuna substitute the central columns of a tetrastyle temple with the Neo-Punic legend *'bdrt* placed on the temple's tympanum, creating an image of synthesis with few parallels in *Hispania*'s coinage (Fig.4). A common use of Phoenician writing and language should not be deduced from such an instance, for the strokes and the inversion of the legend (Faria 1998, p. 243) denote the engraver's evident ignorance of the writing. Although Neo-Punic still survived in the region, as evidenced in graffiti and, at an official level, in late countermarks, such as the one from *Tagilit*, over a coin from Acci issued in the times of Tiberius (García-Bellido 2006, pp. 142-146), we believe that the message enclosed in the legend was different.

The key to these aporias is found in the variable nature of the iconography itself; similar images that reappear at different times, do so for very varied reasons. If earlier coins could be ascribed to their own civic ethno-cultural identity, later they were incorporated into a new, Roman, political reality, in which different communities competed in antiquity and prestige as part of one common polyadic system.

But perhaps the best exponent of the changes experienced by civic identities in *Hispania*, sustained by local aristocracies that were increasingly integrated in the Roman provincial ideal, is the coinage of *Gades*, specifically its issues of *sestertii* and *dupondii* (Fig. 5), minted during the reign of Augustus.[17] Their types and legends have been studied under this light, as good exponents of municipal coinages of *Hispania*,[18] and their undeniable interest is due in part to the possibility of studying them together with the numerous literary sources that comment on this Phoenician city, one of the principal political and economic centres of southern Iberia, transformed through an intelligent and close collaboration between its ruling classes and Rome. Nevertheless, it is increasingly evident from the literary point of view that it constitutes a paradigmatic case of 'identity by prestige', which takes refuge in a mythical and historical past, reinforced both by Herculean and Tartessian (or Phoenician) association (Álvarez Martí-Aguilar 2007, pp. 477-492; Ferrer Albelda, Álvarez Martí-Aguilar 2008, pp. 205-235). Significantly, *Gades* is the only city of Phoenician origin that Strabo describes in his third book in any detail, comparing its foundation to the Greek model, which constitutes a real topos (Cf. *Diod.*, 5.20). It is likewise interesting that Strabo, and later Pliny, recover the ancient polemic concerning the location of the Columns, placing them in *Gades*, i.e., identifying the finis *terrae* with *Gades* itself, yet another element that would contribute to the geographical-religious identity of this city, which traced its prestige to the beginning of historical times in the confines of the world, after the fall of Troy and the end of the 'reign' of Heroes (*Str.*, 3.5 *passim*). While Rome was constructing a cultural and ideological 'Mediterranean civility', based on an overarching framework enveloping diversity,[19] *Gades* was promoting an identity of its own, based on its geographical singularity and the facility to incorporate foundational stories and myths, without the need of differentiating that which was genuinely Greek from what was particularly Phoenician, the indigenous from the foreign.[20]

All things considered, it becomes necessary to differentiate between coinages, according to a series of criteria, such as the number of issues put into circulation and their chronology. Despite the difficulty of establishing the regularity of a mint and its distribution through time,[21] it is convenient to distinguish between mints that issue coinage 'regularly' in the first two centuries BC and the majority, which only mint occasionally. Variations in issues, volume of production, and the possibility of discerning determined typological differences in the reproduction of iconographic programmes,[22] are all to be considered when assessing the impact of coin types referencing civic identities. The group would be comprised of coinages from *Gadir*, *Malaca*, *Sexs*, *Ilipa* and *Carmo*, as well as the more eastern *Castulo* and *Obulco*.

(15) In general, cf., Roldán, Wulff 2002, p. 450 ss. The presence of Pompey and Caesar during the Civil War, and especially of the young Octavian, later Augustus, in *Hispania* - 45 BC, 27-24 B,C. and 15-13 BC – undoubtedly affected legal promotions and administrative organisation in the province, but it must have also influenced local coinages (Abascal Palazón 2006, pp. 75-77).

(16) Probably throughout the second half of the first century BC (Alfaro Asins 1996, pp. 14-18).

(17) *RPC* 1, 77-90. (Ripollès 2010, p. 88 ss.).

(18)Beltrán Lloris 2002, pp. 166-169; López Sánchez 2003, p. 103, 105; Ripollès 2005, p. 91. Furthermore, attention must be called on the quantitative importance of these issues, making *Gades* one of the most productive mints of Baetica (Ripollès, Llorens 1993, pp. 317-318). Nevertheless, data recovered from die studies do not always fit comfortably with finds or with coins from public and private collections of Ancient Iberia.

(19) Str., 3.1.8. Cf. Cic., *Pro Balbo* 29 and his praise of *Gades*.

(20) For Strabo's geography as a cultural and historical geography, *vid.* Cruz Andreotti 2009, pp. 131-144); Dueck, Lindsay, Pothecary (eds.) 2005, *passim*; and Clarke 1999, *passim*.

(21) As noted in the study of the mint of Valentia, although only as an aspect difficult to ascertain (Ripollès 1994-1995, p. 211).

(22) Attempted in the study of *Malaca*, where the introduction of new types and legends in first century AD issues still maintain typological continuities, such as the forceps and astral types (Campo, Mora 1995, pp. 107-113; Mora Serrano 2000b, pp. 161-162).

As for chronology, it is evident that issues dating to the first half of the first century BC experience changes, although irregularly, affecting coin types and legends, as well as technical and metrological aspects, all of which seem to indicate a gradual, although irregular, approximation to Roman models (Ripollès 2005b, p. 197, 199-200). As recently noted, the reasons for these changes must bear in mind the increasing influence of the local elites, and the relevance of Italian emigrants among these (Chaves Tristán 1999; ibidem 2008, p. 362, 366). Although probably inspired in Roman *denarii* of the first century BC, it is still striking that *Obulco* chose to substitute the traditional female head of its obverses for that of Apollo, even if it was still combined with the typical reverses of the mint, such as the plough, wheat ear, and yoke, which secured the continuity of types promoting civic identities (Arévalo 1999, pp. 59-61; Chaves Tristán 2008, pp. 367-369). The adoption of this type in other mints of the region, such as *Carbula* and *Salpensa* may be interpreted as an echo of the growing importance of the cult of Apollo in Rome at the time, which may have also spread its influence in *Ulterior*, as evidenced by these coins and other documents.[23]

In sum, coinage of southern Iberia gives the impression of undergoing a gradual Latinisation as of the first century BC, especially in the Turdetania region (Untermann 1995, pp. 311-313; Ripollès, p. 2005b, p. 198), but this impression must be compared to the evidence contained in the literary sources –e.g. Strabo's famous reference (3.2.15)-, archaeology, and the increasingly numerous inscriptions (Stylow 2005, p. 250). The sanctuaries of Torreparedones (Castro del Río y Baena) and Cerro de los Santos (Montealegre del Castillo) or the sculpture workshop of *Urso* (Osuna) are clear testimonies to the continuity of ancient traditions of undeniable cultural and religious content, although they also experienced the gradual reception of Roman Republican provincial models, especially in the valley of *Baetis*.[24] When considering the wealth of numismatic evidence for *Ulterior*, attention is paid in the first place to those mints with sufficient types and production to carry out a weighted analysis, in order to gain a proportionate image of the complex monetary reality in southern Iberia. Nevertheless, smaller mints are equally worthy of study, for the analysis of their types and legends also afford valuable evidence in the form of curious iconographic and epigraphic testimonies. An example of the former would be the interesting scene depicted on the reverse of a rare fraction, coined by the mint of *iltiraka*, or better *Ildicira*[25] (Fig. 6). Although we do not share the recent ethnic (Oretani) interpretation put forward for this mint -admittedly complex to narrow down- it is nevertheless interesting to link its iconography and meaning to the ancient warrior elites that constructed the Iberian monuments of the Upper Guadalquivir, such as Pajarillo. It thus follows that the existence of a shared foundational myth would have reinforced the urban network of the populations of Upper Guadalquivir (Mozas Moreno 2006, p. 271, 281-285).

As for epigraphic evidence, smaller mints deserve as much attention as the more relevant coinages. The well-known *Ilipa*, for example, produced interesting and rare testimonies of cursive writing (Mora Serrano 2004, p. 116), but there is also relevant information to be gleaned from minor coinages, as modest as they are rich in data. The so-called 'monetiform lead tokens' already captured the interest of 19th C. studies and collections of Roman Republican coinage, as did their counterparts of Italian tradition or origin.[26] We will not deal here with problems concerning their chronology and function (García-Bellido 1986, pp. 25-34; ibidem 1998, pp. 192-196); what interests us is to call attention to the lead tokens that are closest to our civic coinage, which in some cases they seem to complement and in others even substitute.[27]

There is no lack of recent examples to highlight the relevance of these tokens, as evidenced in the Punic use of lead to inscribe the legend *b'b'l*.[28] Nevertheless, the group that interests us most is the assemblage with southern Iberian legends –in South-Eastern (Meridional) script -since they contribute to the reduced catalogue of indigenous Iberian place names found on southern coinage. On the one hand, we have the monetiform lead tokens with the legend *gaidur* (García-Bellido 2001b) (Fig.7), which have been linked to intense metallurgic and mining activity, already documented for the area of Punic coinage in the south-east (Alfaro Asins 2000). Written in Levantine Iberian characters, they reinforce the same influences noted for the coin inscriptions of *Ilturir*, although their interest would be even greater if confirmed that the inscription is actually referencing a geographic elevation, as has been recently suggested (Faria 2008, p. 58).

Excepting the afore mentioned Punic examples, the majority of these monetiform lead tokens of *Baetic* origin share a common factor, the use of Latin, which was largely adopted in coinage of the Turdetania region at an early stage, as evidenced in the first bilingual issue from *Obulco* (Arévalo González 1999, p. 47, 87-88). If we disregard the interesting but complex indigenous issues from **Beuipo/Salacia*,

(23) Rodríguez Oliva 1994, pp.144-146. As in other cases, a local cult may lie behind this classical form (Chaves Tristán 2008, p. 368).

(24) Although there are precedents, it becomes predominant as of the second half of the first century AD. In this case, old assimilation theories have also been left aside, in order to attempt a closer study of the mutual influences flowing between indigenous communities and Italians, while also considering the common Hellenisation phenomenon of the central and eastern Mediterranean (Noguera, Rodríguez Oliva 2008, pp. 381-382, 394-395, 427 ss.).

(25) Arévalo González 2005, pp. 46-47. Nevertheless, this location and interpretation has been repeatedly challenged by other authors (Faria 2008, pp. 77-78).

(26) Their undeniable association with Italian materials (Stannard 2005, pp. 47-61) make them relevant for the study of early Italian influences in southern *Hispania*.

(27) One should distinguish between the use of these tokens as coins (out of need) and the use of lead as a suitable metal for coinage (Faria 1987).

(28) Attributed, not without reservations, to Hasta Regia (García-Bellido, Blázquez 2001, p. 156). Nevertheless, the existence of a similar countermark on *Asido* coins, does not clarify its explanation as a place name or minting formula (Mora Serrano 2007, p. 423).

as well as other considerations concerning the use of Latin, there is no doubt that the coinage of the valley of Guadalquivir and south-western Iberia significantly contributes to the fragmentary image that exists of the indigenous culture (Velaza 2005, pp. 365-366). Some of the scant exceptions known for the use of South-Eastern (Meridional) Iberian script in the south-west during the Republican period are found precisely among these modest monetiform lead tokens.

Together with types from *Carbula*, the *Ocanaca* inscription found on certain lead tokens (Fig. 8) has been identified with *Canaca*, cited by Ptolemy (2.4.10) as located between *Baetica* and *Lusitania*.(29) This exciting suggestion leads us to sense that there are further testimonies to be found inscribed on similar media as well as on inscriptions of 'Turdetani' place names. Coins, which were issued officially, substituted Punic for Latin as the official form of writing, in its varied palaeographic forms.(30) On the other hand, similar media, belonging to a less official or private sphere, such as the monetiform lead tokens, do bear indigenous versions of the corresponding Latin place names. Although *(O)canaca* never minted coinage, if it had, it would have used Latin to portray its civic identity through its coins. We must insist that no mint escaped this tendency, with the exception of the afore mentioned **Beuipo/Salacia* and coinages of Phoenician Punic tradition.

Bearing in mind all the limitations put forth, it is not our intention to elevate numismatics to the category of paradigmatic -or even portray it as a guide fossil- for the issues dealt here. Even so, it is undeniable that the exploitation of Ancient coinage in the Iberian Peninsula was used for identity purposes; images and texts were combined to create messages charged with references to identity that would be understood by the communities that assumed the use of these coins and/or by the elites that ordered their production. All in all, coins constitute an *unicum* for gaugins the complex and dynamic ethno-political world of southern Iberia at such key moments as the first two centuries BC.

Continuity and change, expressed in local variations and iconographic traditions, run parallel to the economic homogenisation of southern Iberia, indicating a possible process, in which 'cumulative identities' were constructed (Phoencian Punic, Italo-Roman, indigenous, coastal, valleys...), although not only in local or cultural terms. This process was congruent with the expansion of Roman rule, using the same civic model that had been successful previously in the region, i.e., during the rapid transformation of ancient Phoenician colonies into Punic *poleis*,(31) subsequently influencing a large part of southern Iberia.(32) Whether these 'cumulative identities' were also expressed politically depends on whether they were used in public or private spheres, on the military and political circumstances of the moment (*vid. Carteia*, infra), and on the impact of their dissemination. The identities and politics at play were not as much a mechanism of resistance as a reaffirmation of a common cultural *koiné* of Hellenic origin and of Roman superiority and expansion.(33)

Coinage of Phoenician Punic tradition: civic and ethno-cultural identities

There are many reasons for a city to undergo the technical and economic effort of minting its own coinage.(34) We will highlight one: the political and propagandistic intentions of local authorities to promote their civic identity to foreigners and their own citizens.

Although there are other references belonging to previous periods,(35) the earliest and most explicit evidence for the use of coinage as an instrument for civic reaffirmation in southern Iberia may be found in *Gadir*, although still not dated with precision. Here, the local authorities decided to incorporate the place name *'gdr* – accompanied by the formula *mp'l* or *mb'l* - to the already established coin types of the ancient Tyrian foundation, which may be referring to the city itself or to the governing civic body in charge of minting these issues (Alfaro Asins 1991, pp. 115-116; Manfredi 1995, pp. 130-132), (Fig. 12). *Gadir* was thus distanced, and not only geographically, from *Ebusus*, which continued using models with no inscriptions. It equally brings to our attention that *Gadir* started using inscription on coins as a form of civic self-affirmation, coinciding with the physical presence of *Carthago* in Iberia as of 237 BC, precisely located in *Gadir* itself.(36) Nevertheless, the impact of this civic formula, incorporated by *Gadir*'s coinage, in southern Iberia and the neighbouring North African territories

(29) Published by Casariego, Cores, Pliego, 1987, p. 4 n. 3-4; Faria 2008, pp. 79-80, even if this reading is not universally accepted.

(30) Domínguez Monedero 2000, p. 64, 66); its use in other contexts and social spheres must have been more restricted (Ripollès 2005b, p. 198). On the other hand, the recent discovery of a Neo-Punic inscription from *Ilipa* (Zamora 2007) provides evidence for a wider use of this kind of writing from what may be gleaned from preserved finds – generally scant, except for graffiti.

(31) A term which is used here only in a chronological sense, in reference to the Late Phoenician period, which starts in the second half of the sixth century BC.

(32) López Castro 2002; these influences culminated in the brief, yet intense rule of the Barcid family in Iberia, whose coinage is well known (Bendala Galán 2009, pp. 21-31).

(33) Cf. *Cic.*, *Ad Quintum*, 1.1,27-28.

(34) (Howgego 1990); for the Iberian Peninsula, there are a multitude of factors involved, complicating the comprehension of this important phenomenon, in which cities played leading roles (Chaves 2007, p. 217 ss.; Ripollès 2005b, pp. 189-193).

(35) Outside our geographical area, southern Iberia, there are earlier precedents in *Emporion* and Rhode, which are also important in assessing the impact of coinage on indigenous populations of the north-east (Campo 2004, p. 348).

(36) Carthage's hegemony over Iberia is disputed, but finds arguments from a political-administrative point of view (Manfredi, 2003, pp. 471-477), in the establishment and later development of *Gadir*'s coinage, which can also be considered from the eccentric position of *Gadir* and its area of influence in relation to the political and administrative –though not cultural and economic- sphere of Carthage in the Mediterranean 'far west' (Mora Serrano 2007, p. 412 ss.).

of the future *Tingitana*,[37] occurs, as with the majority of coinage in the Peninsula, after the Carthaginian defeat in the Second Punic War and the establishment of Rome's hegemony over the region. The emblematic character of these inscriptions is clearly appreciated in certain reverse dies from *Sexs*. The engraver fitted the mint's inscription on a console, added on to the die by four fixing points at the extremes, creating an explicit example of the incorporation of new legends (Mora Serrano 2007, p. 411), (Fig. 10).

The early minting of coin in the Phoenician Punic area of southern Iberia was associated with the use of place names or more complex formulas and underlines the ancient roots of the urban phenomenon in the region, going back to the sixth-fifth centuries, coinciding with profound changes experienced by the previous colonial system.[38] Their transformation into western Phoenician *poleis* (López Castro 2002, pp. 81-84; Ferrer, Fernández 2007) resulted in the creation of a new territorial and economic framework, also affecting ideology, the echo of which may be recognised in the coinage, despite its later chronology.[39] Indeed, the coinage of southern Iberia combined its role as a primary document with a logical adaptation to the particularities and evolution of the region's societies during the second-first centuries BC.

Let us recall that the antiquity and extension of the urban phenomenon in a good part of *Ulterior-Baetica* was not exclusive to Phoenician Punic cities; there are many arguments that allow us to speak of an early urban development in other territories of southern Iberia.[40] One of the main arguments for comes once again from numismatic evidence (Ripollès 2005b, pp. 195-196). Let us not forget the close relationship existing between coin inscriptions and the urban concept and its organisation, expressed in the inclusion of prefixes or suffixes in the city's name that illustrated its civic organization. In some cases, this occurred doubly, like in the name *Ilipense* (Correa 2004, pp. 21-22), where both the root *Il(i)-* and the suffix *-ense* find parallels in Iberian inscriptions of eastern Andalusia, as well as in more ancient precedents from the Spanish Levant and north-east (Perez Almoguera 2001, pp. 28-34; Correa 2004, p. 21).

(37) Led by *Tingi* and *Lixus* (Manfredi 1995, pp. 183-188); (Alexandropoulos 2002, p. 196 ss.).

(38) Despite the complex transmission of the written source -and the very reasonable doubts surrounding it– Moret (Moret 2004, pp. 40-43; ibidem 2006, pp. 42-45 ss.) versus Ferrer Albelda (Ferrer Albelda 2006, pp. 1997-2008), it does not seem coincidental that, from the group of references to southern *poleis* in Hecataeus, those that may be considered 'genuine' from a literary point of view (according to style, language, etc.) are precisely the Phoenician and 'surrounding' cities (frgs. 38, 40, 42, 43 and 44 Jacoby). A summary, including the entire polemic, in Cruz Andreotti (Cruz Andreoti 2010, pp. 32-36); for the problems concerning the term polis in Hecateaus *vid.* Whitehead (Whitehead 1994, pp. 119-120) and more recently Hansen (Hansen 1997, especially pp. 20 and 27).

(39) This approach has been applied to the coinage of *Malaca* (López Castro, Mora Serrano 2002, p. 186 ss., 205 ss.).

(40) Bendala Galán 2005, pp. 26-27, places particular emphasis on the concept of urban ethnicity.

There is no doubt that in the complex ethnic map of southern Iberia, Phoenician Punic traditions stand out from an early stage as especially cohesive. The recognition of these traditions is facilitated by the wealth of coin evidence, thanks to the iconography, but especially to Phoenician legends in Punic, Neo-Punic or singular Neo-Punic scripts, as the 'Lybian Phoenician' may be called. New readings of the literary sources, based on the growing archaeological record, open new trends that may be applied to traditional numismatic approaches to iconography, which has been studied for a long time from very different stand points -different yet often complementary (Domínguez Monedero 2000, p. 65 ss., 70 ss.; Mora Serrano 2003).

Once these different iconographies are put together and considered in all their complexity several regional variations may be appreciated. For example, coastal mints, coinciding with ancient Phoenician Punic foundations, produce more established iconographic models but are also recognisable by the script used on legends and the presence or absence of personal names. Recognisable are too the differences between the Strait and eastern Andalusia (García-Bellido, Blázquez 2001, pp. 59-62), although with notable exceptions, such as *Malaca*, where there are no types or allusions to the Melqart cycle, which is a striking characteristic of *Sexs*, and also to a certain degree in *Abdera* and *Abla* (Chaves Tristán, Marín Ceballos 1992, pp. 173-175; Mora Serrano 2007, pp. 426-429). Regardless of the iconographic language chosen, a common characteristic for the whole assemblage is the religious imprint, which is recognisable in a good portion of the types chosen; these include the more evident anthropomorphic representations, but also zoomorphic and phytomorphic -good examples being the well-known Lascutani altars and the recently reinterpreted altars from *Tagilit*.[41] Nevertheless, despite everything that has been said, there are considerable gaps and a lack of precision in the potential contribution of coin evidence to the Phoenician Punic cultural mapping of southern Iberia, especially concerning territorial influence.

We have already mentioned coinages from *Sacili* and *Nabrissa*; legends, classified as 'uncertain' by numismatic historiography have been reassigned; and Punic presence has been attested in the Turduli *Baeturia* (*Arsa*, *Turriregina*)[42]; nevertheless, of all the relevant cases that could be mentioned, *Carteia* stands out from the rest. Recent archaeological excavations studying its Punic fortifications and their successive remodelling, have argued that, for this emblematic Strait city too, urban and architectural changes that subsequently transformed the ancient Punic-Republican city are not recorded until Augustus, more specifically

(41) Specially interesting is the new reading – as an altar stela to Isis- of one of the types from *Tagilit* (Alfaro Asins 2003, p. 16), although a full understanding of the type depends on the legend (Pérez Orozco 2006, pp. 183-184), which has been read as «minted by *Tagilit* and the assembly», reinforcing the region's tradition of minting civic formulas.

(42) García-Bellido 1995, p. 132; Domínguez Monedero 2000, pp. 70-71. The identification and location of Punic coinage known as 'uncertain' is still problematic, more specifically those attributed by some to *Ituci* and recently to Cortijo de Ebora (Sáez, Blanco 2006).

until the mid first century AD. (Roldán, Blánquez, Bendala et al. 2003, p. 217 ss. 231). Nevertheless, *Carteia*'s coinage, initiated in the late second century BC, seems formally unaware of the Phoenician Punic substrate that dominated the city. While acknowledging other possible readings (García-Bellido, Blázquez 2001, I, 67, II, 87), the evidence seems to indicate a singular situation, which is perceived in the difference in coin types chosen by the local authorities (initially with a marked Roman, and later Hellenic, influence) as well as the magistracies and prosopography of the personal names that are included[43] (Fig. 9). Nevertheless, such a singularity is not unique, but a good reflection of the weight of the Roman Italian adstratum in the region, adopted by the elites of various important localities, first for military and strategic reasons and later also for economic interests. Furthermore, *Carteia*'s coinage is equalled in singularity by the legal status of this colonial foundation -Rome's head of the bridge over the Strait. In this case, cultural and civic identities walk beside each other, but not hand in hand, because of the particular characteristics of the city as a strategic point, subject to various re-foundations.[44]

The existence of 'substrates' and 'adstratum' in these territories and the possibility of recognising them in literary and archaeological sources -including coinage- explains the appearance of new approaches to such a complex theme, aggravated by important knowledge gaps and by the need to combine useful global perspectives on concrete geographical and chronological realities.[45]

Ituci's coinage constitutes a singular example. It was a Punic mint, as evidenced by the coin inscriptions, and its location coincided with one of the best known Tartessian/Turdetani enclaves, now Tejada La Vieja. Archaeologically, Tejada la Nueva (Escacena, Huelva), cannot dispense with its coinage, because it is a key element for addressing the ethnic and cultural mixture of most peoples in the southern Iberian Peninsula, which only further supports the importance of the ancient oriental substrate in the region, which was later reinforced by the equally strong Punic presence. The recent reassessment of the meaning of Tartessoss lies behind all this discussion, and actually comes to explain it.[46]

Ituci acts as a bridge between the Phoenician Punic coinage of the coast and the formally 'early Latinised' great mints of Middle and Lower *Baetis*, evidenced in its choice of coin types (horseman, bull-fish, and especially wheat ears) (Fig. 12) and in the early adoption of Latin inscription combined with conservative Punic script. The continuation of coin types in the Latin issues of *Ituci* spark old debates concerning Punic readings for coin iconographies from different cities in the interior of *Baetica*, including those with no Punic inscriptions. Certain coinages from the *Baetis* valley have taken up most of this discussion, especially *Carmo*.[47] Is it possible for coin iconography to reinforce theories on the continuity of a Hellenized Punic substratum? We would argue that it is, although some iconographies do have multiple readings, such as the Heracles-Hercules and the Hermes-Mercury, also present in North African coin iconography.[48]

There are also other formal analyses, which portray possible influences of Phoenician Punic mints over other 'Turdetani' coinages. For example, the well-known type depicting two wheat ears and a place name may be interpreted as a version of *Gadir*'s reverses (tuna and place name), just like in other North African workshops of the Circle of the Strait (Mora Serrano 1993, p. 75, 78-79; Domínguez Monedero 2000, p. 64). Nevertheless, this possible relationship should not be generally assumed, for there are other adopted types with strong personalities of their own,[49] not to mention differences in metrological behaviour.[50]

Territorial and civic identities: a close up to the mythical geography of Iberia through its coinage

We have stressed throughout the possibility of reading civic identities into the majority of coinage from the south of

(43) Pena 2000, pp. 99-101. There is a preference for certain magistracies - quaestores-, while others are rare *-censores-*; put together with the study of onomastics, one may presume a central Italian influence; contra: Rodríguez Neila 1995, p. 266.

(44) Wulff 1989, pp. 43-57. Curiously, the identification of *Carteia* with Tartessos (*vid.* Str., 3.2.14: Plin., *Nat. Hist.*, 3.7; Mela, 2.96; Sil., *Pun.* 3.396-99; possibly: App.., *Iber.* 63 o Paus., 6.19.3) or with *Heracleia* (Str., 3.1.7) seems to be a strong indicator of Punic identity in the Late Republic and Imperial period, although institutional "Italianization" was occurring at the same time (*vid.* infra. n. 83).

(45) Once again, Punic Turdetania is fertile ground for such an analysis (Ferrer Albelda 2004, pp. 287-288); there is a need to distinguish between archaeological dating and established chronologies, and the inexact translations existing between geographical-literary realities and their ethnic components.

(46) Unlike *Carteia*, which constitutes a paradigmatic example, as well as a very particular case, of Roman response to what seems to be a newly acquired 'symbolic' and political identity, *Ituci* shows no contrasts between the earlier period and later developments. *Ituci*, therefore, constitutes an example of an alternative way of dealing with the shared or 'cumulative' identities we spoke of at the beginning. Put into a general context (*vid.* Álvarez Martí-Aguilar 2007 and Ferrer Albelda 2008, summarised in Cruz Andreotti 2010), at least as of the second century BC, a good part of the southern populations of Semitic origin (not only on the coast) juggled and brought together a more than evident historical heterogeneity, which would ultimately be translated into a Turdetania 'without Turdetani' (Chaves Tristán, García Fernández, Ferrer Albelda 2006, *passim*).

(47) Its oriental past, Punic presence, Barcid influence, and the probable continuity of these Punic influences in Roman cemeteries - summarized in a recent publication on the history and archaeology of a Sevillian locality (Caballos 2001), still confronts different stances on the reading and interpretation of its coin iconographies (Chaves Tristán, García Fernández, Ferrer Albelda 2006, pp. 823-825).

(48) Rodríguez Casanova 1999, pp. 337-338; Manfredi 1995, p. 164 for *Sabratha* types. They have nevertheless also been interpreted, together with the Halos type, as Italo-Roman (Chaves Tristán 2008, p. 370).

(49) Do not depend on the models that are followed and adapted, as has been pointed out for the Janiform heads (Chaves Tristán, Marín Ceballos, 2004, pp. 353-357, 373); (Chaves Tristán 2008, p. 370), offers different adopted models, some of which are typically Roman.

(50) (García-Bellido, Blázquez 2001, pp. 79-82). *Ituci* is, once again, of particular interest for this discussion; its metrology shows an interesting relationship between the weight system of Punic tradition and that of the great mints of the Middle Guadalquivir valley (Mora Serrano 2006, pp. 47-48).

the Iberian Peninsula, by using evidence from several examples that could be multiplied, especially in reference to formal aspects (types and legends), which were used from the very beginning as instruments of self-affirmation. This interpretation is founded on the ancient and deep urban roots present in these territories, and does not rule out other possible interpretations dealing with the afore mentioned 'cumulative identities'. We believe it is thus possible to put forth an interpretation, which combines geographical identity with certain iconographies adopted in various mints of *Ulterior-Baetica*.

In truth, it is common practice to differentiate between the iconographic variety of *Ulterior* and the repetition of types found in most of *Citerior*, mostly known for the combination of male head and horseman.(51) In general terms, this assertion is correct, although with nuances that explain the use of certain types and 'common' symbols by different cities, even if they are not mechanical copies of the images.

We will subsequently draw attention to two distinct groups of images, which nevertheless may both be interpreted as the transmission of ancient myths, linked to the 'far west'.(52) Transformed through time into literary images, they would be recreated and assumed by the urban elites that controlled the mints. Once again, Phoenician Punic coinage stands out as the clearest example for the use of a common type, that of *Gadir*'s Heracles-Melqart, although we should probably be ascribing it to *Hispania* or Iberia. It is worth insisting on the importance and antiquity of the cult in *Gadir*, as well as in other territories of *Hispania*, as attested in the literary sources and archaeology, including numismatics (López Castro 1997; García-Bellido 1991, pp. 49-50, 51-55). This is the case with *Sexs*, an important mint in the south-east that adopted the Melqart-Heracles type in its very first issues, at the end on the third century BC, and transforms in the Late Republic into a striking imitation of *Gadir*'s types and legends (*CNH* 104.5 ss). Aside from other possible explanations,(53) Strabo's famous passage (3.5.5) seems especially relevant; it cites a Phoenician presence in *Sex*, or *Ex*, immediately prior to the foundation of *Gadir*. It would therefore be a mythical image, linked to the origins of the city, i.e., with a meaning and identity of its own, which would explain its depiction on the coins, although it was clearly also linked to a certain territory. This mythical geographical reading is compatible with its civic identity. Furthermore, we believe it is possible to apply this reading to Melqart's images in other south-eastern mints, as found in later coinages of *Alba* (*Abla*, Amería) and *Abdera* (Mora Serrano 2007, p. 432).

This same mythical geographical perspective, reflected in the adoption of common iconographies, may also be applied to the lower and middle reaches of the Guadalquivir valley. Such is the case with the wheat ear and the shad, adopted from an early stage and later disseminated by the coinage of *Ilipa* Magna throughout the region.(54) Interpreting zoomorphic and phytomorphic types, such as those dealt with, is particularly complex, as evidenced by the different readings offered for these interesting images (García-Bellido 1991, pp. 57-59; Chaves Tristán 2007b, pp. 214-215), which are already alluded to in antiquarian literature.(55) Rodrigo Caro, in his famous *Chorografía*, full of references to the region's coin evidence, refers to the types from *Ilipa* as testimonies to the fertility of the earth (wheat ear) and to the proximity to *Baetis* (shad) (Caro 1634, p. 98). These two explanations have also been applied to other coin types, as for example, the wheat ears from *Carmo*, the grape cluster from *Osset*, and the shad from *Cun(u)baria* (Caro 1634, p. 157, 114, 96), (Fig. 13).

It is definitely appropriate to carry out an economic interpretation of these images, for there are numerous archaeological testimonies to the fishing exploitation of the river Guadalquivir,(56) as well as the fertile plains of the interior (Sáez 2006). As highlighted in recent studies, it is even possible to attribute an excessive –we would say modern-economic interpretation for these images, which sees these local divinities as protecting economic resources. The female divinity on the obverses from *Obulco*, conveniently enhanced by the frugivorous images on the reverses, is a good example, but also a clear model for other mints of the region, such as *Abra* and *Ulia* (Chaves Tristán 2008, p. 358; Arévalo González 2000, pp. 46-48).

The use of these images, whether copies or more complex creations, in other mints of southern Iberia, extensive to other types -such as the grape cluster- (Fig. 14) may also be explained as images of bountifulness, associated from old with Tartessos, and later assumed in Turdetania, while recreated by the Late Hellenistic and Roman literature. If our interpretation is correct, coinage from the region could contribute to evidence the existence of an image of territorial identity, Turdetania, which Strabo (3.1.6; 2.3) identifies,

(51) Occasional versions of this type in *Baetica* – Carissa, *Ituci*, armed horseman with round shield, and others from *Obulco*, *Olontigi* and *Laelia* – have not passed unnoticed (Arévalo González 2003, p. 65, 67-68); also mentioned in the search for formal models in Punic areas (Mora Serrano 1993, pp. 73-74; Arévalo González 2003, 70; Noguera Celdrán, Rodríguez Oliva 2008, pp. 397-399).

(52) The bibliography on this topic is extensive. Despite their age, good references are still Ballabriga 1986 and Jourdain-Annequin 1989. We would like to underline the survival and use of ancient mythical geography –practiced by Phoenicians and Greeks-which was transformed in the Roman period, leading to the creation of an Iberian ethnogenesis (Cruz Andreotti 2004, pp. 253-270).

(53) Chaves Tristán, García Vargas 1991, pp. 156-157, offer an interesting explanation for these *Sexs* images as a reflection of a possible commercial route, led by *Sexs* in the south-east, which may have been similar to the gipsy route.

(54) Its numerous issues have been recently analysed (Chaves Tristán 2007b) as part of a joint publication on the city's history and archaeology.

(55) Such as in the *Antigüedades* of Rodrigo Caro, cited and further discussed in reference works of the 19th C. (Delgado 1871, cli-clii).

(56) A proposal based on more recent references (Chic García 2003, p. 62); some archaeological discoveries provide evidence for fishing and the salting of different species, from the shad to the sturgeon, in the same manner as in the coast (Carreras Monfort 2001, pp. 423-424). Cf. Ferrer Albelda, García Vargas, García Fernández 2008, pp. 217-246; and García Vargas, Ferrer Albelda, García Fernández 2008, pp. 247-270.

clearly for the sake of simplification, with the relevance and wealth of *Baetis*.

The contrast between an overwhelming fertility in the confines of the world with the equilibrium found at the centre is a literary construct as ancient as literature itself (Homer, Hesiod); likewise, liminal territories house heroes and gods; nothing could resemble the world of men, who could not live alongside the gods after the Trojan War. After the colonial development and expansion, the mythical image of the 'far west' did not disappear, and survived in popular and marine cosmologies, as well as in literature, especially where Hellenic presence was less stable and purely commercial, not colonial. It is not uncommon for unexplored or unknown territories to be interpreted in familiar cultural and geographical terms, acquiring qualities that contrast with daily life, which is dictated by the common laws of time, space and man (Janni 1973, pp. 445-500; ibidem 1975, pp. 145-178; ibidem 1997 [1998], pp. 23-40; Prontera 1990, pp. 55-82).

Literary sources for Iberia, while being different in genre and intentions, are still covered by this halo of preconceptions surrounding the limits of the world, comparable to other literary constructs like the 'wonderful Ehtiopians' or Scheria of the Phaeacians: Stesichorus (frg. 154 Page), Pherecydes (frg. 17 Jacoby), Anacreon (frg. 4 Gentili), Hecataeus (frgs. 26 ss. Jacoby), Herodotus (I 163 and IV 151 -153) or Herodorus (frg. 2a Jacoby). Be as it may, they are collateral constructs, with no intention of creating -like in the Italian or Sicilian territories- a mythical and heroic foundational geography of colonial expansion, centred for this time period in the Ligurian, Tyrrhenian, and Sicilian Seas, not the Iberian one.

A different matter arises when these territories become part of a well established ecumene, geographically, politically, and by extension, culturally as well. The continuity of images through time carry a different meaning, even if they may also be explained by ancient literary traditions. It is easier now to appreciate how ancient literary topics transform into cultural elements feeding into identities, although not necessarily ethnic, in territories with hitherto unknown or unrecognized histories. Strabo -and possibly his sources (Asclepiades and Artemidorus)- does not follow the main stream, which identifies Tartessian with Phoenician, and chooses to underline the autochthonous character of Tartessos and Turdetania, directly connecting it to a Homeric-Herculean idyllic past, which was rapidly Latinised, as a reflection of civility and prosperity in the Roman times, just as it had been in the remote past. It is as much a literary construct as the reflection of an existing elite identity, which was furthermore not the only one arising as a result of an urban diversity, which found its only common factor in the *Baetis* valley, subsequently becoming the *prouincia Baetica*.[57]

(57) A summary in Cruz Andreotti 2010.

Final reflections

What is there to conclude in all of this? At a glance, there is an evident homogenisation taking place in the traditionally Semitic area, most clearly reflected in the political and territorial creation of the *coventus gaditanus* (*Str.*, 3.4.20). Pressing further, one may consider the unity and diversity of coin types and their 'penetration' in the *Baetic* interior as an indicator of civic, not ethnic, identities. This leads us to the delicate and controversial issue of discerning whether these identities were there from the beginning or were created subsequently. From a historical point of view, the second option is the more likely, taking us into the second question. Is Rome, or rather its locally integrated elites, behind the promotion and reinvention of the ancient/new Phoenician Punic identity, linked to the paradise-like image of its territory? A shared cultural context would allow for a subsequent political and administrative -therefore also cultural- exploitation of the region's main weakness. The cities competed among each other for the more 'glorious past'; while only *Gades* could lay claim to a momentous foundation, all of them could call on a mythology relating to the confines of the earth, conveniently Euhemerised into the cult of Heracles/Hercules and a fertility myth. It possibly may be so; furthermore, coinage, as a civic symbol, became the best instrument and the clearest evidence for this process. The so-called 'Punification' of the *Baetic* interior shares many analogies with the concept of 'Romanisation'. Rome and Carthage were two Hellenistic *poleis*, achieving their true political nature through the expansion of *civitas* and Hellenic culture. This is the only context possible for Strabo's (3.4.3) enigmatic affirmation, describing Asclepiades as "a man who taught grammar in Turdetania and has published an account on the tribes of that region".

Abbreviations

CNH (1994)= Villaronga L. *Corpus Nummum Hispaniae Ante Augusti Aetatem*. Madrid.

RPC1(1992)= Burnett A., Amandry M., Ripollés P. P. *Roman Provincial Coinage, I. From the Death of Caesar to the Death of Vitellius (44 BC to AD 69)*. London-Paris, (reed. 1999) and Suppl. I.1998 and II.2006 [http://www.uv.es/=ripolles/rpc_s2]

References

Abascal Palazón J. M. (2006). 'Los tres viajes de Augusto a Hispania y su relación con la promoción jurídica de ciudades', *Iberia*, 9, pp. 63-78.

Alexandropoulos J. (2002). *Les monnaies de l'Afrique Antique 400 av.J.-C. - 40 ap. J.* Toulouse.

Alfaro Asins C. (1991). 'Epigrafía monetal púnica y neopúnica en Hispania. Ensayo de síntesis', in Ermanno A., *Arslan Dicata, I (Glaux 7)*. Milan, pp. 109-150.

Alfaro Asins C. (1996). 'Avance de la ordenación de las monedas de Abderat/Abdera (Adra, Almería)', *Numisma*, 237, pp. 11-50.

Alfaro Asins C. (2000). 'La producción y circulación monetaria en el sudeste peninsular', in García-Bellido Mª. P., Callegarin L. (coords), *Los cartagineses y la monetización del Mediterráneo occidental*. Madrid, pp. 101-112.

Alfaro Asins C. (2003). 'Isis en las monedas de Baria y Tagilit', *Numisma*, 247, pp. 7-18.

Alföldi M. R. (1989). 'Die Forschungsmethoden der antiken Numismatik', in Alföldi M. R. (ed.), *Methoden der antiken Numismatik*. Darmstadt, pp. 1-42.

Álvarez Martí-Aguilar M. (2007). 'Arganthonius Gaditanus. La identificación de Gadir y Tarteso en la tradición antigua', *Klio*, 89.2, pp. 477-492.

Arévalo González A. (1999). *La ciudad de Obulco: sus emisiones monetales*. Madrid.

Arévalo González A. (2000). 'La moneda hispánica en relación con la explotación minera y agrícola', in *Moneda i administració del territori (IV curs d'historia monetaria d'Hispania 23 i 24 de novembre de 2000)*. Barcelona, pp. 37-55.

Arévalo González A. (2003). 'La moneda hispánica del jinete ibérico: estado de la cuestión', in Quesada Sanz F., Zamora Merchán M. (eds), *El caballo en la Antigua Iberia. Estudios sobre los équidos en la Edad del Hierro*. Madrid, pp. 63-74.

Arévalo González A. (2005). *Sylloge Nummorum Graecorum España. vol. II. Hispania. Ciudades del área meridional: Acuñaciones con escritura indígena*. Madrid.

Ballabriga A. (1986). *Le Soleil et le Tartare. L'image mythique du monde en Greece archaique*. Paris.

Beltrán Lloris F. (2002). 'Identidad cívica y adhesión al príncipe en las monedas municipales hispanas', in Marco Simón F., Pina Polo F., Remesal Rodríguez J. (eds), *Religión y propaganda política en el mundo romano*. Barcelona, pp. 159-187.

Beltrán Lloris F. (2004). 'Imagen y escritura en la moneda hispana', in Chaves Tristán F., García Ferández F. J. (eds), *Moneta qua scripta. La moneda como soporte de escritura (Actas del III Encuentro Peninsular de Numismática Antigua. Anejos del Archivo Español de Arqueología XXXIII)*. Sevilla, pp. 125-139.

Bendala Galán M. (1994). 'El influjo cartaginés en el interior de Andalucía, Cartago, Gadir, Ebusus y la influencia púnica en los territorios hispanos', in *VIII Jornadas de Arqueología Fenicio-Púnica*. Ibiza, pp. 59-74.

Bendala Galán M., Blánquez Pérez J. (2002-2003). 'Arquitectura militar púnico-helenística en Hispania', *Cuadernos de Prehistoria y Arqueología Universidad Autónoma de Madrid*, 28-29, pp. 145-159.

Bendala Galán M. (2005). 'Urbanismo y romanización en el territorio andaluz: aportaciones a un debate en curso', *Mainake*, 27, pp. 9-32.

Bendala Galán M. (2009) 'El privilegio histórico y cultural de la moneda: aliento y compromiso científicos' in Arévalo A. (ed.), *XIII Congreso Nacional de numismática: Moneda y Arqueología*. Vol. 1. Madrid, pp. 17-48.

Bernett A. (2005). 'The Roman West and the Roman East', in Howgego C., Heuchert V., Burnett A. (eds), *Coinage and Identity in the Roman provinces*. Oxford, pp. 171-180.

Blanco J. M., Sáez J. A. (2002). 'La ceca "Libiofenice" de Sacili', *Gaceta Numismática*, 144, pp. 3-16; 145, pp. p. 35-48.

Caballos A. (ed.) (2001). *Carmona Romana*. Carmona.

Caccamo Caltabiano M. (1998). 'Immagini/parola, grammatica e sintassi di un lessico iconografico monetale', in Arslan E. A. et *al.*, *La 'parola' delle immagini e delle forme di scrittura. Modi e techniche della comunicazione nel mondo antico*. Messina, pp. 57-73.

Campo M. (2003). 'Les primers imatges gregues: L'inici de les fraccionàries d'Emporion', in Campo M. (ed.), *Les imatges monetàries: llenguatge i significat*. Barcelona, pp. 25-45.

Campo M. Mora B. (1995). *Las monedas de Malaca*. Madrid.

Campo M. (2004). 'Dinero de metal y moneda en territorio indigente: el testimonio de Mas Castellar (siglos V-III a.C.)', in Chaves Tristán F., García Fernández F. J. (eds), *Moneta qua scripta = La moneda como soporte de escritura: III Encuentro Peninsular de Numismática Antigua*. Sevilla, pp. 345-354.

Caro R. (1634). *Antigüedades y principado de la Ilustrísima ciudad de Sevilla y corografía de su convento jurídico o antigua Chancillería*. Sevilla (ed. fac. Sevilla, 1998).

Carreras Monfort C. (2001). 'Producción de Haltern 70 y Dressel 7-11 en las inmediaciones del Lacus Ligustinus (Las Marismas, Bajo Guadalquivir)', in *Congreso Internacional Ex Baetica Amphorae. Conservas, aceite y vino de la Bética en el Imperio Romano (Écija y Sevilla, 17 al 20 de Diciembre de 1998)*. Vol. I. Écija, pp. 419-426.

Casariego A., Cores G., Pliego F. (1987). *Catálogo de los plomos monetiformes de la Hispania antigua*. Madrid.

Clarke K. (1999). *Between Geography and History. Hellenistic construction of the Roman world*. Oxford.

Cruz Andreotti G. (2004). 'Una contribución a la etnogénesis ibérica desde la literatura antigua: A propósito de la Geografía de Iberia y los iberos', in Candau J. M. et *al.*, *Historia y mito. El pasado legendario como fuente de autoridad.* Málaga, pp. 241-276.

Cruz Andreotti G. (2009). 'La naturaleza histórica de la "Geografía" de Estrabón', *Euphrosyne*, 37, pp. 131-144.

Cruz Andreotti G. (2010). 'Tarteso-Turdetania o la deconstrucción de un mito identitario', in de la Bandera Romero Mª. L., Ferrer Albelda E. (eds), *El Carambolo. 50 años de un tesoro*. Sevilla, pp. 17-53.

Cruz Andreotti G., Mora Serrano B. (eds) (2004). *Identidades étnicas - Identidades políticas en el mundo prerromano hispano*. Málaga.

Chaves Tristán F. (2007). 'Origen, uso y función de la moneda en la sociedad hispana: siglos IV-I a.C.', in Moucharte G. *et al.*, *Liber amicorum Tony Hackens (Numismatica Lovaniensia 20)*. Louvain-la-Neuve, pp. 213-222.

Chaves Tristán F. (2007b). 'Una aproximación a la ceca de Ilipa', in Ferrer Albelda E., Fernández Flores A., Escacena Carrasco J. L., Rodríguez Azogue A. (eds), *Ilipa Antiqua. De la prehistoria a la época romana*. Alcalá del Río, pp. 211-226.

Chaves Tristán F. (2008). 'Moneda local en Hispania: ¿autoafirmación o integración?', in Uroz J., Noguera J. M., Coarelli F. (eds), *Iberia e Italia: Modelos romanos de integración territorial*. Murcia, pp. 353-377.

Chaves Tristán F., García Fernández F. J., Ferrer Albelda E. (2006). 'Relaciones interétnicas e identidades culturales en Turdetania (siglos II a.C. – I d.C.)', *L'Africa romana*, 16, pp. 813-828.

Chaves Tristán F., García Vargas, E. (1991).'Reflexiones en torno al área comercial de Gades: Estudio numismático y económico', in *Homenaje al Dr. Michel Ponsich (Gerión)*. Madrid, pp. 139-168.

Chaves F., Marín Ceballos Mª. C. (1992). 'L'influence phénico-punique sur l'iconographie des frappes locales de la Péninsule Ibérique', *Numismatique et histoire économique phéniciennes et puniques (Studia Phoenicia IX)*. Louvain-La-Neuve, pp. 167-194.

Chaves Tristán F., Marín Ceballos Mª.-C. (2004). 'Las cabezas galeadas en la amonedación hispana', in Caccamo Caltabiano M., Castrizio D., Puglisi M., *La tradizione iconica come fonte storica. Il ruolo della numismatica negli studi di iconografia (Atti del I Incontro di Studio del Lexicon Iconographicum Numismaticae)*. Messina, pp. 351-384.

Chic García G. (2003). 'Nuevas consideraciones sobre la navegación fluvial por el Guadalquivir', in Parodi Álvarez M. J. (ed.), *El Baetis-Guadalquivir, puerta de Hispania, Monografías Sanluqueñas. Vol. I.* Sanlúcar de Barrameda, pp. 39-66.

Correa J. A. (2004). 'Leyenda monetal y toponímia', in Chaves Tristán F., García Ferández F. J. (eds), *Moneta qua scripta. La moneda como soporte de escritura (Actas del III Encuentro Peninsular de Numismática Antigua. Anejos del Archivo Español de Arqueología XXXIII)*. Sevilla, pp. 14-23.

Delgado y Hernández A. (1871). *Nuevo método de clasificación de las medallas autónomas de España. Vol. I.* Sevilla.

Domínguez Monedero A. J. (2000). 'Monedas e identidad étnico-cultural de las ciudades de la Bética', García-Bellido Mª. P., Callegarin L. (coords), *Los cartagineses y la monetización del Mediterráneo occidental*. Madrid, pp. 59-74.

Dueck D., Lindsay H., Pothecary S. (eds) (2005). *Strabo's cultural geography: the making of a kolossourgia*. Cambridge.

Faria A. Marques de (1987). 'Moedas de chumbo, da época romana, cunhadas no actual território português. A propósito do Catálogo de Plomos Monetiformes de la Hispania Antigua', *Numismática Lisboa*, 47, pp. 24-28.

Faria A. Marques de (1998). 'Recensões bibliográficas', *Revista Portugesa de Arqueologia*, 1.2, pp. 241-256.

Faria A. Marques de (2008). 'Crónica onomástica paleohispânica (14)', *Revista Portuguesa de Arqueologia*, 11.1, pp. 57-102.

Farney G. (2007). *Ethnic Identity and Aristocratic Competition in Roman Republic.* Cambridge.

Ferrer Albelda E. (2004). 'Sustratos fenicios y adstratos púnicos: Los bástulos entre el Guadiana y el Guadalquivir', *Huelva Arqueológica*, 20, pp. 283-298.

Ferrer Albelda E. (2006). '¿Mastia en África?', *L'Africa romana*, 16, pp. 1997-2008.

Ferrer Albelda E., Álvarez Martí-Aguilar M. (2008). 'Comunidad cívica e identidad en la Iberia púnica', in Wulff F., Álvarez Martí-Aguilar M. (coords), *Identidades, culturas y territorios en la Andalucía prerromana*. Málaga-Sevilla-Jaén, pp. 205-235.

Ferrer Albelda E., García Vargas E., García Fernández F. J. (2008). 'Inter Aestuaria Baetis. Espacios naturales y territorios ciudadanos prerromanos en el Bajo Guadalquivir', *Mainake*, 30, pp. 217-246.

García-Bellido Mª. P. (1986). 'Nuevos documentos sobre minería y agricultura romanas en Hispania', *Archivo Español de Arqueología*, 153-154, 59, pp. 13-46.

García-Bellido Mª. P. (1992). 'La moneda, libro en imágenes de la ciudad', in Olmos R. (ed.), *La sociedad ibérica a través de la imagen.* Madrid, pp. 237-249.

García-Bellido Mª. P. (1991). 'Las religiones orientales en la Península Ibérica: documentos numismáticos, I', *Archivo Español de Arqueología*, 64, pp. 37-81.

García-Bellido Mª. P. (1995). 'Moneda y territorio: La realidad y su imagen', *Archivo Español de Arqueología*, 68, pp. 131-147.

García-Bellido Mª. P. (1998). 'Los ámbitos de uso y la función de la moneda en la Hispania republicana', in *Actas del III Congreso Histórico-Arqueológico Hispano-Italiano (Toledo, 1993).* Madrid, pp. 177-207.

García-Bellido Mª. P. (2001).'Numismática y etnias : Viejas y nuevas perspectivas', in Villar F., Fernández Álvarez Mª. P. (eds), *Religión, lengua y cultura prerromanas de Hispania (8 CLCPPI).* Salamanca, pp. 135-160.

García-Bellido Mª. P. (2001b). 'Plomos monetiformes con el topónimo ibérico de Gador', *Paleohispanica. Revista sobre lenguas y culturas de la Hispania antigua*, 1, pp. 335-340.

García-Bellido Mª. P., Blázquez C. (2001). *Diccionario de cecas y pueblos hispánicos, con una Introducción a la Numismática antigua de la Península Ibérica.* Madrid.

García Vargas E., Ferrer Albelda E., García Fernández F. J. (2008). 'La romanización del Bajo Guadalquivir: Ciudad, territorio y economía (siglos II-I a.C.)', *Mainake*, 30, pp. 247-270.

Gozalbes M., Ripollès P. P. (2003). 'La fabricación de moneda en la Antigüedad', *XI Congreso Nacional de Numismática.* Zaragoza, pp. 11-34.

Hansen M. H. (1997) 'Hekataios' use of the word polis in his Periegesis', in Nielsen T. H. (ed.), *Yet more studies in the Ancient Greek Polis.* Stuttgart, pp. 17-27.

Howgego C. J. (1990). 'Why did ancient states strike coins?', *The Numismatic Chronicle*, pp. 1-25.

Janni P. (1973) 'Il mondo della qualità. Appunti per un capitolo di Storia del pensiero geografico', *Annali dell'Istituto Orientale di Napoli*, 33, pp. 445-500.

Janni P. (1975) 'Il mondo della qualità. Appunti per un capitolo di Storia del pensiero geografico', *Annali dell'Istituto Orientale di Napoli*, 35, pp. 145-178.

Janni P. (1997 [1998]), 'Los límites del mundo entre el mito y la realidad: evolución de una imagen', in Pérez Jiménez A., Cruz Andreotti G. (eds), *Los límites de la tierra: el espacio geográfico en las culturas mediterráneas (Serie Mediterranea, 3).* Madrid, pp. 23-40.

Jourdain-Annequin C. (1989). *Héraclès aux portes du Soir. Mythe et Histoire.* Paris.

Keay S. (2003). 'Recent Archaeological Work in Roman Iberia (1900-2002)', *Journal of Roman Studies*, 93, pp. 146-211.

Llorens M. M., Ripollès P. P. (2002). 'Las imágenes', in Ripollés P. P., Llorens M. M. (eds), *ArseSaguntum. Historia monetaria de la ciudad y su territorio.* Sagunto, pp. 63-120.

López Castro J. L. (1997). 'Los héroes civilizados: Melqart y Heracles en el Extremo Occidente', in Alvar J., Blázquez J. M. (eds), *Héroes y antihéroes en la Antigüedad Clásica.* Madrid, pp. 55-68.

López Castro J. L. (2001). 'Las ciudades fenicias occidentales y Cartago (c. 650-348 a.C.)', in Tavares A. (ed.), *Os Punicos no extremo occidente.* Lisbon, pp. 57-68.

López Castro J. L. (2002). 'Las ciudades fenicias occidentales', *Valencia y las primeras ciudades romanas de Hispania.* Valencia, pp. 81-92.

López Castro J. L., Mora Serrano B. (2002). 'Malaka y las ciudades fenicias en el occidente mediterráneo. Siglos VI a.C. - I d.C.', *Mainake*, 24, pp. 181-214.

López Sánchez F. (2003). 'Retratística imperial en las series hispanolatinas y estructuración territorial de un far-west romano', in *Les imatges monetáries: llenguatge i significat (VII Curs d'Història Monetària d'Hispània).* Barcelona, pp. 103-118.

Manfredi L. I. (1995). *Monete puniche. Repertorio epigrafico e numismatico delle leggende puniche (Bolletino di Numismatica, Monografia 6).* Roma.

Manfredi L. I. (2003). *La politica amministrativa di Cartagine in Africa.* Roma.

Marín Ceballos M. C. (2001). 'Les contacts entre Phéniciens et Grces dans le territoire de Gadir et leur formulation religieuse; Histoire et Mythe', in Ribicini S., Rocchi S., Xella P. (coords), *La questione delle influenze vicino-orientali sulla religione greca.* Roma, pp. 315-331.

Marín Ceballos M. C., Belén Deamos M. (2002). 'En torno a una dama entronizada de Torreparedones', *Boletín de la Asociación Española de Amigos de la Arqueología*, 42, pp. 177-194.

Mierse W. E. (2004). 'The Architecture of the Lost Temple of Hercules Gaditanus and Its Levantine Associations', *American Journal of Archaeology*, 108.4, pp. 545-576.

Mora Serrano B. (1993). 'Las cecas de Malaca, Sex, Abdera y las acuñaciones púnicas en la Ulterior-Baetica', in *Numismática hispano-púnica. Estado actual de la investigación*

(*VII Jornadas de Arqueología Fenicio-Púnica*). Ibiza, pp. 63-45-

Mora Serrano B. (2000a). 'La interpretación de la iconografía de la moneda hispana en la investigación numismática española del siglo XIX', in *XII International Numismatic Congress*. Vol. I. Berlín, pp. 131-136.

Mora Serrano B. (2000b). 'Las fuentes de la iconografía monetal fenicio-púnica', García-Bellido Mª. P., Callegarin L. (coords), *Los cartagineses y la monetización del Mediterráneo occidental*. Madrid, pp. 157-168.

Mora Serrano B. (2003). 'La iconografía de la moneda hispano-púnica', *Les imatges monetàries: llenguatge i significat (VII Curs d'Història Monetària d'Hispània)*. Barcelona, pp. 47-66.

Mora Serrano B. (2004). 'Notas sobre la escritura latina en la amonedación antigua de Hispania', in Chaves Tristán F., García Fernandez F. J., *Moneta qua scripta: La moneda como soporte de escritura (III Encuentro de Numistática Antigua)*. Sevilla, pp. 113-124.

Mora Serrano B. (2006). 'Metrología y sistemas monetarios en la Península Iberica (siglos V-I a.C.)', in *XII Congreso Nacional de Numismática*. Madrid, pp. 23-61.

Mora Serrano B. (2007). 'Sobre el uso de la moneda en las ciudades fenicio-púnicas de la Península Ibérica', in López Castro J. L. (ed.), *Las ciudades fenicio-púnicas en el Mediterráneo Occidental*. Almería, pp. 405-438.

Mora G. (2000). 'La moneda púnica en la historiografía española de los siglos XVI a XIX', in García-Bellido Mª. P., Callegarin L. (coords), *Los cartagineses y la monetización del Mediterráneo occidental*. Madrid, pp. 168-178.

Moret P. (2004). 'Ethnos ou ethnie? Avatars anciens et modernes des noms de peuples ibères', in Cruz Andreotti G., Mora Serrano B. (coords), *Identidades étnicas - identidades políticas en el mundo prerromano hispano*. Málaga, pp. 31-62.

Moret P. (2006). 'La formation d'une toponymie et d'une ethnonymie grecques de l'Ibérie: étapes et acteurs', in Cruz Andreotti G., Le Roux P., Moret P. (eds), *La invención de una geografía de la Península Ibérica. I. La época republicana*. Málaga - Madrid, pp. 39-76.

Mozas Moreno Mª S. (2006). 'Consideraciones sobre las emisiones de Iltiraka: procedencia y tipología', *Actas del XII Congreso Nacional de Numismática*. Madrid, pp. 269-286.

Noguera Celdrán J. M., Rodríguez Oliva P. (2008). 'Scultura ispànica in epoca repubblicana: note su generi, iconografia, usi e cronologia', in Uroz J., Noguera J. M., Coarelli F. (eds), *Iberia e Italia: Modelos romanos de integración territorial*. Murcia, pp. 379-454.

Pérez Almoguera A. (2001). 'Iltir/iltur = oppidum. Los nombres de lugar y la ciudad en el mundo ibérico', *Faventia*, 23.1, pp. 21-40.

Pérez Orozco S. (2006). 'Los letreros de las monedas fenopúnicas y libiofenicias de Hispania', *Numisma*, 250, pp. 165-196.

Prontera F. (1990). 'L'Estremo Occidente nella concezione geografica dei Greci', in *La Magna Grecia e il lontano Occidente (Atti del ventinovesimo convegno di studi sulla Magna Grecia. Taranto, 6-11 ottobre 1989)*. Taranto, pp. 55-82.

Ripollès P. P. (1994-1995). 'La moneda en los inicios de la romanización: talleres y artesanos', *Arse*, 28-29, pp. 199-215.

Ripollès P. P. (2005). 'Coinage and Identity in the Roman provinces: Spain', Howgego C., Heuchert V., Burnett A. (eds), *Coinage and Identity in the Roman provinces*. Oxford, pp. 79-93.

Ripollès P. P. (2005b). 'Las acuñaciones antiguas de la península ibérica: dependencias e innovaciones', in *XIII Congreso Internacional de Numismática*. Vol. I. Madrid, pp. 187-208.

Ripollés P. P., Muñoz J., Llorens M. M. (1993). 'The Original Number of Dies used in the Roman Provincial Coinage of Spain', in *XI International Numismatic Congress*. Louvain-la-Neuve, I, pp. 315-324.

Rodríguez Casanova I. (1999). 'Consideraciones sobre la iconografía monetal de la ceca de Carmo: el 'Mercurio Africano'', in Centeno R. M. S., García-Bellido Mª. P., Mora G. (coords), *Rutas, ciudades y moneda en Hispania (Actas del II Encuentro Peninsular de Numismática Antigua. Anejos del Archivo Español de Arqueología 20)*. Madrid, pp. 333-340.

Rodríguez Neila J. F. (1995). 'Organización administrativa de las comunidades hispanas y magistraturas monetales', in García-Bellido Mª. P., Centeno R. M. S. (eds), *La moneda hispánica: ciudad y territorio (Actas del I Encuentro Peninsular de Numismática Antigua. Anejos del Archivo Español de Arqueología 14)*. Madrid, pp. 261-274.

Rodríguez Oliva P. (1994). 'Sobre el culto de Apolo en la Baetica', in *Latinitas Biblica et Christiana. Studia philologica varia in honorem Olegario García de la Fuente*. Madrid, pp. 144-158.

Roldán J. M., Wulff F. (2002). *Citerior y Ulterior. Las provincias romanas de Hispania en época republicana*. Madrid.

Roldán L., Blánquez J., Bendala M. et al. (2003). *Carteia II*. Madrid.

Sáez Bolaño J. A., Blanco Villero J. M. (2006). 'Una ceca incierta de la Bética', *Numisma*, 250, pp. 111-138.

Sáez Fernández F. (2006). 'Las Tradiciones Agrícolas Antiguas en el Territorio Andaluz', in *Historia de Andalucía*. Vol. I. Sevilla, pp. 240-251.

Stannard C. (2005). 'Numismatique evidence for relations between Spain and central Italy at the turn of the first and second centuries BC', *Revue Suisse de Numismatique*, 83, pp. 47-79.

Stylow A. U. (2005). 'Fuentes epigráficas para la historia de la 'Hispania Ulterior' en época republicana', in Melchor E. et al. (eds), *Julio César y Corduba: Tiempo y espacio en la campaña de Munda (49-45 a.C.)*. Córdoba, pp. 247-262.

Untermann J. (1992). 'Los etnónimos de la Hispania Antigua y las lenguas prerromanas de la Península Ibérica', in Almagro Gorbea M., Ruiz Zapatero G. (eds), *Paleoetnología de la Península Ibérica (Complutum 2-3. Vol. 1)*, pp. 19-34.

Velaza J. (2005). 'La escritura y la lengua en el mundo ibérico: algunas reflexiones', in Carrasco Serrano G., Oliva Mompeán J. C. (coords), *Escrituras y lenguas del Mediterráneo en la Antigüedad*. Cuenca, pp. 363-379.

Villaronga L. (2000). 'Una nueva emisión monetaria de Sacili', in Castro Hipólito M. et al. (coords), *Homagem a Mário Gomes Marques*. Sintra, pp. 145-148.

Whitehead D. (1994). 'Site-Classification and reliability in Stephanus of Byzantium', in ID. (ed.), *From Political Architecture to Stephanus Byzantius. Sources for the Ancient Greek Polis*. Stuttgart, pp. 99-124.

Woods D. E. (1964). 'A Numismatic Chapter of the Romanization of Hispania', in *Essays in Memory of K. Lehman*. New York, pp. 383-387.

Wulff F. (1989). 'La fundación de Carteia: algunas notas', *Studia Historica Historia Antigua*, 7, pp. 43-57.

Wulff F. (2003). *Las esencias patrias. Historiografía e Historia Antigua en la construcción de la identidad española (siglos XVI-XX)*. Barcelona.

Zamora López J. A. (2007). 'La inscripción sobre fragmento de pizarra hallada en Alcalá del Río: un excepcional epígrafe neopúnico', in Ferrer Albelda E., Fernández Flores A., Escacena Carrasco J. L., Rodríguez Azogue A. (eds), *Ilipa Antiqua. De la prehistoria a la época romana*. Alcalá del Río, pp. 131-147.

1

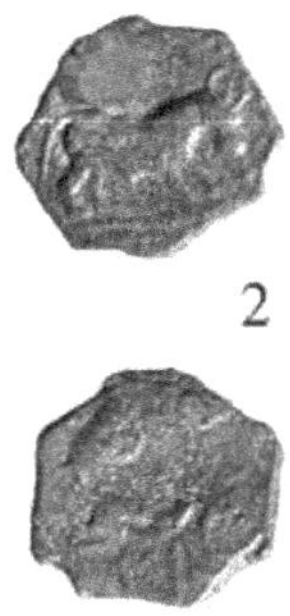

2

3 (x2)

4

5

6

7

8

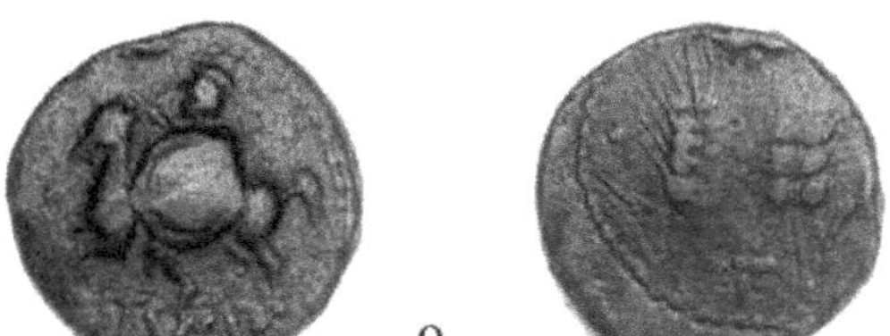

9

10

11

12

13

14

Cities, *Drachmae*, *Denarii* and the Roman conquest of Hispania

Manuel Gozalbes

ABSTRACT

This paper deals with the role played in the Iberian Peninsula by silver coins between the third and first centuries BC, in close connection with the Roman conquest. The Second Punic War resulted in the entry into circulation of a significant range of coins of different cultures and mints. The subsequent withdrawal of this coinage led to the establishment in Hispania of a homogeneous monetary mass based on Roman and 'Iberian' denarii during the second century BC. Classical sources provide little help in numismatic terms, and therefore the coins themselves are the only evidence available to establish the origins, function and use of these local series. Among the subjects to discuss are the different chronology of the mints, their varied output, the supply of metal, the evolution of weights and the authorities involved in this process. In addition, the circulation of the 'Iberian denarii' supports the idea that, in certain places and periods, these local issues were also the only currency available to the Romans.

Introduction

The provinces of Hispania Citerior and Hispania Ulterior were created in 197 BC, soon after the Second Punic War (218-202 BC).[1] This political context encouraged the development of the Iberian and Celtic coinage of Hispania, which took place principally in the presence of the Romans throughout the second and first centuries BC (García-Bellido and Ripolles 1997; Domínguez 1998, 2001 and 2005). A comprehensive catalogue for these series identifies nearly a hundred cities in Hispania Citerior and probably up to sixty in Hispania Ulterior which were minting coins before the arrival of Augustus (*CNH*). This paper deals only with Citerior coinages, a production characterized by (a) a regular use of Iberian script; (b) silver issues; and (c) a well-known degree of homogeneity in their designs. Ulterior coinings, on the other hand, used mainly Latin characters, did not mint silver and used a remarkable variety of coin types.

The Roman occupation of Spain was progressive in nature, expanding control from the eastern and southern lands towards the west and north. Episodes of war were common in Hispania Citerior up to the reign of Augustus, when the occupation of the peninsula was completed. This situation is comprehensible in a broad sense, but there remain a number of difficulties in the way of our developing a better understanding of the origins, function and legal basis of these second and first-century local coinages developed in the presence of the Romans. Many questions remain unresolved in terms of identifying mints with actual sites, ordering coinages and providing them with a reliable chronology and establishing the extent of Roman intervention in this process. A number of contributions have been made to the study of these matters, and this research includes monographic studies identifying the original dies of silver mints, thus creating the basis for further study. This research has estimated the volume of coinage of several mints which produced silver in accordance with different cultural traditions:

1. *Drachmae*: released before, during and after the war at the Greek colony of Emporion (as well as Rhode before the war) (Villaronga 2000, 2002 and 2003), followed by a variety of imitations (Villaronga 1998). Besides these, *drachmae* of a different standard were also produced at the Iberian cities of Arse (Ripollès and Llorens 2003) and Saitabi (Ripollès 2007).

2. *Denarii*: minted exclusively from the second century BC: Kese (Villaronga 1983), Sekaiza (Gomis 2001), Konterbia Karbika (Abascal and Ripollès 2000), Belikiom (Collado 2000), and Turiazu (Gozalbes 2009a). These five examples constitute the sample available, out of 21 cities which minted *denarii*.

As regards *denarii*, the production of Turiazu is noteworthy, as there appears to have been an outstanding production of these coins. The study of these opens up a new approach to the production of silver coins in Hispania Citerior and their role in the Roman conquest (Gozalbes 2009a). But

(1) I am deeply indebted to Fernando López Sánchez for inviting me to write this article. I am also indebted to Mark Temple and Denny Collie for pointing out, in great and careful detail, a number of errors and omissions in the following pages. All responsability for any errors that may remain is, of course, mine.

for a deeper understanding of the whole process, it is necessary to look back at the role played by silver from the Second Punic War onwards, a matter discussed in another recent work (Gozalbes 2009b).

Silver money and the first coins

The Iron Age in the Iberian peninsula, traditionally situated between the sixth and first centuries BC, included both Celtic and Iberian cultures. An increasing amount of evidence from stray finds and hoards reveals that some Greek coins reached the coastal territories of Iberia from the fifth century BC, as a direct consequence of trade movements. This coinage was principally valued for its silver content and its artistic value (Ripollès 2009). In comparison, the local coinage of Iberia was irrelevant, as it was limited to the production of the Greek colonies of Emporion and Rhode in the noth-east from the fifth century onwards (Villaronga 1997 and 2000). The first Iberian mint was that of Arse (the present-day Sagunt), where Greek influence led the city to produce its first coins in Iberian script at the end of the fourth century BC (Ripollès and Llorens 2003; Aranegui 2005). The minting activity of these coastal cities, which followed different weight standards, can be linked to a considerable level of economic development.

Recent works also draw attention to the use of silver bullion in economic transactions, a complex phenomenon which developed approximately between the fifth and second centuries BC and which shows the increasing need of standardised money for transactions. The great rupture in the economic customs of the Iberian and Celtiberian peoples occurred, however, in direct consequence of the Second Punic War, which took place on Iberian soil from 218 BC onwards. It was therefore an episode of war that marked the beginning of an irreversible turning point in the economies of the Iberian peoples, when coins began to become a common form of payment. Even after the War, though, ingots and fragments of silver, many of them originating in war booty, were hoarded together with coins, demonstrating that money was still composed of a mixture of silver objects and coins (Gozalbes, Cores and Ripollès, forthcoming). A fragment from Strabo refers to the inland practice of bartering alongside payments, using small sheets of cut silver (3.3.7), and archaeological finds prove that silver and coins were to a certain extent available only in the southern and eastern territories where the war actually took place. In the north and west, the role of precious metals as a form of money remains more obscure: gold and silver were available, but existing records do not allow us to establish its use in any standardised form. Coins did not reach these territories until the second or even first centuries.

An assortment of coins

Iberia was the scene of the Second Punic War (218-202 BC), where both Carthaginians and Romans employed different strategies to mint coins to cover the costs of the hostilities (Marchetti 1978, pp. 369-430). While the Carthaginians minted their whole production on Iberian territory, Romans arguably produced only victoriatii on Iberian soil (RRC 96), despite recent suggestions that they also produced the rare *simbellae* and *libellae*, which were of minor economic relevance (García-Bellido 2000-2001, pp. 571-573). The significant numbers of hoards are the best evidence in order to study the currency of those years (Marchetti 1978, pp. 355-368; Villaronga 1993, nos. 11-40), as these included silver coins from a variety of origins: (1) Carthaginian (minted in Iberia and elsewhere); (2) Roman (republican, minted in Rome); (3) Greek (including a significant number from Emporion, as well as Rhode, Massalia and a variety of Hellenistic pieces); (4) Iberian imitations of Emporion; (5) Iberian *drachmae* from Arse and Saiti; (6) fractions from uncertain mints; (7) Punic coins from Ebusus or Gadir; and (8) Gaulish. A number of studies identify the different series involved in the conflict (Marchetti 1978; Crawford 1985; Villaronga 1973): the most significant of these were the so-called official productions of both states (1 and 2). This mainstream of production aside, a large number of *drachmae* were minted at Emporion (3) and then imitated by Iberian peoples (4), the former probably in support of the war efforts of the Romans (Villaronga 1987) and the latter for uncertain purposes. These local *drachmae* probably then set a precedent which encouraged the minting of later Iberian *denarii* under the Roman administration.

Second Punic War hoards show high figures for silver coins in circulation, and these formed a heterogeneous monetary mass which was widely available in southern and eastern territories and which made use of a considerable mixture of monetary systems and values. From these hoards three areas of circulation can be established: (a) in the south-east Carthaginian coins were predominant; (b) in the north-east, Roman and Emporitan issues formed the main currency; and (c) a mixture of both models can be found in a central area of contact (Villaronga 1993, p. 72). Furthermore, additional difficulties arise from the different cultural traditions of the territories involved (at very least Iberian, Celtiberian, Greek and Punic), which followed different weight patterns. During this period the use of coins can be closely linked with that of bullion silver, a fact that is becoming clearer with study of the numerous deposits, such as Driebes, Valeria, Cerro Colorado and Armuña de Tajuña, where both types were hoarded together (Gozalbes, Cores and Ripollès, forthcoming). Taking into consideration the fact that coins usually appear in the form of halves and quarters, and that silver bullion fragments cover a wide range of weights (from 0.1 g to great cakes of silver), it is obvious that for specific agreements some payments could only be arranged after checking the weight of particular pieces. In any case, the existence of facilities for standardised transactions are hard to find among this assortment of currency and it is hard to guess whether prices were fixed in a common accounting system. A new monetary background was needed and the new rulers realised that a total retrieval of currency was indispensable for the creation of a new monetary order.

This mixed currency disappeared progressively in the first decades of the second century BC and was no longer hoarded after the Roman retrievals of the 180-170s BC (see 5, below). The creation of the denarius in Rome around 211 BC marked an important milestone for the future introduction of a homogeneous monetary system in Hispania. Scholars wonder about the chronology of the first series of Iberian *denarii*, the coins minted by Iberian cities following the new Roman standard, but evidence for dating is scarce, since these Iberian pieces do not occur in hoards in significant quantities until the final decades of the second century BC.

CONTINUITY AND CHANGE IN SILVER ISSUES

1. *DRACHMAE* AND THE ROMANS

Before the arrival of the Carthaginians and the Romans, silver was fundamentally minted at Emporion, Rhode and Arse. The Greek colonies of Emporion and Rhode were the first cities to mint coins in Iberia, but the earliest coinage to be described as Iberian in a cultural sense was minted at Arse during the fourth century BC, beginning a prolonged production of silver coins with Greek influences which continued over the third and second centuries BC.

New mints for *drachmae* were probably created after the arrival of the Carthaginians in 237 BC. The Punic cities of Ebusus and Gadir minted *drachmae* and fractions, perhaps encouraged by the variety of Carthaginian issues made on Iberian soil following the shekel standard (Villaroga 1973; *CNH*, pp. 63-74). The Romans, however, were also responsible for some coinage after their arrival in 218 BC, and it seems that at first the production of Emporion, their allied city, was handled by the Romans, producing *drachmae* that maintained the traditional style of the Greek colony (Marchetti 1978, p. 382). The designs show continuity, though there is a little renovation from 218 BC onwards: on the reverse, the head of Pegasus turns into a figure of a little man holding his feet with his hands (Figure 1). These series, long accepted as a Roman initiative, constitute an original monetary practice that served the Romans' purposes without making its presence felt through the design.

After the War, and following Emporion, several new Iberian mints adopted this design (Persefone/Pegasus), accompanied by over a hundred different legends. These coins are grouped under the headings *drachmae* imitations of Emporion or Iberian *drachmae* (*CNH*, pp. 36-60; Villaronga 1998). The legends on these coins are somewhat irregular, with several attempting to reproduce, with varying degrees of accuracy, the original Greek legend ΕΜΠΟΡΙΤΟΝ, alongside others with Iberian legends, and many others engraved with unidentifiable characters. These issues shared certain formal features, but it is hard to guess how many authorities were responsible for these series. Some legends state city names with Iberian characters in a more or less comprehensible form, but mints are hardly recognizable, since only a few legends provide names which are clearly related to cities such as ILTIRTAR (*CNH*, p. 41, nos. 32-39), OROSE (*CNH*, p. 42, nos. 40-41), TARANKONSALIR (*CNH*, p. 44, nº 56), BARKENO (*CNH*, p. 51, nº 95) or BELSE (*CNH*, p. 52, nº 105), while the meaning of many others is uncertain (Villaronga 1998, pp. 61-67). A few of these legends could be read as personal names (Villaronga 1998, p. 65), a particular feature of these productions, since later Iberian and Celtiberian legends on *denarii* basically consist of city names.

Fig. 1. *Drachma* minted at Emporion after 218 BC. 18mm.

So how many workshops were responsible for this large output? Despite the variety of legends, many of these pieces share a common style, as if only a few artisans or engravers were responsible for the entirety of these series. It seems unlikely that each issue was created by a different workshop, and if these series were minted by several cities, why are their names usually absent or poorly engraved? It should be remembered that minting was also a business, and the name of the authority seems to be a valuable part of the design, if not the most important. The designs appear to be well finished, but was the skill of the engravers insufficient to trace simple signs in some cases? Were the engravers illiterate, or unable to reproduce Iberian script? Were they in fact Iberians? It could also be the case that epigraphic errors crept in after successive copies.

Diversity in quality could be connected with different origins, but at the same time certain workshops may possibly have minted coins for different cities. It seems as if a travelling workshop may have offered its services widely to local populations which had silver available and wished to obtain money in the form of coins. Should this supposition be true, only a few workshops could be responsible for the entire output of *drachmae*. But why should they have produced poorly-finished imitations of Emporion *drachmae*? This panorama seems to reflect a low level of organisation and the spontaneous development of issues without any structured background. It is hard to suppose that these degenerated legends aimed to reproduce any particular name and perhaps the availability of silver was the only necessary condition for minting coins.

2. SOME VISIBLE ROMAN INFLUENCES

Iberian *drachmae* strictly copied the original Greek design from Emporion, so in formal terms they represented nothing new. But as well as these imitations, the Iberian mints of Saitabi and Iltirke also issued new original designs of *drachmae*, or at least a local standard (García-Bellido 2000-2001, p. 558) which fitted in well with the new Roman context, in accordance with their respective choices:

a. The adoption of a Roman design. Saitabi, located near the present-day Xàtiva (Valencia), issued a series of didrachms, drachms and hemidrachms with a reverse design which copied the republican gold pieces of 60, 40 and 20 *asses* (Ripollès 2007, pp. 33-35). This symbolic choice may establish what is perhaps the first connection between Iberian and Roman silver coinage.

b. A workshop that successively minted *drachmae* and *denarii*. Both denominations can be linked to the work of a single artist, perhaps the finest of all the engravers of Iberian coins. The mints of Iltirke and Iltirta provide a unique example of continuity in the Iberian cities (García-Garrido and Montañès 2007, pp. 46-47). The former minted a *drachma* with the legend ILTIRKESALIR (*CNH*, p. 36, nº 1), while the latter coined *denarii* with the legend ILTIRTASALIRBAN (*CNH*, pp. 176-178, nos. 4, 5, 13, 19), a series which is situated among the earliest productions of this new denomination, if not the very first. The chronology is uncertain for both issues: the *drachma* is dated to the years of the Second Punic War, while the *denarius* appears to fit in well in the first decades of the second century BC. What is interesting is the fact that both of these issues, belonging to different mints and following different metrological standards, used obverse and reverse dies engraved by the same artist (Figure 2). This allows us to surmise that both issues were released in a similar context, which also suggests a chronological proximity, and in addition the existence of this shared workshop makes it viable to posit a similar model for the minting of other Iberian *drachmae*. If Iltirke and Iltirta did share a workshop, it seems no longer relevant to consider different backgrounds for their respective coinages. The change of weight can be seen as a minor innovation or even the choice of the mint. The former *drachmae* workshop turned into one which minted *denarii*, showing continuity in an established business that created high-quality coins and connecting the traditions of *drachmae* and *denarii*. The change, rather than being the consequence of a new monetary policy, seems to be more of an immediate and effective adaptation on the part of a mint to a new weight standard which was lighter and therefore more profitable, enabling the extraction of more coins from the same quantity of silver.

Fig. 2. (a) *Drachma* from Iltirkesalir (b) *Denarius* from Iltirtasalirban [Paris, BnF])

At Arse, Roman influences began to be felt in the third century BC with the production of small bronze fractions with a prow on the reverse (Ripollès and Llorens 2002, cat. 79-81). During the second century BC, the growing power of Rome affected a large number of bronze issues from Arse, with the depiction of a goddess resembling Rome on the obverse and a prow on the reverse. The silver issues of the city, with Greek influences, are, however, more elusive as regards revealing affinities with the new political background, even from a metrological approach (Ripollès and Llorens 2002, pp. 65-94, 153-154).

3. *Denarii* for all

Once the silver currency of the war had disappeared, the slow introduction of the new Roman weight standard began, adopting the new types of the male head and the horseman for local coinages. Hoards do not register, however, a transition between these periods and the example of Iltirtasalirban found no immediate continuity. The retrieval of currency was effective and, at least according to hoard evidence, the new *denarii* did not appear prior to the decade of 170 BC, and were very scarce until the last third of the century. The production of local silver was mainly located around the north-east coast and the Ebro and Duero valleys, and Iberian, Celtiberian and Vasconian peoples were involved in a minting process that extended over a century, ca. 170-70 BC.

Another problem lies in establishing an end point for these issues. Scholars traditionally situate the abandonment of these local silver coinages as coming after the Sertorian War, in a Roman punishment for the supposed loyalty of the mints to the cause of Sertorius. This view is strongly influenced by a presumption that relates the main output of Iberian *denarii* with the cause of Sertorius, i.e. for the financing of his troops: mints like Bolskan, Turiazu or Sekobirikes would have assisted the Sertorian war efforts (García-Bellido 2005, p. 34). The fact that these coins were circulating during the conflict is undisputed, because many of the series had been minted in the previous decades and they constituted the core of the monetary mass at the time. The real difficulty here lies in identifying certain dies that may have been in operation during the Sertorian years, a view which, in the case of Turiazu, cannot be sustained for the main output (Gozalbes 2009a, p. 172), despite the fact that a few dies from this mint could even be dated to after the war.

Celtic, Iberian and Vasconian peoples were neighbours who had their own traditions, but their respective coinages were identical, showing the background of a common influence: the only shared reference point for all these peoples was the Roman presence (Burnett 1987, p. 39). The distribution of silver mints has been studied from a territorial perspective, given that, in a broad sense, production took place from east to west (Burillo 1998, pp. 318-320), including primarily Iberian, Celtiberian and Vasconian cities which can be arranged according to a more precise ethnic attribution (Table 1), and which are subject to different conceptual and chronological interpretations for Celtiberian peoples and their neighbours (Burillo 1998, p. 147, fig. 44; Burillo 1999). The entirety of their issues adopted Iberian signs for their coin legends -a common feature along with the choice of similar designs (male head/horseman) and weights. The typological uniformity of the Iberian, Celtic and Vasconian issues is also a matter to consider, since the bearded/unbearded head and the horseman with spear, palm or other objects were a common feature of Hispania Citerior coinage (Figure 3). Why did such diverse peoples share these designs? It seems plausible that they were copying each other except for minor details, like objects or attributes. The types chosen appear to be related to gods or heroes of local origin (Almagro-Gorbea 1995; Arévalo 2002-2003 and 2003), while, from another perspective, the horseman and a number of secondary designs could be read as Roman provincial themes (Paz and Ortiz 2007; against this argument Gozalbes 2006).The output of these mints was diverse, nevertheless. Some of the cities, which produced huge quantities of *denarii*, rise the interest of scholars. This production of huge quantities of coins were presumably related to the state budget, or significant wages or taxes. For mints with a small production it is difficult to speculate regarding their use, which could, at least to some extent, be quite different. There were 21 cities which minted *denarii*, from a number of different ethnic groups. Despite the fact that some of these were Iberian while others were Celtic or Vasconian, the literature usually groups them under the heading Iberian *denarii*, a designation which is only justified by their common adoption of Iberian script.

A certain mystery lies behind the names of the cities responsible for the main silver issues: places like Sekobirikes, Baskunes, Arekorata, Arsaos or Turiazu are only known through coin legends. It is certain that the most powerful minting centres of Hispania were not cited by any literary source for their minting activities or for any other historical feature, and, furthermore, decades of archaeological, linguistic and numismatic research have still failed to precisely locate these cities or villages. Bolskan, also referred to as Osca, is the only example quoted (Plut., Sert. 14 and 25), but in the context of its later role as the Sertorian headquarters for a number of years at a time when minting activities may have ceased.

Table 1. Ethnicity

Culture	Ethnic group	Mint
Iberian	Kessetani	kese
	Ilergetes	iltirta
	Ausetani	ausesken
	Sedetani	kelse
Celtiberian	Suessetani	sesars, bolskan, sekia
	Belli	belikiom, sekaisa
	Lusones	turiazu
	Arevaci	sekobirikes
	Celtiberi	arekorata, oilaunikos, kolounioku, sekotias
Vasconian	Vascones	baskunes, arsaos, arsakos, bentian
Other	Carpetani	karbika
	Uncertain	ikalesken

Fig. 3. *Denarius* of Belikiom [Paris, BnF]

5. SOURCES

Livy, Appian, Strabo and Plutarch provide isolated and vague references to monetary matters concerning Hispania. Livy's work includes over seventeen references[2] which detail the transport to Rome of precious metals and coins from Hispania in the first decades of the second century BC (García Riaza 1999b). Livy referred to silver bullion, pounds of unspecified coins, on four occasions to *bigati* (197-191 BC), and on three to pieces named *oscensis argenti* and *signati oscensis nummum* (197-195 BC).[3] These much-discussed references, relating to the years 197-195 BC, apparently mention the *denarii* of Bolskan (*CNH*, p. 211-212), later the imperial Osca, and more improbably the Oscan script of southern Italy (Villaronga 1977). The idea of Bolskan *denarii* circulating soon after the Second Punic War is hard to sustain when we consider the fact that these pieces were absent from hoards prior to the last decades of the second century. In addition, the number of *oscenses* coins recorded by Livy exceeds by far the supposed output of the mint at that date, if indeed any early attempt at minting was done.

It appears that Livy's reference lacks the historical accuracy that we are seeking. Even if Livy was referring to a particular issue, coin finds demonstrate that its withdrawal

(2) Livy 28.38.5; 31.20.7; 32.7.4; 33.27.2; 33.27.3; 34.10.4; 34.10.7; 34.46.2; 36.39.2; 39.29.6-7; 39.42.3; 40.16.11; 40.43.4-6; 41.7.2; 41.7.2; 41.28.6; 45.4.1.

(3) Livy 34.10.4 and 7; 34.46.2; 40.43.6.

was effective, so if any issue of Bolskan coinage was withdrawn, this would remain unknown to us. The fact is that the Second Punic War series no longer appear after the first decades of the second century BC, and according to this evidence the value of Livy's words is limited, and can be appreciated only as a Roman literary reference from the Augustan period to a kind of coin (or coins) that circulated much earlier. Crawford also points out that Livy's coverage of monetary matters was somewhat lacking (1969, p. 83), and scholars agree that the expression *argentum oscense* refers to the local coinage of the Second Punic War, including, under different criteria, Emporion *drachmae*, Iberian imitations and Carthaginian issues (Amorós 1957, p. 62; Campo 1998, p. 40; Ripollès 2000, p. 334). As well as these earlier issues, Roman coins like *quadrigati* also disappeared: they were withdrawn and melted down because of their usefulness for minting the new lighter *denarii* in Rome, and thus providing additional profit.

It is perhaps significant that Livy's references to coins are concentrated in a few lines, with all of them coming from six fragments out of a total of 17 which detail the retrieval by Rome of precious metals. Among those which detail coins, three list different kinds, while the other three only include one mention of specific or unspecified coins. Why were a few coins identified and recorded specifying the number of units? The Romans were interested in pounds of silver, but not in precise accounts of foreign pieces which were worthless in Rome. In comparison with records of silver bullion, too, these coins represented only a small amount of wealth. It is possible that the coins that had already been counted before the retrieval were retained because they were useful for making payments, and so they were treated in a different manner to the silver bullion, and also that their grouping under the terms *bigati* and *argentum oscense* could be read in terms of Roman and non-Roman issues, perhaps to facilitate the keeping of records or accounts or even their transfer for specific payments to people who might prefer a particular variety of coin. Livy also listed some booties and taxes for the years 218, 209, 205 and 152 BC.[4] His recording system included pounds (*librae pondo*), talents and sestertii. A variety of studies have focused their interest in these retrievals on listing them (Blázquez 1967, pp. 262-264), calculating income for Rome excluding the coins (García Riaza 1999b), or converting all metals into *denarii*, but including conversions of gold bullion (Ferrer 1999).

Other sources provide very little help regarding the local currency of Hispania, dealing only with quantities of money, mainly local tributes imposed on peoples and cities (García Riaza 2009). Appian mentions at least three cases of Roman imposition of taxes on Celtiberian peoples, and two isolated texts by Strabo and Plutarch also refer to tributes.[5] The historical background to these quotes may be situated prior to the years 140-139 BC, perhaps therefore in a period when the main output of Iberian *denarii* was still to come. In any case, in the context of the historical panorama, the amounts quoted in these texts seem to lack monetary precision.

With the notable exception of Livy's coin records, monetary payments are recorded in different units: *pondo* (Livy), 'αργυρίου τάλαντα (Appian) and τάλαντα (Strabo and Plutarch). From these records, registered in accounting units, it is impossible to establish exactly the kind of silver referred to: bullion, coins, or a mixture of both are all plausible options. The vagueness of these sources appears to complicate any attempt to clarify this question, but a few noteworthy references provide a little more insight into Roman and Iberian monetary matters.

1. Livy specifies that Roman troops were paid by the Iberians on at least two occasions. In 206 BC, Mandonio was forced to contribute coins for the Roman army to be paid, by claiming *pecunia* from him to pay the *stipendium* (Livy, 28.34. 11-12,). Later, in 180 BC, provincials provided troops with *stipendium* and *frumentum* (Livy, 40.35.4).[6]

2. Caton paid 200 talents to the Celtiberians for their help as *auxiliarii* in 195 BC.[7] This reference clearly excludes the possibility of Celtiberians paying their own troops who were serving the Romans, thus revealing a complex background of political agreements and payments for *auxiliarii*.

3. Appian mentions that the Romans lost their money (χρήματα) while it was kept in the city of Ocilis (App. *Ib.*, 47), and also when the city switched its support to the Celtiberians.[8] The text is relevant in a financial sense because it states that Ocilis was where the Romans kept their resources, despite the ambiguous meaning of the term χρήματα.

These texts reveal that, in addition to the problems associated with the storage of money, anyone could pay anyone else with any coin in circulation, at least during the early years of the conquest. The fact that Iberian and Celtiberian peoples accepted Roman coins is not discussed anywhere, and both Livy's text and coin finds show that the Romans also accepted Iberian coins (see below, 13). Once this evidence is accepted, the main question is related to the origin and function of the *denarii* rather than their use once in circulation. It seems certain that Iberian *denarii*, which in practical terms meant 'silver money', were frequently used by the Romans during the conquest.

(4) Livy 21.61.11; 26.47.7; 30.21.3-5; 40.47.10.

(5) App, *Ib.* 48.52 and 79; Str. 3.4.13; Plut, *Cat. Ma.*, 10.

(6) The accuracy of this text is limited; if we understand this as possession of money, it could refer to Roman coins, Iberian coins, or both, with the latter perhaps the most plausible option for a time when the currency was heterogeneous. The possibility that the term refers to authority might also be taken into account, however.

(7) A figure equal to 15.794 pounds or 1.326.000 *denarii* (Plutarch, *Cat. Ma.* 10).

(8) In the following year, Marcellus demanded 30 talents after recovering the city (App. *Ib.* 48).

6. Origins, function, and use

Traditional interpretations of Iberian silver coinage as a means of favouring commercial transactions are now obsolete. From the 1970s onwards, different authors have investigated Iberian coinage, trying to explain its chronology, origins and function and focus regarding the latter has centred on state revenue and expenditures. In many senses, it is impossible to consider Iberian and Celtiberian coinage as a whole: the differences are of fundamental importance, bearing in mind that many mints and territories were involved, including series of bronze and silver minted over a century, and the different extent of their output. In reference to the Celtic and Iberian *denarii* of the northern meseta, in the context of uncertain administrative organisation and without any previous monetary tradition, three controversial aspects must be defined.

Origins. Discussion of the origins of Iberian *denarii* involves addressing chronological and legal questions, both in terms of the date of the first issue and the legal basis of the coinage as regards identifying the authorities involved in the process, a question that remains unresolved for these issues. The legal question seems to us to be particularly valuable, since the creation of mints was progressive and, furthermore, the output of the recent issues was greater than that of the earlier ones. The exact date of the first series of Iberian *denarii*, has long been the subject of discussion, but it can only vaguely be dated back to the first decades of the second century BC, in accordance with the preserved ancient hoard that includes these series (Villaronga 2002b). *Denarii* were a new release, but their continuity with *drachmae* proves the existence of previous attempts at minting, probably arranged on a similar basis.

Function. Coins enter into the monetary mass as a means of paying for products or services. Strictly speaking, only these first payments can be described as "function", though of course different mints and coin issues could have been destined for a variety of purposes. For Iberian, Celtiberian and Vasconian silver coins, however, a homogeneous main function has long been discussed, and so an initial objective consists in determining whether these Iberian *denarii* had a single or a multiple purpose. A different way of looking at the issue is to suppose something like a functional sequence, where coins always circulated in a similar way from their former use, repeating sequentially functions where one payment led automatically to another. It could be that Celtiberians paid their taxes with coins, and that the Romans used those coins mainly to pay wages, creating a kind of routine. Multiple secondary uses are better defined and, logically, not considered to be a primary function according to this perspective.

Use. Iberian and Celtiberian *denarii* were employed for multiple purposes (commercial, civil, fiscal or military), but not before the second century BC (Ñaco and Prieto 1999, p. 207). Of course, local peoples could dedicate silver coins principally for certain purposes, but only suppositions can be made regarding this, and the range of possible uses is wide, and also includes non-monetary purposes (Otero 1998, pp. 133-134). Considerations regarding the multiple uses of these *denarii* exceed the scope of this paper.

For our purposes, only origins and function require a brief discussion. Considering that previous *drachmae* issues were minted in the presence of the Romans, certain similarities could arise in several areas. A valid perspective involves taking into account the fact that the successive minting of *drachmae* and *denarii* only reveals a visible change of typology and weight which formed part of a heterogeneous monetary mass. Underlying this formal renovation, however, it is possible to guess the Roman monetary influence.

7. Continuity and volume of coin issues

These Iberian *denarii*, first minted during the first half of the second century BC, have usually been studied separately from Second Punic War coinages and considered as an independent phenomenon. In other words, the creation of mints for Iberian *denarii* became a challenge for scholars in terms of identifying a new Roman monetary policy for the newly-created province of Hispania. Previous to this, however, the *drachmae* of Emporion and their Iberian imitations played a crucial role in financing the war efforts of the Romans, and perhaps of certain Iberian peoples, thus creating a precedent that encouraged the later issues of *denarii*. Villaronga estimated the dies of different series of *drachmae* (Table 2); his calculations show high figures for a Greek colony such as Emporion and reveal how its designs were slightly modified and its output increased under Roman influence. During the conquest of Greece, the cities of Apollonia and Dyrrachium displayed a similar pattern of minting, adapting their production to the Roman presence (Giovannini 1982, p. 168). The drachms of these cities served Roman purposes when disembarking on the Greek coast and for their journeys along the via Egnatia. The main difference lies in the fact that the Greeks were already largely monetised, while the inhabitants of the Iberian meseta were at this time being introduced to these new small round silver pieces.

At the same time that these Iberian *drachmae* were minted, the Romans were introducing the new denarius system. This new denomination, weighing 4.5 g (72 to the pound), was deliberately intended to be exchangeable with Emporion *drachmae*, the only local coins available in significant quantities and probably also minted under Roman disposition. From an Iberian perspective, this was the new Roman *drachma*, since its weight was the same as that of the Emporion issues, weighing 4.67 g during the third century and 4.62 g from 218 BC onwards. It seems realistic to suppose a similar background for *denarii*: the Romans adopted local issues to their purposes, and at this point reduced the weight to the new standard. The origins and function of Iberian *denarii*, local productions which followed the Roman metrological system, remain obscure, despite the fact that they were of fundamental importance for both

Table 2. Estimated output of *drachmae* coin issues

	Obverse dies		Reverse dies		Source
Series	*Identified*	*Estimated*	*Identified*	*Estimated*	
Emporion *drachmae*. Before 218 a.C.	160	285.5	187	355.66	Villaronga 2000, 123-125
Emporion *drachmae*. Second Punic War	212	280.02	303	451.79	Villaronga 2003, 86-87
Emporion *drachmae*. beginnings 2nd cent. B.C.	94	98.36	129	141.74	Villaronga 2002, 55-56
Iberian *drachmae*		278			Villaronga 1998, 90
Iberian fractions		47.45			Villaronga 1998, 93
Rhode *drachmae*. Before 218 a. C.	41	72.63			Villaronga 2000, 53
Rhode *drachmae*. From 218 a. C.	6	9.43			Villaronga 2000, 53
Rhode *drachmae*. Imitations	95	198.25			Villaronga 2000, 54
Rhode *drachmae*. Groups 5 and 6	?	76			Villaronga 2000, 54

Iberians and Romans during the conquest. In terms of continuity, however, the question of a new release seems inadequate as the sole approach to study. The amount of silver minted in Iberia up to the Second Punic War would have reached approximately 174.174 kg, according to Villaronga's initial estimations (1995b, pp. 8-9).(9) As a merely hypothetical figure, this quantity of silver minted locally in Iberia before the end of the War is very close to the records of coins transported to Roma between the years 199-180 BC as detailed by Livy, which adds up to approximately 182.000 kg.(10) This resemblance seems coincidental, but provides support for the idea that the monetary mass was totally withdrawn in the aftermath of the War.

For some Iberian and Celtiberian mints, an estimation of issues has been made (Table 3), and it may be useful to divide these into three categories according to their respective importance. The highly diverse output of these cities makes it clear that their economic importance varied to a large degree: a few of them played a major role in the economy of the region, while there were others where production had little importance, such as Ausesken, Sekotias or Koulionoku.

8. SILVER

Minting of *drachmae* and *denarii* require silver. So where did Iberian and Celtiberian silver come from? There is no clear evidence concerning metal supplies, but a mixture of origins must be supposed, since Iberia was a rich source of metals, and silver can be easily recycled. The richest mines were located at Carthago Nova, which produced nine million *denarii* per year (Strabo 3.2.10; Blázquez 1978, pp. 32-35): this was highly significant in terms of production, but it was unlikely that there was any intention to mint coins in Hispania after the Second Punic War. Iberian and Celtiberian peoples were familiar with silver, since ingots, jewellery and dishes are often found as archaeological evidence in different areas of Hispania Citerior, and, furthermore, Second Punic War hoards reveal a preponderance of silver fragments over coins. In absolute terms, partially-documented Hacksilber from hoards adds up to 17.5 kg, despite the fact that the weight of silver coins did not exceed 8.73 kg (Gozalbes, Cores and Ripollès, forthcoming). The significance of bullion must have been higher still, though, when one takes into account the records of Livy who provided details of large quantities of silver and gold which were transported to Rome (García Riaza 1999b). This process, which involved significant transfers of metal, could have meant a lack of precious metals among Iberian societies for a few decades (Ripollès 2000, pp. 334-335).

New *denarii* were essential in territories where silver coins were scarce or non-existent after the Second Punic War, and the Romans progressively integrated into their sphere of influence peoples which were new to coin circulation. Silver metallurgy is a field that awaits further research, but it is obvious that some areas rich in minerals were already being exploited when the Romans arrived. Leaving aside well-known areas of Hispania Ulterior such as Carthago Nova or the Sierra Morena, which formed part of a territory that did not mint silver coins, scholars have attempted to find silver ores in the areas of Hispania Citerior that surround known silver mints. There is, however, as yet little evidence linking these phenomena, despite findings that ores from the Sierra Calderona were perhaps used for Arse-Saguntum *drachmae* (Ripollès and Llorens 2002, pp. 162-164), and that Celtiberian mines may have produced far more silver than was required for Celtiberian issues (Sanz 2003).

(9) Including silver fractions (9.786 kg), *drachmae* of Emporion and Rhode (9.588 kg and 4.982 kg), carthaginian issues (99.458 kg, including carthaginian -37.989 kg, 31.204 kg, 27.432 kg-, Gadir -1.100 kg- and Ebusus -1.733 kg-), Emporion under the Romans (39.809 kg), Arse (3.256 kg) and Iberian imitations of *drachmae* (7.295 kg). Later calculations of the same author; 9.112 kg of silver fractions (Villaronga 1997, p. 102) and 13.782 kg of Iberian *drachmae* and fractions (Villaronga 1998, p. 94).

(10) The records of Livy include retrievals of 213.153 bigati (Livy 34.10.4 and 7; 34.46.2; 36.39.2.) 478,740 pieces of *argentum oscense* (see note 2) beside 553,063 pounds of uncertain coins (Livy 33.27.2; 34.10.4 and 7; 34.46.2), equal to about 179.192 kg calculated from a pound of 324 g. Calculating an arbitrary weight of 4 g for 691.893 pieces of bigati and *argentum oscense* it would suppose 2.767 kg more, reaching a total of 181.959 kg.

Table 3. Estimated output of *denarii* mints

	After Villaronga 1995, 75-76	After monographs (obverse, estimated)
Kelse	1	
Kolounioku	2	
Ausesken	4	
Sekotias	4	
Arsakoson	5	
Oilaunu	10.4	
Sekaisa	13.8	20-22 (Gomis 2001, 98)
Bentian	18	
Kese	32.6	
Konterbia	32.7	18 (Abascal and Rippollès 2000, 30)
Sekia	33.5	
Belikio	49.4	37-38 (Collado 2000, 104)
Ikalkusken	52.6	
Iltirta	68.3	
Arsaos	90	
Sekobirikes	136.6	
Sesars	145	
Turiazu	158.3	378-401 (Gozalbes 2009, 161)
Baskunes	222.2	
Arekorata	267.4	
Bolskan	550.7	

Mining activities were the main source of silver, but not the only one. It is possible that once silver mines provided a regular supply, there was less urgent need to send to Rome bullion collected from taxes or booties. After the Second Punic War silver was transferred to Rome in large quantities (according to Livy's records, up to 1,250,000 pounds of silver) but this fact does not exclude the possibility of local peoples keeping some of their resources, with or without Roman consent. Indeed, a Roman policy of leaving no silver at all in this immense territory with many peoples living outside the boundaries of the provinces under control seems unrealistic. Hoards like that of Salvacañete (Cabré 1936) demonstrate that silver bullion was still available at the end of the second century BC. After the main retrievals, later acquisitions by the Roman authorities could have been directly transformed or minted in Hispania rather than shipped to Rome, thus saving costs and the risks of transport. Once the process had been established, transporting silver from mines was a routine activity, unlike other income streams like taxes or booty, which could involve difficult transfers with unforeseen risks.

Coins could also become an immediate source of silver at certain times. The withdrawal of heavier pieces from circulation would allow melting down and the creation of new blanks adapted to lighter standards, with subsequent benefits. The mint of Turiazu reveals that high weight coin issues could be also used for coining new ones of a lighter standard (Gozalbes 2009a, p. 106): the earlier *denarii* of Turiazu weighed nearly 4g, while the later ones were an average of 3.32g. In fact, earlier series are hard to find in hoards, which indicates that even at that time the heaviest pieces were not available. On some occasions, direct overstrikes also took place, thus saving extra work (Gozalbes 2009a, fig. 101).

If during the first half of the second century BC the Roman army was paid in bronze, then silver issues could be regarded as initially of secondary importance. The progressive increase in Iberian silver issues seems to reflect Roman requirements more than those of the local peoples, who had been continuously fighting against the Romans ever since their arrival. Even finds at Numantia may reflect the fact that the monetary mass was organised according to Roman monetary structures. But the real difficulty lies in identifying who directly contributed the silver for minting these *denarii*. Names of cities appear on every issue, but some series seem too large to be the result of civic contributions. Their characterisation as ethnic contributions is impossible to argue, given the absolute lack of evidence for this.

9. DATING LOCAL *DENARII*

Nearly a hundred Iberian, Celtiberian and Vasconian mints produced coins from the century between the beginning of the second century BC and the end of the Sertorian conflict. These local coins of Hispania included silver and copper/bronze issues released at cities incorporated into Roman territory, or simply on the basis of their vicinity to the borders of the latter. Only 21 of these localities, however, minted silver *denarii*, including four that minted *quinarii*, another feature that fits in well with Roman monetary culture (Gozalbes 2009a, pp. 167-168). The mints in question are located mainly in the north-eastern part of the peninsula, with the exact location uncertain in several cases (Figure 4). Indeed, seeking to establish a precise date for the introduction of Iberian *denarii* seems an inappropriate approach to the problem. If Roman permission was necessary for minting, there is no doubt that the initial authorisation could be of particular importance, and it is possible that this could have been arranged for Iltirke or Kese, but the relevance of this fact is perhaps relative, given the earlier minting of *drachmae* at Emporion (Villaronga 1993a, pp. 22-30) and the imitations that followed (Villaronga 1993a, pp. 36-55), possibly with a similar function. In addition, the first series of Iberian *denarii* were scarcer than later ones, and many mints and ethnic groups were involved in the process. Did Iltirtasalirban and Sekobirikes follow the same instructions for minting? The coins of the former, rare as they were, were produced at the beginning of the second century BC, while the extensive issues of the latter were probably minted on the cusp of the second and first centuries BC, at least 50 or 60 years later. Were these issues in accordance with the granting of similar permissions? It is possible that during that period Roman political practice had evolved along with the specific requirements of the conquest.

Numismatic literature places the origins of the first Iberian *denarii* at ca. 180-150 BC (Amorós 1957, p. 62; Jenkins 1958, p. 58; Crawford 1985, pp. 143-144; Beltrán 1998, p. 112; García-Bellido and Blázquez 2001, p. 74, 129-130). What seems clear is that issues were not simultaneous, and that their peak seems to be situated at between approximately 150 and 75 BC. The coastal territory of the north-west housed the earlier Iberian mints, while it was the Upper Ebro and Duero valleys that produced the later ones. It is possible that the first series were released at Kese, Iltirkesalir, Iltirta and Ausesken, and these were then followed by Sesars and Bolskan, and finally mints like Turiazu or Sekobirikes.

The hoard from Francolí confirms that the Iberian *denarii* of Kese can be dated back to the first quarter of the second century BC (Villaronga 2002b, p. 39), and the absence of hoards containing Iberian *denarii* dated prior to this date seems relevant, since there are many deposits from the second century BC. Despite this, and taking into consideration the fact that for the middle decades of the century evidence of hoards is scarce, *denarii* only became common in the hoards buried at the end of the century. There is a notable gap between 170 BC and the fall of Numantia in 133 BC, and no records are available for these crucial decades. In relation to the years 169-133 BC, it is hard to determine the level of payments to the Romans and the role of silver coins, data that would determine the extent of the issues if they were related to the Roman administration. Little new evidence contributes to the establishing of definite chronologies for the progressive incorporation of mints. The recent study of Turiazu suggests that the city was probably minting coins between around 140-130 and 70 BC (Gozalbes 2009a, pp. 145-147).

Dating evidence is scarce for the first series of *denarii*, but taking into account the previous coinages of *drachmae*, and the fact that the establishment of Iberian *denarii* mints was not simultaneous, the importance of this seems to be only relative. A shared workshop for Iltirkesalir and Iltirtasalirban is an evidence of continuity between *drachmae* and *denarii* and probably constitutes an early attempt to introduce the new weight without there being particular instructions or further administrative changes at the mint itself (see also 4.2). During the period of the conquest, general policy can only be understood when validated by study of the Iberian mints and the currency. This panorama of local coinages fits in well with the fact that Roman silver was increasingly important for state payments from 157 BC onwards (Crawford 1985, p. 72, 96, 143), and Iberian bronze coinage seems to have been insufficient for the payment of troops. On the other hand, silver mints could have contributed to this function to some extent, as is demonstrated by the estimation of the original dies used. It seems therefore that *denarii* were minted in large quantities only when it proved necessary.

The closure of the silver mints is another issue which has been the subject of discussion. Evidence from hoards, as well as a troubled political background, has suggested to scholars that Iberian and Celtiberian *denarii* were no longer produced after the Sertorian war. This date constitutes only an approximate reference point, given the fact that a number of mints probably ended their minting activities long before this (as in the cases of Kese, Iltirta, Sesars or Belikiom), and that a few issues (like those of Turiazu) could have continued for some years after the war (Gozalbes 2009a, p. 148).

10. Legal authority and Roman Republican coins

These silver issues seem to bring up an important question: they were created on Roman instructions, or was it a local initiative? By creating Iberian *denarii*, Roman magistrates may have been consciously trying to gain some advantage by introducing new coins with an appearance appropriate to the peoples of the area. If authorisations were arranged individually for each mint, as seems to have been the case, every concession seems equally relevant. In contrast to *drachmae* issues, *denarii* series did not share engravers to any great extent. There are, of course, certain resemblances, but the majority of the output was produced by exclusive engravers. It is possible, however, that a common engraver was responsible for the silver dies of Bolskan-Belikiom-Sekia-Turiazu, and that another one worked at Arsaos and Turiazu (Gozalbes 2009a, pp. 152-154) and perhaps dies from Sekobirikes and Arekorata also show certain formal affinities. But the bulk of the dies from the major centres of production did not share the features that denote a com-

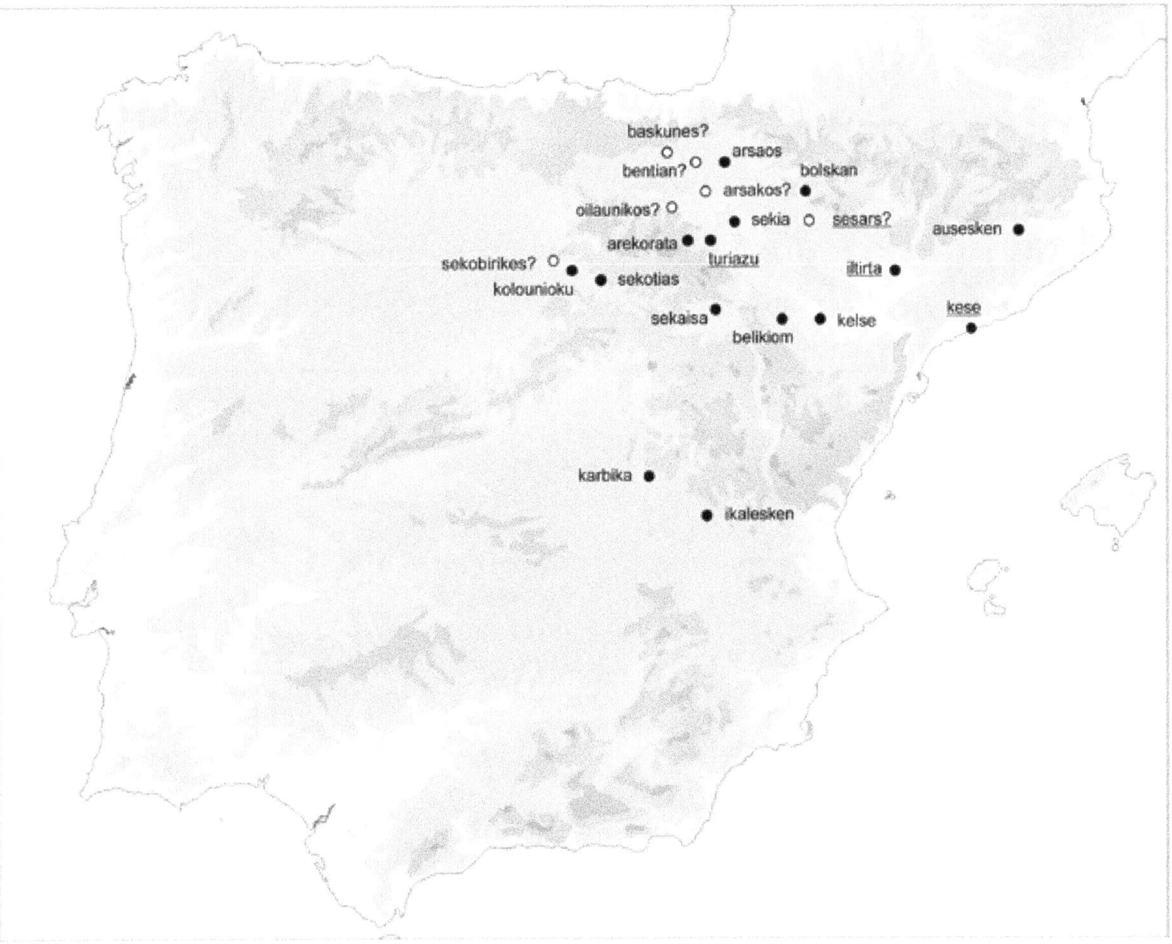

Fig. 4. *Denarii* and *quinarii* (underlined) mints of the second and first centuries BC. White circles indicate an uncertain location

mon hand at work, and further studies of mints will come to reveal the extent to which this is the case.

Their geographical distribution suggests that the establishment of mints was subject to central Roman planning. From a Roman perspective, Iberian coins were the new local currency for Romans travelling in Hispania. By creating this new monetary mass, the Romans enabled Iberian coins to be both guaranteed and accepted everywhere, because of their local appearance. Furthermore, the dots included on several bronze issues served as marks of origin, revealing the Roman influence and linking silver and bronze series in terms of their respective value. *Denarii* did not include value marks which resembled the Roman X or XVI, but other marks like dots or signs could also serve as references of value (Ferrer i Jané 2007). The territorial distribution of mints is closely linked with the Roman advance in a type of frontier production model, but earlier issues were also clearly released by cities firmly under Roman control, as the example of Kese-Tarraco suggests. This city was a Roman military settlement and began to mint coins soon after the arrival of the Romans, including silver issues which share a notable continuity with bronze series. It does not appear to have been a dual Roman and Iberian settlement (Arrayás 2005, pp. 25-28), but the Roman presence encouraged the new minting policy using Iberian script. The monetary mass of this Roman town, easily supplied from the sea, was mainly composed of local issues (Ripollès 1982, p. 375, 380), thus implying that these coins were used by the Romans on a daily basis.

Throghout the first half of the second century BC, the Roman army was paid in bronze coins (Crawford 1985, p. 72; Arévalo-Marcos 1998), and this is supported by the numeous coin finds of Roman Republican bronzes dating back to the second century BC (Ripollès 1984), complemented by certain local bronze issues which were available at the time. The shift from bronze to silver coinage reveals the Roman influence, and the scarcity of silver issues during this period may reflect the fact that *denarii* were not needed for regular payments. Another reason for change could be in direct consequence of extraordinary political situations, like that of the senatorial commission that visited Hispania after the fall of Numantia (Pina 1997).

It must, finally, be questioned whether all these issues could have been the result of different initiatives? It is possible that some, whether silver or bronze, were created on Roman initiative while others were arranged in accordance with local plans, but answers to this question remain elusive, as homogeneity, in a broad sense, is the norm for the majority of the production. As regards deciding on new silver issues, the role of the *quaestores* seems to be significant, given that they held direct responsibility over military expenditure (see also 15).

11. Questions of weight

a) Roman denarii and drachmae

It was a metrological fact that established the basis for naming these Iberian silver issues *denarii*, because of the similarity in their weight to that of the Roman standard. The definitive change of weight of the Roman *denarius* is situated at around 157 BC, when it was reduced from 72 to 84 to the pound, despite certain prior attempts that were made to introduce this standard between 179 and 170 BC (Hildebrandt 1991-1993, p. 205). Crawford, however, is more ambiguous as regards changing patterns for different issues (Crawford 1974, pp. 594-595). At first glance, these chronological landmarks seem to be useful references, because Iberian *denarii* were minted under this new weight. But who copied who? A traditional view would classify Iberian *denarii* as following the new Roman standard, but it is possible that both productions changed the weight of the coins to some degree simultaneously. Attempts to reduce weight had been made previously in the case of *drachmae* issues, where the weight was cut to 4.14g (Villaronga 2002a, p. 108).

Drachmae circulated as part of a wide variety of coins after the War, forming part of a heterogeneous currency that was then removed from Hispania to Rome or melted down for minting new coins. The weight of these coins, far from conforming to a unique standard, was not suitable for exchanging with the Roman *denarius* of 3.86g, and so a formal renovation became necessary. This Roman measure removed from circulation even their own coins (perhaps Livy's *bigati*?), which were retired because of their high weight. Only the renowned cities of Emporion and Arse maintained a production of *drachmae* to some extent after the retrievals, but evidence seems to suggest that silver production there was soon abandoned.

It is therefore not possible to establish two precise metrological stages for local *drachmae* and denarii, and to categorize every issue according to these theoretical models. Complications arise on checking the average weight of single issues and mints, even in the case of Roman Republican *denarii* (Duncan-Jones 1995; Generoso 1993). A progressive reduction in weight did take place, however, including variations within a single mint, as is demonstrated by the example of Turiazu (Gozalbes 2009a, p. 94). Furthermore, Arse minted light *drachmae* at the same time that other cities were minting *denarii*, which is intriguing, given that they were producing coins under a particular standard while the rest of the mints were trying to find some kind of homogeneous system. This particular practice therefore appears to exclude Arse, the allied city of the Romans during the Second Punic War, from strict Roman monetary control.

Metrological stages for Emporion and their imitations may thus be established in the following terms: (1) 4.67 g for issues released before the arrival of the Romans; (2) 4.62g after their arrival in 218 BC, a standard resembling that of the earlier *denarii* of 4.5 g (72 to the pound), making both series exchangeable; (3) 4.56g for Iberian *drachmae*; (4) 4.14g at Emporion, reduced during the second century (Villaronga 2002a, p. 108).

b) Iberian and Celtiberian denarii

The estimated figure of a hundred cities minting in Hispania Citerior is complex. Every mint produced copper or bronze coins, but only 21 minted silver *denarii* and four silver *quinarii*. Because of their relatively late minting, the majority of the Iberian *denarii* fit in well with the Roman standard when this was fixed at 84 to the pound, but some of the earliest attempts at minting local *denarii* suggest the use of a higher standard (Gozalbes 2009a, p. 185), as in the case of the earlier series of Iberian *denarii* which were over the Roman standard of 84 to the pound, like Turiazu (4.06g), Bolskan (3.98g), Arekorata (4.01g) or Karbika (3.98g) (Gozalbes 2009a, p. 95, Table 8). Some of the later ones also show the use of a lighter standard, like those of Sekobirikes (*CNH* 5-10). These weights demonstrate that it is hard to find closed metrological systems, and that for both local and Roman coinages the overall trend was towards the unification of standards.

For over a century, Iberian and Celtiberian *denarii* were the only silver coins available in considerable quantity throughout the meseta. The silver content of these issues is also of interest. While Roman Republican silver series were minted according to a purity of 97% prior to the Sertorian period (Walker 1980, pp. 160-165; Hollstein 2000, p. 115), Iberian and Celtiberian *denarii* were generally coined at a lower quality level, ranging between 85 and 95% (Gozalbes 2009a, p. 130), notwithstanding the fact that the percentages of the heaviest series remain uncertain because of an absence of analysis. This situation can also be read in terms of benefits: Iberian *denarii* did not circulate outside Hispania because of their relatively poor quality, and if these series were used by the Roman administration, it is obvious that they were saving silver to some extent.

12. Units of account and military expenditure

The monetary mass of the Second Punic War was heterogeneous, with different weight systems coexisting in a territory which did not have any previous coin tradition. After the war, therefore, it was necessary to create a standardised mass, as it is hardly possible to conceive of the simultaneous use of two silver standards, a Roman one alongside a local one, as proposed by García-Bellido and Blázquez (2000-2001, pp. 97-99). The military background created the basis for a new economic model which then expanded into territories where coins became the new form of money, and a major requirement for the establishment of a homogeneous *denarius* system involving Roman, Iberian and Celtiberian coins was the creation of a uniform organisation according to weight. Of course, specific local systems could coexist with this, as the Arse *drachmae* demonstrate, but in general terms the tacit or explicit goal was the establishment of a common language for transactions.

In order to attain a serious level of economic organisation, one unique accounting system was necessary, and it is difficult to imagine that this could have been any other than the Roman system. Rather than this being imposed, however, the practice of the new Roman purchasers was perhaps followed once Roman coins became available, and so the system became a reality within a few decades. The matter of military wages, supplies and subsequent payments may also have been relevant for local traders, who adopted the Roman accounting system to facilitate operations. If they shared a currency, it is easy to suppose that payments were calculated and registered in a similar manner.

The transport and storage of money must be viewed as a fundamental issue (Wolters 2000-2001, p. 581). How did the Romans deal with this question in Hispania? In Rome, the *aeraium* was an extraordinarily useful building for this purpose (note the vast income that Livy mentions in relation to the Second Punic War), and some cities in Iberia/Hispania also had their own treasury for storing public resources, as, for example, in Arse (Ripollès 2002, p. 324). For the Romans, the question of where to safely keep resources for military campaigns that took place over vast territories was of great importance, and minting coins was most likely a Roman solution, enabling them to keep at least part of the resources safely.

13. FUNCTION OF ISSUES AND COIN FINDS

One might well question to what degree Iberian *denarii* were a new release. There is no doubt that their creation heralded a new system, with a reduced weight and new designs, but it cannot be guaranteed that they actually reflected a new policy. In the case of Emporion, from 218 BC onwards, the Romans adapted and adopted the Iberian coinage for their own purposes. The terms of this arrangement probably became a model for later releases, in the context of a political background where the common feature was Roman intervention. Later imitations of Emporion coinage could be either Roman or local in origin, but it is not possible at present to establish the extent of Roman intervention in the case of these issues.

It is unanimously considered, however, that silver *denarii* were not originally minted for trade purposes, but in order to facilitate state income and payments, with the most important uses being taxes and army maintenance (Crawford 1969, pp. 83-84; Knapp 1979, p. 465, 468; Crawford 1985, p. 94; Burnett 1987, p. 39; Beltrán 1998, p. 114), including legionary wages (Ñaco and Prieto 1999, p. 213; García-Bellido 1993, p. 108). As regards legionary maintenance and supplies, it is possible that wages did not represent the most costly share, taking into account the fact that legionaries did not receive all their money in cash, as the state deducted from their pay a clothing and food tax. With the exclusion of trade, the only plausible options from a Roman point of view were taxes and the military budget. The volume of the issues is also worthy of consideration. *Denarii* issues from a pair of dies probably came under a different kind of arrangement, if indeed there was one, than those of the cities responsible for a larger output. The extent of Roman intervention in the process is open to question, as mints would not have required authorisation for their own coinages.

There is no mention of local silver mints in Greek and Roman sources (App, *Ib.* 48.52 and 79; Str. 3.4.13; Plut. *Cat. Ma.* 10). Taking into account the fact that in some cases their issues exceeded by far other sums such as civic tributes, which were recorded, it is difficult to understand the reason behind this silence if those cities were strategically significant. Turiazu, whose exact location is unknown to us, minted over one thousand silver talents (Gozalbes 2009a, p. 163). The exact function of this huge production is uncertain, but it is clearly not related to a city budget or something similar, and the spread of Turiazu's silver series is closely linked with the progress of the Roman conquest. If official Roman issues were not available throughout the territory and if legions made any use of coins during their campaigns, then their only option was to pay with Iberian and Celtiberian *denarii*.

More doubts arise regarding the profitability of the issues. Were *drachmae* or *denarii* workshops a Roman business to any extent, or were they handled by local craftsmen? In this sense, coin legends themselves raise a number of questions. Many signs on *drachmae* are indecipherable, revealing the intervention of artists who were illiterate, or at least unable to read Greek characters and to engrave Iberian signs. At the same time, however, the rest of the design was normally cut quite skilfully. Why was the legend treated poorly, given that it constituted an essential part of the coin's value? Did the artisans have insufficient skills? The *corpora* of Iberian and Celtiberian inscriptions over different surfaces prove that writing was a task which usually incorporated minor errors. Only the *drachmae* include non-existent signs which formed invented coin legends. The skill of the engravers seems to have been sufficiently developed to copy a model of a legend, but it is probable that the original model, or even a well-centred one, was not available to them. In terms of the legibility of the legends, there appear to be two groups: some dies were released with legible Iberian legends, while others did not seem to be interested in the legend as a symbol of authority, and simply showed engravings of imaginary signs. A reasonable explanation for this might be that when copies were engraved, they were based on other copies, resulting in increasing illegibility of the legends. What is likely is that most artisans were probably unable to read and write Greek and Iberian names.

Second Punic War hoards reveal that the Romans, the Carthaginians and local peoples all employed a mixture of issues, including to some extent those of their respective enemies, as well as foreign pieces like Greek and Gallic coins. After the war, a new currency was necessary, and as time passed the Romans became interested in establishing a homogeneous currency, and provided the basis for the creation of a new monetary mass, importing coins from Rome and authorizing new Iberian and Celtiberian issues in silver and bronze. Finds demonstrate that where available, principally in the coastal territories and Hispania Ulterior in the south, both Roman and local *denarii* circulated together. The Roman presence in the northern meseta was prolonged, however, and within this territory no significant quantity of Roman *denarii* has been found. The Romans used Iberian bronzes during their time at the camps besieging Numantia (Haeberlin 1929, pp. 241-243), and at towns like Tarraco (see also 10), and did not appear to be concerned about their different weight and designs: they were simply useful and thus accepted in trade. Silver finds, on the other hand, are scarcer because of their higher value.

The boundaries of Hispania Citerior were not static. During the conquest the Roman frontier advanced gradually from the Mediterranean coast towards the west, increasingly affecting the peoples of the northern meseta. In the south-west (Hispania Ulterior), only isolated episodes of war like those involving Viriatus or Sertorius upset the peaceful background of a territory which was brought under control much earlier. Roman *denarii* were largely available in the coastal territories of the east and in the south (Ripollès 2000, Fig. 39), but became very scarce towards the interior. Knapp realised that were no Roman *denarii* in Celtiberia, although he only provided evidence for the early stages of this period (Knapp 1977, pp. 7-8). Villaronga also noted that in Celtiberia and Aragon (that is, the northern meseta in approximate terms), the currency was made up of Iberian *denarii*, and Roman silver was entirely absent (Villaronga 1995a, p. 80), and he also pointed out that in the north-west the only silver production in circulation was its own (Villaronga 1995a, p. 48). It seems that the production of local mints located in the central areas of the Ebro and Duero valleys travelled east to west, as is shown by the finds from Turiazu, Arekorata and Arsaos (Otero 2009, pp. 79-80, Figs. 1-3; Fernández 2009, pp. 478-479, Figs 3 and 5; Gozalbes 2009a, p. 83, Fig 67 and 88, Fig. 71). Some *denarii* mints, however, show the opposite pattern as regards the circulation of their issues. While Turiazu and Arsaos coins travelled westwards, those of Bolskan circulated mainly in an eastwards direction. So why did that difference exist? Was it chronological? Did the people who possessed those coins move in different directions? Or could the patterns be influenced by the fact that the coins were not always wholly or even partially distributed from the minting centres?

There is no doubt, nevertheless, that Roman *denarii* were either scarce or non-existent in the northern meseta. The hoards dated between the second half of the second century and the first half of the first century BC do not include Roman *denarii* to any significant extent (Gozalbes 2009b, p. 99). This very small presence is supported by the lack of hoards composed exclusively of Roman coins in that territory, even from the time of the Sertorian conflict (Marcos 1999, p. 103, Fig. 2), when these were easily available on the Mediterranean coast and in the south (Ripollès 1984; Chaves 1996, p. 574). The most valuable evidence from the coin finds of the north meseta is therefore the scarcity of Roman Republican issues. If Roman troops were indeed paid in silver from 157 BC onwards, then the only coins available where the episodes of war took place were those of Iberian, Celtiberian and Vasconian mints. Furthermore, the arrangement of some productions seem to indicate approximately when Roman payments shifted from bronze to silver, though in this sense it must be emphasised that the sums involved in payments for supplies, which were handled by commanders and involved local peoples or Roman traders based at *cannabae*, probably exceeded cash payments to legionaries.

14. PATTERNS FOR CELTIC COINAGES

Celtic coinages include a number of series which originated in a vast area stretching from Hispania to Germania. All of these were Celtic in character, but it is possible that they were planned and arranged on a variety of different bases. It may be seen that the Hispanic series show evidence of a strong underlying organisation, and the Roman influence is clearly visible in the form of value marks, designs, weights and even the progressive implementation of the various issues. Minting silver in Rome was predominantly a public matter, and as Hispania was a province, its coin production too would have been arranged in Roman fashion. Even during the period of the empire, there is no doubt that, while the western provinces minted bronze with or without permission, silver coinage was always released under imperial control. So why would a similar policy not have been considered for the 'Romanized' issues of the Republic? It is possible that this was organised on a similar basis, but the appearance of the coins concealed their real nature, because of the obvious restrictions which applied to Roman commanders as regards minting. The only singularity in this case may have been the typological choice, though it is well known that the Romans had facilities for maintaining the traditions of other peoples.

A certain number of dies and tools have been recovered from the Celtic world (see Zieghaus, forthcoming), but in the case of Iberian and Celtiberian cultures this kind of finding is non-existent, with the exception of isolated examples such as a die from Turiazu which was recovered from Gaul (Gozalbes 2007). As regards Republican coinage, the situation is again quite similar. It seems as if Iberian and Celtiberian coinages were official productions, with the workshops much more strictly controlled than some of the mints of northern Celtic peoples. Hispanic issues always include the names of places, and finds related to specific workshops are rare, as with the few Roman Republican examples, which are usually described as official products. Northern Celtic tools and dies, on the other hand, could have belonged to travelling workshops which minted coins regularly without any epigraphic references to the authority in question, producing coins without any restriction apart from the availability of silver. This situation was peculiar to territories that were not subject to Roman control. There was no need to destroy the dies after striking either, because these did not incorporate any indication of authority, such as names of people or places, or any specific symbols. This lack of any of the limitations associated with dies obviously worked in favour of both the workshop and the group or individuals that ordered the coins.

15. IBERIAN *DENARII* AND THE ROMAN LEGIONS MAINTENANCE

Authorities such as Mommsen, Lenormant, Hübner and Vives have suggested that there was a close association between the production of Iberian *denarii* and the Roman administration (brief summary in Knapp 1979, pp. 465-466). In recent years, influential authors have also argued that Hispanic silver served mainly to pay the wages of Roman legionaries (Crawford 1969, pp. 83-84; Crawford 1985, p. 94), and recent decades have provided further insight into the major issues surrounding the function of Iberian *denarii* (see 13). The main problem centres on the identification of the specific peoples involved in the process and the mechanisms of circulation. There seems to be little doubt, on the other hand, that the availability of silver bullion marked the starting point of the minting process. By the decade beginning in 170 BC the monetary mass had been severely reduced after the removal of precious metals detailed by Livy (Ripollès 2000, pp. 334-335), which constituted a benefit for the Roman budget, but a considerable reduction in wealth for the peoples of Iberia. The origin of the silver used for later *denarii* issues is uncertain, but it may be surmised that it was either saved from monetary retrievals and stored, or newly obtained from silver ores.

Booties played a crucial role during the conquest (Gabba 1977, p. 20; González Román 1980), and the Latin word *manubiae* refers to the product of selling off this booty (Aulus Gellius 13.25.26). A major concern for Roman commanders was ensuring a regular money supply for their campaigns. It did not really matter how this took place, but local silver did reach Roman army funds and it was then redistributed or converted into money, which was more practical than sending it to Rome, which was a long way away. Appian mentions how early in the second century BC Cato sold off booty to *publicani* or *negotiatores* (App., *Iber.* 40). Sending silver to Rome was a laborious, time-consuming and risky operation that would also require a further remittance back to Hispania, and therefore it was a clever solution to make immediate use of the silver needed in Hispania, as this was faster than sending it and waiting for another shipment in return. It is likely that the *quaestores* played a crucial role in this process, as they were in charge of military funds, and the distribution of booty was one of their responsibilities. It is not difficult to see that the best way to make equal parts was to turn the booty into coins, thereby also obtaining a standardised form of money. This would have provided good business for Iberian cities and workshops, and had the decisive advantage of avoiding problems with the Senate, as the Roman commanders themselves did not act as issuing authorities. It is indeed hard to imagine a course of action more beneficial to the Romans than exchanging booty or taxes for coins that were probably mainly used within Hispania.

The Romans were only able to receive Iberian silver by means of imposing taxes or taking booties, and there only seem to have been three appropriate options for this income: sending it to Rome, distributing it all equally, or storing it for future payments. Keeping bullion and then converting it into coins, or vice versa, was secondary as a problem. It is possible that an important change came about, however, as a result of Roman penetration into the meseta. In the first decades of the Roman presence, there are records of two actions, the minting of local coins at Emporion, and the sending of precious metals and coins to Rome. But from 170 BC onwards, deliveries to Rome disappeared, at least according to the records of Livy. It may be that at the beginning proximity to the coast could have facilitated deliveries to Rome but when distances from the coast increased, booties were reduced considerably and a homogeneous currency was established, other policies were considered more appropriate.

Roman troops serving in Hispania must have regularly received coins, as is demonstrated by examples from the Second Punic War and from Numantia (Liv. 28.25.6; Plin, *NH* 33.141). During the second century, Roman Republican issues were not released in Hispania, and while *denarii* were shipped from Rome and reached the coastal territories and Hispania Ulterior via the Guadalquivir valley, they were absent from the northern meseta. For the Romans, ease of shipping could be considered to be of primary importance, and under these circumstances Roman magistrates may have played an important role. The conquest of Hispania was taking the Romans ever deeper into the meseta, and further away from supplies. There were, of course, similar difficulties during the Second Punic War, but this time the Romans had decided to conquer Hispania in order to stay, meaning that at some moment there was a point of no return. If we look forward in time, we can see that Roman imperial mints were only fully decentralised after a number of centuries.

Unfortunately, in the case of Hispania the practical arrangements of the magistrates were not recorded in the sources available, and, in addition, the changing political and social background provides very little help in isolating the relative importance of factors such as the evolution of Roman political practice, the policies of different magistrates after their isolation from Rome, the attitudes of local peoples, the influence of changing alliances, different tax policies, and the variety of territories involved in the conflicts.

Roman influence in the Iberian Peninsula saw major developments in the production of silver coins, and previous attempts at creating local models, like those initiated at the Greek colony of Emporion or at the Iberian city of Arse, were finally abandoned. Local coin weights were set at the same time that the Romans fixed their own model, but the Iberian coinages preserved a fully autochthonous appearance in terms of design. A number of Iberian, Celtiberian and Vasconian cities developed coin productions, with different chronologies, volumes and functions. These silver coins were scarce until the middle of the second century BC, but abundant by 100 BC, and their minting ceased altogether in the first quarter of the first century BC, though it seems probable that in some places people may have continued using this local currency until the reign of Augustus.

Abbreviations

CNH (1994)= Villaronga L. *Corpus Nummum ante Augusti Aetatem*. Madrid.

References

Abascal J. M., Ripollès P. P. (2000). 'Las monedas de Konterbia Karbika', in Olcina Doménech M. H., Soler Díaz, J. A. (coord.), *Scripta in Honorem Enrique A. Llobregat Conesa, vol. II*. Alicante, pp. 13-76.

Aguilar Guillén M. A. , Ñaco del Hoyo, T. (1997). 'Fiscalidad Romana y la aparición de la moneda ibérica. Apuntes para una discusión. II. 195-171 a.C.: algunos textos polémicos', *Habis*, 28, pp. 71-86.

Almagro-Gorbea M. (1995). 'La moneda hispánica con jinete y cabeza varonil ¿Tradición indígena o creación romana?', *Zephyrus*, 48, pp. 235-266.

Amorós J. (1957). 'Argentum oscense', *Numario Hispánico*, 6, pp. 51-71.

Aranegui C. (2005). *Sagunto. Oppidum, emporio y municipio Romano*. Barcelona.

Arévalo A. (2002-2003). 'Las imágenes monetales Hispánicas como emblemas de Estado', *Cuadernos de Prehistoria y Arqueología, Universidad Autónoma Madrid*, 28-29, pp. 241-258.

Arévalo A. (2003). 'La moneda hispánica del jinete ibérico: estado de la cuestión', in Quesada F., Zamora M. (eds), *El caballo en la Antigua Iberia*. Madrid, pp. 63-74.

Arévalo A., Marcos C. (1998). *El depósito monetal de Torelló d'en Cintes*. Barcelona.

Arrayás I. (2005). *Morfología histórica del territorio de Tarraco. Ss. III-I a.C. (Collecció Instrumenta 19)*. Barcelona.

Beltrán M. (1986). 'Sobre la función de la moneda ibérica e hispano-Romana', *Estudios en Homenaje al Dr. Antonio Beltrán Martínez*. Zaragoza, pp. 889-914.

Beltrán M. (1998). '*De nuevo sobre el origen y la función del denario ibérico*', *La moneda en la societat ibèrica. II Curs d'Història monetària d'Hispània*. Barcelona, pp. 101-117.

Beltrán M. (2006). 'El origen y la función del denario ibérico', in Burillo F. (ed.), *Segeda y su contexto histórico entre Catón y Nobilior (195 al 153)*. Mara, pp. 105-115.

Blázquez J. M. (1967). 'Roma y la explotación económica de la Península Ibérica', in Gómez-Tabanera J. M. (ed.), *Las raices de España*. Madrid, pp. 253-282.

Blázquez J. M. (1978). *Historia económica de la Hispania romana*. Madrid.

Burillo F. (1998). *Los celtíberos. Etnias y estados*. Barcelona.

Burillo F. (1999). 'Etnias, ciudades y estados en la Celtiberia', in Villar F., Beltrán, F. (eds), *Pueblos lenguas y escrituras en la Hispania Prerromana*. Salamanca, pp. 109-140.

Burnett A. (1987). *Coinage in the Roman World*. London.

Cabré J. (1936). 'El tesoro de plata de Salvacañete (Cuenca)', *Archivo Español de Arte y Arqueología*, 12, pp. 151-159.

Campo M. (1998). 'Les primeres monedes dels ibers: el cas de les imitacions d'Emporion', *La moneda en la societat ibèrica. II Curs d'Història monetària d'Hispània*. Barcelona, pp. 27-47.

Chaves Tristán F. (1996). *Los tesoros en el sur de Hispania. Conjuntos de denarios y objetos de plata durante los siglos II y I a.C.* Sevilla.

Collado E. (2000). *La ceca de Belikiom*. Tesis de Licenciatura. Universitat de València.

Crawford M. H. (1969). 'The financial organisation of Republican Spain', *The Numismatic Chronicle*, 7th Series, vol. 9, pp. 79-93.

Crawford M. H. 1974. *Roman Republican Coinage*. Cambridge.

Crawford M. H. 1985. *Coinage and money under the Roman Republic*. London.

Domínguez A. 1998. 'Las acuñaciones ibéricas y celtibéricas de la Hispania Citerior', Alfaro Asíns *et alii*, *Historia Monetaria de Hispania Antigua*. Madrid, pp. 116-193.

Domínguez A. 2001. 'La moneda celtibérica', *Catálogo de la exposición Celtas y Vettones*. Ávila, pp. 218-227.

Domínguez A. 2005. 'Moneda: la imagen pública de los celtíberos', in Chaín A., de la Torre J. I. (eds), *Celtíberos. Tras la estela de Numancia*. Soria, pp. 387-394.

Duncan-Jones R. (1995). 'Change in the Late Republican Denarius', *The Numismatic Chronicle*, pp. 109-117.

Fernández Gómez J. (2009). 'Arsaos. Reflexiones históricas, geográficas y tipológicas en torno a una ceca indígena en territorio vascón', in Andreu J. (ed.), *Los vascones de las Fuentes antiguas: en torno a una etnia de la antigüedad peninsular*. Barcelona, pp. 437-480.

Ferrer i Jané J. (2007). 'Sistemes de marques de valor lèxiques en monedes ibèriques', *Acta Numismàtica*, 37, pp. 53-73.

Ferrer Maestro J. J. (1999). 'El botín de Hispania, 205-169 a. C.', in Alonso Ávila A. (coord.), *Homenaje al profesor Montenegro (Estudios de Historia Antigua)*. Valladolid, pp. 243-255.

Gabba E. (1977). 'Esercito e fiscalità a Roma in età repubblicana', *Armées et Fiscalité dans le Monde Antique (Paris, 14-16 October 1976)*, pp. 13-33.

García-Bellido M. P. (1993). 'Origen y función del denario ibérico', in Heidermanns F., Rix H., Seebold E. (eds), *Sprache und Schriften des antiken Mittelmeerraums. Festschrift für J. Untermann zum 65. Geburtstag*. Insbruck, pp. 97-123.

García-Bellido M. P. (2000-2001). 'Roma y los sistemas monetarios provinciales. Monedas romanas acuñadas en Hispania en la Segunda Guerra Púnica', *Zephyrus*, 53-54, pp. 551-577.

García-Bellido M. P. (2005). 'La moneda hispánica en los horizontes bélicos peninsulares', in Pérez González C., Illarregui Gómez E. (eds), *Arqueología militar romana en Europa*. Segovia, pp. 29-44.

García-Bellido M. P., Blázquez Cerrato M. C. (2001). *Diccionario de cecas y pueblos hispánicos*. Madrid.

García-Bellido M. P., Ripollès P. P. (1997). 'La moneda ibérica: prestigio y espacio económico de los iberos', in *Los Iberos. Príncipes de Occidente*. París-Barcelona-Bonn, pp. 205-272.

García Garrido M., Montañés J. (2007). 'La dracma de Iltirkesalir', *Acta Numismàtica*, 37, pp. 41-51.

García Riaza E. (1999a). 'La financiación de los ejércitos en época Romano-republicana', *Moneda i exèrcits, III Curs d´Història monetària d´Hispania*. Barcelona, pp. 39-58.

García Riaza E. (1999b). 'El cómputo del metal precioso en los botines de guerra hispano-republicanos', *Historia Antiqua*, 23, pp. 119-136.

García Riaza E. (2009). 'La moneda dels ibers a les fonts literàries', in Campo M. (dir.), *Els ibers, cultura i moneda*. Barcelona, pp. 56-59.

Generoso C. (1993). 'Il problema del rafforzamento ponderale del denario romano nella segonda metà del II sec. a.C. attraverso l'esame statistico', in Hackens T., Van Driessche V. (dir.), *Proceedings of the XIth International Numismatic Congress. Bruxelles 1991*. Lovain-la-Neuve, pp. 129-132.

Giovannini A. (1982). 'La circulation monétaire en Grèce sous le protectorat de Rome', in Camilli L., Porise N. F. (eds), Stato e moneta a Roma fra la tarda republica e il primo Impero, *Annali del Istituto Italiano di Numismatica*, 29, pp. 165-181.

Gomis M. (2001). *Las acuñaciones de la ciudad celtibérica de Segeda/sekaiza*. Teruel-Mara-Zaragoza.

González Román C. (1980). 'Economía e imperialismo: a propósito de los praeda-manubiae durante el s. II a. de C.', *Actas del Coloquio Formas de intercambio durante la Antigüedad (Memorias de Historia Antigua 4)*. Oviedo, pp. 139-150.

Gozalbes M. (2006). 'Jinetes sin escudo. Las representaciones ecuestres en la Citerior', *Numisma*, 250, pp. 295-317.

Gozalbes M. (2007). 'Un cuño para fabricar denarios celtibéricos de turiazu', in Travani L., Bolis A. (eds), *Conii e scene di coniazione*. Roma, pp. 253-257.

Gozalbes M. (2009a). *La ceca de Turiazu. Monedas celtibéricas en la Hispania republicana (Serie Trabajos Varios del SIP 110)*. Valencia.

Gozalbes M. (2009b). 'Circulación y uso de los denarios ibéricos', *Ús i circulació de la moneda a la Hispània Citerior, XIII Curs d'història monetària d'Hispània*. Barcelona, pp. 83-103.

Gozalbes M., Cores G., Ripollès P. P. (forthcoming). 'Trading with silver in Spain during the third century BC The silver bullion from the hoard of Armuña de Tajuña (Guadalajara, Spain)', in XIII *International Numismatic Congress*. Glasgow.

Haeberlin E. J. (1929). 'Die Münzen aus der Stadt Numantia den Lagern des Scipio und den Lagern bei Renieblas', in Schulten A., *Numantia* IV. Munich, pp. 235-283.

Hollstein W. (2000). 'Denarprägungen des 3. und 2. Jh. v. Chr.', in Hollstein W. (ed.), *Metallanalytische Untersuchungen an Münzen der Römischen Republik*. Berlín, pp. 114-123.

Hildebrandt J. (1991-1993). 'Vergleichende Metrologie spanischer und römischer Münzen der römischen Republik aufgrund einer neuen Theorie', *Acta Numismàtica 21-23 Homenatje al Dr. Leandre Villaronga*, pp. 199-212.

Jenkins G. K. (1958). 'Notes on Iberian *Denarii* from the Cordova Hoard', *American Numismatic Society Museum Notes*, 8, pp. 57-70.

Jimeno A. (coord.) (2005). *Los celtiberos, tras la estela de Numancia.* Junta de Castilla y León.

Knapp R. C. (1977). 'The date and purpose of the Iberian *denarii*', *The Numismatic Chronicle*, 7th Series, vol. 17, (vol. 137), pp. 1-18.

Knapp R. C. (1979). 'Celtiberian conflict with Rome: policy and coinage', in Tovas A., Faust M., Fischer F., Koch M. (eds), *Actas del II Coloquio sobre Lenguas y Culturas Prerromanas de la Península Ibérica. Tübingen 17-19 junio de 1976.* Salamanca, pp. 465-472.

Kraay C. M. (1984). 'Greek coinage and war', in Heckel W., Sullivan R. A. (eds), *Ancient coins of the Graeco-Roman world. The Nickle Numismatic Papers.* Waterloo-Ontario, pp. 3-18.

Llorens M. M., Ripollès P. P. (1998). *Les encunyacions ibèriques de Lauro.* Granollers.

Marchetti P. (1978). *Histoire économique et monetaire de la deuxième guerre punique.* Brussels.

Ñaco del Hoyo T., Prieto Arciniega A. (1999). 'Moneda e historia monetaria en la Hispania republicana: ¿economía, política, fiscalidad?', *Studia Historica, Historia Antigua*, 17, pp. 193-241.

Otero P. (1998). 'Uso y función de las monedas ibéricas', *La moneda en la societat iberica. II Curs d'Història monetària d'Hispània*, pp. 119-140.

Otero P. (2009). 'La difusion de las emisiones de Arekorata', Ús i circulació de la moneda a la Hispània Citerior, *XIII Curs d'història monetària d'Hispània.* Barcelona, pp. 65-82.

Paz Peralta J. A., Ortiz Palomar E. (2007). 'El jinete en la moneda ibérica y celtibérica. Su imagen e interpretación: un arte provincial romano', *Numisma*, 251, pp. 87-136.

Pina F. (1997). 'Las comisiones senatoriales para la reorganización de Hispania (App., Iber., 99-100)', *Dialogues d'Histoire Ancienne*, 23.2, pp. 83-104.

Ripollès P. P. (1982). *La circulación monetaria en la Tarraconense Mediterránea (Serie Trabajos Varios del SIP 77).* Valencia.

Ripollès P. P. (1984). "Los hallazgos de moneda romano-republicana en la Tarraconense Mediterránea y las Baleares", *Italica*, 17, pp. 91-126.

Ripollès P. P. (2000). 'La monetización del mundo ibérico', Ibers. Agricultors, artesans i comerciants. III Reunió sobre Economia en el Món Ibèric, *Saguntum*, Extra-3, pp. 329-344.

Ripollès P. P. (2007). *Las acuñaciones de la ciudad ibérica de Saitabi.* Valencia.

Ripollès P. P. (2009). 'El dinero en la Contestania en los siglos V-III a.C.', in Olcina M., Ramón J. (eds), *Huellas griegas en la Contestania ibérica.* Alicante, pp. 62-75.

Ripollès P. P., Llorens M. M. (2002). *Arse-Saguntum. Historia monetaria de la ciudad y su territorio.* Sagunto.

Sanz Pérez E. (2003). 'La minería de la plata en la Celtiberia: Una aproximación', *Cuadernos de Estudios Borjanos*, 46, pp. 15-49.

Tarradell M. (1986). 'Las cecas ibéricas: economía o política?', *Estudios en Homenaje al Dr. Antonio Beltrán Martínez.* Zaragoza, pp. 915-917.

Villaronga L. (1973). *Las moneda hispano-cartaginesas.* Barcelona.

Villaronga L. (1977). 'Nueva interpretación a Argentum Oscense', *Gaceta Numismática*, 44, pp. 11-17.

Villaronga L. (1987). 'Uso de la ceca de Emporion por los romanos para cubrir sus necesidades financieras en la Península Ibérica durante la Segunda Guerra Púnica', *Studi per Laura Breglia, Supl. al Bollettino di Numismatica*, 4, pp. 209-214.

Villaronga L. (1983). *Les monedas ibèriques de Tarraco.* Barcelona.

Villaronga L. (1993b). *Tresors monetaris de la Península Ibérica anteriors a August: repertori i anàlisi.* Barcelona.

Villaronga L. (1995a). *Denarios y quinarios ibéricos. Estudio y catalogación.* Barcelona-Madrid.

Villaronga L. (1995b). 'La masa monetaria acuñada en la Península Ibérica antes de Augusto', in García-Bellido Mª P., Centeno R. M. S., *La moneda hispánica. Ciudad y territorio. Actas del I Encuentro Peninsular de Numismática Antigua (Anejos AEspA 14)*, pp. 7-14.

Villaronga L. (1997). *Monedes de plata emporitanes dels segles V-IV aC.* Barcelona.

Villaronga L. (1998). *Les dracmes ibèriques I llurs divisors.* Barcelona.

Villaronga L. (2000). *Les monedes de plata d'Emporion, Rhode i les seves imitacions. De principi del segle III a. C. fins a l'arribada dels Romans, el 218 a. C.* Barcelona.

Villaronga L. (2002a). *Les dracmes emporitanes de principi del segle II a. C.* Barcelona.

Villaronga L. (2002b). 'Troballa del Francolí. Testimoni per a la datació del denari ibèric de Kese', *Acta Numismática*, 32, pp. 29-43.

Villaronga L. (2003). *La plata emporitana. De la Segona Guerra Púnica, final del segle III a. C.* Barcelona.

Walker D. R. (1980). 'The Silver Contents of the Roman Republican Coinage', in Metcalf D., Oddy W. A. (eds), *Metallurgy in Numismatics. Vol. I (Royal Numismatic Society Special Publication 13)*. London, pp. 55-72.

Wolters R. (2000-2001). 'Bronze, silver or gold?. Coin finds and the pay of the roman army', *Zephyrus*, 53-54, pp. 579-588.

Zieghaus B. (2002). 'Ein neuer keltisher Münzstempelfund aus dem Nördlinger Ries (Schwaben)', *International Numismatic Newsletter*, 39, pp. 3-5.

Zieghaus B. (2011). 'Celtic workmanship and die production in the West and the East', in García-Bellido Mª P., Callegarin L., Jiménez A. (eds), *Barter, Money and Coinage in the Ancient Meditarranean (10th-1st centuries BC) (Actas del IV Encuentro Peninsular de Numismática Antigua. EPNA)*. Madrid, pp. 289-299.

The Coinage of C. Annius Luscus

Borja Antela-Bernárdez*

ABSTRACT

During the Sertorian Wars (82-73/72 BC), two interesting characters under the names of L. Fabius Hispaniensis and C. Tarquitius Priscus are referred to in textual evidence as quaestors of C. Annius, the governor sent to Hispania by L. Cornelius Sulla with a remit to pursue Q. Sertorius. Two men with similar names and who where in the service of Sertorius are referred to in literary sources as having been exiled under Sulla's proscriptions. An in-depth study of the numismatic evidence highlights a possible new way of understanding both the coinage of C. Annius during his service in Hispania and the importance of these two individuals in the politics of the time.

The *denarii* of the proconsul G. Annius Luscus and the quaestors L. Fabius Hispaniensis and C. Tarquitius Priscus (*RRC* 366)

The coin series of Gaius Annius Luscus -silver *denarii* minted during the hunt in Hispania for the fugitive Q. Sertorius- stand out as a remarkable case among known coin issues of the period of the Roman Civil Wars. Despite being featured in the major works of reference on Roman Republican Coinage (*RRC* 366, 1-4; Sydenham 748),(1) and despite the extent of its production and the variety of its types and mint marks, these coins have received scant scholarly attention, and indeed its analysis has in later years often been reduced to mere descriptions. Nevertheless, there are a number of problematic issues which make it worth taking another look, and the aim of this paper is none other than to put forward a new explanation for these coins.

A female bust wearing diadem to right, with a winged *caduceus* around and scales occasionally beneath the chin, is depicted on the obverse of the two main groups and nine varieties catalogued by M. Crawford (*RRC* 366 1-4). Victory in *quadriga* or *biga*, holding reins in her left hand, and palm-branch in her right hand is depicted on the reverse. C[aius]· ANNI(VS)· T[iti]· F[ilius]· T[iti]· N[epos]· PRO· CO[n]S[ul]· EX·S[enatus]· C[onsulto] is the obverse legend adopted by the engravers for all the varieties existing for this particular type. L[ucius]· FABI[us]· L[ucii]· F[ilius]· HISP[aniensis] and C. TARQUIT[ius]· P[riscus]· F[ilius] are the two legends chosen for the reverses. Above or below the *quadriga* or the *biga* a "Q[uestor]" is also added (Fig. 1,2).

There seems little doubt that the names referred to in these coin issues are C. Annius Luscus and his quaestors, L. Fabius Hispaniensis and C. Tarquitius Priscus, and that the coins would therefore appear to be alluding to their military campaigns against Q. Sertorius.(2) All of the characters and events involved with these coins deserve close consideration, beginning with a clarification of the historical context.

The nature of C. Annius Luscus, L. Fabius and C. Tarquitius Priscus' commands in Spain

During the winter of 82/1 BC,(3) Q. Sertorius abandoned Italy for Spain, where he had probably been invested with proconsular authority.(4) The exact position held by Q. Sertorius in his arrival in the Iberian Peninsula has been the object of intense debate, especially as regards the reference in Plut. *Sert.* 6. 6, where Q. Sertorius is cited as the governor of Iberia. Exuperantius (8. 9), on the other hand, states directly that his jurisdiction was actually Citerior (*Citerioris* Hispania). In his classic paper Badian defended the possibility of Q. Sertorius being in command of the whole

*This paper has been elaborated as part of the Research Projects "Politiques Públiques de Reconstrucció de la Pau" (2009RICIP-00001) funded by the Institut Català Internacional per la Pau, and 'La gestión política de las 'crisis humanitarias' en el mundo grecorromano (ss. IV-I a.C.)' (HAR2010-19185) funded by the Government of Spain, both directed by Dr. Antoni Ñaco del Hoyo. The author would like to thank Dr. Fernando López, Antoni Ñaco, Isaias Arrayás and John Strisino for all their useful commentaries. Nevertheless, both the opinions and possible errors are no-one's fault but the author himself. This paper is lovingly dedicated to Mireia Bosch Mateu, *uxor atque mater.*

(1) *RRC*, pp. 381-386, pl. XLVII; Sydenham (1952), p. 121.

(2) There is unanimity regarding the dating and identification of the names. Nevertheless, in his classic work, Eckhel 1792-98, V, 134-5 discusses the uncertain assignation of this coin series.

(3) Plut. *Sert.* 6.5 seems to indicate that he crossed the Pyrenees in the first weeks of winter, Konrad 1987, pp. 85-9.

(4) Keaveney 1982, p. 197.

Fig. 1.- AR Denarius, Obv.: C. ANNI. T F T N PRO COS EX S C, Draped, diademed female bust r. scales, caduceus, Rev.: L FABI L F HISP / Q, Victory in quadriga r., holding palm-branch. *RRC* 366/1b.Trustees of the British Museum. 18mm

Fig. 2.- AR Denarius, Obv.: C. ANNIVS. T. F. T. PRO. COS. EX. S. C Diademed female bur to r., Rev.: [C.] TARQVITI. [P. F] in exergue/ Victory in biga right; XXXXII above, Q below, *RRC* 366/4. Trustees of the British Museum. 18mm

of the Iberian Peninsula, a hypothesis which would allow for reconciliation with Plutarch as well as explain the subsequent command held by C. Annius. Such an unprecedented degree of control over both Iberian provinces would presumably have been the result of a lack of able officials to take up positions in the Roman Republic during the decade of the 80s.(5) Nevertheless, Chic points out that Q. Sertorius could well have been a *propraetor*, given that all *praetores* and *propraetores* in Hispania enjoyed proconsular authority. This possibility would reconcile as well the statements of Exuperantius and Plutarch, at least if it were accepted that his official authority was ascribed to Citerior.(6) Moreover, Q. Sertorius' prior knowledge of the region, having served as a military tribune in the Peninsula under Titus Didius in 97 and 93 BC,(7) provides another argument in support of his appointment to such an office.

When Q. Sertorius arrived in Hispania, he was faced with the strange situation of not finding any Roman authority to relieve of its command or any opposition on the ground.(8) This may, of course, have been favourable to his interests. Shortly afterwards, C. Annius Luscus(9) was sent by L. Cornelius Sulla to govern the two provinces of Hispania, and therefore to depose Q. Sertorius, albeit indirectly.(10) Once again the nature of C. Annius' command is surrounded with uncertainty, although in the light of what has just been stated, and following Brennan, he may have also been just a *propraetor,*(11) even if his coins designate him as the proconsul.(12) Likewise, it has often been suggested that the two quaestors mentioned on *RRC* 366 correspond to C. Annius' authority over the two provinces of Hispania.(13) There is one particular question that remains unresolved, however. According to Crawford,(14) while the first coin series were minted in Rome, probably by L. Fabius, the second must have been issued in Hispania, perhaps after the expulsion of Q. Sertorius from the Peninsula, with a view to financing the recruitment of troops that would allow C. Annius to secure his newly-achieved position. It is not strictly necessary, therefore, to assume that both figures held their positions simultaneously: one may have replaced the other at any given point in time. Furthermore, the second coin issues are related to the maritime conflict between C. Annius and Q. Sertorius, and probably also with the former's expedition to the Pityuses,(15) where he once again defeated the Sertorian forces and left 5,000 soldiers, according to Plutarch.(16) This event will be dealt with later.

In legal terms, the nomination of C. Annius meant that Q. Sertorius' proconsular command was over. Now proscribed, his own life and that of his followers was put at risk by the imminent arrival of C. Annius. Q. Sertorius must have considered these risks, as it seems apparent that his intention was to safeguard the lives of the *populares* of Hispania. These circumstances, among other reasons, must have influenced his decision to flee from his persecutor as an outlaw and abandon the Iberian Peninsula.(17)

There are several issues, however, that merit further con-

(5) Badian 1964, pp. 88-96.

(6) Chic 1986.

(7) Sal. *Hist.* I. 88M; Plut. *Sert.* 3.3; García Mora 1990; Hinard 1985, p. 398.

(8) Brennan 2000, II, p. 502.

(9) On the improbability of Luscus as cognomen, Konrad 1994,p. 100.

(10) Plut. *Sert.* 4. 5; Sal. *Hist.* I, 95M; I, 97M; Plut. *Sert.* 7.1; García Mora 1991, p. 28ff; Keaveney 1984,p. 138 contemplates the possibility of Annius and Sertorius having met personally in Rome, during the period of Cinna's government.

(11) Brennan 2000, II, p. 505. Schulten 1926, p. 45; Badian 1964 and Ridley 1981 maintain that Annius received the command of both provinces in Hispania, with the object of persecuting Sertorius more effectively, without any jurisdictional territorial limitations.

(12) Konrad 1996,p. 100.

(13) Badian 1964, p. 88. Schulten 1926, 45 note 231 defends that if C. Annius was in the same position as Q. Sertorius, his province was then the Hispania Citerior.

(14) Crawford 1974, I, 386.

(15) Plut. *Sert.* 7.5.

(16) García Riaza, Sánchez León 2000, p. 62. Likewise, the conclusions of Costa Ribas, 678 are also interesting. On the other hand, as pointed out by Konrad 1996, 103, we do not know how C. Annius was provided with his ships. Although perhaps Q. Sertorius left some behind when he fled Carthago Nova, the truth is that part of the series issued by Tarquitius P. could be related, not only with recruitment, but also with the payment of a fleet. Campo 1976, 15 describes Sertorius' steps, but makes no mention of coinage, even though the iconography seems to relate to the campaign, as will be shown supra. Likewise, Padrino Fernández 2005 avoids any mention of the Annius' *denarii.*

(17) Plut. *Sert.* 7-9; Sal. *Hist.* 1.95-102; Val. Max. 7. 3. 6; Flor. 2. 10. 2; Aug., *Civ. Dei* 3. 30; Oros. 5. 21.3; Eutrop. 6. 1. 2; Amp. 18.1; Hinard 1985, pp. 398-399.

sideration. The first of these is the appointment of C. Annius Luscus and his orders to march to Hispania and oppose Q. Sertorius. The son of T. Annius Rufus (cos. 128) and the grandson of T. Annius Luscus (cos. 153),[(18)] C. Annius was no stranger to those who made up the *optimates factio*,[(19)] for he had already served with Quintus Caecilius Metellus Numidicus during the war against Jugurtha.[(20)] Nevertheless, some authors have viewed C. Annius as a representative of a moderate political stance, somewhere in between the two opposing factions.[(21)] We know nothing of him until his appointment as proconsul -or propraetor- of Hispania, and the sources here remain confusing: it is unclear whether his mission was to take over the government of both provinces, or whether his priority was to catch Q. Sertorius, a prestigious and dangerous renegade. Whatever the motive might have been, there is no evidence that the new magistrate had any previous knowledge of the territory where he was to hold office, which of course worked to the advantage of Q. Sertorius.[(22)]

After the elimination of the main popular leaders, it is likely that Q. Sertorius was the last of this faction to hold any degree of power, and he confronted L. Cornelius Sulla, who was already established as *dictator*. Such a scenario is supported by the significant number of proscribed citizens, who joined the ranks of Q. Sertorius.[(23)] This hypothesis would explain the Sertorian initiative of visiting other possible nuclei of Marian supporters, which detracts somewhat from the argument that Q. Sertorius was fleeing from the military pressure exercised by C. Annius.[(24)] Even if the difference in military strength influenced his decision,[(25)] it is also true that Q. Sertorius was militarily and strategically capable of confronting C. Annius,[(26)] as is shown later by his fight against Q. Caeclius Metellus and Pompey. Nevertheless, it seems possible that the arrival of the proconsul mighthave caught Q. Sertorius in a position of material inferiority.

All things considered, the assumed 'flight' of Q. Sertorius seems to be crying out for careful reassessment. Information from literary sources on certain events which took place after his departure shed some light on the interests of the popular faction in Hispania, and specifically of the followers of Q. Sertorius. During his stay in Mauritania,[(27)] Q. Sertorius received a Lusitanian embassy, which presented itself to him to ask for his leadership. Plutarch comments that such a degree of trust was enjoyed with "those who had formerly known him",[(28)] and he might be referring to a previous relationship between Q. Sertorius and certain Lusitanians, perhaps enrolled as auxiliaries in Titus Didius' army when Q. Sertorius first arrived in Hispania as the military tribune of the Roman general. This possibility does not seem very valid, however, and it is much more straightforward to believe that when Q. Sertorius arrived in the Iberian Peninsula in 82 BC, some of his followers attempted to establish ties with the local population,[(29)] while he tried to secure allies abroad, at the same time distracting C. Annius into hunting him down rather than dealing with other Sertorian agents. The contingent that left for Hispania from Italy in 82 BC included senators,[(30)] and probably other figures in search of exile and protection. Given the events that followed Q. Sertorius' 'flight', it is difficult to imagine this group of individuals willingly facing military persecution, marches, siege and naval combat, and it is therefore highly probable that they were left to establish links with the different communities of Hispania. Such is the picture that may be gleaned from Plutarch's reference to the *philoi* of Q. Sertorius, as argued by Konrad.[(31)] The success of these negotiations eventually crystallized in the alliance between Sertorians and Lusitanians.

Worthy of mention is the puzzling coincidence of L. Fabius Hispaniensis[(32)] and C. Tarquitius,[(33)] quaestors of C. Annius having the same names as two figures, later recorded as belonging to the intimate circle of Q. Sertorius.[(34)] It appears that by a strange twist of events the two quaestors, persecutors of Q. Sertorius, became his collaborators and them-

(18) Broughton 1951-2: II, 77; Grueber 1910, II, p. 352 note 2.

(19) This term deserves clarification: Seager 1972.

(20) *Sal. Iug.* 77. 4.

(21) Keaveney 1984, esp. 138, followed by García Mora 1991, p. 28ff.

(22) Such is the situation gleaned from the confrontation between the Sertorian J. Salinator and C. Annius Luscus in the Pyrenees, where Sertorius succeeded in halting the enemy's army, who did not know the passes, with a single strategic movement: Plut. *Sert.* 7. 1-3.

(23) Hinard 1985, pp. 157-158 identifies a total of 19 Sertorian followers from a total of 75 proscriptions.

(24) Antela-Bernárdez 2011.

(25) Plut. *Sert.* 6. 9 specifies the tasks undertaken by Sertorius in Hispania at his arrival from Italy, a whole series of military preparations among them, including: recruitment, the construction of war machinery, and the possible preparation of some kind of fleet. These new forces would have been added, certainly, to the military effects, which accompanied him from Italy. Moreover, Plut. *Sert.* 7.4 clearly states that the Sertorian troops could not rival in number with C. Annius, and therefore, they sought refuge in Carthago Nova, from where they later set sail to abandon Hispania, Blázquez 1961.

(26) Cadiou 2004 has brilliantly revised modern historiographical perceptions of Sertorius' military actions, deconstructing the well established idea of his use of guerrilla warfare, successfully proving the contrary, i.e., that he instructed his troops in established Roman tactics, further enhancing his quality as a capable and brilliant statesman, portrayed in diverse instances throughout the literary sources.

(27) Mauritania's numerous berths favoured this destination, allowing for clandestine movement, Gonzalbes Cravioto 2002. Important contributions may likewise be found in Molina Vidal 1997.

(28) Plut. *Sert.* 10.1.

(29) Konrad 1987, esp. p. 524 ff.

(30) García Mora 1991, p. 18.

(31) Konrad 1987, pp. 525-526.

(32) Broughton 1951-2, II, p. 77; III, 86; Wiseman 1971, p. 230 (who interestingly makes no reference to his service under C. Annius). The cognomen *Hispaniensis* must undoubtedly refer to a Roman from Hispania: Gabba 1954, p. 301. Also on the term, Syme 1937, p. 133; Castillo 2006; Migliorati 2006.

(33) Broughton 1951-2, II, p. 95, 121; III, pp. 203-204; Wiseman 1971, p. 264. Cichorius 1922, pp. 167-168 is probably the best compilation of information relating to this historical figure. Likewise, also Heurgon 1953, p. 407 note 5.

(34) L. Fabius Hispaniensis: Sal., *Hist.* 3. 4; C. Tarquitius: Front., Strateg. 2. 5. 31. Konrad 1994, p. 211.

selves outlaws. These two historical figures have sparked much scholarly debate on whether C. Annius' quaestors could actually be the same individuals who later came to form part of the Sertorian General Staff.

The identity of these figures has been fully dealt with in the studies of Konrad and Hinard, who, despite using different approaches, arrived at similar conclusions. Both agree as regards discarding the identification of C. Annius Luscus' monetal magistrate, C. Tarquitius P., with the Sertorian general Tarquitius Priscus. As far as L. Fabius Hispaniensis is concerned, Konrad accepts the possibility that there was only one individual but is not certain of it, while F. Hinard rejects it, as in the case of Tarquitius Priscus. The truth is that this issue is so complicated that any reflection on it must go into a great deal of detail, starting with an enumeration of both Konrad's and Hinard's arguments.

In the case of L. Fabius Hispaniensis, Konrad recalls that during the elections which followed the establishment of Sulla's control over Rome, the new magistrates were all fully involved with the senatorial faction and the government of Sulla: that is, the elected magistrates were all approved of by the *dictator*.[35] L. Fabius Hispaniensis, therefore, must have obtained the position of quaestor with the connivance of Sulla, a circumstance which Konrad deems impossible if there had been any slight suspicion of support for the popular cause. As for C. Tarquitius, Konrad bases his argument on palaeographic evidence, namely the difference between Tarquitius, as found on the Asculum Bronze, and Tarquinius, as used without exception in the manuscripts of the literary sources.[36] This solution is not entirely satisfactory, however, because the form *Tarquinius* could very likely be a variation of the name *Tarquitius*, and so this is not a conclusive argument.[37]

Konrad and Hinard coincide in disowning Gabba's hypothesis.[38] According to Gabba, C. Tarquitius and L. Fabius could have been proscribed after taking part in the sedition of M. Aemilius Lepidus, but no proscription took place after the revolt, with the proscription lists being definitively closed on the 1st of June in the year 81 BC.[39] Both authors begin by referring to Sallust (*Hist.* 3.83M), who uses the term *senator ex proscriptis* to describe L. Fabius. While Konrad accepts the possibility that L. Fabius was first elected quaestor in November 82 BC, and later included in the proscriptions, perhaps due to a personal dispute, before he then fled to Hispania in search of refuge and finally joined Q. Sertorius.[40] Hinard does not accept such a hypothesis,[41] given the implications of such a proscription: it would have been impossible for an individual susceptible to being considered an enemy of the Republic to have been elected quaestor just a few months earlier.[42] Hinard therefore puts the presence of a L. Fabius Hispaniensis in the factions of both Sulla and Q. Sertorius down to a homonymous coincidence, and views the ensuing historiographical debate as simply the unsound result of the inherent complexity of Roman prosopography.[43] To sum up, both figures seem to have maintained strong links to Hispania, which leads Hinard to suggest that the coincidence in names might reflect the interest of certain families in keeping a foot in both factions in the conflict, with the aim of securing the survival of at least some of their members.[44]

During the period of the Civil Wars, many Roman families did look to protect their own by maintaining an interest on both sides of the conflict, but in this particular case the homonymy between the subordinates of C. Annius and Q. Sertorius does not seem to be a matter of simple coincidence. The fact of the homonymous names is further complicated by difficulties of interpretation, but even more suspicious is the simultaneous presence of both figures in both scenarios. It appears that the Rome of 82 BC throws up an L. Fabius Hispaniensis and a C. Tarquitius Priscus, both subordinates of C. Annius, and there was likewise an L. Fabius Hispaniensis and a C. Tarquitius Priscus at Q. Sertorius' mortal banquet. As is argued by Konrad and Hinard, then, this appears to be possible, even if they were in fact different individuals. What is suspicious, nonetheless, and is not taken into consideration by the hypothesis of either, is their simultaneous presence: coincidence transcends homonymy, and both figures are to be found together in each set of circumstances. It is this that leads us to the conclusion that we are in fact dealing with the same people in both cases.

Let us carefully consider the information available regarding both figures. L. Fabius Hispaniensis must have belonged to the gens Fabia[45]. By the end of the second century, the Fabii had missed a generation in terms of consulship[46], and their absence from this post is surprising, considering the distinction of the family in Roman politics, a tradition reflected in a wide range of testimonies[47], but also because of the renewed importance of the gens under Caesar, which later continued under Augustus. In this respect, the absence from the consulship of any Fabius between 116 and 45 BC speaks for itself. Viewed in the light of the events linked to the latter date, the family's political recovery in the time of Augustus reveals an interesting link between

(35) Konrad 1987, p. 520. Hinard 1991, p. 117. Likewise, Badian 1964b, p. 216, 220.

(36) Konrad 1987, p. 523-524.

(37) Hinard 1991, p. 115 uses a somewhat hostile language against Konrad's arguments. Later, this author responds in a similar way in Konrad 1994, p. 211.

(38) Gabba 1973, pp. 300-301.

(39) Cic. Rosc Amer. 128.

(40) Konrad 1987, p. 521.

(41) Hinard 1991, p. 116.

(42) Hinard 1991, p. 117.

(43) Hinard 1991, p. 117

(44) Hinard 1991, pp. 118-119.

(45) Roddaz 2006, p. 105: "Les Fabii constituent la famille la plus représentée dans les inscriptions de la péninsule Ibérique".

(46) Syme 1939, p. 18.

(47) Martínez-Pinna 2002.

the Fabii and Marius' popular *factio*, which was inherited by Caesar and later by Augustus. Even if the gens as a whole cannot be considered to have been opposed to the *optimates*, it seems likely that at least some of its members were close to the popular faction of Marius and Caesar.(48) Likewise, the Fabii would also have maintained an influential position in Hispania, as it is seen in Valentia, a very important city for the Sertorians.(49) On the other hand, links between the gens Fabia and Lusitania may also be gleaned from numismatic evidence and from their participation in the fight against Viriatus.(50) Relations between the Marians and the gens Fabia seem therefore to have been likely, at least among those members of the family who still had direct ties to Hispania, which must have been the case of L. Fabius Hispaniensis, as is reflected in his cognomen.

Q. Tarquitius Priscus also constitutes an interesting case. Roman history established direct links between the end of the ancient Tarquinian kings and the inheritors of their power, among whom the Fabii were prominent. Even if the Etruscan monarchy might be considered to be very remote in relation to the Sertorian War, both Konrad and Hinard highlighted the similarity between the noun *Tarquinius* and the name of the Sertorian Tarquitius, as well as the potential political interest in assimilating these two names. In regard to this, it is well known that an important part of the Sertorian general staff was dominated by Etruscans, described as an 'Etruscan circle' in Q. Sertorius' government.(51) It is not therefore either surprising or strange to find one more Etruscan under Sertorian orders, and furthermore it seems probable that these Sertorian Etruscans were related to those Etruscan families which arrived in the Iberian Peninsula,(52) and in many cases later settled, becoming distinguished landowners and merchants.(53)

The relationship between C. Tarquitius and Q. Sertorius may, nevertheless, date back to before the Civil Wars. Indeed, a certain Tarquitius is recorded as being one the officers of Gnaeus Pompeius Strabo during the Social War,(54) a period in which Q. Sertorius himself was under the orders of Strabo,(55) leading some authors to suggest that the two already knew each other before the Sertorian War. All things considered, therefore, the presence of C. Tarquitius among the Sertorian ranks is clearly justified by his Etruscan descent as well as by his career.

The real problem, though, is posed by the numismatic evidence. If it were only a question of the literary sources, there would be no reason for doubt as to which faction L. Fabius Hispaniensis and C. Tarquitius Priscus belonged to. The only evidence that suggests a change of sides, or at very least that these two figures lived through a peculiar situation during the Sertorian War, is to be found in the coinage. In spite of everything that has been written, however, the truth is that discussion has rarely revolved around C. Annius.

C. Annius is a dark figure, like many others from the period of the Roman Civil Wars. Not much is known about him, as we have already seen. It is indeed surprising that we should know so little of someone who was apparently capable of subduing Q. Sertorius and making him flee, and who invariably cut short his advances, at least according to the interpretation put forward by scholars. Despite all of this apparent success, though, C. Annius disappears without a trace just after the Ebussus episode, and moreover it does not seem that the termination of his command was planned in any way, given the subsequent power vacuum in the Iberian Peninsula. According to Plutarch, Sulla's government eventually sent Vibius Pacciecus(56) to hunt down Q. Sertorius, which again indicates the existence of very unusual circumstances. It seems improbable that this Pacciecus, a mere *privatus*, would have held any *imperium* from the government in Rome which might have bestowed upon him leadership responsibilities in the region sufficient to hunt down the rebel forces of Q. Sertorius.(57) The presence of Pacciecus seems therefore to denote the absence of any competent authority able to take charge and face Q. Sertorius (such as C. Annius, had he still been operating in the Peninsula). Pacciecus' opposition to Q. Sertorius seems to have been voluntary in nature, motivated as it was by a desire to gain prestige in the eyes of the *optimates*: according to Plutarch, his actions were linked to the designs of Sulla,(58) although there must also have been commercial motivations. Q. Sertorius' presence in North Africa would have created instability in the traditional North African and Western Mediterranean markets,(59) endangering the

(48) Syme 1939, p. 423: "Of the dynastic houses of the patrician nobility now renascent, Aemilii and Fabii stood closely bound by ties of kinship or personal alliance with the Caesarian house".

(49) Gallego Franco 2000. On Valentia and the Sertorian faction, Konrad 1994, p. 97. Likewise, the fact that Valentia remained loyal to Perperna and the other conspirators, killers of Sertorius, only confirms that the links of the city with the Sertorian faction were not limited to their leader, but probably originated from other members of the faction: Konrad 1994, p. 172.

(50) For example: Florus, 1. 32.17.

(51) Antela-Bernárdez 2011.

(52) Blázquez 1989.

(53) Good examples of this process, and of particular interest for the Sertorian War, because of the links with Lusitania, are found in the work of Navarro Caballero 2006, who uses detailed prosopography to highlight the relevance of Italian families of Etruscan and Campanian origins in Lusitania: *Clatius, Cossutius, Curiatius, Curius, Loreius, Orbius, Rubrius, Tarquius, Trebonius, Vrsius*... many of them with important commercial links in the Eastern Mediterranean.

(54) *CIL* VI/IV/III 37045 (1933, pp. 3801-3804); Chichorius 1992, p. 131; Critini 1970, pp. 16-26.

(55) Plut., *Sert.* 4, 2. Konrad 1994, p. 56; Rijkhoek 1992, p. 99ff; Likewise, the collaboration between Sertorians and some of the men in the *turma Salluitana* seems to be attested by the presence in the inscription, listing Strabo's troops, of Q. Hirtuleius, brother of L. Hirtuleius, Sertorius' officer, and L. Insteius: Konrad 1994, p. 56. Furthermore, a possible relative to Annius, T. f. Ouf(entina), was indeed a member of Pompeius Strabo's *consilium*: Cichorius 1922, 128 note 12.

(56) Hernández Fernández 1998.

(57) García Mora 1991, p. 50.

(58) Plut. *Sert.* 9.5. Konrad 1994, pp. 112-113.

(59) Taking into consideration the strategic importance of passing through Ebusus and North Africa for the safest naval routes: Molina Vidal 1997, p. 81, 84.

economic interests, probably commercial in nature, of the Pacciecus family in the region, which is why it proved necessary to oppose Q. Sertorius in the defence of these interests.(60)

In his biography of Q. Sertorius, Plutarch records how Sertorius confronted the four *strategoi*.(61) C. Annius, however, was not among them, and my thesis in this respect is a straightforward one: C. Annius must have died at some point during the Sertorian War. Although there are no records that might confirm this hypothesis, the fact that his name is no longer recorded during the range of conflicts that derived from the Civil Wars, as well as the context of subsequent events (e.g. the revolt of Lepidus), proves that C. Annius was no longer active. Badian has correctly already stressed the significance of the lack of governors during this period, which only reinforces such a hypothesis.(62) C. Annius, an experienced soldier, would have participated in other conflicts of the time if it had been possible for him to do so, or at the very least he would have retained the command of the province after his victories.(63) Konrad,(64) on the other hand, expresses an alternative view, suggesting that C. Annius might have been deposed after his quaestors' abandonment of him and change of faction.

It must be mentioned, nevertheless, that if they were elected as quaestors for the mission in Hispania, neither L. Fabius, nor C. Tarquitius, would initially have seemed to present any danger to Sulla's government. It appears that while Sulla did punish many who opposed him, others who did not openly support a faction or take part directly in the war against the Senate or against Sulla himself could not be considered guilty. Therefore, it is probable that L. Fabius and C. Tarquitius played no part in Cinna's government, or indeed in any warlike or political action that might have turned them into traitors or opponents of Sulla. They would have been elected as quaestors because of their contacts in Hispania and their knowledge of the territory, as has been pointed out above.

As is noted by Hinard, it is not the fact that L. Fabius and C. Tarquitius were elected as magistrates that is surprising, but the fact that they changed sides. Because of this, we are obliged to ask ourselves whether these figures previously harboured the intention of acting against C. Annius, as this would imply that their collaboration with the forces sent to repress Q. Sertorius was actually the result of a plan much more wide-ranging than can be gleaned from the information available. Their betrayal could, however, also have been motivated by one of many specific events that took place after they had taken up office.

In order to support his hypothesis, Hinard argues that it is impossible that an individual such as L. Fabius, closely related to the enemy, should have held office in Sulla's Rome of 81 BC.(65) Nevertheless, there are many known cases of politicians who, while being ideologically close to the Marian faction, decided to stay loyal to Rome and carry out their duties under the authority of Sulla. Among such cases were that of M. Aemilius Lepidus, and even that of M. Perperna, both of whom based their decision on Sulla's good intentions.(66) Most noteworthy among these examples, however, are L. Magius and L. F Annius, two men who shared certain remarkable similarities with L. Fabius Hispaniensis and C. Tarquitius Priscus. Marian politicians who at some point worked in the organisational structure of Sulla's government must indeed have been more common than one might initially assume: in effect, many Marian supporters would have decided to stay within the bounds of legality and acknowledge Sulla's government, but even if they did not, they nevertheless did not entirely relinquish the hope of eventually being able to continue the fight. L. Fabius Hispaniensis and C. Tarquitius Priscus would seem, in principle, to match this profile. Although Marian supporters, they decided to accept the legal government of Rome, led by Sulla, and simply wait, like many others, for a more appropriate moment to act. There seems little doubt that their links with Hispania influenced their nomination for office, as well as their initial acknowledgement of Sulla's government.

Hinard(67) creates a major problem by accepting the thesis of Carcopino,(68) who, basing his view on Appian,(69) suggests that Sulla held consular elections in 82 BC in order to name the consuls for the following year, concluding that he did the same for the other magistracies. Nevertheless, this interpretation is flawed in two specific respects. Firstly, it presupposes some form of action, which may constitute an over-interpretation of the sources: it appears to be normal that Sulla would have controlled the consular elections, but this does not mean that he applied the same iron fist policy as regards the remaining magistracy elections. Secondly, it assumes that Sulla engaged in a formal reconstruction of Republican politics, taking advantage of his monopoly over the *optimates* faction. However, the image portrayed by Keaveney of C. Annius, as belonging to a moderate political group in Roman politics, questions the role of those who avoided involvement during the Civil War, who kept within the bounds of legality so as to, given the right moment, lend their support to the victor, who would ultimately also be the legal head of Republican politics. While the majority of known cases of people switching sides were to

(60) On this family in Baetica, Melchor Gil 2006, pp. 253-254, with bibliography. Nevertheless, the members of this family have not been fully explained, and could well be the subject of a monograph investigation, in order to better explain the change in alliances taking place in the family during the Sertorian and Caesar's Civil Wars.

(61) Konrad 1994, p. 127; Brennan 2000, I, p. 506.

(62) Badian 1964a, pp. 88-96.

(63) García Mora 1991, p. 29

(64) Konrad 1987, p. 521

(65) Likewise, Hinard 1991, p. 115 discards the romantic vision of deserting for political ideals.

(66) Plut. *Sul.* 28.1.

(67) Hinard 1985, p. 121

(68) Carcopino 1931, pp. 40-41.

(69) App. *B.C.* 1. 103, pp. 478-479; Hinard 1991, p. 117 and note 26.

the benefit of Sulla, there are also examples of individuals who chose not to become involved in the civil conflict, and it seems logical to assume that these *neutral* figures were later incorporated by Sulla into the administrative sphere of the Republic. On one hand, as pointed out by Badian, there was a great need for able men capable of holding a magistracy or a military office, and furthermore this *neutral* group was probably more numerous than any other one faction and its supporters. The policy of restoration of the Republic under Sulla was therefore obliged to ally itself with these moderate politicians, who guaranteed the continuity of order in the system. In addition, the news of the proscriptions must have been late in arriving at Annius' army, and so L. Fabius may have well maintained his position until what was very probably the summer of 81 BC, at least. This circumstance may be related to a change in quaestors from L. Fabius to C. Tarquitius, who were not necessarily appointed simultaneously, as we have already seen.

Finally, there are other possible explanations too, especially those which relate to Sallust's expression *senator ex proscriptis*, made in reference to L. Fabius Hispaniensis. The degree of veracity of this affirmation remains unknown: after all, Appian considered Q. Sertorius to be a senator,[70] a statement which in itself directly questions any possible interpretation of this expression. Several authors have accepted that L. Fabius was included in the proscriptions as a senator in order to differentiate him from his homonymous counterpart in the Sertorian faction. Nevertheless, the same authors later went on to study L. Fabius in relation to his condition as Hispaniensis, that is, as a member of a family which had only recently achieved citizenship, according to the information contained on the Asculum Bronze.[71] In the view of the author, such an approach cannot be valid, because if we accept that L. Fabius was indeed a senator, we would also have to accept the possibility that he was proscribed by Sulla, and moreover, if his family had only recently obtained citizenship, he could hardly have belonged to the senatorial *ordo*, thus making his proscription extremely improbable. There is, therefore, room to doubt the reliability of the reference in Sallust, which was perhaps a mere reflex action of the author at the moment of recording the information, which is of course, in another order of events, quite logical, considering the historical context described. On the other hand, and in contrast to the view of Spann, who sees L. Fabius as occupying a secondary role in the Sertorian faction,[72] Konrad correctly pointed out his influential position: otherwise, he would not even have been present at the banquet at which Q. Sertorius was killed.[73] Lastly, although the expression *senator ex proscriptis* might respond to a conjecture of Suetonius explaining the presence of L. Fabius in the closest circle of the Sertorian general staff, it is also quite common to find falsifications in the proscription lists,[74] and if this were indeed a falsification, it would have been the result of L. Fabius switching sides after his election as quaestor. To sum up, the information to be gleaned from *ex proscriptis* is in no way conclusive.

(70) App. *B.C.* 1. 65.

(71) For example, Roddaz 2006, pp. 104-106.

(72) Spann 1987, p. 131.

(73) Konrad 1987, p. 522, note 10.

Anna Perenna and the beginning of the military season in 82 BC

Returning to the coinage of C. Annius, it is worth re-examining the information contained on these coin issues in the light of the interpretations that have been expressed above. Traditionally, the figure on the obverse has been identified with Anna Perenna,[75] a divinity associated with the gens Annia and with the beginning of spring celebrations.[76] Equally notable is the date of the festivity, the Ides of March,[77] which coincides with the beginning of the season of war. The presence of Anna Perenna on the obverse of the coin therefore requires further consideration, even though the general interpretation, which views C. Annius as simply paying homage to his gens, remains a valid one. The break in the Roman calendar marked by the second Equirria ended with the festivity of Anna Perenna, a boundary in the transition towards the New Year, and, in some way, a powerful reminder of the restoration of order and prosperity for Rome.[78] Anna represented a perfect symbol for Sulla's political propaganda, as a metaphor of spring and of life itself, and the presence of Anna Perenna in *RRC* 366 would also be an invitation to reflect on the time of year of C. Annius Luscus' journey to Hispania, perhaps serving as a chronological indicator related to the beginning of the season of war. This could serve to situate C. Annius' departure at around the time of the festivity of Anna Perenna and the Ides of March, in the year 82 BC.

The next question concerns the reason why C. Annius decided to highlight in his coin issues so obvious a circumstance, namely that his persecution of Q. Sertorius started at the time of year at which warfare was validated once more. The mark EX SC on the *denarii* seems to reflect a more complex reality behind the use of the image of Anna Perenna, which after all constitutes an exception for Roman coins of this period. It is worth reflecting that a reference

(74) For example, Fezzi 2003, pp. 36-38.

(75) Ovid. *Fast.* 3.523c.; Daremberg, Saglio A-B, 1877: s.v. "Anna Perenna, 270; Piranomonte 2002.

(76) Some authors have questioned the identification of the female figure with Anna Perenna, proposing other possibilities, such as Moneta or Aequitas: Eckhel 1792-98: V, pp. 134-135. It is worth noting that these *denarii* break iconographically with other coinages of the same period by using a female figure, whether Anna Perenna or any other. In regards to this, and considering the message contained in Sulla's coins of the following years, with terms such as *Triumphalis* and *Imperator*, one cannot discard the possibility that the female bust may be directly representing the Republic itself. Nevertheless, in view of this analysis, Anna Perenna seems to be the most viable option.

(77) Macrob. *Sat.* 1. 12; Woodard 2002, p. 96.

(78) Woodard 2002, p. 97: "the restoration of order by the arrival of the Ides, the celebration of the New Year's feast of Anna Perenna, and the swelling of the ranks of the *iuvenes* under the watchful eye of *Juventas*, goddess of youth and guarantor of the vitality of Rome".

to the festivity of Anna Perenna and to the Ides of March would only make sense if those responsible for the coining had the intention to generate a specific message, and the hypothesis of this author is therefore that the production of the coins did not take place right after the Ides of March, but before them. This circumstance would explain the desire to explicitly validate a rupture in traditional minting practice, by putting the persecution of the Sertorians a few months forward. To support this hypothesis, it is important to bear in mind firstly that Sulla took control of the city of Rome at the beginning of November 82 BC, and that from that point onwards until the Ides, there was an interval of five months, time enough for Q. Sertorius to establish a foothold in Hispania and to bolster his resistance. Nevertheless, if C. Annius did set sail before that, the possibility that he would be able to confront Q. Sertorius successfully is hightened. In fact, haste seems to be a key concept behind the iconography of the *denarii RRC* 336, as is evidenced by the position of the *quadriga/biga* on the reverse, signalling movement, and often clearly representing a race. Annius' campaign was, after all, a race to stop the Sertorian "menace".[79]

It has generally been assumed that these coin issues were minted after the confrontation between C. Annius and Q. Sertorius, and that their iconographies reference the victory over the Sertorians in the Pyrenees.[80] This traditional interpretation is rendered untenable, however, for various reasons. In the first instance, no such victory existed: according to the sources, C. Annius was able to prevail against the forces confronting him in the Pyrenees thanks to treason, rather than to military combat.[81] Indeed, there is no further evidence during the period of persecution of any episode meriting the appellation of victory through military action. The reference to the *quadriga* and raised palm-branch was not at all surprising in *RRC* 366, given the victorious character of the *denarii*, and these coin motifs should therefore be explained from a different standpoint, that of the Civil Wars, and viewed in relation to a wider series of military actions. Considering the historical context, this interpretation does seem to be more appropriate.

There is one final iconographic element depicted in some of the *denarii RRC* 366 that also deserves attention, namely the presence of the *caduceus* and the scales. The traditional interpretation views both of these as expressing religious significance, but the *caduceus*, the staff of Hermes, may also be understood in a narrower interpretation, as referring to the tutelar god of commerce, and even more so if it appears next to some scales, both being very obvious symbols of commercial activity. In the light of this, the numismatic elements present in C. Annius' coinage would appear to imbue the Sertorian conflict with a broader Mediterranean dimension, as a central episode in the Roman Civil Wars. The motivation behind both defections may also be related to two factors specific to the period. The first of these is Sulla's action in Etruria shortly after taking control of Rome, whereby he decided to establish a significant number of his troops in Etruscan lands, probably with the objective of controlling the territory through the presence of his supporters.[82] Expropriations and the imposition of troops ensued, which constituted a good reason for figures such as L. Fabius and C. Tarquitius to rebel and change sides, considering the interests of their families in the region. As regards the second factor, Roddaz has pointed out the implications of events related to the First Mithridatic War for Italian merchants who had settled in the East and who then migrated to the West in search of peace, settling in significant numbers in the valley of the Tagus and along the Lusitanian coast.[83] As mentioned elsewhere,[84] Sulla's actions throughout the First Mithridatic War were not driven only by military objectives, but were also pragmatic in nature. The Marian faction was strong in the East, and the war destroyed the client networks of Italian merchants settled throughout the eastern ports and commercial enclaves, who were later substituted by new agents who could be relied upon to act in benefit of Sulla's interests. Throughout the duration of Sulla's actions in Greece during the First Mithridatic War, there was therefore an important shift in the political orientation of Italian merchants in the East. Commerce in the region was no longer controlled by the faction of the *populares*, but instead was now subject to the interests of Sulla and the *optimates*. Many of the merchants displaced by the war were probably close to the Marians, and therefore likely to have had a favourable view of Q. Sertorius subsequently. Nevertheless, by aiding him in his fight against Sulla's government,[85] these merchants were positioning themselves outside the legal framework, and some may even have been considered as pirates.

It is now possible to contrast these so-called Sertorian 'pirates', who were in fact merchants who supported Q. Sertorius, with those other merchants to whom Annius' coinage seems to refer. The fight between C. Annius and Q. Sertorius over the Western Mediterranean may ultimately be viewed as one more proof of the existence of conflict and competition between these two groups of merchants[86] due to the important commercial interests of Ebussus,[87] and of

(79) Roddaz 2006, p. 102.

(80) Pierfitte 1946, pp. 121-122.

(81) Plut. *Sert.* 7.1-3. Konrad 1994, pp. 99-101.

(82) Amela 2003, p. 66.

(83) Roddaz 2006, p. 107.

(84) Antela-Bernárdez 2009a.

(85) Perhaps by supplying ships: Roddaz 2006, p. 107 and note 67.

(86) Competition between two opposing groups of merchants would explain to a certain extent contradictory accounts in the sources on the relationship between Sertorius and piracy, sometimes in collaboration (Plut. *Sert.* 7. 5; vid. García Mora 1991, p. 201) and others in clear opposition (vid. Plut. *Sert.* 8. 2). Worthy of noting is the work of Mariotta 2002, 1872, mentioning a fragment in Sallust, which refers to Cilician pirates as 'genus Graecorum', i.e., of Greek origin, a piece of information, which is interesting in considering East-West relations during the Sertorian conflict. The Ebusus episode is, without a doubt, an exception, as has been noted by Prieto 1987, p. 273.

(87) Likewise, let us recall, following Molina Vidal 1997, p. 81 and 84, that sailing was subject to certain technical needs, and that in order to navigate the marine circulating currents affecting any journey from North Africa to the Iberian Peninsula, it was necessary to bypass Ebussus, which would mean that Sertorius was forced to approach it on his return from Africa;

the fact that each group was linked with one of the bands involved in the Sertorian conflict. Legitimation for this hypothesis is to be found in a series of direct precedents, especially in the case of the merchants of the Eastern Mediterranean linked to Marius before the First Mithridatic War and later substituted by supporters of Sulla, as we have shown elsewhere[88]. In the context of the fight against Q. Sertorius and the activities of the Ebusitanian pirates, it seems very probable that the events that took place on the island were a direct result of this commercial confrontation[89]. The presence of two factions of pirates, one favouring and the other opposing Q. Sertorius[90], seems to confirm the existence of two groups of sailors in the conflict, reaffirming the hypothesis of a war of commercial interests which provided the motivation for a large part of the movements of both factions.

In conclusion, this analysis aims to demonstrate how the conflicts which derived from the Social War and the Civil Wars came to broaden Rome's hold on the world. It views the persecution of Q. Sertorius, as reflected in the analysis of the *denarii* minted by C. Annius Luscus, as a crucial and culminating point in the process that saw Rome's expansion beyond the defined limits of the *Urbs* into the global context represented by the Mediterranean Sea.

Abbreviations

CIL VI/IV/III (1933)= Bang M. *Corpus Inscriptionum Latinarum. Insciptiones Urbis Romae Latinae. Partis Quartae. Fasciculus Postremus. Additamentorum Auctarium.* Berlin.

Daremberg, Saglio A-B (1877)= Daremberg M. CH., Saglio E. *Dictionnaire des antiquités greques et romaines d'après les texts et les monuments, Tome premier. Première partie (A-B).* Paris.

RRC (1974)= Crawford M. *Roman Republican Coinage.* Cambridge, 2 vols.

Sydenham (1952)= Sydenham E. A. *The coinage of the Roman Republic* (Revised with indexes by Haines, G. C.; edited by Forrer L., Hersh C. A.) London.

References

Amela Valverde L. (2003). *Cneo Pompeyo Magno.*

Antela-Bernárdez B. (2009a). 'Sila no vino a aprender Historia Antigua: el asedio de Atenas en 87/6 a. C.' *Revue des Etudes Anciennes*, 111, pp. 475-491.

Antela-Bernárdez B. (2009b). 'Entre Delos, Atenas, Roma y el Ponto: Medeo del Pireo', *Faventia*, 31. 1-2, pp. 49-60.

Antela-Bernárdez B. (2011).'Q. Sertorio. La búsqueda de aliados', *Athenaeum*, 99, pp. 399-409.

Antela-Bernárdez B. (2012). 'Economía, comerciantes e intereses durante las Guerras Sertorianas', *Latomus.*

Badian E. (1964a). 'Notes on the Provincial Governors from the Social War down to Sulla's Victory' in Badian E. (ed.) *Studies in Greek and Roman History.* New York, pp. 71-104 (originally published in Proceedings of the African Classical Associations, 1, 1958, pp. 1-18).

Badian E. (1964b). 'Waiting for Sulla' in Badian E., *Studies in Greek and Roman History.* New York, pp. 206-234 (originally published in Journal of Roman History, 52, 1962, 47-61).

Blázquez J. M. (1961). 'Las relaciones entre Hispania y el Norte de África durante el gobierno bárquida y la conquista romana (237-19 a. C.)', *Saitabi*, 2, pp. 21-43.

Blázquez J. M. (1989). 'Etruscos en la Hispania Romana', Maetzke G. (ed.), *Atti del Secondo Congresso Internazionale Etrusco (Firenze 26 Maggio - 2 Giugno 1985).* Rome, pp. 1495-1500.

Brennan T. C. (2000). *The Praetorship in the Roman Republic.* 2 vols. Oxford.

Broughton T. S. (1951-2). *Magistrates of the Roman Republic.* 2 vols. New York.

Cadiou F. (2004). 'Sertorius et la guerrille' in Auliard C., Bodiou L. (dir.), *Au jardin des Hespèrides: Histoire, sociéte et épigraphie des mondes anciens (Mélanges offerts à Alain Tranoy).* Rennes, pp. 297-314.

Campo M. (1976). *Las monedas de Ebusus.* Barcelona.

Carcopino J. (1931). *Sylla ou la monarchie manquée.* Paris.

Castillo C. (2006). 'Hispaniensis e Hispani en la Bética' in Sartori A., Valvo A. (a cura di), *Hiberia-Italia, Italia-Hiberia.* Milan, pp. 87-98.

Chic G. (1986). 'Quinto Sertorio, procónsul', in *Actas de la Reunión sobre Epigrafía Hispánica de Época Romano-Republicana.* Zaragoza, pp. 171-176.

Cichorius C. (1922). *Römische Studien. Historisches Epigraphisches Literargeschichtliches aus vier Jahrhunderten Roms.* Lepizig.

Costa Ribas B. (2002). 'La ocupación de Ebusus por Sertorio' in Khanoussi M., Ruggeri P., Vismara C. (a cura di), *L'Africa Romana. Lo spazio marítimo del Mediterraneo oc-*

therefore Annius needed to establish the mentioned reinforcements, in order to prevent possible dangers arriving from Africa, where the Marians, although controlled, were still very numerous, as has just been outlined.

(88) Antela-Bernárdez 2009b, note 36.

(89) On this matter, vid. Antela-Bernárdez 2011.

(90) In favour: Plut. *Sert.* 7.5; against: Plut. *Sert.* 9.2.

cidentale: geografia storia ed economica.1. Sassari, pp. 665-680.

Critini N. (1970). *L'epigrafe di Asculum di Gn. Pompeo Strabone*. Milan.

Eckhel J. H. (1792-98). *Doctrina numorum veterum*. 9 vols. Vienna.

Fezzi L. (2003). *Falsificazione di documenti pubblici nella Roma Tardorepubblicana (133-31 a.C.)*. Firenze.

Gabba E. (1954). 'Le origini della guerra sociale e la vita politica romana dopo 189 a. C.' *Athenaeum*, 32, pp. 41-114, 293-345.

Gabba E. (1973). *Esercito e società nella tarda repubblica romana*. Florence.

Gallego Franco H. (2000). 'Los Sertorii: Una Gens de origen republicano en Hispania romana', *Iberia*, 3, pp. 243-252.

García Mora F. (1990). 'Quinto Sertorio: 100-98 a. C. Trienium sine armis?', *Florentia Iliberritana*, 1, pp. 137-145.

García Mora F. (1991). *Un episodio de la Hispania Republicana: La guerra de Sertorio*. Granada.

García Riaza E., Sánchez León M. L. (2000). *Roma y la municipalización de las Baleares*. Palma de Mallorca.

Gozalbes Cravioto E. (2002). 'El papel económico de los puertos de la Tingitana' in Khanoussi M., Ruggeri P., Vismara C. (a cura di), *L'Africa Romana. Lo spazio marítimo del Mediterraneo occidentale: geografia storia ed economica. vol. I. Sassari*, pp. 550-552.

Grueber H. A. (1910). *Coins of the Roman Republic in the British Museum*. 3 vols. London.

Hernández Fernández J. S. (1998). 'Los Vivii Pac(c)iaeci de la Baetica: una familia de hispanienses mal conocida', *Faventia*, 20.2, pp. 163-176.

Heurgon J. (1953). 'Tarquitius Priscus et l'organisation de l'ordre des haruspices sous l'empereur Claude', *Latomus*, 12, pp. 402-417.

Hinard F. (1985). *Les proscriptions de la Rome républicaine*. Rome.

Hinard F. (1991). 'Philologie, prosopographie et histoire à propos de Lucius Fabius Hispaniensis', *Historia*, 40, pp. 113-119.

Keaveney A. (1982). *Sulla. The Last Republican*. London.
Keaveney A. (1984). 'Who were the Sullani', *Klio*, 66, pp. 114-150.

Konrad C. F. (1987). 'Some friends of Sertorius', *American Journal of Philology*, 108, pp. 519-27.

Konrad C. F. (1994). *Plutarch's Sertorius. A historical commentary*. Chapel Hill-London.

Lovano M. (2002). *The Age of Cinna: Crucible of Late Republican Rome*. Stuttgart.

Mariotta G. (2002). 'Le Historiae di Sallustio e le imprese di Sertorio', in Khanoussi M., Ruggeri P., Vismara C. (a cura di), *L'Africa Romana. Lo spazio marítimo del Mediterraneo occidentale: geografia storia ed economica*. Vol. 3, pp. 1863-1873.

Martínez-Pinna J. (2002). 'Sobre el origen mítico de la Gens Fabia', in Martinez-Pinna J. (coord.), *Mito y Ritual en el Antiguo Occidente Mediterráneo*. Málaga, pp. 117-141.

Melchor Gil E. (2006). 'Corduba, caput prouinciae y foco de atracción para las élites locales de la Hispania Ulterior Bética', *Gerión*, 24, pp. 251-279.

Migliorati G. (2006). 'Il nome *Hispaniensis* della legio IX', in Sartori A., Valvo A. (a cura di), *Hiberia-Italia, Italia-Hiberia*. Milan, pp. 327-338.

Molina Vidal J. (1997). *La dinámica comercial romana entre Italia e Hispania Citerior*. Alicante.

Navarro Caballero M. (2006). 'L'emigration italique dans la Lusitanie côtière: une approche onomastique', in Caballos Rufino A., Demougin S. (eds), *Migrare. La formation des élites Dans l'Hispanie romaine*. Burdeos, pp. 69-100.

Padrino Fernández S. (2005). *Una aproximación a la circulación monetaria de Ebusus en época romana*. Ibiza.

Pierfitte G. (1946). 'Monnaies de la République Romaine', *Mélanges de la Société Toulousaine d'Études Classiques*, 1.

Piranomonte M. (2002). *Il santuario della musica e il bosco sacro di Anna Perenna*. Rome.

Prieto A. (1987). 'Un punto oscuro en la invasión romana de las Baleares: la piratería', *Habis*, 18-19, pp. 271-275.

Rijkhoek K. G. (1992). *Studien zu Sertorius: 123-83 v. Chr.* Bonn.

Ridley R. T. (1981).'The extraordinary commands of the Late Republic', *Historia*, 30, pp. 280-297.

Roddaz J.-M. (2006). 'D'une péninsule à l'autre: l'épisode sertorien', in Sartori A., Valvo A. (a cura di), *Hiberia-Italia, Italia-Hiberia*. Milan, pp. 99-115.

Schulten A. (1926). *Sertorius*. Leipzig.

Seager R. (1972).'Factio: Some observations', *Journal of Roman Studies*, 62, pp. 53-58.

Spann Ph. O. (1987). *Quintus Sertorius and the legacy of Sulla*. Fayetteville.

Syme R. (1937). 'Who was Decidius Saxa?', *Jounal of Roman Studies*, 27, pp. 127-137.

Syme R. (1939). *The Roman Revolution*. Oxford.

Wiseman T. P. (1971). *New men in the Roman Senate, 139 BC- AD 14*. Oxford.

Woodard R. D. (2002). 'The disruption of time in myth and epic', *Arethusa*, 35, pp. 83-98.

Garrisons, coins and war stress (89-63 BCE) in Late Hellenistic towns

Toni Ñaco del Hoyo*

ABSTRACT

War stress, caused by the garrisoning and billeting of foreign armies in Hellenistic towns, is a historical phenomenon which may be traced throughout the period of the Mithridatic Wars. Coinage sometimes constitutes the most relevant piece of evidence available to the modern historian in order to reveal such war stress. In this paper I shall focus on a number of case studies from the Thracian coast of the Black Sea, which suffered extreme pressure on the part of both Roman and Pontic sides.

Collateral damage suffered by Late Hellenistic towns forced to billet foreign troops was initially analysed in a recent article (Ñaco 2010, pp. 929-940), and this paper follows up on some of the suggestions presented there. Numismatic evidence allows modern historians to clarify some of the conclusions emanating from the study of other historical sources, such as ancient literature and epigraphy, although sometimes coinage constitutes the sole evidence for the existence of these garrisons. The autonomous coins from the Illyrian city of Rhizon provide one such example. Towards the end of the Third Macedonian War (168-167),[1] the coinage disappeared completely, probably owing to the presence of a Roman garrison in the city,[2] A similar phenomenon may have occurred during the Mithridatic Wars (89-63), a conflict involving two hegemonic powers of the eastern Mediterranean, Rome and Pontus, but which also affected a large number of *poleis* in continental Greece, the Aegean islands and Asia Minor. A wide variety of factors played a part in this historical scenario, and although they are highly disparate in nature, they should be analysed within this same context (Ñaco, Antela, Arrayás and Busquets 2009, pp. 34-38, fig. 1). These include the Pontic invasion of Asia and the minting of silver coins to finance military activity such as the movement of armies, the defence of a city, or the payment of war indemnities. The presence of military garrisons among the civil population and war compensations handed out by the victorious faction at the end of the war are other important influences. After the cold war that preceded the First Mithridatic War (89) and for the following quarter of a century, the eastern Mediterranean suffered widely from the consequences of the confrontation between Mithridates VI Eupator and Rome. Greek urban society was deeply fragmented, forcing its political leaders and *demos* to side with one faction or the other according to circumstances and ultimately to answer for their alliances before their own people, as well as before the victorious power. The purpose of this paper is to relate in one interpretative framework the war stress created in the majority of the *poleis* affected directly or indirectly by the situation through the long period of cold war, conflicts and intervals of peace. The aim will be to achieve this through the analysis of two of the phenomena affecting the conflict, namely the widespread use of garrisons by both factions and the eventual effect which this had on coinage during this period. In particular, a few relevant case studies where numismatic evidence can contribute new approaches to the topic have been singled out, though this does not obviate the need for other kinds of historical evidence (Ñaco 2010, pp. 935-936).[3]

Garrisoning, billeting and Late Hellenistic towns

After the invasion of continental Greece by the Pontic Archaelaos (87), the Roman faction tried to maintain strategic control over Boeotia at all costs, charging with its defence Q. Bruttius Sura, legate pro *quaestore* of the governor of Macedonia, C. Sentius Saturninus (pr.94). The name of the latter appears on some of the reissued tetradrachms of

* ICREA Research Professor at UAB, and MCR at Wolfson College, Oxford. I want to thank the editor, Dr. Fernando López-Sánchez, for his kind invitation to take part in this book, and, particularly, for his patience with my long-awaited manuscript. This paper has been possible thanks to the support given by the research projects: RICIP2009-00001, HAR2010-19185, 2011-00004, and 2009SGR18. I also want to thank Dr. Isaías Arrayás for letting me read some of his unpublished work, and Dr. López-Sánchez for comments, references, and discussions on the topic.

(1) All dates are BCE unless stated otherwise

(2) *Praesidio imposito Gabinium praefecit, Rhizoni et Olcinio, urbibus opportunis.* Ujes 2004, p. 162.

(3) As will be seen ahead later, the analysis of several coin issues has led to the identification of potential military garrisons in various Hellenistic towns, especially along the coast of the Black Sea. This is one of the most relevant, albeit controversial, contributions of De Callataÿ 1997, pp. 145-150, 254-256.

Asillas and Thasos, which may have been used to pay the troops that were stationed at intervals in Chaironeia, a very important strategic location for that region of continental Greece.[(4)] In this case, fortunately, there is plenty of historical evidence available to assess the impact of these garrisons on the Boeotian town, a common but nevertheless important phenomenon in the history of the Hellenistic world, especially during its late period. A famous passage by Plutarch describes the revolt led during the winter of 88-87 by the young aristocrat Damon, together with other members of the Ephebia, against the commander of the Roman garrison, who had previously seduced that young Chaironeian boy (Plut. *Cim.*1-2; Ñaco, Antela, Arrayás and Busquets 2009, pp. 36-37).

Likewise, an inscription from the same city honoured Amatokos, a Thracian in command of a winter garrison at some time after 87. According to other texts, some months later, Sulla set up a military tribune at the request of several of his soldiers, perhaps unsurprisingly natives of Chaironeia themselves, who were afraid that a Pontic advance would eliminate their town (Plut. *Sull.*16.8;17.5).[(5)] From all this, one may conclude that the two Roman garrisons, which practically succeeded each other in chronological terms, had a direct impact on the city, affecting its civic institutions but also its social make-up, which probably never recovered from some of the events mentioned because of increasing differences between pro-Roman and anti-Roman factions, especially after the billeting of foreign armed forces within the town. Significantly, however, Chaironeia does not seem to have issued coinage during the conflict or the preceding decades: the Boeotian town did not see any need to finance military expenditure with its own coinage. In this case, surprisingly, the numismatic evidence does not serve to clarify the collateral damage produced by the two Republican garrisons, which are on the other hand reflected in numerous instances to be found in other historical sources (Head 1881, p. 93).[(6)]

Neither is Chaironeia an isolated example in the Hellenistic world, even prior to the Roman-Pontic conflict. Garrisons, made up of either mercenaries or auxiliaries, were established temporarily or permanently under the authority of Hellenistic monarchs, guaranteeing their military, political and even fiscal control over a civil population, which lived with the constant pressure of sharing their urban centre with armed contingents.[(7)] During the winter season in particular, the idle soldiers belonging to these contingents were temporarily demobilised in their fortresses, or more commonly billeted in allied cities and housed, fed, and even paid for by the civil population. The elite social groups, which sustained the local finances and carried the burden of the military presence together with the rest of the population, must have considered this a necessary evil for the interests of the polis.[(8)]

A passage in Plutarch specifically refers to the advantages of wintering in a Greek town, especially if the soldiers had endured more than one campaign: in these cities the Roman legionaries were billeted at the expense of their lodgers and enjoyed the comforts that were lacking in the camps (Plut. *Luc.* 33.4).[(9)] In other cases, the garrisons were only in charge of offering logistical aid to armies forced to winter nearby. Such was the case of the city of Smyrna, which suffered the legions of Sulla during the winter of 85-84 after the defeat of Mithridates (Tac. *Ann.*4.56; Oros. 6.2.8).[(10)] While there was a long tradition behind such practices in the Greek world,[(11)] some of their major consequences are more easily observed during the Mithridatic Wars, a period of intense military activity with significant collateral damage, which was caused by the hegemonic aspirations in the Aegean of two great economic and military powers.[(12)] For a quarter of a century including periods of cold war and open confrontation, the Roman Republic and the kingdom of Pontus forced many towns into accepting military garrisons within their walls for strategic reasons related to developments in the war, but also for the sake of realpolitik, i.e. the preservation of political, military and

(4) Broughton 1952, vol. 2, 50 (87 BC); De Callataÿ 1998, pp. 115-117; Picard 2008, pp. 478-479. Likewise, according to De Callataÿ 2009, p. 65, the sole function of this kind of coinage was to pay Thracian mercenaries enrolled in the Roman army, so that once their mission concluded and they returned to their homes, the money would be treasured simply as a proof of value, and would circulate only in a very limited form.

(5) *REG* 32, 1919, pp. 320-337. Honorary inscriptions such as the one dedicated to Amatakos, were probably instigated by local factions with political or even commercial interests, in connivance with forces from the same faction outside the city. Nevertheless, none of this provides with information relevant to possible damage inflicted on the local population: Launey 1987, vol. 2, pp. 642, 649-650; Mackay 2000, pp. 103-104.

(6) There is no mention either of the coin issues from Chaeroneia: Fossey 1990, pp. 249-253.

(7) Launey 1987, vol. 2, pp. 633-723; Chaniotis 2002, pp. 99-113; Ma 2002, pp. 115-122; Couvenhes 2004, pp. 77-113; Chaniotis 2005, pp. 88-93; Couvenhes 2006, pp. 401-411; Billows 2008, p. 306; see, most recently, a different approach to this topic in López Sánchez 2010, pp. 17-52.

(8) Baker 2000, pp. 177-196; Baker 2001, pp. 193-194; Ñaco 2001, pp. 63-90.

(9)'Well, then, Sallust says that his soldiers were ill disposed towards him at the very beginning of the war, before Cyzicus, and again before Amisus, because they were compelled to spend two successive winters in camp. The winters that followed also vexed them. They spent them either in the enemy's country, or among the allies, encamped under the open sky. Not once did Lucullus take his army into a city that was Greek and friendly' (Loeb Transl.). Wintering in a Greek town contributed to the well being of the soldiers and diminished the risk of mutiny, a real menace during spells of inactivity or when there was a lack of war spoils, a situation experienced by Lucullus in 67 (Dio 36.16). Ballesteros 1996, pp. 262-263; or Fimbria in 86 (Dio 31. 104): Magie 1951, vol. 1, p. 227, vol.2, p. 1109; Muñiz 1995-1996, p. 262.

(10) Magie 1950, vol. 1, p. 234, vol. 2, n. 7 (1112); Lewis 1991, pp. 126-129. Smyrna coined gold staters when it supported Pontus at the beginning of the First Mithridatic War, but when it defected to the Romans (86-85), it ceased to do so, as did a majority of Asian cities, probably because they were no longer forced to billet the Pontic garrisons, well provisioned with coinage: Head 1887, p. 593; Kinns 1987, p. 110; De Callataÿ 1997, p. 290.

(11) As evidenced for example on an inscription from Skythopolis in the Seleucid kingdom (early second century BC), in which Ptolemy solicits an exemption from billeting soldiers on his properties: Robert and Robert 1970, pp. 472-473.

(12) General essential reading: McGing 1986; Ballesteros 1996. See more recently Madsen 2009a, pp. 191-201; Madsen 2009b, pp. 223-236; Ñaco, Antela, Arrayás and Busquets (2011).

commercial interests in the region. It is not difficult to imagine that these measures brought with them much wider repercussions than simply those resulting from the battles themselves.[13] In fact, the support of one faction not only led to the alignment of state allies and enemies, but also deepened existing internal tensions in the towns, which ultimately affected the immediate future of the population and its alliances after the end of the conflict. For example, after the defeat of Mithridates in 63, Rome denied promotions to former allies of Pontus and awarded benefits to its own allies, i.e. those which had lent support to Roman garrisons and the prefects, or *phrourarchoi*, that commanded them. These individuals benefitted personally from their service to Rome from this time on.[14]

It is well known that one of the measures decreed by Sulla (85) as a reprisal on the Roman towns that defected the Republican faction in the first months of conflict, and played an active role in the mass murder of *romaioi* instigated by Mithridates (88), concerned the mandatory billeting of armed contingents.[15] It was in fact in that same year that Stratonicea (Caria), after enduring Pontic pressure for several months, finally fell to the influence of Mithridates, whose troops had already swept through Rome's Asia province. A garrison was left in the late Rhodian city, either for logistical reasons or simply as a guarantee of military control (App. *Mithr.* 21). This detachment was probably charged with collecting the financial penalties imposed for having shown unwavering loyalty to the Republic, as is evidenced by one of Sulla's letters of the year 81. It contains a *senatus consultum* in which Rome explicitly recognised the great costs incurred in resisting Mithridates and offered autonomy and free status to Stratonicea and other cities loyal to the Republic, which were also significantly affected by the same offensive.[16] According to Meadows, coinage constitutes the best evidence available for the assessment of this resistance. Silver coins from Stratonicea, known as group 3, were minted within a very short timespan and served to finance the city's war efforts, as it had done during previous periods of stress, while group 2 was also minted for similar purposes during the war against Aristonicus (133-129). By way of contrast, it seems that during intervals of peace and throughout the post-war period, the town only demanded bronze coinage, which continued to be minted after the expulsion of the Pontic forces without any significant change. Stratonicea's silver coinage of the year 88 was a one-off issue, the result of the pressure of lone resistance by the town which was finally unable to prevent occupation by foreign troops and the subsequent depletion of its financial resources.[17]

Messembria and the Greek towns of the western Black Sea: a case study

Rome had ambitions for a greater level of control over the western coast of the Black Sea. Commercial interests were at play after the restructuring of public finances in the new Asia province, between the end of the war against Aristonicus (129) and the promulgation of the *Lex Sempronia Asiae* (123), and throughout the last quarter of the second century BC. Such interests are demonstrated by a number of factors, including Rome's active participation in the Thracian Wars (114-106), the treaty with the city of Callatis (probably signed in the last decade of that same century), and finally by the data contained in the copy of the *lex portorii asiae*, recently discovered as part of the *monumentum ephesenum*, which describes the limitations of Roman influence in northern part of the province of Asia. All of this signal the Thracian Bosphorus as a buffer region abutting the territory controlled by Mithridates VI (Mitchell 2002, p. 42; Mitchell 2008, pp. 178-182, fig. 2). Nevertheless, towards the end of the second century, more pressing issues in other regions of the Mediterranean put on hold the Republic's interest in the area, which then passed very quickly to Pontic control.[18]

It is thus possible, as noted by Reinach back in 1890, that several coin series bearing the portrait of Mithridates VI in the image of Alexander, found in Messembria and other Greek cities of the Thracian coastline, may be the result of a conscious policy for the deployment of military garrisons at the service of the Pontic kingdom.[19] As regards the specific function of this coinage, there has been conjecture that it was used to pay Thracian mercenaries or soldiers based at Mithridatic garrisons of the Black Sea region.[20] To ac-

(13) Arrayás 2010a, p. 380, in relation to the effort of various benefactors, such as Diodoros Pasparos in Pergamon, who helped to ameliorate the disastrous effects caused by the *hospitum militare*, which also affected the majority of Asian towns. This was especially the case after Rome took control of the city in 85 BC.

(14) Tibiletti 1953, pp. 64-100; Corsaro 2003, pp. 373-396; Labarre 2004, pp. 221-248; Ñaco 2009, pp. 179-195.

(15) Plut. *Sull.*25.2; *Luc.* 4.1; App. *Mithr.* 62: in fact, the dismantling of Pontic garrisons was one of the conditions imposed on Archelaos by Sulla in the peace treaty negotiations (App. *Mithr.* 55); Frank 1938, pp. 517-518; McGing 1986, p. 141; De Callataÿ 1997, p. 258; Ñaco 2001, pp. 82-83; Santangelo 2007, pp. 111-113; Mayor 2009, pp. 13-26.

(16) Magie 1950, vol. 1, p. 215, 234-235, vol. 2, pp. 1112-1113, n. 9; Sherk 1984, num. 63; McGing 1986, pp. 140-141; Kallet-Marx 1995, pp. 268-272; Santangelo 2007, p. 53. Rome granted similar privileges to the Carian town of Tabai, which also resisted Mithridates: Crawford and Reynolds 1974, pp. 289-294; Labarre 2004, p. 244, jointly with Aphrodisias and Alabanda: Kallet-Marx 1995, p. 276, n. 61; Ferrary 2001, p. 105.

(17) Meadows 2002, p. 116 *ff*; a similar instance of emergency coinage may be found at Rhodes. In this case it was used to finance the town's resistance to siege, a few months after the events that took place at Stratonicea, according to Ashton 2001, pp. 53-66.

(18) Ferrary 2001, pp. 100-101; Avram 2005, pp. 175-177; Ferrary 2007, pp. 321-322.

(19) Reinach 1890, p. 75. On Mithridatic coinage: De Callataÿ 1997, pp. 118-119; De Callataÿ 2005, pp. 119-136. For a more critical view on the possibility of identifying Pontic garrisons in these *poleis* solely on the basis of numismatic evidence: McGing 2009, pp. 210-212. Nevertheless, Hojte 2009, pp. 9-10, notes that the distribution of civic bronze coinage throughout the Pontic kingdom could actually reflect a garrison policy, especially when some of the place names inscribed may be identified not so much as towns, but as small, fortified enclaves. See fig. 3, a silver issue from Odessos.

(20) App. *Mithr.* 41 describes the heterogeneous make-up of the Mithridatic armies during the battle of Chaironeia, a text of great historical significance according to De Callataÿ 1997, pp. 257-258; App. *Mithr.* 69 also mentions the recruitment of Thracians during the Third Mithridatic War: Launey 1987, p. 389; Couvenhes 2007, pp. 419-426; Weber 2001, pp. 14-16;

cept this would also be to acknowledge a relatively stable Pontic presence in all of these coastal towns, at least from the beginning of the first century BCE until the advance of Lucullus' brother, even if only some of the issues may be dated after the time of Mithridatic control over the region. The truth is that during the first war with Rome (89-85), port conditions along the Thracian coastline offered an excellent anchoring point from which to dispatch soldiers and supplies to the Pontic armies operating in continental Greece. The region's value may therefore have been fundamentally strategic, which in turn allows us to speculate on the presence of Pontic garrisons, even though the data is not conclusive in this regard.[(21)] In the case of Histria, a recently-published decree honours a *strategos* who commanded the Pontic garrison in the Greek town, probably in the initial period of the conflict, and who, according to the inscription, was a mercenary originating from Amastris or Amisos (Avram and Bounegru 1997, pp. 155-165).[(22)]

A similar phenomenon may also have occurred on the other side of the Black Sea. According to Strabo, Mithridates controlled up to fifteen small fortifications in the Colchis region, where he had placed part of his treasure (Str. 12.3.28).[(23)] It is therefore logical to conclude that there were Pontic garrisons among these, though specialists do not always agree on the identification of these garrisons, especially when this implies accepting certain coin issues as conclusive historical evidence. For some, the discovery in the same archaeological context (the Georgian city of Vani, Colchis) of a Mithridatic stater, some tetradrachms and several copper coins constitutes sufficient evidence for the existence of a Pontic garrison in the town, thus confirming Strabo's testimony. Others, on the other hand, believe that there are simpler explanations for this. Linking the coins to the religious importance of the urban sanctuary would refute any hypothetical link with a military garrison, and in this regard, there is also a lack of direct evidence in the data collected from urban archaeological interventions: there are no signs from this period of defence works or restructuring, which would have been desirable in the event of a significant Pontic attack.[(24)]

In fact, a large number of these coastal *poleis* of the western Black Sea suffered harsh reprisals at the hands of Roman advances from the year 72 onwards, very probably due to the existence of hostile garrisons in the region. There is, however, no conclusive historical proof for this other than the numismatic evidence, as existing literary sources are too imprecise (Eutr.10.6; Str.7.6.1). The geopolitical control held by Pontus over the western Black Sea underwent a radical change during the early years of the Third Mithridatic War, and specifically around the summer of 72, when Mithridates carried out a strategic retreat, after the loss of a large part of the Aegean fleet. This coincided with the advance of Lucullus towards Pontus' forces (Memn.29.5), and his besieging and later taking of towns like Amisos and Eupatoria. Almost simultaneously, according to Eutropius, his own brother, M. Terentius Varro Lucullus, turned his attention to several Greek cities on the Thracian coast, destroying Apollonia and taking Callatis, Parthenopolis, Tomis and Histria, thus bringing an end to Pontic control over this region of great strategic importance (Eutr.6.10).[(25)]

The Roman siege of Apollonia was followed by the town's destruction. Such brutality has sometimes been explained as the result of the hypothetical resistance of a Pontic garrison in the town, the existence of which has been confirmed in an inscription honouring one of the Pontic commanders in charge of defending Mithridatic interests (*IGBulg* I2 392).[(26)] However, historical evidence to support a widespread presence of garrisons in the Greek towns of the region has generally been inconclusive, leading to disagreement among scholars, for instance, as regards the interpretation of data extracted from coinage. A good example of this may be found at Tomis. The town's second issue of staters, dating roughly to the decades of Mithridatic conflict, has been identified by De Callataÿ as belonging to a Pontic garrison, with no other proof than the existence of these coins. On the other hand, it is Poenaru Bordea's view that such an identification lacks credibility, given the small size of the town in comparison to others in the region that never minted coins, as well as the absence of other kinds of evidence which is present at other sites. The truth is that in a majority of cases the only evidence for the possible existence of Mithridatic garrisons in the *poleis* of the Thracian coastline of the Black Sea comes from a very specific method of interpreting the existence of Pontic coinage in these cities.[(27)]

Zahariade 2009, pp. 46-50. On the Thracian mercenary tradition: Griffith 1935, pp. 188-190; Launey 1987, pp. 366-398; Sánchez-León 1997, pp. 392-398; De Callataÿ 2009, p. 59 *ff.*

(21) The influence of Pontus over the colonies of this Black Sea region is normally attributed to an undefined moment after the young king's journey to Crimea (Gaggero 1976, p. 296; McGing 1986, p. 50), thanks to the study of an inscription mentioning the Armenian population of Olbia, located in a slightly more northern part of the Black Sea coast. This same author identifies this with a Pontic garrison (55 and n. 50), although De Callataÿ (1997, p. 253) prefers to interpret this episode as a movement of population. A more recent inscription, also from Olbia, provides evidence for the existence of a Pontic garrison commander in the city in the year 78/77: Krapivina and Diatroptov 2005, pp. 168-170.

(22) On the autonomous silver coins from Histria, belonging to the last period prior to Roman control: De Callataÿ 1997, pp. 145-146; Talmatchi 2006, pp. 37-39.

(23) An inscription from Phanagoreia in the Bosphorus (*SEG* 41, 625), dated to 88-87, contains a decree in honour of the resident Mithridatic mercenaries, who earned a variety of rights and compensation after their fighting alongside the town's own citizens: Vinogradov and Wörrle 1992, pp. 159-170; Avram 2005, pp. 163-185, 171; Saprykin 2007, p. 310; Molev 2009, pp. 323-326.

(24) Dundua and Lordkipanidze 1979, pp. 2-3; Lordkipanitze 1991, p. 193, n. 112; De Callataÿ, 1997, p. 254 and n.72; Kacharava and Kvirkvelia 2008, pp. 50-79.

(25) Oros.6.3.4; Liv.*Per.*97; Amm.27.4.11; App. *Illyr.* 30; Gaggero 1976, pp. 299-300; Ballesteros 1996, pp. 235-238, 244-245; Arrayás 2010b, pp. 941-948. See fig. 2.

(26) Pippidi 1975, p. 168; Gaggero 1976, p. 298; De Callataÿ 1997, pp. 118, 256.

(27) De Callataÿ 1997, p. 148 n. 28; *contra.* Poenaru 1999, p. 159; Buzoianu and Barbulescu 2003, pp. 296-297. See fig. 4.

A significant exception to this is to be found in the Greek town of Messembria (Nessebar, Bulgaria), located in the same coastal region. Its coinage portrays the bust of Mithridates (Nawotka 1997, pp. 42-43; Preshlenov 2003, pp. 180-181; fig. 5.), but other relevant data may be found in two inscriptions normally dated to the period of the Mithridatic conflict, which provide evidence for the existence and activities of military garrisons outside the control of the civic authorities. The first of these is an honorific inscription (*IGBulg* I, 315) which sheds some light on what the situation of the town might have been prior to Roman intervention. More specifically, Glaucias, a distinguished physician of this community who was probably active during the periods of conflict, was honoured by the civic institutions of Messembria with a statue and with important privileges. Among the most significant of these honours was an exemption from taxes and local liturgies, as well as from housing, feeding, and in some cases even paying members of a foreign garrison, duties which the majority of citizens of Messembria were obliged to comply with.(28) This obligation was so much of a burden for the entire population that it became a privilege to be exempted from it, as in the case of Glaucias, who was honoured in this way, exceptionally and in individual terms. The inscription is generally dated to the first half of the first century BC, although epigraphic criteria has not confirmed the chronology with complete certainty, and it would also be possible to date it to the Mithridatic years or to after the year 71, when the town was completely under Roman control (*IGBulg.* I, 315, Mikhailov 1970, pp. 275-278).

The second honorific inscription from Messembria (*IGBulg.* I, 314) contains a dedication by the local authorities to a *C.Cornelius c.f., eparchos*, previously unknown, but probably the head of the military garrison based in the city by Terentius Varro from at least the winter of 72-71. In principle, it is very unlikely that an inscription honouring a Roman prefect should shed any light on the secondary effects caused to the civic institutions and daily life of Messembria by his contingents, which had after all supported Rome's enemy.(29) Even so, the data contained in both inscriptions respond to the same reality, and hence they should be interpreted in tandem. Even though the authorities of Messembria were keen to comply with the new Roman *phrourarchos*, as is shown by the first inscription, there is sufficient data in the second to allow speculation regarding the serious damage that the presence of an armed contingent would have inflicted on the population, to the point of it being considered a privilege to be exempted from the obligation to provide hospitality, one worthy of one of the town's most outstanding citizens, distinguished for his services to the community. This same scenario may also have taken place, however, in the preceding decades. As is the case of the other Greek cities of the Thracian Black Sea coast, the coinage may testify to the presence in Messembria of a Pontic garrison, and it is not preposterous to think that this might also have inflicted collateral damage on the civil population, enough perhaps to justify the privileges granted to the physician Glaucias.(30) In fact, the dedication of honorific inscriptions to physicians who had served professionally in military garrisons is nothing new in the Hellenistic context, as in the case of the decree honouring the doctor Eukrates, in Halasarna.(31)

Whatever the case may be, numismatic evidence does seem to confirm that Roman intervention implied important consequences for the history of the town's coinage. More specifically, and as may be easily inferred, the arrival in 72/71 of a Roman *eparchos* in 72/71 to command the garrison saw the end of the minting of the Mithridatic silver coinage, which was linked to the previous alliance between Messembria and Pontus and the fluid contacts with the inland Thracian tribes, which probably served the Pontic garrison with mercenaries. Messembria was not destroyed, though, unlike other cities in the region such as Apollonia. From this moment onwards, however, the town was incorporated into the *imperium romanum* by the force of events. Several decades later, it minted several series of bronze coins, probably signalling a certain revival of the civic institutions during the new Roman rule in the region. To sum up, when coinage is considered in conjunction with other historical evidence, it stands out as an important testimony of the terrible consequences caused by war stress on the Greek towns during the whole of the conflict -and in particular, of war stress suffered during the first years of the Third Mithridatic War.(32)

Conclusions

Throughout the Mithridatic Wars, Hellenistic towns suffered the consequences of war stress, owing to their direct

(28) This kind of reward was not uncommon in Greek towns of the period, as in the case of this well-known *Senatum Consultum*, in which exceptions are made to the obligation to comply with instructions for the billeting of soldiers: Raggi 2001, pp. 92-93; see in general: Arrayás 2010a, pp. 379-380, and n. 47.

(29) *SEG* 47, p. 1137; Tibiletti 1953, pp. 69-74 compares the events in Messembria with the known case of a Gades prefect who was denounced before the Senate in 199 BC for presumed offences (pp. 68-69); Robert-Robert 1954, pp. 150-151; *IGBulg*, 314, Mikhailov 1970, pp. 272-275; Sherk 1984, num. 73; Broughton 1986 (vol. 3), 61; Ñaco, Antela, Arrayás and Busquets 2009, pp. 34-38.

(30) Launey 1987, p. 696 and n. 7; Nawotka 1997, p. 186; Samarra 2003, num. 093, (pp. 192-193, and n. 75; general comments in p. 55 and n. 100); Vespasian regulated the exemptions granted to physicians in 74 AD, according to an inscription in Pergamon, num. 189); Avram 2005, p. 176, n. 29. The term used on this occasion to describe the exemption from billeting obligations (lín.17: ἀνεπιστάθμευτον) does not seem to be very frequent: Plb.15.24.2; 3; *IG* VII, 2413; 3074; *SEG* 37, 859 B-D; *SEG* 37, 1003; *SEG* 39, 1244.

(31) *SEG* 53-2, 844, see Maiuri 1925, num. 675, pp. 234-235. The importance granted to certain physicians in Hellenistic society transcended politics. Worth mentioning in this regard is Asclepiades of Prusias, a physician from Bithynia, who lived in Rome before the outbreak of the First Mithridatic War. He received from a Pontic delegation a personal invitation from Mithridates VI Eupator to become part of his court, a petition that Asclepiades very gracefully turned down, despite the gold he was offered (Plin.*Nat.* 25.6): Fernoux 2004, pp. 124-128.

(32) Not all mints of the eastern Mediterranean closed down with the arrival of Roman rule, as has been described in relation to this particular region. After the agreements signed with Pompey in 66, the Armenian king Tigranes was able once more to issue silver coinage as a friend and ally of Rome: Mousheghian and Depeyrot 1999, p. 38.

participation in the conflict, or because of the strategic importance of their territories. Both of these situations may be observed in the serious damage inflicted by the military garrisons on civic institutions, defence systems and on the civil population. In many cases, this took the form of billeting, and in the particular case of the Greek towns of the western Black Sea, with the exception of two important inscriptions from Messembria, coinage constitutes the main historical source for the study of war stress. Although there is a lack of unanimity among scholars, it seems likely that a large part of the Mithridatic coinage served to pay foreign contingents, and most probably Thracian soldiers, almost certainly billeted in these coastal towns as part of the Pontic garrisons. This situation remained unchanged until the advance of M. Terentius Varus Lucullus, who ended Mithridatic hegemony over the region in 72/71. At the same time, the production of silver coinage ceased, continuing in some cases in bronze only during the following decades, evidencing a radical change in the geopolitical scene, which forced surviving towns to bow to the new Roman order.(33) This new political scenario was further enforced, although perhaps only at specific moments in time, by the establishment of Roman military garrisons in towns like Messembria, where the arrival of an *eparchos* to watch over these forces is attested to in honorary inscriptions. Both Pontic and Roman garrisons contributed to the undermining of the political independence of Greek towns in different periods of their history, and in the use of their ports as logistic bases for their own military interests. Coinage thus constitutes an excellent source for the study of war stress suffered by the Thracian coast of the Black Sea, as it would surely also be for other regions of the eastern Mediterranean which were similarly affected, directly or indirectly, by the Mithridatic conflict.

Abbreviations

IGBulg I (1970)= Mihailov G. *Inscriptiones Graecae in Bulgaria Repertoir. Vol. I. Inscriptiones Orae Ponti Euximi*. Sofia.

IG VII (1893 [1903])= Dittenberger W. *Inscriptiones Megaridis et Boeotiae*. Berlin.

REG 32 (1919)= Holleaux M., 'Décret de Chéronée relatif à la première guerre de Mithradates', *Revue d'Études Grecques*, pp. 320-337.

SEG 37/1987 (1990)= Pleket H. W., Stroud R. S. *Supplementum Epigraphicum Graecum*. Amsterdam.

SEG 39/1989 (1992)= Pleket H. W., Stroud R. S. *Supplementum Epigraphicum Graecum*. Amsterdam.

SEG 41/1991 (1994)= Pleket H. W., Stroud R. S. *Supplementum Epigraphicum Graecum*. Amsterdam.

SEG 47/1997 (2000)= Pleket H. W., Stroud R. S., Chamiotis A., Strube J. H. M. *Supplementum Epigraphicum Graecum*. Amsterdam.

SEG 53-2/2003 (2007)= Chaniotis A., Corsten T., Stroud R. S., Tybout R. A. *Supplementum Epigraphicum Graecum*. Leiden-Boston.

References

Arrayás I. (2010a). 'El impacto de las guerras mitridáticas en la creación de una nueva clase dirigente. Evergetas y evergetismo en Asia Menor', *Klio. Beiträge zur alten Geschichte*, 92.2, pp. 369-387.

Arrayás I. (2010b). 'Amiso. Reflexiones entorno a la destrucción y a la restauración de una ciudad póntica durante la III Guerra Mitridática', in López Barja de Quiroga, P. et alii (eds.), *Dialéctica histórica y compromiso social. Homenaje al Profesor Domingo Plácido Suárez*. Madrid, pp. 941-948.

Ashton R. A. J. (2001). 'Rhodian Bronze Coinage and the Siege of Mithridates VI', *The Numismatic Chronicle*, 161, pp. 53-66.

Avram A. (2005). 'La défense des cités en mer Noire à la basse époque hellénistique', in Frölich P., Müller Ch. (eds), *Citoyenneté et participation à la basse époque hellénistique*. Paris, pp. 163-185.

Avram A., Bounegru O. (1997). 'Mithridates al VI-Lea Eupator si coasta de vest a Pontului Euxin', *Pontica*, 30, pp. 155-165.

Baker P. (2000). 'Coût des garnisons et fortifications dans les cité à l'époque hellénistique, in *Économie antique. La guerre dans les économies antiques. Entretiens d'archéologie et d'histoire, Saint-Bertrand-de-Comminges*, pp. 177-196.

Baker P. (2001). 'Quelques remarques sur les Institutions Militaires dans les cités de Thessalie à l'époque hellénistique', *The Ancient World*, 32.2, pp. 191-206.

Ballesteros Pastor L. (1996). *Mitrídates VI Eupátor, rey del Ponto*. Universidad de Granada.

Billows R. (2008). 'International Relations', in Sabin Ph., Van Wees H., Whitby M. (eds), *The Cambridge History of Greek and Roman Warfare*, vol. 1. Cambridge, pp. 303-324.

Broughton T.S.R. (1952). *The Magistrates of the Roman Republic*, vol. 2. New York.

Broughton T.S.R. (1986). *Supplementum to the Magistrates of the Roman Republic*. Atlanta.

Buzoianu L., Barbulescu M. (2003). 'Tomis', in Grammenos D.V., Petropoulos E.K. (eds), *Ancient Greek Colonies in the Black Sea*, vol. 1. Thessaloniki, pp. 287-335.

(33) Karaiotov 1995, p. 65; De Callataÿ 1997, p. 119; Lazarov 1997, p. 20. On the link between Messembria's bronze coinage and the Thracians: Karaiotov 2000, p. 82.

Chaniotis A. (2002). 'Foreign soldiers – native girls? Constructing and crossing boundaries in Hellenistic cities with foreign garrisons', in Chaniotis A., Ducrey P. (eds), *Army and Power in the Ancient World*. Stuttgart, pp. 99-113.

Chaniotis A. (2005). *War in the Hellenistic World*. Oxford 2005.

Corsaro M. (2003). 'Prefetti romani in città provinciali: il caso di Entella', in Corda A.M. (a cura di), *Cultus splendore. Studi in onore di Giovanna Sotgiu*. Senorbì, pp. 373-396.

Couvenhes J.-Ch. (2004). 'Les cites grecques d'Asie Mineure et le mercenariat à l'époque hellénistique', in Couvenhes J.-Ch., Fernoux H.L. (dir.), *Les cites grecques et la guerre en Asie Mineure à l'époque hellénistique*. Tours, 77-113.

Couvenhes J.-Ch. (2006). 'La place de l'armée dans l'économie hellénistique: quelques considérations sur la condition matérielle et financière du soldat et son usage dans les marchés', in *Approches de l'économie hellénistique. Entrétiens d'Archéologie et d'Histoire*. Saint-Bertrand-de-Comminges, pp. 397-436.

Couvenhes J.-Ch. (2007). 'L'armée de Mithridate VI Eupator d'après Plutarque, Vie de Lucullus, VII.4-6', in Bru H. et alii (eds), *L'Asie Mineure dans l'Antiquité. Échanges, populations et territoires*. Rennes, pp. 415-438.

Crawford M. H., Reynolds J. (1974). 'Rome and Tabae', *Greek, Roman and Byzantine Studies*, 15.3, pp. 289-294.

De Callataÿ F. (1997). Histoire des guerres mithridatiques vue par les monnaies (*Numismatica Lovanniensia* 18). Louvain-la-Neuve.

De Callataÿ F. (1998). 'The coins in the name of Sura', in Burnett A., Wartenberg U., Witschonke R. (eds), *Coins of Macedonia and Rome: Essays in honour of Charles Hersh*. London, 113-117.

De Callataÿ F. (2005). 'Coins and Archaeology: the (Mis) use of Mithradatic Coins for Chronological Purposes in the Bosporan Area', in Stolba V.F., Hannestad L. (eds), *Chronologies of the Black Sea Area in the Period c. 400-100 BC*. Arhus, pp. 119-136.

De Callataÿ F. (2009). 'Armies poorly paid in coins (the Annabasis of the Ten-Thousands) and coins for soldiers poorly transformed by the markets (the Hellenistic Thasian-type tetradrachms) in Ancient Greece', *Revue Belge de Numismatique et Sigillographie*, 155, pp. 51-70.

Dundua G.F., Lordkipanidze G.A. (1979). 'Hellenistic coins from the site of Vani in Colchis, Western Georgia', *The Nimismatic Chronicle*, 139, pp. 1-5.

Fernoux H.-L. (2004). *Notables et élites de Bithynie aux époques hellénistique et romaine (IIIè. Siècle av. J.-C. – III siècle ap. J.-C.). Essai d'histoire sociale*. Lyon.

Ferrary J.-L. (2001). 'Rome et les cités grecques d'Asie Mineure au IIè siècle', Bresson A., Descat R. (eds), *Les cités d'Asie Mineure occidentale au IIè siècle a.C.*. Bordeaux, pp. 93-106.

Ferrary J.-L. (2007). 'L'essor de la puissance romaine dans la zone pontique', Bresson A., Ivantchik A., Ferrary J.-L. (eds), *Une Koinè pontique. Cités grecques, sociétés indigènes et empires mondiaux sur le litoral nord de la Mer Noire (VII s.a.C. - III s.p.C.)*. Bordeaux, pp. 319-325.

Fossey J. M. (1990). 'The Cities of the Korais in the Roman Period', *Papers in Boiotian Topography and History*. Amsterdam, pp. 220-267.

Frank T. (1938). 'Roman Asia Minor', in *An Economic Survey of Ancient Rome*, vol. 4. Baltimore, pp. 499-916.

Gaggero E. S. (1976). 'Relations politiques et militaires de Mithridate VI Eupator avec les populations et les cités de la Thrace et avec les colonies grecques de la Mer Noroccidentale', *Pulpudeva*, 2, pp. 294-305.

Griffith G. T. (1935). *The mercenaries of the Hellenistic World*. Cambridge.

Head B. V. (1881). *On the Chronological Sequence of the Coins of Boeotia*. London.

Head B.V. (1887). *Historia Nummorum: a manual of Greek numismatics*. Oxford.

Højte J.M. (2009). 'Introduction', in Højte J.M. (ed.), *Mithridates VI and the Pontic Kingdom (Black Sea Studies 9)*. Arhus, pp. 7-14.

Kacharava D., Kvirkvelia G. (2008). 'The Archaeology of Vani', in Chi J. Y. (ed.), *Wine, worship and sacrifice: the golden graves of Ancient Vani*. Princeton, pp. 50-79.

Kallet-Marx R. (1995). *Hegemony to Empire. The Development of the Roman Imperium in the East from 148 to 62 BC*. Berkeley - Los Angeles - London.

Karaiotov I. (1995). *The Coinage of Messambria*. Agabar.

Karaiotov I. (2006). 'Mesambria and the rulers of the coastal Thrace (according to numismatical evidence)', *Bullétin du Musée National de Bourgas, 3. Studia in Memoriam Ivani-Galabov*. Burgas, pp. 66-82 (rus., summary in English).

Kinns Ph. (1987). 'Asia Minor', in Burnett A.M., Crawford M.H. (eds), *The Coinage of the Roman World in the Late Republic (BAR International Series 326)*. Oxford, pp. 105-119.

Krapivina V. Diatroptov P. (2005). 'An inscription from Mithridates VI Eupator's governor from Olbia', *Ancient*

Civilizations from Scythia to Siberia, 11, pp. 3-4, 167-180.

Labarre G. (2004). 'Phrourarques et phrouroi des cités grecques d'Asie Mineure à l'époque hellénistique', in Couvenhes J.-Ch., Fernoux H.L. (dir.), *Les cites grecques et la guerre en Asie Mineure à l'époque hellénistique*. Tours, pp. 221-248.

Larazov L. (1997). 'An interesting autonomous bronze coin of Mesambria', *Revue Belge de Numismatique et Sigillographie*, 143, pp. 17-20.

Launey M. (1987). *Recherches sur les armées hellénistiques*. Réimpression avec addenda et mise à jour, en postface par Garlan Y., Gauthier Ph., Orrieux C. Paris, 2 vols.

Lewis G. (1991). 'Sulla and Smyrna', *Classical Quarterly*, 41.1, pp. 126-129.

López Sánchez F. (2010). 'Numidian Kings and Numidian Garrisons during the Second Punic War: Coins and History', *Potestas. Revista del Grupo Europeo de Investigación Histórica*, 3, pp. 17-52.

Lordkipanitze G.A. (1991). 'Vani, an ancient city of Colchis', *Greek, Roman and Byzantine Studies*, 32.2, pp. 151-195.

Ma J. (2002). 'Oversexed, overpaid and over here'. A Response to Angelos Chaniotis', in Chaniotis A., Ducrey P. (eds), *Army and Power in the Ancient World*. Stuttgart, pp. 115-122.

Mackay Ch. S. (2000). 'Damon of Chaeoronea: the Loyalties of a Boeotian Town during the First Mithridatic War', *Klio, Beiträge zur alten Geschichte*, 82.1, pp. 91-106.

Magie D. (1951). *Roman Rule in Asia Minor*. 2 vols. Princeton.

Madsen J.M. (2009a). 'The ambitions of Mithridates VI: Hellenistic Kingship and Modern Interpretation', in Højte J.M. (ed.), *Mithridates VI and the Pontic Kingdom (Black Sea Studies 9)*. Arhus, pp. 191-201.

Madsen J.M. (2009b). 'Mithradates VI Rome's perfect enemy', *Proceedings at the Danish Institute at Athens*, 6, pp. 223-236.

Maiuri A. (1925). *Nuova Silloge Epigrafica di Rodi e Cos*. Florence.

Mayor A. (2009). 'Kill them all and Let the Gods to Sort them Out", *The Poison King. The Life and Legend of Mithradates, Rome's Deadliest Enemy*. Princeton, pp. 13-26.

McGing B.C. (1986). *The Foreign Policy of Mithridates VI Eupator King of Pontus*. Leiden.

McGing B.C. (2009). 'Mithridates VI Eupator: Victim or Agressor?', in Højte J.M. (ed.), *Mithridates VI and the Pontic Kingdom*. Arhus, pp. 203-216.

Meadows A.R. (2002). 'Stratonikea in Caria: the Hellenistic City and its Coinage', *The Numismatic Chronicle*, 162, pp. 79-134.

Mitchell S. (2002). 'In search of the Pontic community in Antiquity', in Bowman A., Cotton H. M., Goodman M., Price S. (eds), *Representations of Empire. Rome and the Mediterranean World (Proceedings of the British Academy, 114)*. Oxford, pp. 35-64.

Mitchell S. (2008). 'Geography, Politics, and Imperialism in the Asian Customs Law', in Cottier M. et alii (eds), *The Customs Law of Asia*. Oxford, pp. 165-201.

Molev E.A. (2009). 'Bosporos under the rule of Mithridates VI Eupator', in Højte J.M. (ed.), *Mithridates VI and the Pontic Kingdom*. Ahrus, pp. 321-328.

Mousheghian A., Depeyrot G. 1999. *Hellenistic and Roman Armenian Coinage (1st.C. BC - 1st. C. AD)*. Wetteren.

Muñiz Coello J. (1995-1996). 'C. Flavius Fimbria, consular y legado en la provincia de Asia (86-84 a. C.)', *Studia Historica. Historia Antigua*, 13-14, pp. 257-275.

Nawotka K. (1997). *The Western Pontic Cities. History and Political Organisation*. Amsterdam.

Ñaco del Hoyo T. (2001). 'Milites in oppidis hibernabant. El hospitium militare invernal en ciudades peregrinas y los abusos de la hospitalidad subtectis durante la República', *Dialogues d'Histoire Ancienne*, 27.2, pp. 63-90.

Ñaco del Hoyo T. (2010). 'Guarniciones republicanas y los 'daños colaterales' en ciudades helenísticas: algunos ejemplos', in Fornis C., Gallego J., López Barja P., Valdés M. (eds), *Dialéctica histórica y compromiso social. Homenaje al Prof. Domingo Plácido Suárez - Universidad Complutense de Madrid*. Madrid, pp. 929-940.

Ñaco del Hoyo T., Antela B., Arrayás I., Busquets S. (2009), 'The impact of the Roman intervention in Greece and Asia Minor upon civilians (88-63 BC)', in Antela B. and Ñaco del Hoyo T. (eds), *Transforming Historical Landscapes in the Ancient Empires (BAR., Internatioanal Series 1986)*. Oxford, pp. 33-51.

Ñaco del Hoyo T., Antela B., Arrayás I., Busquets S. (2011). 'The Ultimate Frontier between Rome and Mithridates: War, Terror and the Greek Poleis (88-63 B.C.)', in Hekster O., Kaizer T. (eds), *The Frontiers of the Roman World (Durham University, April 16th-19th 2009)*. Leiden-Boston, pp. 291-304.

Picard O. (2008). 'Les trétradrachmes à types thasiens et les guerres thraces au début du Ier siècle avant notre ère', *Académie des Inscriptions et Belles Lettres. Comptes rendus, avril-juin*, 2, pp. 465-493.

Pippidi D.M. (1975). 'Les premiers rapports de Rome et des cités de l'Euxin', Scythica Minora. *Recherches sur les colonies grecques du litoral roumain de la mer Noire*. Bucharest, pp. 159-171.

Poenaru Bordea G. (1999). 'À propos du Pont occidental et du bas-Danube à l'époque de Mithridate VI Eupator', *Revue Belge de Numismatique*, 114, pp. 155-164.

Preshlenov H. (2003). 'Mesambria', in Grammenos D.V., Petropoulos E.K. (eds), *Ancient Greek Colonies in the Black Sea*, vol. 1. Thessaloniki, pp. 157-208.

Raggi A. (2001). 'Senatus Consultum de Asclepiade Clazomenio Sociisque', *Zeitschrift für Papyrologie und Epigraphik*, 135, pp. 73-116.

Reinach Th. (1890). *Mithridate Eupator roi de Pont*. Paris.

Robert J., Robert L. (1954) 'Bulletin Épigraphique', *Revue des Études Grecques*, 67, pp. 150-151.

Robert J. Robert L. (1970) 'Bulletin Épigraphique', *Revue des Études Grecques*, 83, pp. 472-473.

Sánchez-León Mª.L. (1997). 'Les Thraces dans l'armée d'Eumène III de Pergame', in Roman P. (ed.), *The Thracian World at the Crossroads of civilisations*, vol. 2. Bucharest, pp. 392-398.

Santangelo F. (2007). *Sulla, the Elites and the Empire. A Study of Roman Policies in Italy and the Greek East*. Leiden-Boston.

Samarra E. (2003). *Les médecins dans le monde grec. Sources épigraphiques sur la naissance d'un corps médical*. Paris.

Saprykin S. (2007). 'The Kingdom of Bosporus at the Turn of the Common Era: Barbarian and Roman Impact', in Bresson A., Ivantchik A., Ferrary J-L. (eds), *Une Koinè pontique. Cités grecques, sociétés indigènes et empires mondiaux sur le littoral nord de la Mer Noire (VII s.a.C. - III s.p.C.)*. Bordeaux, pp. 309-317.

Sherk R. K. (1984). *Rome and the Greek East to the death of Augustus*. Cambridge.

Talmatchi G. (2006). *Les monnaies autonomes d'Istros, Callatis et Tomis. Circulation et contexte*. Wetteren, pp. 37-39.

Tibiletti G. (1953). 'Governatori romani in città provinciali', *Istituto Lombardo di Scienze e Lettere. Rendiconti (Classi di Lettere e Scienza Morali e Storiche 86)*, pp. 64-100.

Ujes D. (2004). 'Autonomous coinage of Rhizon in Illyria', in Cabanes P. , Lamboley J.-L. (eds), *L'Illyrie méridionale et l'Épire dans l'Antiquité - IV (Actes du IV colloque international de Grenoble. 10-12 octobre 2002)*. Paris, 149-168.

Vinogradov J.G., Wörrle M. (1992). 'Die söldner von Phanagoreia', *Chiron*, 22, pp. 159-170.

Weber Ch. (2001). *The Thracians 700 BC - AD 46*. Osprey, Oxford.

Zahariade M. (2009). *The Thracians in the Roman Imperial Army. From the First to the Third Centuries A.D. I. Auxilia*. Cluj-Napoca.

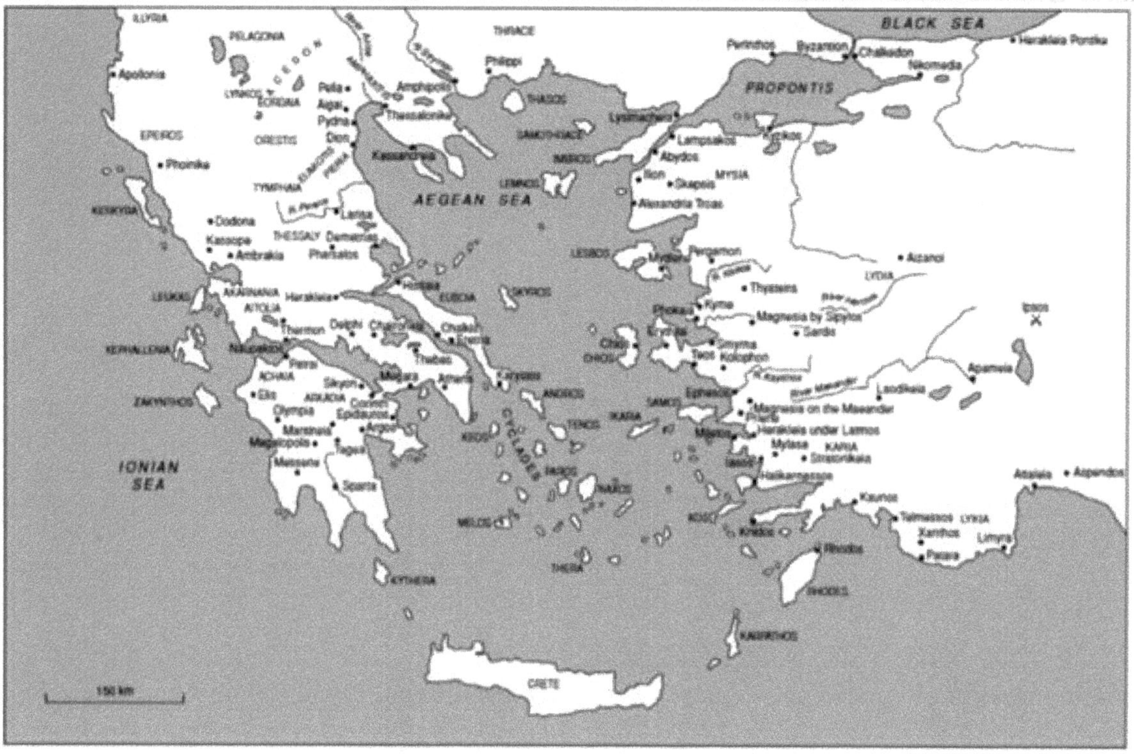

Fig. 1. Mainland Greece, the Aegean, and Asia Minor, after A.Chaniotis, *War in the Hellenistic World*. Blackwell, Oxford 2005, p. 254

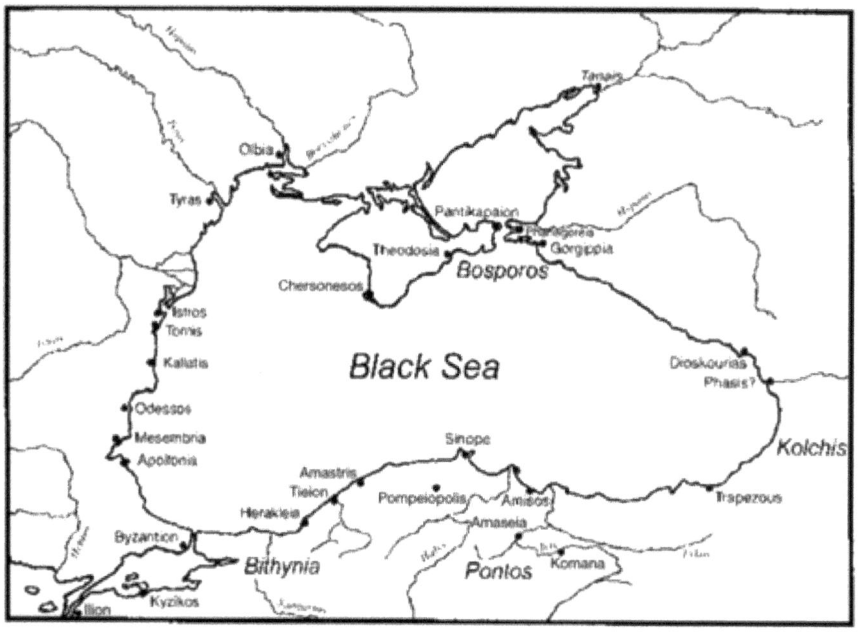

Fig. 2. The Black Sea Region, after J. Munk Hokte, 'Introduction', in Hokte J. M. (ed.), *Mithridates VI and the Pontic Kingdom*. Aahrus University Press 2009, p. 9

Fig. 3. AR Tetradrachm. Mithradatic War issue. Odessos mint, in the name of Alexander the Great, ca. 120-90 B.C. www.coinarchives.com (January 19th, 2011)

Fig. 4. AV stater. First Mithradatic War issue. Tomis mint, in the name of Lysimachos, ca. 88-86 B.C. www.coinarchives.com (January 19th, 2011)

Fig. 5. AR Tetradrachm, Mithridatic War issue, in the name of Alexander (posthumous), Messembria mint, c.125-65 BC. www.forumancientcoins.com (January 19th, 2011)

AGRIPPINE LA JEUNE ET LA MONNAIE : DE LA PRINCESSE À LA« RÉGENTE »

Virginie Girod*

ABSTRACT

En digne descendante des *Iulii*, Agrippine la Jeune était animée par une grande ambition politique. Le fait d'être une femme réduisait cependant à néant toutes ses velléités de pouvoir. Pourtant, à force de manœuvres et de manipulations tant familiales que politiques, elle parvint au faîte de l'Empire. Le monnayage de l'atelier impérial de Rome témoigne de son ascension politique insolente. D'abord timidement associée au rayonnement politique et social de Caligula au même titre que ses autres sœurs, elle devint ensuite la première impératrice vivante à voir son nom, son titre et son buste figurer sur les monnaies romaines. S'imposant par la suite comme la régente de Néron, elle fut représentée un temps dans l'iconographie monétaire de l'*Vrbs* comme la dirigeante de l'Empire. Quelques mois après le début du règne de Néron, elle fut finalement chassée du Palatin et son portrait disparut à jamais des monnaies émises par l'atelier de Rome. Le programme iconographique monétaire du début du règne de Néron connut une véritable rupture dans le courant de l'année 55 au moment de la disgrâce de l'impératrice. Les sources littéraires et numismatiques prouvent ainsi qu'*Agrippina Augusta* exerçait le pouvoir avec un programme politique propre dont l'iconographie monétaire était le support.

Agrippine *Minor* fut sans conteste la femme la plus puissante de la dynastie Julio-Claudienne. Elle réussit à surpasser, non seulement en prestige mais aussi en pouvoir personnel, Livie, son aïeule qu'elle aurait été jalouse d'égaler (Tac., *Ann.*, 12.69). Grisée par le pouvoir, elle n'a pas perçu à temps les limites politiques que lui fixaient sa condition de femme et, immolée par son propre fils sur l'autel de son ambition,[1] elle laissa, au travers des sources littéraires, l'image d'une femme parée de tous les vices, couverte de tous les opprobres.

Toute femme qu'elle était, c'était le sang d'Auguste qui coulait dans ses veines et elle a exercé le pouvoir à Rome pendant près de six mois (Barrett 1996, p. 238) jusqu'à ce qu'elle soit chassée du Palatin par Néron sur les encouragements de Sénèque et de Burrus qui devaient eux-mêmes à l'*Augusta* l'influence qu'ils exerçaient sur le jeune *princeps*.[2] Sa participation active aux affaires politiques de l'Empire est attestée par plusieurs sources: «Il abandonna à sa mère l'administration souveraine de toutes les affaires publiques et privées» (Suet., *Nér.*, 9); «Quant à ce qui est d'Agrippine (...), elle s'acquittait, au commencement, pour Néron de tous les devoirs du gouvernement» (Dio, 61.3). Les sources présentent *Agrippina Augusta* comme une régente ayant dirigé l'empire pour le compte de son fils. Cet état de fait est corroboré par les monnaies des années 54-55 qui marquent l'avènement de Néron et de sa mère. Ces monnaies sont le symbole de l'apothéose de la « carrière politique » de cette femme hors normes. Pour la première fois dans l'histoire de Rome, la *potentia* d'une femme y est représentée. Cela induit une influence plus ou moins importante de l'*Augusta* dans le choix des types monétaires. Mais l'effigie d'Agrippine avait déjà trouvé sa place dans le monnayage de l'*Vrbs* depuis Caligula. Sœur, nièce, épouse, mère d'empereurs,[3] elle fut tout ce qu'une femme pouvait être pour un *princeps* et la numismatique d'Agrippine, dans le cadre des ateliers impériaux,[4] est le parfait reflet de son ascension politique comme de sa chute.

*Docteur en Histoire de l'Université Paris IV-Sorbonne, UMR 8167. Je souhaite adresser mes plus sincères remerciements à Dominique Hollard pour les conseilles pleins de sagesse qu'il me prodigue sans parcimonie aucune.

(1) Tac., *Ann.*, 14.9.3: «Cette fin, bien des années auparavant, Agrippine en avait cru et méprisé l'annonce : en effet, comme elle les consultait au sujet de Néron, les Chaldéens lui répondirent qu'il règnerait et qu'il tuerait sa mère ; et elle «Qu'il tue, dit-elle, pourvu qu'il règne !»».

(2) Suet., *Nér.*, 7; Dio, 60.32. C'est Agrippine qui avait choisi Sénèque comme précepteur pour son fils afin que ce dernier soit formé au pouvoir par un esprit reconnu par tous comme étant des plus brillants. Il s'enrichit considérablement grâce à elle. De plus, c'est elle qui, dans ce but, le fit rappeler d'exil et lui obtint la préture (Tac., *Ann.*, 12.8.2.) Selon Dio (61.10), ils auraient aussi été amants.

(3) Tac., *Ann.*, 12.42: « (...) pour une femme, née d'un *imperator*, sœur, femme et mère de celui qui occupait le pouvoir, cas unique jusqu'à nos jours».

(4) Pour cette étude, nous ne prendrons en compte que le monnayage des ateliers impériaux de Lyon et Rome, c'est-à-dire les ateliers qui émettent les monnaies dont il est fait usage à Rome. Ainsi, les ateliers impériaux de Césarée de Cappadoce et d'Ephèse qui frappent respectivement des didrachmes et des cistophores ne seront pas étudiés dans la mesure où les types qui y sont frappés sont réservés à l'Orient romain (*BNCMER*, II, p. 4-6).

Du statut de princesse à celui d'*Augusta*

Agrippine *Minor* naquit le 6 novembre 15 ou 16 après J.-C. à Cologne (*Ara Vbiorum*). Elle est la fille d'Agrippine *Maior* et de Germanicus. Par sa mère, elle descend en droite ligne d'Auguste dont elle est l'arrière-petite-fille. Par son père, elle est l'arrière-petite-fille de Livie, d'Octavie et de Marc Antoine. Ainsi, elle procède des hommes et des femmes les plus puissants de la fin de la République et du début du Principat. Tibère était son grand-oncle du côté de Germanicus avant de devenir son grand-père adoptif.[5] Agrippine concentre en elle le sang des *Iulii* et celui des *Claudii*. En tant que femme, elle n'a pas accès au pouvoir, mais tout enfant né d'elle pourrait prétendre un jour à la pourpre. De fait, Tibère la maria, en 28 de notre ère, avec Cn. Domitius Ahenobarbus, petit-fils d'Octavie et de Marc Antoine par sa mère et de la *gens Ahenobarba*, famille patricienne et consulaire (Suet., *Nér.*, 1), par son père. De ce mariage naquit Néron (Suet., *Nér.*, 4) le 15 décembre 37 qui, bien que né dans les hautes sphères du patriciat n'était déjà plus sur le chemin balisé de la succession directe d'Auguste. Néron naquit neuf mois après la mort de Tibère, sous le principat de cet oncle qu'il admira tant : Caligula (Suet., *Nér.*, 30).

En 37, Caligula devient le troisième *princeps* de l'Empire. Avant que ne lui échoie la pourpre, il avait passé une partie de son adolescence, après la mort de son père, entouré de femmes. Il avait habité chez Livie, puis chez Antonia avec ses sœurs (Nony 1986, p. 93). Ayant perdu son père, ses frères puis sa mère, il rendit, tout au long de son principat, de nombreux hommages aux femmes qui l'entourèrent. En multipliant les honneurs dont bénéficiaient ses aïeules, sa mère et ses sœurs, il augmentait considérablement son propre prestige et sa légitimité.[6] Les honneurs qu'il attribua sans parcimonie aucune aux femmes de sa famille se reflètent dans son monnayage.[7] Jamais il n'avait été vu à Rome autant de matrones sur les monnaies.[8] Et c'est dans le cadre des frappes de l'avènement de 37-38 qu'Agrippine *Minor* apparaît, pour la première fois, sur des sesterces frappés à Rome (n° 1). Elle n'est cependant pas seule à être représentée au revers de l'effigie en buste couronné de lauriers de son frère. Agrippine est accompagnée de ses deux jeunes sœurs. Les noms des trois princesses encadrent le champ sur trois côtés. Chacune d'elle personnifie une divinité protectrice de Rome. À gauche, Agrippine, appuyée sur une colonne, symbole de stabilité et tenant une corne d'abondance, incarne la *Securitas*. Elle est la personnification de la sécurité de la vie publique et privée. Cette sécurité assure du même coup la prospérité de Rome et de son empire (Mikocki 1995, p. 111). La figure d'Agrippine appuie sa main libre sur l'épaule de Drusilla, personnifiant la *Concordia*. À droite du champ, Livilla prête son image à *Fortuna*. De la même façon que Caligula avait souhaité que les serments et les rapports des consuls ajoutent les noms de ses sœurs à celui de César,[9] les trois princesses incarnent de manière symbolique le bonheur, la concorde et la stabilité qui règnent sur Rome sous le principat de leur frère. Elles sont associées, de cette manière, au rayonnement politique et social de Caligula.

En 37, les sources ne nous laissent pas clairement entrevoir les prétentions au pouvoir d'Agrippine. Aussi pouvons-nous nous demander si elle prit vraiment part au complot monté par M. Aemilius Lepidus en 39.[10] Quoi qu'il en soit, Lepidus est condamné pour adultère et complicité dans une conspiration menée contre Caligula. Agrippine et Livilla, elles, sont condamnées ensemble à l'exil sur l'île de Ponza, non loin de Rome, pour adultère (Suet., *Cal.*, 24). Ainsi l'effigie d'Agrippine disparut-elle des monnaies, mais pour un temps seulement.

Agrippine et sa jeune sœur furent rappelées d'exil par Claude (Dio, 60.4.1). Agrippine recouvra ses richesses et même plus encore grâce à l'héritage laissé par Crispus Passienus. Suétone rapporte que le crédit et la puissance d'Agrippine augmentèrent tant que Messaline en vint à craindre pour la succession de Britannicus.[11] La mort de Messaline (Tac., *Ann.*, 11.38) ouvrit une voie pavée d'or à l'ambition d'Agrippine. Avant de devenir la femme du *princeps*, il lui fallut vaincre deux rivales, Ælia Pætina et Lollia Paulina (Suet., *Cl.*, 24). Elle possédait, pour remporter ce concours, deux alliés précieux. Tout d'abord Pallas qui expliqua à Claude comment une fille de Germanicus à la fécondité éprouvée «siérait bien à la dignité impériale (Tac., *Ann.*, 12.2.3)». Ensuite, son charme assorti de son statut de nièce de l'empereur qui lui permettait d'approcher ce dernier et de le séduire (Tac., *Ann.*, 12.3.1). Pour que le mariage fût contracté, il fallut que le sénat admît, dans le souci du bien de l'État, que cette union eût lieu. En effet, un mariage entre un oncle et sa nièce était alors considéré comme un inceste. Une loi fut ainsi votée, autorisant pour tous les Romains ce type d'union (Suet., *Cl.*, 25). En 49, le mariage fut célébré et dans les premiers mois de l'année 50, Agrippine obtint le surnom d'*Augusta* (Tac., *Ann.*, 12.26.1) puis, aidée de Pallas, elle parvint à faire adopter Néron par Claude (Tac., *Ann.*, 12.25.1; Suet., *Cl.*, 27). Plus âgé que Britannicus de trois ans, le jeune Domitius, désormais Néron, était en première place pour succéder (Tac., *Ann.*, 12.25.2)

(5) Dio, 55.12 : Auguste adopta Tibère le plaçant ainsi à la première place pour lui succéder. Afin de préparer la succession de Tibère, il contraint ce dernier à adopter Germanicus alors qu'il avait lui-même un fils.

(6) Dio, 59.3: Il multiplie les honneurs faits à Livie, à Antonia et à sa mère et donne les privilèges des vestales à ses sœurs.

(7) Ginsburg 2006, p. 66. Les monnaies aux effigies des femmes s'inscrivent dans le programme iconographique plus large de réhabilitation des honneurs faits à Germanicus et à Agrippine.

(8) À peine l'effigie de Livie était-elle apparue plus que timidement sur les monnaies de Tibère (*RIC*, I², 35, 43, 46, 47).

(9) Suet., *Cal.*, 15: «Pour honorer ses sœurs, il prescrivit d'ajouter à tous les serments : «je ne serais pas plus attaché à moi-même ni à mes enfants que je ne le suis à Gaius et, immédiatement après lui, à ses sœurs » ; de même aux rapports des consuls : « pour le bonheur et la prospérité de C. César et de ses sœurs ». »

(10) Cogitore 2002, pp. 196-197: L'auteur se pose la question de la participation réelle des deux sœurs de Caligula à ce complot. Selon elle, Lépide aurait pu nouer certains liens avec elles, mais les deux femmes n'avaient rien à gagner dans cette histoire. La douceur des conditions de leur exil prouverait que Caligula ne les craignaient pas vraiment.

(11) Suet., *Nér.*, 6 : Ce serait à ce moment que Messaline aurait fomenté une tentative d'assassinat contre Néron encore enfant mais le crime échoua.

à son nouveau *tata*. De surcroît, à la même époque, pour assurer davantage de légitimité à son fils, Agrippine obtint qu'il fût fiancé à la jeune Octavie (Dio, 60.32).

La promotion d'Agrippine au rang d'épouse impériale portant, en outre, le surnom d'*Augusta*[12] fut célébrée sur des monnaies d'or et d'argent (nos 2, 3). L'*aureus* et le denier à l'effigie du couple impérial ont dû être frappés dès 50-51 en leur honneur. Nous assistons alors à la réalisation d'un type monétaire résolument nouveau: celui du *princeps* et de son épouse, dont les bustes occupent chacun une face de la monnaie (Ginsburg 2006, p. 69). Dans l'atelier impérial de Lyon,[13] seule une femme avait été représentée en buste au revers d'une monnaie d'un empereur également en buste. Il s'agissait d'Agrippine *Maior* qui figurait ainsi au revers de l'effigie de son fils, mais elle était déjà décédée lors de l'émission (*RIC*, I², 7, 21). Livie n'avait eu le privilège d'être ainsi représentée avec Auguste que dans des ateliers orientaux (*RPC*, I, 1427, 2338, 2496, 2829). Même le cas de Julie n'est pas comparable à celui d'Agrippine. Elle avait figuré certes, en buste, au revers d'une monnaie à l'effigie de son père mais elle était assimilée à Diane (*RIC*, I², 403).

Cette nouveauté constitue presque une dérive monarchique du pouvoir impérial.[14] Cette iconographie, que l'on pourrait assimiler à celle d'un roi et d'une reine, a toujours été évitée sous les principats d'Auguste[15] et de Tibère. L'utilisation du double portrait est la preuve que la légitimité de la dynastie Julio-Claudienne est reconnue de tous (Kunisz 1980, pp. 135-142). Aussi, peut-on lire au droit la titulature impériale de Claude dans le style le plus classique: TI CLAVD CAESAR AVG GERM P M TRIB POT P P. La tête de Claude est laurée. Quant à Agrippine, on remarque que sa titulature est au datif et qu'elle est passablement lapidaire : AGRIPPINAE AVGVSTAE. L'usage du datif dégage une impression de dédicace que l'empereur ferait à son épouse en faisant la publicité de son surnom d'*Augusta* en lettres d'or et d'argent sur les monnaies. Néanmoins, pour Agrippine, ce fut probablement une première victoire éclatante qui se faisait l'écho de la place qu'elle tenait auprès de Claude.[16] Son visage, son nom et son surnom figuraient sur des *aurei* et des *denarii* et cela pouvait être vu par chaque personne qui manipulait ces monnaies (Grant 1952, p. 79). Toutefois, le buste d'Agrippine possède un attribut un peu étonnant: une couronne d'épis. Il est vrai qu'il s'agit d'un attribut des plus féminins[17] qu'Antonia avait porté avant elle (*RIC*, I², 65, 66, 67, 68, p. 124, n). Mais le port de cette couronne, dans l'esprit de tous les Romains, renvoie à une assimilation à Cérès (Mikocki 1995, pp. 90-91). De fait, Agrippine, sur cette série représentant le couple impérial, n'est pas encore tout à fait elle-même, elle reste, au travers de Cérès, une protectrice symbolique de la fertilité de l'Empire. Sous Claude, il a été considéré qu'il fallait encore avoir recours à l'alibi de l'assimilation à une divinité pour représenter le buste d'une femme vivante sur le numéraire en métal précieux, dont l'usage est réservé aux plus hautes couches de la société et à l'armée nonobstant le fait que sa légende, *a contrario* de celle de l'empereur, soit au datif.

En 51, Néron s'affirma encore d'avantage comme étant le successeur de Claude lorsqu'il devint prince de la jeunesse. Cet événement fut célébré lors de plusieurs frappes monétaires[18] où le jeune homme était représenté au revers de Claude (*RIC*, I², 82, 83) et au droit d'instruments de culte (*RIC*, I², 76, 77) qui signifiaient sa participation aux affaires religieuses. Dans ces deux cas, Néron était représenté tête nu, à gauche, entouré de la légende NERO CLAVD CAES DRVSVS GERM PRINC IVVENT. Ce type à l'effigie de Néron semble également avoir été utilisé pour une monnaie d'or où figurait sur l'autre face l'effigie d'Agrippine, mais pas n'importe quelle effigie puisqu'il s'agissait du type qui avait été utilisé pour les monnaies avec Claude (revers des n° 2 et 3). Nous sommes donc en présence d'un hybride (n° 4). Cette monnaie d'or, n'étant connu qu'à un seul exemplaire, est regardée avec méfiance par H. M. Von Kaenel (Von Kaenel 1986, p. 19). Toutefois, cet *unicum* proviendrait de fouilles qui la dateraient indubitablement du début de l'époque Néronienne (Von Kaenel 1986, p. 19). La piste du faux moderne est alors à exclure. Au regard de ce fait, W. Trillmich la considère comme étant une monnaie authentique bien que la découverte d'autres hybrides identiques pourraient infirmer ou confirmer cette hypothèse (Trillmich 1978, p. 56). Pour T. Fischer, dont la monnaie a été portée à sa connaissance par H. A. Cahn, l'authenticité de cet *unicum* laisse peu de doute. Cependant, il explique l'hybridité de cette monnaie par le fait qu'elle aurait été frappée aussitôt après l'accession de Néron au pouvoir (Fischer 1967, p. 43), ce qui laisse entendre que des coins de 51 auraient été ainsi recyclés. Or, il est très peu probable qu'on ait réutilisé ces coins qui dataient de 51 et qui commémoraient le statut de prince de la jeunesse de Néron alors que celui-ci venait de devenir empereur. Ainsi, ou bien cet hybride est le fruit d'une erreur émanant de l'atelier puisqu'il s'agit de monnaies qui, selon toute vraisemblance, datent toutes de 51,[19] comme le pense H. Mattingly (*RIC*, I, 100;

(12) Seule Livie, avant elle, avait porté ce surnom de son vivant, pendant de celui d'Auguste mais après la mort de celui-ci. Elle pouvait d'autant plus s'enorgueillir de le porter si vite que Messaline ne l'avait jamais obtenu. (Dio, 60.12).

(13) Giard 1990, pp. 175-180. Sous Claude, seul l'atelier impérial de Lyon frappe des monnaies en métal précieux.

(14) Martin 1994, p. 387 et s. Auguste devait utiliser le vocabulaire de la République pour instaurer un régime qui était en réalité une monarchie. Voilà pourquoi Livie n'apparaît jamais dans le monnayage impérial. Elle reste une matrone et ne devient pas une reine consort.

(15) Auguste avait gardé en mémoire les types monétaires aux couples qu'avaient fait frapper Marc Antoine avec Octavie (*RRC*, I, 527) d'une part, mais surtout avec Cléopâtre (*RPC*, I, 4094, 4771) d'autre part. Marc Antoine, au travers de son philhellénisme exacerbé, avait montré son goût pour la monarchie dans sa relation avec la reine d'Égypte.

(16) Dio, 60.33 : «Agrippine était souvent à côté de Claude en public, soit lorsqu'il s'occupait des affaires de l'État, soit lorsqu'il donnait audience à des ambassadeurs, assise sur une tribune particulière».

(17) Bastien 1992, p. 121. Exceptionnellement, on trouve des bustes couronnés d'épis pour des hommes (Hadrien et Gallien) ce qui est sujet à débat.

(18) Tac., *Ann.*, 12.41.1. Voir aussi: Grau 2009, p. 131.

(19) Von Kaenel 1986, p. 94, 100. Les monnaies de Claude et Agrippine (n° 2) et de Claude et Néron prince de la jeunesse (*RIC*, I², 82, 83) sont toutes les deux datées de 51. Je puis en déduire avec certitude que la date de l'hybride est également 51.

RIC, I^2, 75 n). Mais, cela témoignerait d'une légèreté peu crédible de la part des monétaires. Ou encore, et cela est plus plausible, cette monnaie a été spécialement créée pour associer Agrippine à la promotion politique dont venait de bénéficier son fils. En tant qu'*Augusta*, elle était le lien qui unissait Claude à son successeur, l'épouse et la mère, la donatrice de légitimité.[20]

Si l'*aureus* est unique, dix deniers sont connus (n° 5). Hélas, au moins deux numismates aguerris ont prouvés qu'ils étaient tous faux. En effet, J.-B. Giard a montré que l'exemplaire de la Bibliothèque nationale de France, comme celui du British Museum, sont deux faux modernes coulés et provenant du même moule ! (*BNCMER*, II, 5, p. 173). Quant aux autres, l'impitoyable H. M. Von Kaenel a réduit leur authenticité à l'état de chimère (Von Kaenel 1986, pp.18-19). Toutefois, comme l'*aureus*, dans l'attente de la preuve du contraire, est considéré comme vrai, rien n'indique que des deniers n'aient pas, eux aussi, existés. Que cet hybride ait été frappé uniquement sur l'or ou également sur l'argent, sa rareté s'explique du fait même de son hybridité puisqu'il devait s'agir d'une frappe exceptionnelle dédiant la promotion de son fils à Agrippine, dont la légende est toujours au datif.

Dès la fin de l'année 51, Agrippine avait posé tous les jalons qui conduiraient son fils à la pourpre. Elle-même était la deuxième *Augusta* vivante de l'histoire et tout l'éclat de sa condition apparut dans un sesterce (n° 6) frappé entre 51 et 54. En 51, Agrippine s'était vu concéder un immense privilège, celui de se déplacer en certaines occasions en *carpentum* (Tac., *Ann.*, 12.42). Ce char était l'apanage des prêtresses depuis l'abrogation de la *lex Oppia* (Abaecherli 1936, p. 5), en 195 avant J.-C. Livie, en tant que prêtresse d'Auguste, avait joui de cette prérogative consacrée sur un sesterce de l'époque Tibérienne (*RIC*, I^2, 50, 51). Toutefois, les monétaires n'avaient pas jugé utile de faire apparaître le portrait de la veuve d'Auguste sur cette monnaie. Messaline avait eut également l'insigne privilège de suivre Claude en *carpentum* lors du triomphe de ce dernier (Dio, 60.22; Suet., *Cl.*, 17), mais aucune monnaie ne le célébra. Seule la mère d'Agrippine avait vu son portrait assorti du *carpentum* sur un sesterce lors du principat de Caligula (*RIC*, I^2, 55), mais elle était déjà décédée; il s'agissait d'une monnaie qui commémorait son souvenir et le char y jouait un rôle funèbre. Seule Agrippine put se prévaloir de posséder son image au droit d'un sesterce montrant au revers le convoité *carpentum* alors qu'elle n'était ni morte, ni prêtresse.[21] La légende de droit est AGRIPPINA AVG GERMANICI F CAESARIS AVG. Pour la première fois, il est possible de constater une titulature pour une femme vivante, imitant le genre de titulature que l'on pourrait trouver pour un homme. En effet, le nom est au nominatif et mentionne l'envié *cognomen* d'*Augusta*. Ensuite, et ceci afin de souligner le prestige inhérent à sa condition, le monétaire obligeant a ajouté sa filiation avec Germanicus, l'enfant chéri des Romains, et précise qu'elle est l'épouse de l'empereur régnant. Enfin, l'iconographie du revers rehausse si bien le prestige de l'arrière-petite-fille d'Auguste qu'elle est anépigraphique. L'utilisation de ce char sans être une prêtresse confère à Agrippine une sorte de statut de mère de la patrie (Pagnotta 1977-1978, pp. 169-170) en corollaire au titre de *pater patriae* qui apparaît sur les monnaies de Claude dès 50-51.[22] La frappe de ce sesterce dans l'atelier de l'Vrbs représente la quintessence de tous les privilèges et honneurs qu'elle était parvenue à conquérir en quelques années. Elle était déjà la femme la plus puissante de l'Empire romain. Son fils était le successeur désigné de Claude. L'historien sagace peut déduire qu'il ne lui restait plus qu'un seul exploit à accomplir : la participation effective aux affaires politiques de l'Empire, comme le fit parfois Livie du temps du principat de son fils.[23]

« LE MONNAYAGE D'AGRIPPINE », RÉGENTE DE NÉRON

Au début de l'année 54, Agrippine avait reçu tous les honneurs qu'une Julio-Claudienne pouvait recevoir. Quant à Néron, au vu de son ascendance Julienne et Claudienne, de son adoption par l'empereur et de son mariage avec Octavie (Tac., *Ann.*, 12.58) en 53, personne dans tout l'Empire n'avait plus de légitimité que lui pour prendre la succession de Claude. Pourtant, les sources sont formelles. Des mots échappés de la bouche de Claude dans l'ivresse[24] ou dits en confidence à Britannicus[25] firent craindre à Agrippine de voir le fils de Messaline recouvrer ses droits à la succession et de se voir elle-même exclue du Palatin.[26]

Aussi, dut-elle se résoudre à abréger les jours du *princeps* avant que le sénat et l'armée ne réclamassent, conformément aux hypothétiques vœux de l'empereur, Britannicus à la succession. Les craintes d'Agrippine étaient-elles fondées ? Était-elle seulement pressée d'arriver au pouvoir avant que son fils ne fut trop âgé pour l'écouter ? Les ré-

(20) Flory 1998, pp. 113-138. L'auteur montre qu'une Augusta est celle qui, le plus souvent, a engendré un empereur et est l'épouse du précédent. Elle est le lien qui unit un *princeps* à son successeur.

(21) Ce fut la seule dans ce cas car toutes celles qui bénéficièrent de cette iconographie après elle était déjà morte et parfois même divinisées. Voir à ce sujet: Girod 2008, pp. 27-47.

(22) *RIC*, I^2, 51 à 64 pour le monnayage d'or et d'argent de Claude frappé à Lyon. Les titulatures de l'empereur portent dès 50-51 la mention *P(ater) P(atriae)*.

(23) Dio, 56.47 : « (...) Si j'ai ajouté le nom de Livie, c'est qu'elle aussi s'occupait des affaires comme si elle eût le pouvoir suprême.»; 57.12 : «les lettres de Tibère portèrent même le nom de Livie et celui du prince, et on écrivait pareillement à l'un et à l'autre. (...) Elle se vantait d'avoir fait Tibère empereur, et pour cela elle prétendait avoir moins une autorité égale à la sienne, qu'une autorité supérieure».

(24) Tac., *Ann.*, 12.64: «Mais la plus tourmentée par la crainte était Agrippine. Une parole échappée à Claude dans l'ivresse la faisait trembler: il avait dit que sa destinée était de supporter les désordres de ses femmes et de les punir ensuite. C'est pourquoi elle résolut d'agir et au plus tôt (...)».

(25) Suet., *Cl.*, 43: Citations de Claude à Britannicus: «Grandis, je te rendrais compte de toutes mes actions» et «Celui qui t'a blessé te guériras aussi». En lui faisant prendre la toge virile: «C'est pour que le peuple romain ait enfin un véritable César».

(26) Dio, 60.34. « (...) Claude s'apprêta à renverser Agrippine et à nommer son fils successeur à l'empire. Quand Agrippine fut instruite de ces projets de Claude, elle fut saisie de crainte et résolut de le prévenir par le poison. (...)»; Fl. Jos., *Ant. Jud.*, 20.8.1: il évoque également l'empoisonnement.

ponses à ces questions se trouvaient peut-être dans les mémoires d'Agrippine.(27) Hélas, ces écrits se perdirent dans les limbes du temps. Quoi qu'il en fût, dans la première moitié d'octobre 54, Claude mourut vraisemblablement empoisonné.(28) Agrippine aurait retardé l'annonce de sa mort afin de laisser le temps à Burrus (Fl. Jos., *Ant. Jud.*, 20.8.2) d'amener Néron devant les prétoriens pour qu'il se fît acclamer tout en ayant retenu Britannicus et Octavie au chevet de leur père (Tac., *Ann.*, 12.68 ; Suet., *Cl.*, 45). Le 13 octobre 54, à midi, Néron devint le cinquième César (Tac., *Ann.*, 12.69).

Néron avait une conscience aigüe du fait qu'il héritait de la pourpre grâce aux manigances ourdies par sa mère, comme en témoigne le mot d'ordre qu'il aurait donné au tribun prétorien de garde le jour même de son acclamation : «*Optima Mater*» (Tac., *Ann.*, 13.2.3 ; Suet., *Nér.*, 9). En outre, l'*Octavie* du Pseudo-Sénèque, écrite entre la chute de Néron et l'avènement d'Hadrien,(29) prouve combien chaque Romain savait qui était l'instigatrice du pouvoir de Néron.(30) Un jeune Néron qui n'avait que dix-sept ans, qui aimait les arts (Suet., *Nér.*, 20, 21), les courses de chevaux (Suet., *Nér.*, 22; Dio, 61.6), les balades nocturnes dans la *Subura* (Suet., *Nér.*, 26; Dio, 61.8) mais qui craignait encore sa mère.(31)

C'est ainsi qu'au premier jour du règne de son fils, et parce que celui-ci n'était pas encore désireux de s'occuper à plein temps de politique, qu'Agrippine devint la régente de l'Empire (Dio, 61.3; Suet., *Nér.*, 9 ; Tac., *Ann.*, 12.64). Son intelligence lui permettait d'accomplir les tâches administratives avec application. Mais, elle imaginait, à tort, que parce que Sénèque lui devait son rappel d'exil, il serait son allié (Tac., *Ann.*, 12.8). Ainsi, au vu des types monétaires frappés entre 54 et 55, nous pouvons imaginer que la toute puissante *Augusta* a pu manifester l'expression de son pouvoir au travers du choix, direct ou indirect, des types monétaires dans les premiers mois du règne de son fils.

Très peu de temps après son arrivée au pouvoir, Néron promit un *donatiuum* à l'armée d'un montant de quinze mille sesterces pour chaque soldat (Suet., *Cl.* 10), comme l'avait fait son père avant lui (Tac., *Ann.*, 12.69.2; Dio, 61.3), des distributions de quatre-cents sesterces par tête au peuple de Rome et une allocation annuelle aux sénateurs ruinés (Suet., *Nér.*, 10). Cela nécessita que l'on battît monnaie pour cette occasion qui célébrait l'accès à la pourpre du jeune *princeps*. C'est dans ce contexte de largesses que furent frappés les *aurei* et les deniers de la série de fin 54 avec Néron et Agrippine (nos 7, 8), sans doute largement destinés aux *donatiua* et à la noblesse. L'idéologie véhiculée par le type de cette monnaie est absolument extraordinaire car elle symbolise la gloire d'Agrippine en tant que régente, statut qu'elle se donna officieusement elle-même. Au droit, on peut lire AGRIPP AVG DIVI CLAVD NERONIS CAES MATER. La titulature est au nominatif. Son surnom d'*Augusta* est précisé ainsi que sa condition de veuve d'un *diuus* et celle de mère du nouveau César. Encore une fois, ce type de légende est totalement novateur dans la numismatique impériale. Ce qui pouvait être perçu comme particulièrement choquant pour les vieux Romains conservateurs, c'était de constater que la titulature de l'empereur passait au revers de la monnaie: NERONI CLAVD DIVI F CAES AVG GERM IMP TR P. Chose encore plus singulière, alors même que le nom d'Agrippine est au nominatif, celui de Néron est au datif. Il s'agit d'un cas unique sous son propre principat.(32) Aussi Agrippine apparaissait-elle comme étant l'autorité émettrice.

Toutefois, Agrippine avait dû se croire prudente sur le choix de l'iconographie du droit. Les bustes apparaissent affrontés,(33) Néron à gauche et Agrippine à droite. Certes, elle n'apparaît pas seule au droit comme une souveraine, une nouvelle Cléopâtre, mais son portrait est à droite, le côté dominant alors que le *princeps* est à la *sinistra*. Enfin, le jeune Néron est tête-nue, comme du temps où il était prince de la jeunesse, alors qu'Agrippine, à défaut d'autres attributs qui auraient fait scandale, apparaît dans se dignité de matrone, portant la *stola* et la *palla*.

L'iconographie du revers, une couronne de chêne entourant les lettres EX SC, soulève d'épineux problèmes d'exégèse. La couronne de chêne est une récompense militaire donnée à un homme qui a sauvé la vie d'un citoyen Romain (Maxfield 1981, p. 70). L'hypothèse selon laquelle Néron aurait reçu la *corona ciuica* par vote du sénat (Kraft 1962, pp. 7-49) est intéressante mais peu crédible car ni Tacite, ni Suétone n'en font état. Pour C.H.V. Sutherland (*RIC*, I², p. 134), cela exprimerait la participation du sénat à la frappe monétaire sur métal précieux. Or, on ne retrouve pas ce EX SC entouré de la *corona ciuica* sur toutes les monnaies en métal précieux sous le principat de Néron.(34) De surcroît, l'atelier impérial de Lyon, créé par Auguste, a continué de

(27) Tac., *Ann.*, 4.53: Tacite a lu les mémoires d'Agrippine qui aurait narré sa propre vie et celle de sa famille.

(28) Tac., *Ann.*, 12.66-67. Ces deux chapitres insistent sur la préméditation du meurtre et la perfidie d'Agrippine. Il est dit qu'Agrippine méditait depuis longtemps ce crime alors qu'en XII, 64, elle aurait voulu «agir au plus tôt». Ces éléments contradictoires ont pour but de la dénigrer. Suet., *Cl.*, 44.

(29) Bonnet 2006, pp. 202-222. Selon l'auteur, l'*Octavie* aurait été écrite sous Trajan pour lui montrer l'importance que revêtait le choix d'un successeur dans la perversité du système dynastique plutôt qu'une attaque contre Néron écrite peu après sa chute.

(30) Ps.-Sen., *Octav.*, 3.601-602 : «et la récompense que me valut le don de l'Empire: la nuit de mon déplorable naufrage».

(31) Tac., *Ann.*, 12.64.3. «Agrippine, au contraire [de Lépida], ne lui [à Néron] montrait qu'un visage sévère et menaçant».

(32) Il n'existe que trois exemples différents de légende de Néron explicitement au datif, sur des monnaies frappées à Rome et à Lyon, et encore datent-ils du principat de Claude. *RIC*, I², 78, 79, 108.

(33) Bastien 1996, p. 661s. Les bustes affrontés représentant deux hommes existent depuis la fin de la République dans le monnayage romain. Cette configuration au profit d'un homme et d'une femme est utilisée pour la première fois avec Agrippine. On retrouve le même cas de figure avec Trajan et Plotine puis cela deviendra assez courant à partir de Commode.

(34) *RIC*, I², p. 151: plusieurs émissions avec une légende de revers contenant les fonctions de *pontifex maximus, pater patriae* ainsi que les consulats et les puissances tribuniciennes sont ornées de la couronne de chêne et de la mention EX SC.

fonctionner sans ingérence de la part du sénat jusqu'à la réforme monétaire de 64 où la frappe des monnaies d'or et d'argent a été transférée à Rome (Giard 1990, p. 179). Donc, l'hypothèse de C. H. V. Sutherland n'est pas pleinement satisfaisante.

N'oublions pas que les Julio-Claudiens étaient passés maîtres dans l'art de manipuler les images (Zanker 1992, p. 350) et l'iconographie choisie pour les monnaies contribuait à affermir leur idéologie.

L'étude de ce revers doit être effectuée, autant que faire se peut, en utilisant les indices découverts dans les sources littéraires. Les Julio-Claudiens, de règne en règne, rappelaient souvent des épisodes glorieux des principats de leurs prédécesseurs dans le but d'augmenter leur prestige. Aussi peut-on imaginer une autre hypothèse, plus symbolique. La couronne civique était un apanage permanent de la famille impériale depuis Auguste, qui l'avait reçu du sénat. Elle figurait sur le toit de la maison du Palatin, à la vue de tous.[35] Chaque nouvel empereur s'inscrivait dans la continuité du premier *princeps* et continuait de sauver la patrie en l'empêchant de tomber dans le chaos des guerres civiles.[36] Sous Claude, cette couronne civique était toujours au faîte de la maison du Palatin car il fit accrocher, à côté de cette dernière, une couronne navale (Suet., *Cl.*, 17). Mais la couronne civique gardait toujours sa valeur d'emblème[37] de la dimension salvatrice de la *domus Augusta*. C'est sans doute cet héritage augustéen qu'Agrippine et Néron[38] voulurent montrer au revers de la monnaie qui glorifiait le jeune César et surtout l'*Augusta* dans le but de légitimer leur pouvoir.

Les reliefs du *Sebasteion* d'Aphrodisias font un très bel écho iconographique à cette monnaie. En effet, cela est plus audacieux dans la composition, mais il se situait en terre grecque: la statue d'Agrippine fut représentée couronnant celle du jeune Néron (Smith 1987, p. 128-129).

Le deuxième type, frappé sur des monnaies d'or et d'argent datant de 54, fut en l'honneur du *diuus Claudius*[39] (nos 9, 10). Il s'agit un corollaire à la monnaie du couple impérial mère-fils. Cette monnaie célèbre l'entrée dans le panthéon romain de Claude en illustrant au revers le quadrige tirant l'image ou la statue du nouveau dieu dans un char ressemblant à un petit temple (Abaecherli 1936, p.7). La légende de revers est simplement EX SC, ce qui implique l'accord du sénat pour la divinisation. Au droit, la légende est tout aussi simple: DIVVS CLAVDIVS AVGVSTVS avec un buste de Claude lauré. Si Agrippine a certainement voulu faire frapper dans un délai aussi bref une monnaie en l'honneur de Claude divinisé, c'est bien sûr pour l'honorer mais pas uniquement. Le plus important aux yeux de l'*Augusta*, résidait dans le fait qu'elle devenait l'épouse d'un dieu, par conséquent elle devenait aussi sa prêtresse, recevait dans ce cadre deux licteurs (Tac., *Ann.*, 13.2.3), alors que Livie n'en avait eu qu'un en tant que flaminique d'Auguste (Dio, 56.46), et enfin, son fils-*princeps* était le fils d'un nouveau dieu.

Le dernier type frappé sous l'égide d'Agrippine dans la première moitié de 55 est une sorte de nouvelle fresque du pouvoir (nos 11, 12). Encore une fois, il s'agit du monnayage d'or et d'argent. Mais Agrippine, si arrogante dans l'expression de son pouvoir en 54, semble avoir voulu ou accepté de redonner une place plus naturelle à Néron. Au droit, nous pouvons lire la titulature impériale de Néron au nominatif : NERO CLAVD DIVI F CAES AVG GERM IMP TR P COS. À l'inverse de l'émission de 54, l'empereur a de nouveau sa titulature au droit, ce qui est censé être une norme absolue dans l'Empire, puisque que le droit illustre l'autorité émettrice. La légende d'Agrippine est ainsi reléguée au revers: AGRIPP AVG DIVI CLAVD NERONIS CAES MATER. Elle est identique à celle de 54. L'iconographie du droit cependant, a quelque peu changé en moins de six mois. Le buste de Néron occupe le centre du champ, orienté à droite. Le buste d'Agrippine est seulement accolé à celui de son fils. On ne voit émerger du profil du *princeps* qu'une partie du visage de sa mère toujours drapée de la *stola* et de la *palla*.

En suivant notre postulat de départ selon lequel Agrippine aurait contribué à choisir ou influencer les types monétaires du début du règne de Néron, nous assistons, sur cette monnaie de 55, à un premier recul du pouvoir de l'*Augusta*. Cette nouvelle mise en scène de la régence s'avère plus prudente. Agrippine est toujours là, mais elle semble seconder son fils dans ses tâches politiques, elle lui laisse le premier plan. A. Barrett et J. Ginsburg ne pensent pas que cette monnaie soit l'expression du début de l'évincement politique d'Agrippine. Pour J. Ginsburg, les personnes avançant une telle hypothèse interprètent de manière erronée le matériel numismatique à la lumière des sources littéraires ! (Ginsburg 2006, p.73). Ainsi, reprend-elle l'idée de S. Wood selon laquelle il s'agirait simplement d'une variante de la représentation de Néron et Agrippine sur les monnaies (Wodd 1999, pp. 293-294). Or la monnaie, frappée qui plus est sur métal précieux, est un puissant vecteur d'idéologie et les monétaires ne devaient pas créer de nouveaux coins tous les six mois juste pour faire des variantes (Burnett 1988, p. 70 s). Ce qui justifie un changement d'iconographie si rapide ne peut être que la critique acerbe

(35) Dio, 52.16. «Ainsi on avait décrété que les lauriers seraient placés devant son habitation souveraine et qu'une couronne de chêne y serait suspendue, comme s'il ne cessait de vaincre les ennemis et de sauver les citoyens».

(36) *RIC*, I², 404: au revers d'une de ses monnaies, Auguste avait fait représenter sa fille, Julie, entre ses deux fils. Le buste de Julie était surmonté d'une couronne civique. Julie poursuivait l'œuvre salvatrice de son père en lui donnant des descendants du sang.

(37) Maxfield 1981, p. 72: «The civic crown, (...), was also adopted as an imperial emblem».

(38) Suet., *Nér.*, 10: «[Néron] déclara qu'il gouvernerait selon les principes d'Auguste ». Reprendre les emblèmes d'Auguste était un bon moyen de montrer que Néron imiterait ses principes. Par ailleurs, Auguste est celui de tous les Césars Julio-Claudien qui a utilisé le plus la couronne civique dans son monnayage (cf. *RIC*, I², p. 43, 47, 62, 64, 69).

(39) Suet., *Nér.*, 9; Tac., *Ann.*, 13.2.3.

des contemporains d'Agrippine.[40] Par ailleurs, le choix de ce second type a pu être inspiré par les monnaies ptolémaïques[41] représentant des bustes accolés du roi et de la reine au second plan.[42]

Quant à A. Barrett, il suggère que les deux émissions ont été frappées en partie de manière contemporaine (Barret 1996, p. 167). Or, la série de 54 a été frappée en vue de distributions (Barret 1996, p. 167) et la série de 55 inaugure le premier consulat de Néron (Tac., *Ann.*, 13.11.1). La série de 54 n'a plus de raison d'être frappée puisque la légende de Néron est devenue obsolète dès janvier de l'année suivante. Le *RIC* I^2 indique, de surcroît, que les deux types sont relativement rares (*RIC*, I^2, p. 150), ce qui argue en faveur de la thèse selon laquelle ces deux séries n'ont été frappées que durant un court laps de temps.

Enfin, le revers de la série d'*aurei* et de *denarii* de 55 rend hommage à Claude divinisé. Encore une fois, mais il s'agira de la dernière, il est possible de déceler l'influence directe d'Agrippine qui chercha à placer son règne et celui de son fils dans la continuité de celui de Claude.[43] En effet, c'est dans cette série que *Diuus Claudius* apparaît une ultime fois dans le monnayage impérial du principat de Néron.[44] Claude, fraîchement divinisé avec l'accord du sénat, comme le montre les lettres EX SC dans le champ, y est représenté sur un char d'éléphants à côté de la *fides praetorianorum*.[45] La personnification anthropomorphe de la confiance des prétoriens est figurée sous les traits d'une femme tenant un sceptre surmontée d'un aigle. Cette personnification, déjà usitée dans la numismatique de Claude (*RIC* I^2, 6, 7, 19, 20, 36, 37), représente la confiance dont les prétoriens avaient témoigné envers ce dernier, en le promulguant empereur après l'assassinat de Caligula (Suet., *Cl.*, 10). Sur la monnaie de 55, la *fides praetorianorum*, symbolise les prétoriens qui, toujours fidèle à Claude, ont acclamé Néron (Tac., *Ann.*, 12.69.1), car Néron, devenu prince de la jeunesse, était perçu comme le successeur désigné au détriment de Britannicus.

Après cette émission, l'influence d'Agrippine disparut à jamais du monnayage impérial. Et pour cause, Burrus et Sénèque menèrent contre l'*Augusta* une guerre perfide et hypocrite qui devait l'écarter du gouvernement (Tac., *Ann.*, 13.2.2; Dio, 61.3). Comme l'avènement de Néron était en réalité celui de la fille de Germanicus,[46] ils firent tout ce qui était en leur pouvoir pour encourager Néron à se détourner de sa mère et à l'éloigner du Palatin. Pour cela, ils le poussèrent dans les bras de la douce Acté (Tac., *Ann.*, 13.12.1-2) dans l'espoir que l'affection d'une autre femme l'aiderait à ne plus rechercher celle d'Agrippine.[47] Ensuite, ils firent en sorte de limiter la participation de la régente auto-promulguée aux affaires politiques, comme le prouve l'affaire de l'ambassade d'Arménie (Tac., *Ann.*, 13.5.1-2; Dio, 61.3). Enfin, Pallas fut chassé du Palatin et révoqué des fonctions que lui avait confié Claude (Tac., *Ann.*, 13.14.1-2). La chute de l'affranchi ne faisait que précéder celle de sa patronne. Agrippine se vit privée de sa garde qu'elle avait reçu en tant qu'épouse de Claude avant de devoir déménager dans l'ancienne maison d'Antonia (Tac., *Ann.*, 13.18. 2-3; Suet., *Nér.*, 34). Bien sûr, l'*Augusta* continua à se battre pour reprendre le pouvoir, au moins dans l'ombre. L'entreprise fut vaine. Arriva alors l'ennemie ultime, la trop belle Poppée qui aiguillonna le cœur de Néron vers le matricide.[48]

À la fin du mois de mars 59, Agrippine mourut dans sa villa de Baules, sous les coups d'Anicetus.[49] De nombreuses sources précisent qu'elle aurait ordonné à son bourreau de frapper au ventre (Tac., *Ann.*, 14.8.5; Dio, 61.13). Est-ce une légende ? L'historien honnête ne peut trancher cette question mais il est possible qu'une femme dotée d'un si fort tempérament ait pu le dire.

(40) Tac., *Ann.*, 14.11.1. À en croire Tacite, Agrippine avait exigé plus que le choix des types monétaires. S'il est vrai qu'elle avait fait jurer fidélité aux cohortes prétoriennes, qu'elle répondait au courrier des ambassadeurs, qu'elle faisait venir le sénat au Palatin pour pouvoir écouter les séances en cachette (Tac., *Ann.*, 13.5.1), elle avait dû accumuler suffisamment d'ennemis en quelques mois pour adoucir l'image de sa participation au gouvernement de l'Empire sur la seconde émission monétaire du règne de son fils. Dion Cassius corrobore le fait qu'Agrippine s'acquittait de toutes les tâches administratives et s'occupait notamment des rois et ambassadeurs étrangers: Dio, 61.3.

(41) Bastien 1992, p. 649. Il est très possible que les monétaires aient pris pour référence le monnayage ptolémaïque. Néron, de la même façon que Ptolémée III, s'est fait représenter avec une couronne radiée de son vivant. C'est une preuve de l'influence du monnayage lagide. Voir à ce sujet Poole, 1892, p. xxxix.

(42) Par exemple, une monnaie de Ptolémée III où il apparaît accolé à Arsinoé II avec, au revers, Ptolémée II accolé à Bérénice (*SNG*, Cop., 133). Dans le cas lagide, les femmes légitiment le pouvoir des hommes. En Thrace, on trouve ce même type de représentation pour Auguste et Livie au revers des monnaies du roi Rhoemetalces et de la reine consort Pythodoris (*RPC*, I, 1708). Cependant, avec Agrippine, c'est la première fois que l'on voit un tel mode de représentation pour un fils et sa mère à Rome.

(43) Tac., *Ann.*, 13.5. Agrippine tenta, mais en vain, de faire suivre à Néron la politique de Claude concernant le sénat.

(44) Au printemps 55, Sénèque publia *L'Apocoloquintose du divin Claude* qui glorifiait Néron et ridiculisait ouvertement Claude. Dès lors, Néron n'insista plus sur la dimension divine de son père adoptif. En outre, Néron aboli le culte de Claude divinisé qui ne fut rétablit que sous Vespasien (Suet., *Cl.*, 45).

(45) *BNCMER* II, 10: Il s'agit de l'interprétation de J.-B. Giard, que je partage.

(46) Tac., *Ann.*, 13.6.2. «Qu'attendre d'un enfant gouverné par une femme?»

(47) Cizek 1982, p. 33. L'auteur a bien mis en exergue la complexité des liens qui unissent Néron et sa mère. Agrippine était d'une extrême exigence envers son fils. C'était sans doute pour lui plaire qu'il lui laissa en grande partie les rênes du pouvoir en 54. Mais Sénèque, Burrus et les courtisans étant tout sucre et tout miel avec le jeune *princeps* parvinrent à stimuler sa haine contre Agrippine.

(48) Tac., *Ann.*, 16.1.3: «Ces traits, que les pleurs et l'art d'une amante rendaient plus pénétrants, on n'y opposait rien : tous désiraient l'abaissement d'Agrippine, et personne ne croyait que la haine d'un fils dût aller jamais jusqu'à tuer sa mère». Même Tacite, pourtant misogyne et ne prêtant aucune sympathie à Agrippine semble choquer par ce recours extrême. Dio, 61.12. Dion Cassius est tout aussi conscient de l'horreur du matricide: «meurtre impie».

(49) Dio, 61.13: L'auteur ajoute que Néron n'osa pas envoyer les prétoriens pour accomplir le matricide car ces derniers respectaient Agrippine comme étant la fille de Germanicus. C'est Anicetus et des marins qui se chargèrent du forfait.

Même si ce terme est plutôt impropre à une femme de l'antiquité romaine, Agrippine *Minor* a eu une «carrière politique» dont les différentes étapes sont perceptibles dans le monnayage impérial où elle est représentée. Dans un premier temps, ce sont les autres qui se servent de son image. D'abord utilisée de manière quasi hiératique par son frère (n° 1), elle devient le parangon de l'*Augusta* sur les monnaies frappées à Lyon et à Rome sous Claude (nos 2 à 6). Ses titulatures, son buste mais aussi ses privilèges honorifiques sont représentés dans le monnayage entre 50 et 54 comme cela n'avait jamais été fait auparavant pour aucune femme vivante de la *domus Augusta*. En cela, elle avait déjà défié les limites politiques que la société romaine imposait à une femme. Mais ses ambitions allaient bien au-delà. Son but ultime était de gouverner l'empire avec ou pour son fils (Tac., *Ann.*, 12.64; Dio, 61.3). Elle parvint effectivement à administrer l'empire dans les premiers mois de son principat. Les sources littéraires le disent, les monnaies le prouvent. Évincée du Palatin vers le milieu de l'année 55, les thèmes monétaires de l'iconographie néronienne changèrent. Agrippine disparaissait pour toujours du monnayage impérial.[50] Dès lors, Néron, devenu sans doute très méfiant quant aux ambitions politiques des femmes ne représenta plus jamais les femmes de la *domus Augusta* sur ses monnaies.[51] *Diuus Claudius* disparaissait également du monnayage car Néron se réclamait de l'héritage d'Auguste et non de celui de son père adoptif,[52] ce dont témoigne l'abandon du culte de ce dernier et la parution de l'*Apocoloquintose* en 55 qui glorifiait Néron et ridiculisait Claude.

Tous ces éléments prouvent que arrivée au sommet de sa carrière politique, Agrippine a directement influé sur le choix de l'iconographie des types monétaires. A-t-elle formé des vœux précis quant à la composition des coins ? A-t-elle choisi parmi plusieurs solutions proposées par les graveurs ? Il est impossible de répondre à cette question mais il est certain que Sénèque et Burrus n'ont alors pas pu faire prévaloir leurs avis, sans quoi la fabuleuse monnaie de 54, sur laquelle Agrippine apparaît comme l'autorité émettrice, n'aurait jamais existé (nos 7 et 8). Les monnaies frappées lors de la présence d'Agrippine au Palatin établissaient un discours idéologique cohérent où Agrippine était la régente de l'empire pour le compte d'un fils encore trop jeune. Elle se revendiquait de l'héritage claudien du pouvoir et émettait des monnaies en l'honneur de sa divinisation. Jusqu'à la mi-55, l'iconographie monétaire est axée sur elle plus que sur Néron ou Claude (nos 7 à 12). Elle instaura une trinité impériale dont elle était, en pratique, le personnage central. En 55, sans doute en partie déjà vaincue par Sénèque, Burrus et le début de révolte de Néron,[53] elle atténua l'image qu'elle donnait de son pouvoir personnel en limitant son effigie à l'état d'ombre derrière son fils (nos 11 et 12). Son évincement du Palatin, qui coïncidait avec sa disparition du monnayage, confirme l'existence, durant quelques mois, de ce que l'on pourrait nommer, comme le feraient les numismates pour un empereur, le «monnayage d'Agrippine».

Catalogue

Caligula

1 : Rome, sesterce, émission de 37-38.
A/ C CAESAR AVG GERMANICVS PON M TR P, buste de Caligula lauré à gauche.
R/AGRIPPINA (à gauche) DRVSILLA (en haut) IVLIA (à droite) S·C à l'exergue, les trois sœurs de Caligula debout, de face : à gauche, Agrippine est appuyée sur une colonne et tient une corne d'abondance ; au centre, Drusilla tient une patère et une corne d'abondance ; à droite, Julia Livilla tient un gouvernail et une corne d'abondance. Elles personnifient la *Securitas*, la *Concordia* et la *Fortuna*.
RIC I^2, 33; *BMC* I, 37; *BNCMER* II, 47*.

Claude

2 : Lyon, *aureus*, émission de 51.
A/ TI CLAVD CAESAR AVG GERM P M TRIB POT P P, tête laurée de Claude à droite.
R/ AGRIPPINAE AVGVSTAE, buste drapé d'Agrippine couronnée d'épis à droite.
RIC I^2, 80; *BMC* I, 72; *BNCMER* II, 76*.

3 : Lyon, denier, émission de 51.
A/ même description que n° 2.
R/ même description que n° 2.
RIC I^2, 81; *BMC* I, 75 ; *BNCMER* II, 82*.

4 : Lyon, *aureus*, émission de 51.
A/ AGRIPPINAE AVGVSTAE, buste d'Agrippine couronnée d'épis à droite.
R/ NERO CLAVD CAES DRVSVS GERM PRINC IVVENT, buste nu de Néron à gauche.
RIC ^{2}, -; Münzen und Medaillen AG, 43, 12-13 novembre 1970, n° 303* = und Münzzentrum, 64, 15 avril 1988, n°102.

5 : Lyon, denier, émission de 51.
A/ même description que n° 4.
R/ même description que n° 4.
RIC I^2, 75; *BMC* I, 82*; *BNCMER* II, 5.

6 : Rome, sesterce, émission de 51-54.
A/ AGRIPPINA AVG GERMANICI F CAESARIS AVG, buste d'Agrippine drapé, à droite.
R/ Anépigraphe, *carpentum* tire par deux mules à gauche.

(50) *A contrario*, elle reste très présente dans le monnayage provincial jusqu'en 59. Près de 71 types différents sont connus pour Agrippine, cf. *RPC*, I. C'est tout de même un peu moins que pour Livie.

(51) À Rome, Claudia Augusta, la fille de Néron, n'est représentée que sur des tessères de plomb. Poppée n'apparaît que sur quelques monnaies provinciales. Cf. *RPC*, I.

(52) Tac., *Ann.*, 13.5.1: Néron, au début de son principat, avait prit des mesures en faveur du sénat en dépit du fait qu'Agrippine pensait que cela était contraire à la politique de Claude. Cela prouve encore la distance que prenait Néron par rapport à son père adoptif.

(53) Suet., *Nér.*, 34: Néron, excédé par les reproches de sa mère, aurait menacé d'abdiquer et de partir à Rhodes. Il s'agit d'une allusion à relation entre Tibère et Livie. Tac., *Ann.*, 13.13.1: Néron se rebelle contre sa mère qui ne supporte pas sa relation avec Acté.

RIC I^2, 103; *BMC* I, p. 195, n. (Berlin)*.

« ***Monnayage d'Agrippine*** »

7 : Lyon, *aureus*, émission d'octobre à décembre 54.
A/ AGRIPP AVG DIVI CLAVD NERONIS CAES MATER, tête de Néron à gauche face à Agrippine, drapée à droite.
R/ NERONI CLAVD DIVI F CAES AVG GERM IMP TR P, au centre d'une couronne de chêne, EX S C.
RIC I^2, 1; *BMC* I, 1; *BNCMER* II, 4*.

8 : Lyon, denier, émission d'octobre à décembre 54.
A/ même description que n° 7.
R/ même description que n° 7.
RIC I^2, 2; *BMC* I, 3; *BNCMER* II, 8*.

9 : Lyon, *aureus*, émission d'octobre à décembre 54.
A/ DIVVS CLAVDIVS AVGVSTVS, buste lauré de Claude à gauche.
R/ EX S C, quadrige tirant un char à droite et surmonté d'une Victoire.
RIC I^2, 4; *BMC* I, 4; *BNCMER* II, 1*.

10 : Lyon, denier, émission d'octobre à décembre 54.
A/ même description que n° 9.
R/ même description que n° 9.
RIC I^2, 5; *BMC* I, 6; *BNCMER* II, 3*.

11 : Lyon, *aureus*, émission de janvier au printemps 55.
A/ NERO CLAVD DIVI F CAES AVG GERM IMP TR P COS, tête de Néron jointe au buste d'Agrippine, drapée à droite.
R/ AGRIPP AVG DIVI CLAVD NERONIS CAES MATER, dans le champ, EX S C, quadrige d'éléphants sur la plate-forme duquel se trouvent deux personnages. Au premier plan, *Diuus Claudius*, arborant la couronne radiée, tient une patère. Derrière lui, une femme, probablement une représentation anthropomorphique de la *fides praetorianorum*, tient un sceptre surmonté d'un aigle.
RIC I^2, 6; *BMC* I, 7; *BMCMER* II, 10*.

12 : Lyon, denier, émission de janvier au printemps 55.
A/ même description que n° 11.
R/ même description que n° 11.
RIC I^2, 7; *BMC* I, 8; *BMCMER* II, 13*.

ABRÉVIATIONS

BMC I= Mattingly H. (1923). *Coins of the Roman Empire in the British Museum. Vol. I. Augustus to Vitellius.* London.

BNCMER II= Giard J.-B. (1976). *Catalogue des monnaies de l'empire romain II. De Tibère à Néron.* Paris.

RIC I^2= Sutherland C. H. V./Carson R. A. G. (1984). *The Roman Imperial Coinage. Vol. I. Revised Edition. From 31 BC to AD 69.* London.

RÉFÉRENCES

Abaecherli A. L. (1935-1936). 'Fercula, Carpenta, and Tensae in the roman Procession', *Bolletino dell'Associazione internazionale studi mediterranei*, 6, pp. 1-20.

Barrett A. (1996). *Agrippina, mother of Nero.* Londres.

Bastien P. (1992). *Le buste monétaire des empereurs romains.* Wetteren.

Bonnet G. (2006). 'Forme et datation de l'Octavie: une nouvelle hypothèse', *Revue d'Études Latines*, 84, pp. 202-222.

Burnett A. (1988). *La numismatique romaine de la République au Haut-Empire* (trans. Depeyrot, G.). Paris.

Cizek E. (1982). *Néron.* Paris.

Cogitore I. (2002). *La légitimité dynastique d'Auguste à Néron à l'épreuve des conspirations.* Rome.

Fischer Th. (1967). 'Bemerkungen zur spätclaudischen Münzprägung', *Revue Suisse de Numismatique*, 46, pp. 34-49.

Flory M. (1998). 'The meaning of Augusta in the Julio-Claudian period', *American Journal of Ancient History*, 13.2, pp. 113-138.

Giard J.-B. (1990). 'L'atelier monétaire de Lyon', dans Pelletier A., Rossiand J. (dir.), *Histoire de Lyon: des origines à nos jours, vol. 1.* Lyon, pp. 175-180.

Girod V. (2008). 'Le carpentum dans la numismatique romaine: évolution et signification', *Cahiers Numismatiques*, 175, pp. 27-47.

Ginsburg J. (2006). *Representing Agrippina.*Oxford.

Grant M. (1952). 'Roman coins as propaganda', *Archaeology*, 5.2, pp. 79-85.

Grau D. (2009). 'Néron, héritier d'Auguste: perspectives numismatiques', *Revue Numismatique*, 165, pp. 129-152.

Kraft K. (1962). 'S(enatus) C(onsulto)', *Jahrbuch für Numismatik und Geldgeschichte*, 12, pp. 7-49.

Kunisz A. (1980). 'La propagande de l'idéologie monarchique sur les monnaies romaines du Ier siècle de notre ère', *Actes du colloque international sur l'idéologie monarchique dans l'Antiquité (Cracovie-Mogilanu, du 23 au 26 octobre 1977, Prace Historyczne, Zeszyt 63)*, pp. 135-141.

Martin P. (1994). *L'idée de royauté à Rome, haine de la royauté et séduction monarchique, vol. 2.* Clermont-Ferrand.

Maxfield V. (1981). *The military decorations of the roman army*. Londres.

Mikocki T. (1995). *Sub specie deae, les princesses et les impératrices romaines assimilées à des déesses: étude iconologique (Supplemento 14 alla rivista di archeologia Rome)*. Rome.

Pagnotta M. A. (1977-1978). 'Carpentum, privilegio del carro e ruelo sociale della matrona romana', *Annali della facoltà di littere e filosofia, Università degli studi di Perugia*, 15.1, pp. 159-170.

Poole Stuart R. (1892). *Catalogue of Greek coins of Alexandria and the nomes*. Londres.

Smith R. R. R. (1987). 'The imperial reliefs from the Sebasteion at Aphrodisias', *Journal of Roman Studies*, 77, pp. 88-138.

Trillmich W. (1978). *Familienpropaganda der Kaiser Caligula und Claudius*. Berlin.

Von Kaenel H. M. (1986). *Münzprägung und münzbildnis des Claudius*. Berlin.

Wood S. (1999). *Imperial women: a study in public images, 40 B.C.-A.D. 68 (Mnémosyne, suppl. 194)*. Boston - Cologne.

Zanker P. (1992). *The power of images in the age of Augustus*. Michigan.

1

2

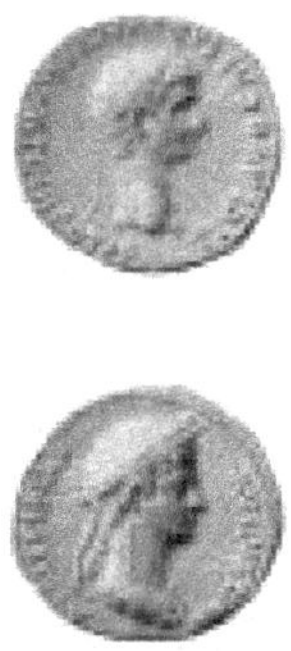

3

4

5

6

7

8

9

10

11

12

The Coinage of Carthago Nova and the Roman fleet of Missenum: Imperial triumphs and local *deductiones*

Fernando López Sánchez*

ABSTRACT

Most coin issues from Carthago Nova may be linked to *deductiones* of Roman veterans. Discharged soldiers were settled in Roman colonies or *municipia* in especial ceremonies, which in the case of Carthago Nova were conducted by the *duoviri quinquennales*, who appear on almost every one of the city's coin issues. Most of the veterans settled in Carthago Nova served in the imperial fleet of Missenum and took part in a number of military campaigns in the period between 31 BC and 41 AD. The coin issues depicting military and religious motifs (*RPC*1 149, *RPC*1 162-164, *RPC*1 174-177, and *RPC*1 157, 169, 172-174) form the main focus of this article and some of these will be reclassified in chronological terms, with reference to commonly-used reference catalogues.

Introduction: the complexity of Carthago Nova's coin issues

From the date of its foundation in the late third century BC, Carthago Nova was for almost two decades the main Carthaginian city in Iberia. Although road communications also played a role, its real importance lay in its maritime connections with a number of different Mediterranean harbours, lying as it did between the Mediterranean and the Atlantic Ocean. After the fall of Carthage, it remained the most important harbour in Roman Hispania and was a key port of call of the Western Mediterranean, connecting North Africa, Sicily and the Atlantic. Furthermore, well before the late first century BC, the route linking the city to the Latium and Campania via Ibiza and Sardinia experienced a major boost (Map 1).(1)

Despite its extraordinary infrastructure and the constant traffic of people and goods, Carthago Nova was never granted the distinction of being named the provincial capital by any of the Julian emperors. Such an honour was reserved, from the very beginning, for Tarraco. Although Carthago Nova was much closer to the rich mines of the Sierra Morena than Caesaraugusta, Tarraco, or Emerita Augusta, and at roughly the same distance as Colonia Patricia (Córdoba), the city did not mint a single imperial coin issue in gold or in silver during the Augustan period, in contrast to these other cities. Neither did Carthago Nova even mint a single coin between 209 BC and around 40 BC (Ripollès 2005, p. 82; Ripollès 1998, p. 346) and when it did, between circa 40 BC and 41 AD, it never attained the rate of production of Caesaraugusta or Emerita Augusta (Ripollès 1998, pp. 347, 361-362).

These breaks in coin production are no less mysterious than the chronological seriation of its issues. Numismatic classification has not proved an easy task, since neither the name of the city nor the minting authorities are always present (Ripollès 1998, p. 347). There is a clear preference for military types, featuring important Italian and Mauritanian names, characteristics which are atypical in modest civic coin issues such as these. The intention here is not to carry out a re-evaluation of Carthago Nova's coin series from a technical or metrological point of view, or indeed to present any previously unpublished issues or surprising new varieties. There are already notable works on this which may be easily referred to. There are, nevertheless, certain coins which have traditionally attracted the attention of numismatists and historians alike and these coins are studied here from a different perspective.

In this article, the study of Carthago Nova's coin issues is divided into five sections. The first of these addresses the series *RPC*1 149, with a trophy and the legend *SABI-NVS/ C-M/ IM-P* on the reverse. One of the first coin issues to be minted in Carthago Nova, this has generally been considered to refer to the city's foundation. The second section analyses the series *RPC*1 163 and 164, in which Agrippa is mentioned as *duumvir quinquennalis 'in absentia'*, with two military trophies on the reverse. A third, section is dedicated to the coins of *RPC*1 172-174, which play a key role among all the other coin types of Carthago Nova. The obverse depicts a triumphal parade, which can scarcely be linked to Carthago Nova and probably in fact refers to Rome. The reverse depicts a temple, which may be con-

* University Jaime I (Castellón, Spain); Wolfson College (Oxford, UK).

(1) Masstoni, Spanu, Zucca 2005, pp. 64-66. See also Stannard 2005.

nected to other examples from the cities of Turris Libisonis and Caralis (Sardinia). A fourth section, meanwhile, studies the coin series *RPC*1 157, 169 and 172/173. The first of these issues chose for its most descriptive coin type (obverse or reverse?) a Victoria walking towards the right, with a palm branch and a wreath. Other issues, *RPC*1 169 and 172/173, though, celebrate Juba II as a Mauritanian *rex* and as a *duumvir quinquennalis* of Carthago Nova, while Ptolemy, on the other hand, appears only as an African *rex*. This section explores the possible connections between Carthago Nova and Mauritania in the early first century AD. Our final conclusions are presented in the fifth and last section, in which Carthago Nova's coinage is considered in relation to the current debate regarding the role of civic coin issues in the Roman world. It will be argued that the city's minting activity coincided with successive *deductiones* of Roman veterans (usually one every five years) which were linked to a significant extent to the personnel of the imperial Roman fleet of Missenum. In the period roughly between 31 BC and 4 AD important detachments of this fleet operated regularly from the port of Carthago Nova plying the routes from Africa and even, sometimes, probably all the way to the Bay of Biscay.

Carthago Nova and the maritime victory *ex Hispania* of C. Calvisius Sabinus (28 BC)

One of the first coin issues minted at Carthago Nova, *RPC*1 149, reads *HEL POLLIO ALBINVS II Q(V)* on the obverse, and depicts a female head with veil and diadem – *Pietas* or *Concordia* (Fig. 1).[2] The reverse, on the other hand, shows a military trophy, with the legend *SABI-NVS/ C-M/ IM-P* in three horizontal lines. For Grant, the *Sabinus* mentioned here refers to C. Calvisius Sabinus a commander, favoured by both Caesar and Octavian, who was proconsul in Hispania between 31 and 29 BC (Curchin 2004, pp. 132-134). Grant goes on to argue that the initials CM stand for *Constitutor Municipi* (FITA, pp. 160-161) and Beltrán agrees with him with regard to this coin issue celebrating the foundation of the colony, though Beltrán prefers to read the inscriptions *C-M/ IM-P* as *Gnaeus Magnus Imperator*. The Spanish numismatist explains the presence of a *G* instead of a *C* by basing his view on Cassius Dio (43.30), who narrates how Pompey the Great was acclaimed *Imperator* after taking the city in 47 BC. The *Sabinus* in the coin legend would also therefore be related to this event, and, according to Beltrán, does not refer to C. Calvisius Sabinus, but to a certain M. Minatius Sabinus, proquaestor of Gnaeus Pompeius in certain *denarii* struck in 46/45 BC (*RRC* 470/1a).[3]

It is easy to argue, however, that Beltrán's *G* for 'Gnaeus' is actually a clear *C* in every single coin of this issue and that the transliteration of *CM* into 'Gnaeus Magnus' and the subsequent association with M. Minatius Sabinus is therefore no more than pure speculation. It might also be argued that a recently-captured city would not choose to celebrate its captor in one of its first coin issues and in this sense C. Calvisius Sabinus seems a better fit than Pompey the Great as the man related to this coin issue of *RPC*1 149, as Grant indeed proposes. One argument against the interpretation of the latter, however, is that the development of *CM* as *Constitutor Municipium* is not very convincing, as our Sabinus is hailed in *RPC*1 149 as *Imperator*, and not as *Constitutor*. Furthermore, his name is linked to a military trophy and not to a city founder ploughing the *pomerium* with a yoked bull and cow. The meaning behind the initials *CM* must therefore be sought in the circumstances which led C. Calvisius Sabinus to obtain the title of *imperator* and also of *ex Hispania*[4] on the 26th of May in 28 BC.

As regards C. Calvisius Sabinus, Shipley notes that "we have no information as to his governorship in Spain, or the campaign for which he celebrated his triumph" (Shipley 1931, p. 34). What we do know is that he served Caesar and Pompey in 48 BC, during the maritime crossing of the Strait of Otranto which led to the landing at Oricus (Caes. *BC*. 3. 34, 35, 56[55]). During 38 and 37 BC, C. Calvisius Sabinus also served as the admiral of Octavian's fleet, against another Pompey (Sextus) (App. BC. 5. 80-102; Dio Cassius 48. 46-48,54). Given Sabinus' maritime record and experience prior to being named proconsul in Hispania between 31 and 29 BC, it may safely be concluded that the victory celebrated in *RPC*1 149 probably took place at sea. The *denarii RRC* 511/2b, minted in 42 BC and in honour of the proconsul Sextus Pompey, serve as a clear example of this, as a naval trophy on the reverse is depicted along with the legend *Praef(ectus) Class(is) et Orae Marit(imae) ex S(enato) C(onsulto)*, i.e. 'Prefect of the fleet and of the shores of the sea by decision of the senate' (Fig. 2). The legend and trophy refer explicitly to Sextus Pompey's victory over Q. Salvidenus Rufus, when he was hailed *imperator* for the second time (*Mag. Pius Imp. Iter.*) Therefore the abbreviation *CM* on *RPC*1 149 coins may be interpreted in a similar way to the *RRC* 511/2b, with the semantic fields being considered as possibly related to '*Classis*' and/or '*Maritimae*'.

Appian (5. 80), when describing C. Calvisius Sabinus' confrontation with Sextus Pompey in the Tyrrhenian Sea in 38 BC, mentions that Octavian "ordered the building of new triremes at Rome and Ravenna". This passage foreshadows the creation of the Roman fleets (of Missenum and Ravenna) which were to watch over the western and eastern Mediterranean respectively during the Empire. The exact dates for the inauguration of the Missenum fleet and its subsequent attachment to the Bay of Naples are unknown. Viereck believes that the western Mediterranean fleet was permanently linked to Missenum at some time between 27 and 18 BC (Viereck 1975, pp. 252-279; Morrison 1996, p. 172), though Pitassi, on the other hand, believes that this could only have taken place as of 22 BC (Pitassi 2009, p. 203). Nevertheless as has been pointed out by Meloni, "it is now widely accepted that the Misenensis fleet was not

(2) *RPC*1, p. 92.

(3) Llorens 1994, p. 46; Beltrán 1953, p. 60.

(4) Tab. Triumph. Barb.: c.cALVislVS.sABINVS.EX.HISPANIA. VII. K. IVN/ TR/V/MPHAVI /T P/L M A M · D E D IT; Shipley 1931, p. 34.

always and entirely based at Missenum"[5] and indeed it may be perfectly possible that the fleet's assignment did not take place until sometime after its creation. In this regard, Pitassi points out that Agrippa first used his fleet at Missenum before sailing to take part in the battle of Actium with it (31 BC). It therefore appears possible that the official inauguration of the Missenum fleet took place in that same year of 31 BC, immediately after the Battle of Actium (the 2nd of September).

C. Calvisius Sabinus could have commanded the Missenum fleet in Spain in the years following Agrippa's command, i.e. 31-29 BC. If this were the case, *CM* could logically be read as *Classis Missienensis* or *Classis Missenatis*. Furthermore, it is possible that Cassius Dio (51.20) informs us of the exact victory and area of operation in Spain which could be attributed to C. Calvisius Sabinus and his fleet. The Bithynian historian does not mention any Roman fleet in 51.20, but nevertheless he states that the Roman general T. Stilius Taurus defeated *Cantabri*, *Vaccaei*, and *Astures* in northern Spain in 29 BC, only a year before Sabinus celebrated his triumph (28 BC). An inscription found in 1621 in Ilici (Elche, Alicante, Spain) also mentions that this very same T. Statilius Taurus was named *imperator* for a third time (T. STATILIO/ TAVRO. IMP./ III. COS. II. PATRONO).[6] Ilici is a nearby Roman colony in the Levantine region, very similar in its characteristics to Carthago Nova.[7] If C. Calvisius Sabinus enjoyed a military triumph in Hispania in 28 BC, apparently thanks to the Missenum fleet, it does not therefore seem too far-fetched to assume that T. Statilius Taurus should have led the same forces in 29 BC in northern Spain as his successor to the command. Likewise, C. Calvisius Sabinus could have defeated the same *Cantabri*, *Vaccaei*, and *Astures* as T. Statilius Taurus in 28 BC, or at very least the *Cantabri* and *Astures*, coastal communities of the northern Atlantic coast.

Carthago Nova and Agrippa's *terra marique* trophies (19/18 BC)

The coin issues *RPC*1 162, 163, and 164 not only display major similarities to each other but were also minted in part by the same civic magistrates, indicating that they were coined at almost the same time. As *RPC*1 162 and 164 explicitly mention Agrippa as *duumvir quinquennalis* (*in absentia*) of Carthago Nova (HIBERO PRAE. M. AGRIP. QVIN.) (Fig. 3), there can be no doubt regarding the chronology of these coins, which were surely minted successively during the year between 19 and 18 BC. It was then that Agrippa travelled to Hispania to put an end to the wars in the north that had at that time been dragging on for a number of years.

The coin types of *RPC*1 162-164 show several parallels with *RPC*1 149, in particular the depiction of a trophy on their reverses. Nevertheless, there are also differences between them. The engraver of *RPC*1 149 inscribed the legend on the reverse in three discontinuous horizontal lines, arranged around the trophy (*SABI-NVS/ C-M/ IM-P*), while the engraver of *RPC*1 162-164 preferred to follow the established conventions, inscribing the legend around the coin rim without any interruptions. This allowed sufficient space for the depiction of shields and spears at the base of the trophy and *RPC*1 162/3 even includes a curious V-shaped frame surrounding the trophy (Fig. 4). The bronze coins of *RPC*1 162/3 are quite similar to the *denarii RIC*12 265 (30/29 BC), which depict a trophy set on the prow of a galley to the right and a crossed rudder and anchor in a V shape at the base around the trophy (Fig. 5). The V-shaped frame around the trophy in *RPC*1 162/163 (19/18 BC) could therefore be viewed as nothing other than a highly schematic rudder and anchor, similar to those depicted in *RRC* 507/1a (Fig. 6). The types *RPC*1 162 and 163, like the coin issues *RIC* I^2 265, must therefore also refer to one of Agrippa's naval victories. It seems likely that the engraver of *RPC*1 149 did not see any need to add an anchor or rudder to his coins because he was already alluding to C. Calvisius Sabinus' maritime victory with the initials *CM* (*Classis Missenatis*). Likewise, the engravers who depicted an anchor and a rudder in *RPC*1 162 and 163 – even if only in a schematic form – did not require any inscription to highlight the contribution of the Missenum fleet to Agrippa's campaign in Hispania. The differences between the campaigns of C. Calvisius Sabinus and M. Vipsanius Agrippa in Hispania can therefore be inferred on the basis of the choice of coin type. While *RPC*1 149 only seems to refer to a maritime victory of C. Calvisius Sabinus in Hispania, *RPC*1 162-164 suggests that M. Vipsanius' success was a great deal more extensive.

*RPC*1 162 and 163 seem to celebrate a purely Roman maritime victory but the same cannot be said of *RPC*1 164. This last issue features numerous shields at the base of the trophy, seemingly representing a Roman victory on land, rather than at sea (Fig. 3). To this effect, the figure-of-eight shields depicted in the gold coins of *RRC* 507/1a, minted by M. Junius Brutus (*imperator*) and S. Casca Longus, resemble those engraved on *RPC*1 164, the only difference between them being the absence in *RPC*1 164 of war prows, which do however appear on *RRC* 507/1a. These final coin issues combined military and naval trophies, with prows and shields at the base, because they sought to emphasise the totality of the Roman victory, both on land and at sea (*terra marique*). The double military nature of *RRC* 507/1a is expressed separately in *RPC*1 162/3 and *RPC*1 164, and yet when they are considered in tandem, it is clear that they repeat the *terra marique* references of *RRC* 507/1a.[8] The

(5) Meloni 1958, p. 93 (è ormai comunemente anmeso che la flota misenese no staziona sempre ed interamente a Miseno); Vegetius, 4. 31: *Nam Misenatium classis Gallian Hispanias Mauretaniam Africam Aegyptum Sardiniam atque Siciliam habebat in proximo.*

(6) *CIL* II 3556.

(7) *Act. Triumph.*: Cap., ann. 719 =720 Varr.= 34 B. C.T.STATILIVS. T. FTAVRVS.PROCOS ANN.BCCXIX/ EX.AFRICA PR DIE. K. IVL; Tab. *Triumph. Barb.*: T.STATILIVS.TAVRVS. EX. AFRICA. PRID. K. IVL. TRIUMP. PALMAM. DEDIT.

(8) See also *RRC* 335 and *RRC* 393, Useful comments on the subject on *RRC* I, p. 335.

iconographic code chosen for the Carthago Nova coin issues of Agrippa of 19/18 BC is not to be considered random or capricious in any way. On the contrary, Agrippa's campaign in north-western Iberia is better understood as forming part of a dual strategy, both maritime and terrestrial. Viewed in this light, its geographical focus also acquires a new significance.

Agrippa's campaign in the Atlantic is only briefly narrated by Cassius Dio (54.11.2-5). The author (53.25) regards the *Cantabri* and the *Astures* as enemies of Rome between 26-19 BC, though in connection to the rebellion of 19 BC he only mentions the *Cantabri*. This fact has led most authors to accept that Agrippa did not fight against the *Astures* in 19/18 BC and did not go beyond the territory of the *Cantabri* (Roddaz 1984, p. 406), but despite the apparent modern consensus on this, Cassius Dio (54.11.2) is actually far more subtle in his words. The Bithynian historian says that "the *Cantabri*, who had been captured alive in the war (22 BC) and sold, had killed their masters in every case and returning home, had induced many to join in their rebellion" (Cary 1980, pp. 309-311). If read carefully, Cassius Dio does not limit Agrippa's sphere of action to ancient Cantabria, but on the contrary he specifies that the *Cantabri* captured in 22 BC took refuge among other more powerful warriors than themselves, namely not *Cantabri*, but just as strong as if they were, and indeed so strong that they caused the loss of "many of his [Agrippa's] soldiers" (Cassius Dio 54. 11.4).[9] These powerful warriors could be none other than the *Astures*.

Although current scholarship prefers to speak of the 'Cantabrian Wars', the truth is that Cassius Dio 53. 25.8 focused his narrative largely on the greater power of the *Astures*, and, furthermore, mentions no culminating defeat of the *Astures* before 19 BC. For example, when P. Carisius occupied Lancia, the main Asturian stronghold, in 25 BC, there is no mention of a previous assault on the site. It is stated simply that "Carisius took Lancia, the principle fortress of the *Astures* after it had been abandoned". The *Cantabri* were, on the other hand, much easier to defeat (Cassius Dio. 54.5.3) and for this reason Rome reserved its best general, P. Carisius, for the Asturian campaigns (Cassius Dio 54.5.1), while less reliable commanders – including the emperor Augustus – took charge of the Upper Ebro Valley (Cassius Dio 54.5.1). When P. Carisius turned his attention to the *Cantabri*, he was so effective that "most of them and the fiercest element perished" (Cary 1980, p. 293), while the survivors were reduced to slavery (22 BC). The *Cantabri* who in 19 BC fled from their masters and took refuge among more powerful warriors (54.5) must have taken refuge among the *Astures* inhabiting the present-day Spanish provinces of Lugo, Orense, Oviedo and parts of León and Zamora. In this context, it may therefore be understood that in 19/18 BC Agrippa launched his double campaign, by land and sea, against the *Astures*, and not against the *Cantabri*.

(9) Cary 1989, p. 311.

Agrippa's 19/18 BC land-and-sea campaign against the *Astures*, alluded to in *RPC*1 162-164, forced him to travel from the south of Hispania to the north[10]. Although Asturias and Galicia were ultimately incorporated into the province of *Hispania Citerior*, with its capital in Tarraco, these two regions were, during Agrippa's campaign, linked to Lusitania.[11] Pliny is quite clear in this respect (*H.N.* 4. 118), noting that *Lusitaniam cum Asturia et Gallaecia patere longitudine DXXXVI, Agrippa prodidit.* The building of the theatre in Emerita in honour of Agrippa (M. AGRIPPA. L. F. COS. III/ TRIB. POT. III)[12] supports the idea of a Roman land-based incursion starting from the south of Hispania in 19/8 BC, perhaps incorporating veteran contingents from this city and probably also from Colonia Patricia and Ulia (*CIL* II 1527). Likewise, the maritime campaign alluded to in *RPC*1 162-163 connected Carthago Nova, where Agrippa was named *duumvir quinquennalis* and patron,[13] with the city of Gades (Roddaz 1984, p. 409), where he was also made patron (*RPC*1 77-84).[14] Furthermore, the aplustres represented on some Gades coins (*RPC*1 81-84) (Fig. 7) demonstrate the role played by the Strait for the Missenum fleet (Maps 1 and 2), as it journeyed from Carthago Nova towards the Atlantic Ocean. The foundations of *Braccara Augusta*, *Lucus Augusti* and *Asturica Augusta* just after Agrippa's campaign (Roddaz 1984, p. 409) also support the idea that the main object of the 19/18 BC campaign was Asturias and Galicia and not Cantabria.

Agrippa declined all triumphal honours after his campaign in honour of Augustus (Cassius Dio 54.11.6), and therefore his victory in Asturias and Galicia is not represented explicitly in *RPC*1 162-164, contrary to the case of *RPC*1 149. When Cassius Dio (53.26.1) mentions the settling of veterans in Emerita Augusta in 25 BC ("Augustus discharged the more aged of his soldiers and allowed them to found a city in Lusitania, called Augusta Emerita")[15], he is not necessarily restricting the events to one year: other instances of the settlement of veterans could perfectly well have taken place afterwards, as Roman military activity in Iberia and Africa continued until well after this year. The constant references in Carthago Nova's coin issues to the magistrates involved in Roman colonies and *municipia* in the admission of new citizens in the city's census – the *duoviri quinquennales* – strongly suggest a continuous settlement of veterans in the city during a significant period of time. It is therefore logical to hold the view that the Roman campaigns in both northern and southern Spain between the years 28 and 18 BC were very similar in nature to the martial activity which

(10) He was also patron of Ampurias, although his interests in this city were probably more connected with activities in southern Gaul in 20 BC, and not with Ulia and Gades, both located in Baetica.

(11) Roddaz 1984, p. 411 and note 134; Trannoy 1981, p. 146 ss.

(12) *CIL* II 474; Roddaz 1984, pp. 416-417.

(13) *M(ARCO) AG(RIPPAE)/ L(VCI) F(ILIO), CO(N)S(VLI) (III, QVIN(QVENNALI)?) PATRON(O, COLONI)*; Koch 1979, pp. 205-214; Roddaz 1984, p. 414; Llorens 1994, p. 60.

(14) With *legends Agrippa/ Municipi Paren(s) or Municipi (patronus) parens)* Roddaz 1984, pp. 414, 604-605; Llorens Forcada 1994, p. 60 and note 143.

(15) Cary 1980, p. 261.

linked the Levant and Galicia in 138 BC. During that year, D. Junius Brutus fought in a campaign in Gallaecia with a large number of Lusitanian soldiers, moving from the south towards the north (App. *Ib.* 74) and after the campaign he rewarded them in the usual Roman manner with "land and town, which is called Valentia (*agros et oppidum dedit, quod vocatum est Valentia*" (Livy. *Per.* 55).[16]

CARTHAGO NOVA AND AUGUSTUS' ELUSIVE TRIUMPH OVER THE *ASTURES* AND THE *CANTABRI* (24 BC)

The Quadrans and Semis coin issues of *RPC*1 174-177, featuring the *duoviri quinquennales* P. Turullius and M. Postumius Albinus, depict on the obverse a quadriga (looking right or left, sometimes galloping and sometimes standing), preceded by a *vexillum* (Figs. 8, 9). Over the quadriga, the legend reads *V (R) I N K*, usually interpreted as *V(R)(bs) I(ulia) N(ova) K(arthago)*.[17] A tetrastyle temple is depicted on the reverse, with the legend *Augusto* (in the dative case) inscribed inside the tympanum. The temple is placed on a podium, sometimes depicted as a block (*RPC*1 174, 176, 177) and on other occasions in tiers (*RPC*1 175). In the Augustan period, there are no parallels in Hispania for a temple of such elegance (Llorens Forcada 1996, p. 73), neither in archaeological evidence nor in ancient texts (Etienne 1958, pp. 388-389, and note 8). Beltrán suggests that Carthago Nova may have followed in the wake of Tarraco's demand in 15 AD and petitioned Tiberius at some time around 19 AD[18] for the construction of a temple in honour of *Divus Augustus* (Tac. *Hist.*, 1.78).[19] Despite the attractiveness of this theory, it might be argued that there are many examples on Roman coins of tympanums which bear longer inscriptions, and the coin engraver would have had no difficulty in inscribing *Divo Augusto* instead of Augusto on the architrave of series *RPC*1 174-177. On the other hand, because the fact that Tarraco petitioned Rome for a temple honouring *Divus Augustus* does not imply that Carthago Nova necessarily did the same. The quadriga with *vexillum* in *RPC*1 174-177 depicts a triumphal march, which could only have taken place in the city of Rome and it is therefore more likely that the temple was linked to specific military victories- and as such would have been located in Rome itself on the Capitoline Hill- and not in Carthago Nova or Hispania.

The *denarii RRC* 385/1, coined by M. Volteius and dated at around 76 BC, depict on the reverse a tetrastyle temple in honour of *Jupiter Capitolinus* (Fig. 10). This was the sanctuary that was usually associated in Rome with the triumphal march of a victorious Roman general. The stylistic resemblance between this and the building in *RPC*1 174-177 is striking. The temple itself was dedicated by M. Horacius Pulvius in 509 BC, although it later burned down in a fire and was reconstructed by Sulla in 69 BC as a hexastyle building (Fig. 11), which was then dedicated by Q. Lutatius Catulus.[20] Although this hexastyle temple could not have served as a model for the coin in question, another more feasible link may be made to the temple to *Jupiter Feretrius*, also located on the Capitoline Hill. This relatively small tetrastyle temple was named after the "Thundering Jupiter" serving, as it did for several centuries, as a repository for war trophies (Fig. 12). The temple of *Jupiter Feretrius* had to be rebuilt by Augustus in 31 BC, owing to previous neglect and the loss of its roof (Sprincer 1954, p. 31). Such a building would have witnessed the march of the triumphal quadriga of Augustus after 31 BC and housed the trophies won in combat, and therefore it would seem highly plausible to identify the temple depicted on Carthago Nova coin issues *RPC*1 174-177 with this one.

Octavian's triple triumph over Dalmatia, Actium and Egypt was celebrated in Rome between 13 and 15 August of 29 BC. At the time, Octavian had not yet received the title of Augustus (which occurred on 16 January in 27 BC), so this celebration may not be linked to the series *RPC*1 174-177, which mentions *Augusto*. Neither is the ceremony returning the standards lost by Crassus to the Persians, which took place in Rome in 19 BC[21], a possibility, as this would not have involved a triumphal quadriga. As was pointed out by Cassius Dio (54. 8.2), the emperor "rode into the city on horseback" before the standards were placed in the corresponding temple. Augustus clearly considered the 19 BC celebration as a simple ovatio rather than a formal *triumph*, or he would have rode over the Capitoline Hill on a quadriga (Cary 1980, p. 300, and note 1). Furthermore, the standards were deposited in a heavily-adorned hexastyle temple dedicated to *Mars Ultor* (Fig. 13) - very different from the austere, tetrastyle temple of *Jupiter Feretrius*.

The representation of the triumphal march on a Carthago Nova coin would logically refer not to a victory in the Balkans or in the East but to one in Hispania. It is worth noting that it was not rare for a Roman military triumph to be depicted on a local issue, at least in the Mediterranean of Octavian's time. Many civic issues of the period depicted a tetrastyle temple facade with closed doors (set on a podium and sometimes with a globe or an eagle standing with its wings stretched out) and acroteria and antefixes along the line of the roof. This is the case, for example, of the coin series *RPC*1 622 and 624, from Turris Libisonis (Porto Torres) and Caralis (Cagliari) in Sardinia (Fig. 14, 15, Map 3). Grant, an acknowledged expert on the coin issues of these cities, generally assumes, as he does for Carthago Nova's *RPC*1 149, that the legends and im-

(16) Schlesinger 1959, pp. 52-53; Martí Matías 2005, pp. 3-7 proposes another *Valentia*, rather than the present-day Valencia, as regards the reference in Livy. Nevertheless, the truth is that neither Livy's passage nor any other reference found in inscriptions, texts or coins, provide proof for the creation of a *Valentia* in Lusitania. Furthermore, the present-day *Valentia* seems perfectly suited to Junius Brutus' *deductio*.

(17) Llorens Forcada 1994, p. 71.

(18) Beltrán 1953, p. 58; Llorens Forcada 1994, p. 73.

(19) Llorens Forcada 1994, pp. 72-73.

(20) Green 2004, p. 102; Nevertheless, as late as the beginning of 62 BC Caesar claimed, in bringing charges against Catulus, that many parts of the temple were still but half finished and that he wished to see Pompey entrusted with the completion of the work (Dio Cassius, 37.44.1; 43.16.6.).

(21) Cary 1980, p. 301.

ages on these coins are foundational in nature (FITA, pp. 205-206). The obverse legend of *RPC*1 622, M.L.D.C.P.(?) is therefore interpreted by this author as *M. Lurius Deductor Coloniae Patronus*, in reference to the supposed founder of the colony, M. Lurius, in 40 BC[22]. With regard to the *RPC*1 624 series from Caralis, the *RPC* editors follow Grant in assuming that "the occasion of this series could be the *constitutio* of the new municipium".[23] Nevertheless, as is shown by *RPC*1 (p. 162), Grant's proposed abbreviation for *RPC*1 622, M.L.D.C.P., appears highly unlikely and the interpretation of M. Lucius as the city's *patronus* is even more problematic. Furthermore, just as in Carthago Nova, there is no evidence of any temple in the Sardinia of the Augustan period being depicted in the style of *RPC*1 622, and so there is no way of proving that this was linked to any kind of civic and foundational ceremony around the time of 40 BC. Bearing all these factors in mind, it seems more plausible to suggest that a hitherto unknown magistrate with the initials 'P.M.L.' served as *Deductor Coloniae* in Turris Libisonis, and that this magistrate was in charge of settling discharged soldiers at some time after 40 BC, though not exactly 'in 40 BC'. The same may also be said of the Caralis issue *RPC*1 624, which mentions in the legend two entirely unknown suffetes (*ARISTO MVTVMBAL RICOCE SVF*).[24]

The tetrastyle temple depicted in the Sardinian series *RPC*1 622 and 624 cannot, however, be linked with certainty to the temple of *Jupiter Feretrius*. It is nevertheless true that these "Sardinian" temples emphasize highly visible closed doors on their facades, as do the homologous "Spanish" temples. Visibly closed doors at the temple of Janus in the *Forum Holitorium* were usually linked to Roman *imperatores* on the occasion of major military victories which brought subsequent peace within the Roman world. It is therefore highly unlikely that *RPC*1 622 and 624 were minted in celebration of the foundation of Turris Libisonis and Caralis around 40 BC, but much more plausible that they actually commemorated a military triumph that took place in Rome at a later date. The striking similarity in style between the two coin types allows us to conclude that the military victory commemorated on both coins was actually one and the same. It must be understood that such a triumph also involved Sardinia directly, and in this respect Cassius Dio (55.28.1) notes that it was precisely in 6 AD when "pirates overran a good many districts, so that Sardinia had no senator as governor for some years, but was in charge of soldiers with knights as commanders. Not a few cities rebelled, with the result that for two years the same men held office in the provinces which belonged to the people and were appointed instead of being chosen by lot" (Cary 1980, p. 467). Cassius Dio (56.17.1) goes on to state that in 9 AD "Germanicus announced the victory, and because of it, Augustus and Tiberius were permitted to add the title of *imperator* to their other titles and to celebrate a triumph" (Cary 1980, p. 37). Although on this occasion the triumphs were won ex *Pannonia et Dalmatia* in particular (Shipley 1931, pp. 41- 42) , it is more than likely that they were also associated with the island of Sardinia. Cassius Dio himself (55.28.1) links the military problems on the island with the great campaigns in Pannonia and Dalmatia, even though he does not go into detail regarding the Sardinian disturbances ("I shall not go into all these matters minutely, for many things not worthy of record happened")[25]. In this regard, Meloni has recently succeeded in completing the narrative of the Bithynian historian, proving via hard evidence from the epigraphy that the three military Roman campaigns (the Pannonian, the Dalmatian and the Sardinian) all concluded with the same joint triumph in Rome (Meloni 1958, p.15).

The temple depicted on *RPC*1 622 and 624 may therefore logically be associated with the temple of *Janus* in Rome because of the conclusion of all wars in the Roman world, and the magistrates named on these coin issues could perhaps be linked with the Roman generals who were in action in Sardinia between 6 and 8/9 AD. Their association with the temple of *Janus* might perhaps imply that these generals received the *ornamenta triumphalia* in Rome at the deferred triumph of Tiberius[26] on 16 January in 12 or 13 AD (Vell. 2.104; 2 121. 3) and that, once they had returned to Sardinia, they settled their veterans in Turris Libisonis and Caralis.[27]

The Sardinian coins depicting the temple of Janus in Rome do not, however, include a quadriga and a *vexillum*. This surely indicates that only the coin issues *RPC*1 174-177 allude to a victory of Augustus himself. Cassius Dio, the main source for the entire topic, once again provides the key to interpreting the differences on the reverses from Carthago Nova. In 53.26.4-5, the author recounts how, after fighting in Hispania against *Cantabri* and *Astures* in 26 and 25 BC, Augustus was saluted as *Imperator VIII* and the temple of Janus closed in consequence in 25 BC, both because of the final pacification of Spain after 200 years of war and because of six triumphs *ex Hispania* in the preceding decade.[28]

Cassius Dio states that Augustus did not care to celebrate his triumph in Spain, but he also adds that M. Vinicius was associated with Augustus' victories because of his "successes in the German war (Cassio Dio 53.26.4) and that "a triumphal arch was erected in the Alps" (Cary 1980, p. 263).

(22) *RPC*1, 162.

(23) *RPC*1, p. 163. See also Sollai 1989, pp. 63-66.

(24) Sollai 1989, 54-61.

(25) Cary 1980, p. 467.

(26) In 17 AD Tiberius dedicated the temple of Janus in the *Forum Holitorium* (Tac. *Ann.* 2. 49) and it seems highly plausible that the completion of the works in this temple should be connected with the *manubiae* of the triumph; Shipley 1931, p. 42.

(27) Other cities in the Mediterranean also depict the temple of Jupiter Feretrius without a quadriga, as is the case of Thaena, *RPC*1 803-805. L. Passienus Rufus is explicitly mentioned in Thaena *RPC*1 804, and we do know that he received the *ornamenta triumphalia* in 3 AD. The Gades coin issue *RPC*1 95 may also be identified with this temple and may be related to Agrippa in 19/18 BC.

(28) Vell. 2.90; Hor. *Carm.* 3.14 compares Augustus with Hercules, benefactor of mankind.

In this last passage, Cassius Dio implicitly suggests that Augustus closed the doors of the Janus temple in Rome in 25 BC, hut this event probably in fact took place after his arrival in Rome in the spring of 24 BC for the marriage of his daughter Julia to Marcellus, his nephew (Lacey 1996, pp. 42-43). Veterans of P. Carisius had been settled at Augusta Emerita in Spain (Cassius Dio 53.26.1), but it is quite logical too that the discharged veterans of Augustus were waiting for their settlements. Many demands were made on him after 24 BC via petitions of the Senate, including "to consent both to being named dictator and to becoming commissioner of the grain supply" (Cassius Dio 54.1.3),[29] and implying that Augustus took care of many different affairs after his arrival. He was also asked to become censor (54.2.1),[30] so that he could give priority to matters of a military nature such as the settlement of discharged veterans. The composition depicted in *RPC*1 174-177 may therefore be viewed as a portrayal of the triumphal honours accorded to Augustus in 25 BC, to the closure of the Janus temple in Rome, and to the arrival of Augustus in the spring of 24 BC. It is very likely that Augustus was accompanied into Rome by veterans from his campaign against the *Cantabri* and the *Astures*. As had occurred with the colonies of Turris Libisonis and Caralis, it may also be assumed that some of the veterans who took part in his entry in Rome were settled in Carthago Nova with a *deductio* made in 24 BC, on the occasion of the closure of the temple of Janus.

Carthago Nova and the Roman-Mauritanian victories of 6/7, 17/18 and 23 AD.

The victorious type chosen for the Carthago Nova coin issue *RPC*1 157 (Fig. 16) is very similar to many of the victorious types minted by Juba II (25 BC - 24 AD) in North Africa (Fig. 17). The legend reads C. AQVINVS MELA II VIR QVIN, with a *Victoria* walking towards the right, holding a wreath and a palm branch. *RPC*1 assigns this coin to the reign of Augustus, although with a question mark, and makes no more precise attribution regarding its chronology (*RPC*1, p. 93). Llorens Forcada, on the other hand, catalogues it as the '8th coin issue' of Carthago Nova, dating it to after 31 BC. It is her view that the Hispanic *Victoria* with the wreath and palm branch is a reproduction of the Cyrenaican reverses of P. Scarpus, struck in 31 BC (*RRC* 546) (Fig. 18). This same author goes on to suggest that the *signa* on the obverse (associated with the legend P BAEBIVS POLLIO II VIR QVIN) allude to the first settlement of veterans in Carthago Nova (Llorens Forcada 1996, pp. 56-57).

RRC 546 could very well have inspired other coin series, too, outside the Cyrenaican region. *Victoria* walking towards the right with a palm and a wreath is certainly a type used by Juba II between 5 and 23 AD (years XXX-XXXXVIII according to the king's royal calendar).[31] The Cyrenaican *denarii* of P. Scarpus are nevertheless rare and chronologically restricted to the first months of 31 BC[32], while on the other hand the Mauritanian and Iberian series provide an exact match, both in the style of their reverses and in the bronze material used. Lastly, there are no examples of the Cyrenaican type found in an archaeological context in Hispania, but the Mauritanian one is present, as is evidenced by the bronze excavated near Sagunto, dated to Juba's year XXXXXVIII (23 AD)[33]. Another find originating in Carthago Nova, coined under the name of *Rex Ptol(omeus)* and recorded in an archaeological context in Iol Caesarea/Cherchell[34] (Map 2), provides further support for the existence of maritime contacts between the kingdom of Juba II and Ptolemy in Africa and Hispania, something which cannot, on the other hand, be demonstrated for Cyrenaica in the time of P. Scarpus. If it is understood that *RPC*1 157 does in fact follow a Mauritanian model rather than a Cyrenaican one, then its chronology should also be ascribed to 5-7 AD (Juba's regnal chronology XXX-XXXII),[35] 15 AD (Juba's XXXX),[36] 17/18 AD (Juba's XXXXIII),[37] 21/22 AD (Juba's XXXXVI),[38] or 23/4 AD (Juba's XXXXVIII).[39] It was during these years that Juba II minted the *Victoria* walking to the right type (with the palm branch and the wreath) and this coincided with Roman-Mauritanian victories in North Africa. It might also be suggested that the Carthago Nova type *RPC*1 157, too, could well have been coined in connection with these Romano-Mauritanian triumphs.

The victorious Mauritanian type first appeared in Juba II's years XXX, XXXI and XXXII (5-7 AD),[40] coinciding with the joint triumph of G. Cornelius Lentulus Cossus and the forces of the African king. The same type appeared in the year XXXX (15/16 AD) celebrating a similar victory as in 5-7 AD although unfortunately barely anything is known about it (Coltelloni-Trannoy 1997, p. 50). A similar issue appeared at the start of the war against Tacfarinas, in XXXXIII (17/18 AD), celebrating the victories of M. Furius Camillus, once again in coalition with the forces of Juba II.[41] In 20 AD, however, instability intensified in the north of Africa to such an extent that the *legio IX Hispana* was summoned there to join the *legio III Augusta*, under the command of the proconsul L. Apronius.[42] With these means at his disposal, Q. Junius Blaesus achieved, apparently without any significant Mauritanian contribution, a great victory in XXXXVI (21/22 AD), earning him a triumph and the

(29) Cary 1980, p. 285.

(30) Cary 1980, p. 287.

(31) Mz. nos. 193-203, 282-289; Coltelloni-Trannoy 1997, pp. 49-51, 53; Roller 2003, pp. 110-113.

(32) López Sánchez 2010.

(33) Gozalbes, Ripollès 2002, p. 233 and 520, no 44.

(34) Llorens Forcada 1994, p. 112, note. 39; Tarradell 1963, p. 14.

(35) Mz. nos.194-201, 282.

(36) Mz. nos. 283.

(37) Mz. nos. 202-203, 284.

(38) Mz. nos. 285-287.

(39) Mz. nos. 288.

(40) Mz. nos. 280-282.

(41) Mz, nos. 202, 203, 284; Coltelloni-Trannoy 1997, pp. 50-51 and note 17.

(42) Tac. *Ann.* 3. 20-21; 4. 13.3-5 Vell. 2 116; Coltelloni-Trannoy 1997, p. 51.

title of *imperator*. In XXXXVIII (June of 23 AD), the Roman-Mauritanian troops won another great victory which practically brought the war to an end and it was only then that the *legio IX Hispana* finally left Africa for Pannonia (Coltelloni-Trannoy 1997, p. 51). The military operations of 24 AD were in fact the last of the long series of wars which united Rome and the Mauritanian monarchy in North Africa and immediately after this Ptolemy was recognised by Rome as Mauritanian *rex* (Tac. *Ann.* 4. 23-26).

Many years of conflict transpired between the first Roman-Mauritanian triumphs of 5-7AD and the final victories of 23 and 24 AD, during which Hispania played a major role in Africa. Referring to a slightly later period, Rebuffat even speaks of a "[military] avalanche espagnole" (Rebuffat 1997, p. 292). The numerous issues coined by Tiberius in Sagunto which depict a war ship on the reverse (occasionally crowned by a Victory) may perhaps be related to the years during which the emperor oversaw the African conflict (15/6-24 AD) (Fig. 19).[43] Rome supplied important logistical and maritime support from Hispania, presumably making use of the Missenum fleet, which left a mark on cities such as Gades[44] and Carthago Nova, where Juba II was made patron (*CIL* II 3417, Llorens Forcada 1996, p. 66), like Agrippa before him. Again following in the footsteps of Agrippa, who had been named *duumvir quinquennalis* of Carthago Nova in 19/18 BC, Juba II also received the same honour, as is indeed portrayed in *RPC*1 169 (CN ATELLIVS PONTI II V Q/IVBA REX IVBAE F II V Q) (Fig. 20). It is the view of Roller that such an honour reflected the "politics and economy in the contemporary western Mediterranean" (Roller 2003, p. 156). Juba II's actions in Gades and Carthago Nova form an exact replica of Agrippa's dispositions in 19/18 BC, given that both aimed to exert military control over the two main ports of the Iberian 'Mediterranean-Atlantic'. The position of patron and *duumvir quinquennalis* of these two cities was probably linked to the coordination of the movements of the imperial fleet of Missenum between Africa and Hispania.

Throughout his reign in North Africa Juba II was supported by Rome and he must therefore have reciprocated by the provision of aid. One of the clearest opportunities to do this would have been in the settlement of veterans in Roman colonies and *municipia* and it seems that it was precisely with this in mind that Juba II was chosen as *duumvir quinquennalis* of Carthago Nova. This also lies behind the representation of the Roman lustral instruments of the *duumvir* Laetilius Apalus in *RPC*1 169, both on the reverse and obverse and accompanied by the African-Egyptian symbols of Juba II. The lotus and the crescent are frequently explained in these Hispanic coins from a purely economic or religious perspective[45] despite the fact that, when symbols of Isis are found on Mauritanian coins, they also carry military and dynastic connotations.[46] Isis is frequently depicted as *Regina* in the Mauritanian kingdom and therefore most of the African-Egyptian symbols that accompany her on coins – the crescent, the sun, the globe, the cow or ox and the *uraeus* – are also connected to military and regal aspects (Coltelloni-Trannoy, 1997, pp. 177-181). All of this leads us to conclude that Juba II and his colleague Laetilius Apalus took part in the lustral ceremony and were involved in the drawing-up of a new census of citizens at the time of the issue of *RPC*1 169. The new citizens that were settled in Carthago Nova by Apalus and Juba II may be assumed to have been discharged soldiers (perhaps Mauritanian auxiliaries?), who had played a role in some of the famous African victories of 6-23 AD.

The *RPC*1 172/173 coin issues are similar in many ways to the *RPC*1 169 series, though of course on this occasion it was Ptolemy, and not Juba II, who was being celebrated as a Mauritanian king (Fig. 21). The name Ptolemy, as *rex*, appears inside a wreath on the reverse of the coin, mirroring the way that the name Augustus, as emperor, appears on the obverse. In contrast to *RPC*1 169, there is in this issue no precise indication as to whether Ptolemy was named *duumvir quinquennalis*, or any correlation on obverse or reverse between the Roman lustral symbols and the African-Egyptian ones of the Mauritanian kingdom (which only appear, minimised, in *RPC*1 172/80). It may therefore be concluded that the authority responsible for these issues was Juba II and not the new royal prince. These coins seem to have appeared immediately after the presentation of Ptolemy as the successor of Juba II in Caesarea in 5 AD,[47] a hypothesis backed up by most of the scholars interested in these coin issues.[48] If *RPC*1 172-173 was indeed coined straight after 5 AD, then it could also be related to the celebration in 6/7 AD of the joint victory of C. Lentulus Cossus and Juba II in Africa,[49] which in turn also explains why the Mauritanian monarchy was at the time interested in Carthago Nova as a settlement town for veterans. Besides, coin series like *RPC*1 160 seem to have accompanied the settlement of a contingent of soldiers in Carthago Nova, and the character of these coins, even more than in the case of *RPC*1 172/173, point towards a *deductio* of former Mauritanian auxiliaries.

Out of the three possible time periods for the Carthago Nova series analysed here (5-7, 17/18, and 23/24 AD), 17/18 AD provides the best match for the quinquennial issues of *RPC*1 169. In 23/24 AD, Juba was already dead or on the point of dying and in this context the *RPC*1 172-174 series appears to fit in well with the presentation of the new *prin-*

(43) Ripollès et alii, 2002, p. 478, no. 416; p. 509, no. 517.

(44) Avienus, *Ora Maritima*, 5. 277-283; Llorens Forcada, 1994, p. 66.

(45) Economic interpretation in Roller 2003, p. 157 and note 216; Religious considerations in García-Bellido 1991, pp. 76-77; Llorens Forcada 1994, pp. 65-66 and note 176, follows here.

(46) Coltelloni-Trannoy, 1997, p. 180, links the symbols of Isis as they appear on coins with triumphal ornaments in Caesarea (Mz. No. 195), in relation to a victory involving "une communauté de Romains (ou indigènes en voir de romanisation?)".

(47) Year in which Ptolomy assumed the *toga virilis* Roller 2003, p. 244 and note 3.

(48) The lotus and crescent are linked to this city during this specific time period Mz. nos. 351-356, Alexandropoulos, nos. 209, 212.

(49) Benabou 1976, p. 64 and note 79; Coltelloni-Trannoy 1997, p. 49 and notes 10-11; Roller 2003, p. 110.

ceps, who became *rex* in 5 AD. The years of 23/24 AD, the transition period in between the kings Juba II and Ptolomy then appear as the only serious proposal for the coin issues *RPC*1 157, as no Mauritanian royal symbols or Mauritanian names are visible on them. The reverse of this coin type is identical to that of Juba II's triumphal series (*Victoria* with palm branch and wreath) except that it includes complete Roman *signa* on the obverse. For this reason, it is possible that on this occasion the veteran *deductio* did not include any Mauritanian auxiliaries.

Conclusions: the Missenum fleet, veteran *deductiones* and the issues of Carthago Nova

Numismatists studying the local coinage minted during the Julian dynasty in Hispania are divided between those who consider that the army played a significant role and those who believe that this has been overvalued. García-Bellido, in her numerous studies on Hispano-Roman coins, has defended the relationship between civic coinage in Iberia and the Roman army, pointing out that there were "very clear administrative routes through which the army was provided with small bronze coinage of small denominations in coin issues from mints that were involved with the supply of the army, coinage that was transported in particular to the north-west of Hispania for the maintenance of troops".[(50)] Ripollés represents the opposing view, on the other hand, preferring to interpret Iberian coinage as strictly civic and local in character. In this regard, he points out that "civic coinings must be connected with local needs more than with the needs of the Roman state or with state-driven coin issues". Furthermore, he emphatically adds that "in *Hispania* it is not possible to link the production of the towns with payments to the army or with any other state expenditure".[(51)]

These academic discrepancies among Spanish scholars also have their counterparts on an international scale among those who study other areas of the Roman world. Mitchell, for instance, has attempted to prove, through a variety of different texts and inscriptions, that in the third century AD the cities of Anatolia and Asia Minor were expected to aid Roman military expedition forces crossing the region (Mitchell 1983, pp. 133-134). This essentially represents the archaeological theory proposed by Green, who back in 1941 linked the cities of Asia Minor and their products with legionary and auxiliary garrisons along the Danube (Gren 1941). While many of the civic communities of Asia Minor were never actually approached physically by any army, this did not mean, according to these authors, that the presence of the army was not felt (Mitchell 1983, p. 142). Ziegler went on to apply Green's theories to coinage, pointing out that, as regards the exchange of products between different regions, "numismatics is able to contribute more to the subject of the 'Roman army in the East' than ancient historians have previously assumed" (Ziegler 1996, p. 119). Rebuffat, on the other hand, has published a comprehensive study of the second and third-century AD coin issues of Asia Minor bearing Roman standards, going as far as asserting that it was the imperial legates or proconsuls, not the civic authorities, who were the true promoters of many of the local issues in the region (Rebuffat 1997, p. 414).

Disputing the views of Ziegler and Rebuffat, Katsari points out that imperial bronze coinage did not easily meet the needs of troops operating in a frontier region (Katsari 2011, pp. 235-236), and, following in the footsteps of Elton, she also expresses the opinion that "the intermittent process of minting and the large chronological space [of many of these minting cities], lasting one or more decades, could suggest the exact opposite of Ziegler's theory" (Katsari 2011, p. 216). For Katsari, neither the movements of armies or the presence of established garrisons are helpful in explaining patterns in the production of local coinage and in the dispersal of civic money. She suggests instead that "extensive trading activities and the development of urban centres (are) the main factors for the monetisation of a region" (Katsari 2011, p. 220). With prudence and common sense, Elton also warns that "the reasons for striking local issues are not well understood" and he asserts that we do not know "how many coins were struck in any given period" (Elton 2005, p. 299). He concludes that "local minting was not necessary to facilitate the supply process" (Elton 2005, p. 297-298). Klose points out also that local festivities and other regional events, rather than the army, often prompted many of these local coin issues (Klose 2005).

These pages have not been written with the intention of defending or attacking any of these positions concerning the production and distribution of local coinage in Hispania. Nevertheless, the study of certain coin issues from Carthago Nova which might be considered to be particularly relevant demonstrates that there are certain aspects of both these divergent stances which seem to apply to this Iberian city. It may be argued, for example, that religious objects such as the *simpulum*, the *aspergillum*, the *securis* and the *apex* (Figs. 20, 22) are as common in the issues of Carthago Nova as are military artefacts. These religious objects were related, however, not only to the *pontifex maximus* or *augur* serving a Julian prince in Rome, but also to the local *lustrum* officiated over by the *duoviri quinquennales*[(52)] (Fig. 23). The main role of the *duoviri quinquennales* (local censors) in a Roman colony or *municipium* was to register citizens and administer the census and, as in Rome,

(50) García-Bellido 2006, p. 674, and note 1 ("vías administrativas muy bien fijadas por las que se abastecía al ejército de numerario menor, de bronce, en partidas monetarias procedentes de unas cecas comprometidas con el abastecimiento militar y especialmente llevadas al NO (de Hispania) para el mantenimiento de la tropa"). See also the author's bibliography as regards this data, pp. 721-722.

(51) Ripollès 1998, p. 384 ("las acuñaciones cívicas han de conectarse con las necesidades locales antes que con las necesidades del estado romano o con programas monetarios de origen estatal ... en *Hispania* no es posible relacionar la producción de las ciudades con la remuneración al ejército o con cualquier otro gasto estatal").

(52) Despite the term *quinquennalis*, few believe nowadays that the positions held by these *duoviri* were actually five years in duration. Instead, they probably lasted only one year, Llorens Forcada 1996, p. 29 and note 31, with bibliography.

to look after the *lectio senatus* and *recognitio equitum*, as well as the management of local finance and public works (Daremberg & Saglio II (a), p. 993). The census, commissioned to *IIviri* or *IVviri quinquennales*, took place in Roman colonies and *municipia* at the same time as in Rome, as was established in the *lex Iulia municipalis* (Daremberg & Saglio II (b), p.1000). Significantly, all of the magistrates recorded in issues from Carthago Nova were *duoviri quinquennales*, and not simple *duoviri* (Llorens Forcada 1996, p. 29). In addition, many of these *duoviri quinquennales* were very high dignitaries, as in the case of Agrippa (*RPC*1 164) (Figs. 3-4), Tiberius Nero (*RPC*1 166), the Mauritanian king Juba (*RPC*1 169) (Fig. 20), Nero and Drusus (*RPC*1 179-181) (Fig. 24) and Caligula (*RPC*1 182-184) (Fig. 25). Other (unknown) *duoviri quinquennales* of the city bore Italian names unrecorded in Hispania and probably had closer links to Italy than to Carthago Nova itself. In any case, all of these figures can be directly or indirectly linked to veterans settled in the colony of Carthago Nova. It is because of this and not merely for reasons of prestige that high Italian and Mauritanian dignitaries accepted civic responsibilities in the city. It seems then clear that Carthago Nova was not just another Roman city in Hispania. It is very likely that its magnificent port housed significant detachments of the imperial fleet of Missenum in the time between the Battle of Actium (31 BC) and the incorporation of Africa (41 AD)[53].

After analysing a few highly significant coin issues from Carthago Nova, it seems plausible to assert that Carthago Nova coins were to a large extent linked to the different settlements of Roman veterans in the city and it might also be suggested that there were probably as many coin issues in Carthago as there were *deductiones*. In partial response to the aforementioned question of Elton, the volume of production of civic coin series in Carthago Nova[54] was probably contingent on the number of veterans discharged on each occasion, which does not necessarily mean, of course, that the coin issues of Carthago Nova were produced to supply each veteran soldier with small-denomination coinage. Nevertheless, it does appear logical to believe that the production of these coins was linked to the roles undertaken by the local censors – the *duoviri quinquennales*. This role specifically included officiating at lustral ceremonies, and this was probably accompanied by speeches, marches and public manifestations of loyalty towards the family of the *Iulii*, both in Imperial Rome and in Carthago Nova. Lastly, the diverse iconography displayed in these coin issues may be attributable to the different circumstances surrounding the discharge of each group of veterans. *RPC*1 174-177 implicitly indicates, for example, that the veterans who were settled in Carthago Nova in 24 BC took part in the victorious arrival of Augustus into Rome. The veterans settled in 6/7 and in 17/18 AD (*RPC*1 169, 172-174) fought, on the other hand, in the contemporary African wars and Mauritanian auxiliaries were probably included within their ranks.

Elton, Katasari and Ripollès are right to emphasise the essentially local characteristics surrounding the minting and distribution of small-denomination civic coinage in the Roman world, but, similarly, the influence of the international events behind these celebrations cannot be ignored. Had there been no Missenum fleet or regular military campaigns in Iberia or Africa linked to Carthago Nova, then the coinage dating roughly between 31 BC and 41 AD would never have been issued in the city. Future studies of the coin series of Hispania and Africa could perhaps explore further the role played by these 'local festivities' which are the veteran *deductiones* both in colonies and municipalities throughout the entire Mediterranean. In this regard, it may also be stated that it is probably no coincidence that the end of civic minting in the West should have coincided with the end of the Julian dynasty and its military campaigns across the Mediterranean.

(53) The thesis is defended by Gimeno 1994: for references and further discussion, see also Arrayás Morales 2005, p. 80.

(54) Llorens Forcada 1994, p. 95 estimates the total number of dies produced for every single coin issue.

ABBREVIATIONS

Act. Triumph.= Mommsen Th. (ed.) (1863). *Corpus Inscriptionum Latinarum (CIL I). Inscriptiones Latinae Antiquissimae. Acta Triumphorum.* Berlin, pp. 453-461.

Alexandropoulos= Alexandropoulos J. (2000). *Les monnaies de l'Afrique antique 400 av. J.-C.-40 ap. J.-C.* Toulouse.

Cary= Cary E. (1980). *Dio's Roman History. VI Volume, With an English translation.* The Loeb Classical Library, Cambridge (Mass.) - London (first printed 1917).

CIL II= Hübner A. (ed.) (1869). *Corpus Inscriptionum Latinarum. Inscriptiones Hispaniae Latinae.* Vol II. Berlín.

Daremberg & Saglio II(a)= Daremberg M. Ch., Saglio E. (1887). *'Censor' Dictionnaire des antiquités grecques et romanies d'après les texts et les monuments.* Tome Premier, Deuxième partie (C). Paris, pp. 990-999.

Daremberg & Saglio II(b)= Daremberg M. Ch., Saglio E. (1887). *'Censor' Dictionnaire des antiquités grecques et romanies d'après les texts et les monuments.* Tome Premier, Deuxième partie (C). Paris, pp. 999-1001.

FITA= Grant M. (1946). *From Imperium to Auctoritas: A Historical Study of Aes Coinage in the Roman Empire 49 B.C.-A.D. 14.* Cambridge.

Mz= Mazard J. (1955). *Corpus nummorum Numidiæ Mauretaniæque.* Paris.

RIC I²= Sutherland C. H. V., Carson R. A. G. (1984). *The Roman Imperial Coinage. Vol. I. Revised Edition. From 31 BC to AD 69.* London.

*RPC*1= Burnett A. M., Amandry M., Ripolles P. P. (1992). *Roman Provincial Coinage. Vol. 1. From the death of Caesar to the death of Vitellius (44 BC-AD 69)*. London.

RRC= Crawford M. (1974). *Roman Republican Coinage. 2 vols*. Cambridge.

Tab. Triumph. Barb.= Mommsen Th. (ed.). *Corpus Inscriptionum Latinarum (CIL I). Inscriptiones Latinae Antiquissimae. Tabulae Triumphorum Barberinianae*, pp. 477-479.

Schlesinger= Schlesinger A. C. *Livy with an English Translation. XIV. Summaries, Fragments and Obsequens*. London - Cambridge (Mass.).

References

Arrayás Morales I. (2005). *Morfología histórica del territorio de Tarraco (ss. III-I. a.C.) (Collecció Instrumenta 19)*. Barcelona.

Benabou M. (1976). *La résistance africaine à la romanisation*. Paris.

Beltrán A. (1953). 'Los monumentos en las monedas hispano-romanas', *Archivo Español de Arqueología*, 26, pp. 39-66.

Coltelloni-Trannoy M. (1997). *Le royaume de Maurétanie sous Juba II et Ptolémée (25 av. J.-C.-40 ap. J.-C.). Études d'Antiquités Africaines*. Paris.

Curchin L. A. (2004). *The Romanization of Central Spain: complexity, diversity and change in a provincial hinterland*. London.

Klose D. O. A. (2005). 'Festivals and Games in the Cities of the East during the Roman Empire', in Howgego C., Jeuchert V., Burnett A. (eds), Coinage and identity in the Roman Provinces. Oxford, pp. 125-133.

Elton H. (2005). 'Military supply and the south coast of Anatolia in the third century AD', in Mitchell S., Katsari C. (eds), *Patterns in the Economy of Roman Asia Minor*. Swansea, pp. 289-304.

Etienne R. (1958). *Le culte impérial dans la péninsule ibérique d'Auguste à Dioclétien*. Paris.

García Bellido Mª. P. (1991). 'Las religiones orientales en la península ibérica', *Archivo Español de Arqueología*, 64, pp. 37-81.

García Bellido Mª. P. (2006). 'Ejército, moneda y política económica', in García Bellido M.ª P. (coord.), *Los campamentos romanos en Hispania (27 a.C.-192 d.C.). El abastecimiento de moneda. Volumen II (Anejos de Gladius. Consejo Superior de Investigaciones Científicas)*. Madrid.

Gimeno J. (1994). 'Plinio, Nat. Hist. III, 3, 21: reflexiones acerca de la capitalidad de Hispania Citerior', *Latomus*, 53, pp. 39-79.

Gozalbes M., Ripollès P. P. (2002). 'Circulación y dispersión', in Ripollès P. P., Llorens Mª M. (eds), *Arse-Saguntum. Historia monetaria de la ciudad y su territorio*. Sagunto, pp. 215-256.

Green S. J. (2004). *Ovid, Fasti 1: a commentary*. Leiden.

Gren E. (1941). *Kleinasien und der Ostbalkan in der wirtschaftlichen Entwicklung der römischen Kaiserzeit*. Uppsala.

Katsari K. (2011). *The Roman Monetary System. The Eastern provinces from the First to the Third Century AD*. Cambridge.

Koch K. (1979). 'Agrippa und Neukarthago', *Chiron*, 9, pp. 205-214.

Lacey W. K. (1996). *Augustus and the Principate. The Evolution of the System (ARCA = Classical and medieval texts. Papers and Monographs)*. Leeds.

López Sánchez F. (2010). 'Military Units of Mark Antony and Lucius Verus: Numismatic Recognition of Distinction', *Israel Numismatic Research*, 5, pp. 123-138, pl. 21.

Llorens Forcada Mª M. (1994). *La ciudad de Carthago Nova: las emisiones romanas*. Murcia.

Manconi D., Pianu G. (1981). *Sardegna (Guide archeologiche laterza 14)*. Roma-Bari.

Martí Matías M. R. (2005). *Una Fundación de Valencia (Hispania). Antítesis de la tesis actual (BAR International Series 1443)*. Oxford.

Masstoni A., Spanu P. G., Zucca R. (2005). *Mare Sardum. Merci, mercati e scambi maritime della Sardegna antica (Colla del Dipartimento di Storia dell'Univesità degli Studi di Sassari 26)*. Roma.

Meloni P. (1958). *L'amministrazione della Sardegna da Augusto all'invasione vandálica*. Roma.

Mitchell S. (1983). 'The Balkans, Anatolia, and Roman Armies across Asia Minor', in Mitchell S. (ed.), *Armies and Frontiers in Roman and Byzantine Anatolia. Proceedings of a colloquium held at University College, Swansea, in April 1981 (British Institute of Archaeology at Ankara. Monograph No. 5) (Bar International Series 156)*. Oxford, pp. 131-150.

Morrison J. S. (with contributions by Coates J. F.) (1996). *Greek and Roman Oared Warships 399–30 B.C. (Oxbow 62)*. Oxford.

Pitassi M. (2009). *The Navies of Rome*. Woodbridge - Rochester.

Rebuffat F. (1997). *Les enseignes sur les monnaies d'Asie Mineur. Des origines à Sévère Alexandre*. Athens.

Ripollès P. P. (2005). 'Coinage and Identity in the Roman Provinces: Spain', in Howgego C. J., Heuchert V., Burnett A. (eds), *Coinage and Identity in the Roman Provinces*. Oxford, pp. 79- 93.

Ripollès P. P. (1998). 'Las acuñaciones cívicas romanas de la península ibérica (44 a.C. -54 d.C.)', in Alfaro C. et alii, *Historia monetaria de Hispania antigua*. Madrid, pp. 335-395.

Ripollès P. P. et alii (2002). *Arse-Saguntum: historia monetaria de la ciudad y su territorio*. Sagunto.

Roddaz J.-M. (1984). *Marcus Agrippa (Bibliothèque des Écoles Françaises d'Athènes et de Rome 253)*. Rome.

Roller D W. (2003). *The world of Juba II and Kleopatra Selene. Royal Scholarship on Rome's African Frontier*. New York - London.

Shipley F. W. (1931). 'Chronology of the Building Operations in Rome from the Death of Caesar to the Death of Augustus', *Memoirs of the American Academy in Rome*, 9, pp. 7-60.

Sollai M. (1989). *Le monete della Sardegna romana*. Sassari.

Sprincer L. A. (1954). 'The cult and Temple of Jupiter Feretrius', *The Classical Journal*, 50.1, pp. 27-32.

Stannard C. (2005). 'Numismatic Evidence for Relations between Spain and Central Italy at the Turn of the Second and First Centuries BC', *Revue Suisse de Numismatique*, 84, pp. 47-80.

Tarradell M. (1963). 'Notas de Numismática Antigua norteafricana', *Numisma*, 13, pp. 9-16.

Trannoy A. (1981). *La Galice romaine: recherches sur le nord-ouest de la péninsule Ibérique dans l'Antiquité*. Talence - Paris.

Viereck H. D. L. (1975). *Die römische Flotte: Classis Romana*. Hertford.

Ziegler R. (1996). 'Civic coins and imperial campaigns', in Kennedy D. L., (ed.), *The Roman Army in the East (Journal of Roman Archaeology. Supplementary Series 18)*, pp. 119-134.

List of Figures

1.- *RPC*1 149, Obv.: HEL POLLIO ALBINVS II Q (V), Female bust, r., wearing veil and diadem; rev: SABINVS CM IMP, trophy. Trustees of the British Museum
2.- *RRC* 511/2b, Sex. Pompeius, Obv.: MAG PIVS IMP ITER, Head of Neptune right, trident over shoulder; Rev.: PRAEF CLAS ET ORAE MARIT EX SC, Trophy with trident above and anchor below, prow-stem on left and aplustre on right, two heads of Scylla at base. Trustess of the British Museum
3.- *RPC*1164, HIBERO PRAE(F) M AGRIP QVIN, bare head (of Agrippa?), r.; L. BENNIO PRAEF, trophy. Trustees of the British Museum
4.- *RPC*1163, Obv.:L. BEN PRAE IMP CAES QVIN, bare head (of Augustus?), rev: Q VARIO PRAEF, trophy. Trustees of the British Museum
5.- RIC I² 265a, Obv.: Bare head right, Rev.: IMP CAESAR, trophy set on prow of galley right; crossed rudder and anchor at base
6.- *RRC* 507/1a, Brutus Imp with Casca Longus, Obv.: BRVTVS IMP, Head of Brutus r., laurel-wreath as border; Rev.: CASCA LONGVS, Trophy with curved sword and two spears on l., and figure-of-eight shield on r.; at base, on either side, prow and sword with squared handle. Border of dots. Trustees of the British Museum
7.- *RPC*1 80, Obv.: AGRIPPA, head of Agrippa, l., wearing rostral crown; Rev.: MVNICIPI (PATRONVS) PARENS, aplustre. Trustees of the British Museum
8.- *RPC*1 175, Obv.: P TVRVLL(IO) V (R) I N K II VIR QVIN(QVEN), quadriga walking, l.; in front, vexillum; Rev.: V I N K M POSTV(M) ALBINV(S) II VIR QVINQ(V) ITER, tetrastyle temple, inscribed AVGVSTO. Trustees of the British Museum
9.- *RPC*1 174, Obv.: P TVRVLL(IO) V I N K II VIR QVIN(QVEN), quadriga walking, R.; in front, vexillum; Rev.: V I N K M POSTV ALBINVS II VIR QVINQ ITER, tetrastyle temple, inscribed AVGVSTO. Trustees of the British Museum
10.- *RRC*. 385/1, Obv. : Head of Jupiter laureate to r., Rev.: M. VOLTEI. M. F. tetrastyle temple of Jupiter Capitolinus with closed portal and thunderbolt in tympanum. Trustess of the British Museum
11.- *RRC* 487/1, Obv.: CAPITOLINVS, Bare head of Jupiter r., Rev.: Temple of Jupiter Capitolinus: richly decorated hexastyle temple with three garlands hanging between columns; PETILLIVS in exergue. Trustess of the British Museum

12.- *RRC* 439/1, Obv.: MARCELINVS, Head of the consul M. Claudius Marcellinus righ,t before, triskeles behind; Rv.: MARCELLVS /COS QVINQ , M. Claudius Marcellinus carrying trophy towards tetrastyle temple. Trustees of the British Museum
13.- *RIC* I² 105b, Obv.: CAESARI AVGVSTO, bare head left / MAR VLT, Temple of Mars Ultor: round-domed, hexastyle temple with acroteria set on podium of three steps; within, aquila between two *signa*. Trustees of the British Museum
14.- *RPC*1 622: Obv: M·L·D·C·P·, head, r., below, plough; Q·A·M·P·C·II·V·, hexastyle temple. Trustees of the British Museum
15.- *RPC*1 624. Obv: ARISTO MVTVMBAL RICOCE SVF, jugate heads, r. VENERIS, tetrastyle temple, in exergue, KAR. Trustees of the British Museum
16.- *RPC*1 157, Obv: P BAEBIVS POLLIO II VIR QVIN, Victory standing, r., holding wreath and palm branch; Rev.: C AQVINVS MELA II VIR QVIN. Trustees of the British Museum.
17.- Obv.: [RE]X IVBA, Diademed and draped bust of Juba, right; border of dots, Rev.: IVB[A] REX XXX, Victory, right, holding a wreath and a palm-branch. Trustess of the British Museum
18.- *RRC* 546/2a; Obv.: M·ANTO·COS·III·IMP· IIII, Head of Jupiter Ammon right; Rev.: SCARPVS IMP, Victory advancing right, holding wreath and palm branch. Trustees of the British Museum
19.- *RPC*1 202, Obv.: TI CAESAR DIVI AVG (F) ACG(VS), bare head r., Rev.: L. SEMP GEMIN(O) L VAL SVRA II VIR, galley r., SAG above. www.coinarchives.com
20.- *RPC*1 169, Obv: CN ATELLIVS PONTI II V Q(V), apex, securis, aspergillum and simpullum; Rev.: IVBA REX IVBAE F II V Q(V), crown of Isis. Trustees of the British Museum
21.- *RPC*1 172, Obv: AVGVSTVS DIVI F, bare gead, r.; Rev: C LAETILIVS APALVS II V Q, diadem (with crescent and lotus above) enclosing REX PTOL. The Trustess of the British Museum
22.- *RPC*1 167, Obv.: AVGVSTVS DIVI F, laureate head, r.; Rev. C VAR RVF SEX IVL POL II VIR Q, simpulum, aspergillum, secures and apex. Trustees of the British Museum
23.- *RPC*1 170, Obv.: AVGVSTVS DIVI F, laureate head, r.; Rev.: M POSTVM ALBIN L PORC CAPIT II VIR Q, togate male standing, holding simpulum and branch. Trustees of the British Museum
24.- *RPC*1 179, Obv: TI CAESAR DIVI AVGVSTI F AVGVSTVS P M, bare head, l.; Rev. C V I N C NERO ET DRVSVS CAESARES QVINQ, confronted heads of Nero and Drusus. Trustees of the British Museum
25.- *RPC*1 182, Obv.: TI CAESAR DIV(I) AVG(V) F AVG(VSTV) P M, laureate head, l.; Rev. C CAESAR TI N QVIN(Q) IN V I N K, bare head, l. Trustees of the British Museum

1

2

3

4

5

6

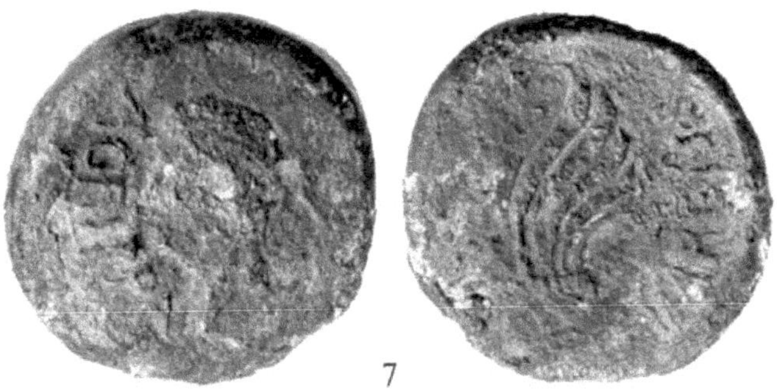

7

8

9

10

11

12

13

14

15

16

17

18

19

20

21

22

23

24

25

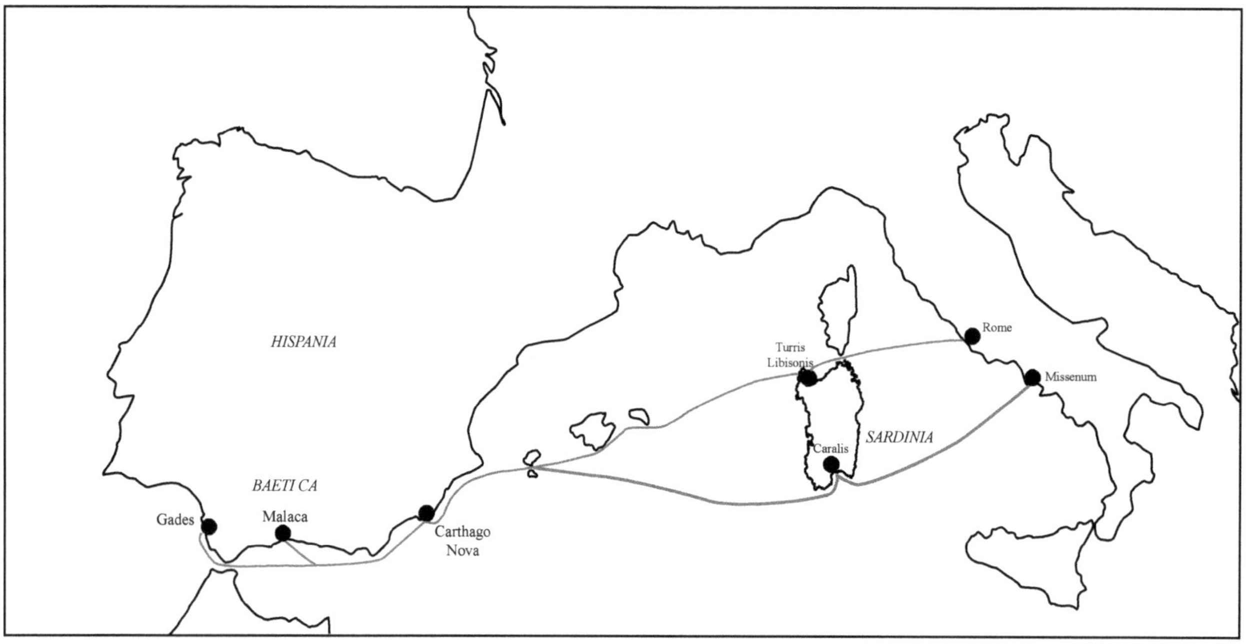

Mapa 1.- The maritime road to Carthago Nova. Drawing F. López Sánchez

Map 2.- Cities in Spain and Mauretania. *RPC*1, Map 2

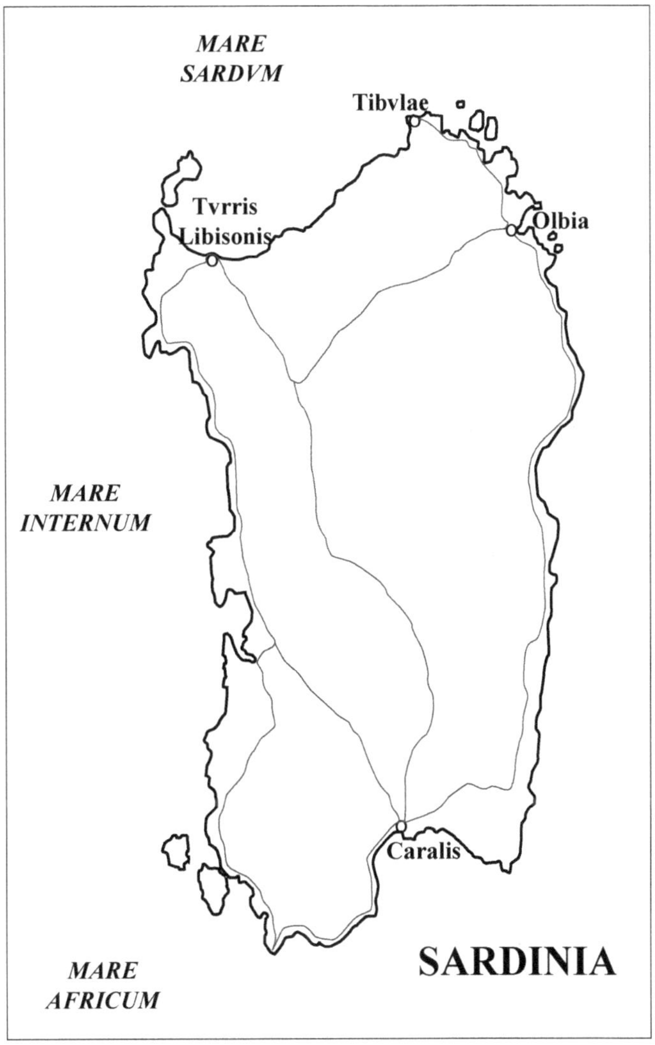

Map 3.- Turris Libisonis (Porto Torres) in the north of Sardinia, and Caralis/Carales in the south. Drawing F. López Sánchez

Monuments, myth and small change in Buthrotum (Butrint) during the Early Empire

Richard Abdy

ABSTRACT

The ancient city of Butrint lies towards the southern tip of Albania, directly across from the island of Corfu (Corcyra), which looms across a narrow strait. Corfu adds to an already appealing natural setting and the monumental centre of the ancient city, including the forum-agora and theatre district, cleared by pre-war and Communist-era excavators is now a pleasant archaeological park. Modern excavations and heritage development has been carried out by the Butrint Foundation (www.butrintfoundation.co.uk).

Geographical and mythological setting[1]

Butrint falls into two distinct areas (Fig. 1). It is dominated by a fairly compact hill now surmounted by an Ottoman fort containing the site museum. The hill represents the old city centre that was once surmounted by its acropolis. Further down the slope nestles the forum-agora-theatre complex (Fig. 2) which is the main source area of the site museum's fine statuary. Butrint hill forms a peninsula separated from a wide plain (the Vrina plain) by a channel (the Vivari channel).

This narrow strip of water is less than 50m wide at the point where a modern pontoon ferry, big enough for two cars, provides a crossing on the road to the Greek border. This is the setting of Butrint's foundation myth. The Trojan refugee and seer Helenus and his men having made camp opposite the hill resolved to sacrifice a bull. However, the animal proved reluctant to participate and made off. It swam across the channel and up the future acropolis before it was overcome; this omen prompted the Trojans to found a city on the spot. The Greek name of the city seems to carry this bull association (βους; Βουθρωτον) (Ceka 1999, p. 11). Virgil's hero Aeneas is an early visitor to this new foundation, receiving a prophecy from his fellow refugee (*Aeneid*, 3.268-505). Indeed, it is the Virgilian link that prompted the Italian archaeologist L. M. Ugolini to search out Butrint and reveal its ancient monuments through the earliest excavations in the 1920s-30s (Ugolini 1937).

The Vivari channel is narrower today than it was during antiquity[2], but it was bridged then; a feat not yet matched today. Archaeologists have cleared the footing of the bridge (Fig. 3) on the city centre side as well as the piers of an aqueduct, which converge with the bridge and lead to a nymphaeum (Ceka 2002, pp. 64-5; Ceka 1999, p. 51). The bridge leads directly across to the plain while the aqueduct footings march off to the mountains beyond where they once collected the water source.[3] It is clear from recent excavations that the plain functioned as a vast suburb, facilitating the expansion of the city in the imperatorial and early imperial period. It is barely a couple of kilometres from the city down the Vivari channel to the shore opposite Corfu (now guarded by a Venetian fort on earlier foundations associated with the notorious Ali Pasha at the beginning of the 19th century[4]). On the other side of the city the channel opens out dramatically into the spacious sea-lake of Butrint that once ran up to the harbour of Phoenice, the one time capital of Epirus.

The mixed economy of the lake and the countryside beyond supported substantial villas, as is attested by the site of Diaporit which now lies partly under the modern lake (Ceka 1999, p. 63). Thus the city's bridge-aqueduct functioned both as the sea gateway to this rich hinterland and, as we will see from the coinage, as a marble monument providing the town's signature building in a similar way to London's tower bridge.

The coin types of Butrint and civic identity

Production of coinage at Butrint spans about a century: from the inception of the city as a Roman colony in 44BC through to the reign of Nero. The coin types promote the city's status through its mythological and monumental

(1) The present author's involvement with the site was as an assistant to the excavation numismatist during the busiest periods of the dig (2003-2007). I would like to express my thanks to Sam Moorhead of the British Museum for his guidance in the field. Also to Pippa Pearce of the British Museum for conservation of the coins and Shpresa Gjongecaj, Director of the Albanian Institute of Archaeology for her kind advice.

(2) Compare Fig. 1 aerial view and reconstruction. Also illustrated on p.14 of Ceka 1999.

(3) Fig. 11.13 on p. 202 of Hansen, Hodges 2007.

(4) http://en.wikipedia.org/wiki/Ali_Pasha_Castle

concerns. The sacrificial bull is seen repeatedly: *RPC*1 1378, 1384-6, 1393 (coupled with the sacrificial tripod), 1395, 1399, 1401, 1403, 1406, 1408, and 1410. *RPC*1 1399 is particularly dramatic, showing the bull swimming in its desperate escape bid (Fig. 4).(5) The visitor Aeneas's ascent to the acropolis is probably to be seen in *RPC*1 1380. *RPC* itself views this as the *Genius* of the city depicted as a Trojan in *Phyrigian* cap, but the Aenean identity of the figure has been cogently argued by S. Moorhead.(6)

The next most prolific theme after the bull is Butrint's symbolic bridge-aqueduct. It first appears on Butrint's Augustan issues: *RPC*1 1382 and 1388. The type is revived under Nero: *RPC*1 1400, 1402, 1404, 1405, 1407 (Fig. 5), and 1409. Although the same feature appears to be depicted in both periods – three spans of a bridge – the proportions are distinctly different. The first Augustan type shows an upper feature that could easily be interpreted as a pipe on lofty stilts set away from the edge of the bridge as would be suggested by the archaeology uncovered to date. The Neronian is less clear as this superstructure is somewhat shrunk to the point of appearing almost like a railing; although on some examples it does seem to be set away from the edge. The second Augustan type is somewhat in between, and, if there is any clear artistic intention perhaps the trend over time was to emphasise the massive bulk of the bridge from boat-level. Recent excavations have uncovered two interesting new Buthrotum types, both from the 2007 season. SF1005 is a Claudian bronze and the first type of that reign which appears to feature the aqueduct (Fig. 6). Preservation is extremely poor but the elaborate reverse seems to show Artemis with quiver on shoulder and bow(?) in crook of arm. She is riding a chariot left past arches surmounted by a small male(?) figure reclining left but with head turned back towards the approaching goddess. It seems possible that he is a water elemental and is sitting on the upper aqueduct level while the goddess passes on the bridge level below (although clearly she would not necessarily have to be on the bridge itself). In addition, Neronian bronze SF6543 seems to show an additional detail to the left of the aqueduct, possibly a cascade of water (Fig.7). If so this would orientate the viewer by understanding the structure to be seen from the seaward side – the monumental approach – with the nymphaeum on the left forming the first city centre deposition of the water supply. It would also count against the alternative idea that the coin type shows a two-tier aqueduct over land rather than the bridge (Hansen, Hodges 2007, p. 202).

The visual abbreviation of the structure appears on the coins almost as a bridge with a 'railing' as opposed to, for example the famous Pont du Guard with its massive triple levels of arches which had to span a far deeper gorge. In the first place, the aqueduct was a much more gracile structure than the massive bridge upon which it once stood. It had the appearance more of a 'pipe on stilts' in comparison to the Pont du Gard's bulk (Gilkes pers. comm).

(5) The significance of the swimming bull has escaped *RPC* (p. 276).

(6) Publication forthcoming.

If Artemis is riding into town on the bridge (she is hardly likely to be depicted deserting the city), this too helps to orientate the aqueduct to the landward edge of the bridge; further explaining the foreshortening when viewed from the seaward approach. Butrint museum's current reconstruction graphics are probably inaccurate as they position the aqueduct on the seaward side of the bridge.(7) However, the archaeological plan does show the aqueduct pillars marching to the landward side of the bridge gate (Ceka 2002, p. 65). Both plan and reconstruction do give a good impression of how close the nymphaeum cascade would have been to the end of the bridge (although the reconstruction understandably does not conjecture anything more than the connecting tank in front of the semi-circular nymphaeum pool).

The third most important subject centres on Butrint's sanctuary of Asklepios which was located in the Forum-Agora (Ceka 2002, pp. 45-6; Hansen, Hodges 2007, pp. 23-8): *RPC*1 1379 (club and snake-staff), 1387 (snake-staff on reverse), 1389 (snake), 1411 and 1413 (both bust of Asklepios). The remaining miscellaneous subjects on Butrint's coinage hint at the city's marine connections: *RPC*1.1392 (dolphin and trident), 1396 (uncertain male figure holding anchor – possibly the *Genius* of the city(8)), and 1416-7 (fish) or more generic religious themes: *RPC*1 1378 (Zeus), 1391 (priest's *lituus*), 1387 and 1397 (both *Concordia*). Zeus was particularly important to the region given the god's primal oracle site at Dodona. *Concordia / Homonoia* is a natural choice on provincial coins wishing to demonstrate their allegiance to Rome.(9)

Further types lack immediate significance: a palm tree adorns Claudian and Neronian coins *RPC*1 1398, 1412 and 1414 while a Victory/*Nike* can be seen on Neronian coin *RPC*1 1415. The palm tree certainly seems an obscure subject for a European mint site, but palms in general were an attribute of Victory, and together with *Nike* such coin types may simply be copying the types produced at Rome or a generic reference to events in the wider Empire. To the *RPC* corpus can be added the new type SF516 which is a variant of *RPC*1.1415 in that *Nike* is in a different pose with a new reverse legend format (Fig. 8).

Butrint as a temporary mint for Mark Antony?

The reverse of *RPC*1 1383 has a distyle temple containing roundel. This appears to copy a *denarius* type of Mark Antony, *RRC* 496/1, where the roundel can clearly be seen as containing a bust of Sol. A temporary mint at Butrint for Antony seems plausible (*RPC*1, p. 275). However no speci-

(7) Fig. 11.12 on p. 201 of Hansen, Hodges 2007.

(8) *RPC*1 p. 276.

(9) There seems little need to seek a hypothesis linking the event of 11 BC noted by Dio (4.35.2) where Augustus diverted a subscription for a statue of himself towards funding statues of *Salus*, *Concordia* and *Pax* instead – see *RPC*1, p. 275.

mens of the *denarius* type have yet been found on site and *RPC*1.1383 is an Augustan issue so could hardly have been contemporary (although this does not preclude the revival of an earlier type known at the mint).

The production of coinage was quite sporadic. Most of the named colleges specify the individuals as *IIvir*; *duoviri*. These issues of the joint heads of the city council of decurions, are sometimes explicitly by decree of the decurions; *D D - decreto decurionum* (Butcher 1988, p. 50).

Magistrates and chronology The magistrate sequence of the early coinage of Butrint is presented in *RPC*		
	Moneyers	**Ethnic abbreviation**
1.	*P.Dastidius, L. Cornelius D D IIvir q.a.*	
2.	*J, Sura IIvir iter*	*C.I.BVT.*
3.	*Q.Naevi. Sura, A. Hirtul. Niger ex D D*	*C.A.BVT.*
4.	*T. Pompon, G. Iulius IIvir quinq.*	*BVTHR*
5.	*T. Pomponius, A. Cocceius IIvir iter ex*	*BVTHR DD*
6.	*M. Pullienus, L. Ateius Fuscus quinq*	*BVTHR*
7.	*Graecinus, Milesius*	*BVTHR*
8.	*P. Pomponius Gr., M. Pullienus quin*	*BVTHR*
9.	*Graecinus, Silvius quinq iter*	*BVTHR*
10.	*Graecinus quinq ter*	*BVTHR*

The title *Q A* accompanying the first magisterial college has been hypothetically expanded to *quaestor aerarii*; treasury official. As it only appears on the first college *RPC* assumes this title is connected to the organisation of the new colony (*RPC*1, p. 275). There is a hiatus between the Augustan coinage and the Claudio-Neronian by which time the magistrates' names had disappeared in favour of the names and titles of the emperor alone. This development is not unexpected since the use of magistrates names on the base metal coinage at Rome did not outlast the reign of Augustus. The lenghty career of Graecinus, the town's most successful politician, was particularly useful in working out the magistrate sequence. He also has a surviving inscription in the museum at Butrint (Fig. 9). First Graecinus appears as *duumvir*, then subsequently as *duumvir quinquennalis*, the most prestigious civic office when the *duoviri* had to organise the five yearly tax census. Finally, he became *duumvir quinq tert* (Fig. 10); showing that he achieved the very top office of *duumvir quinquennalis* three times.

Also noteworthy from the sequence is the name of the colony, which is subsequently but temporarily changed under Augustus to *Colonia Augusta Buthrotum* (*C. A. BVT*) when his portrait first appears on the coinage. *Colonia Iulia Buthrotum* (*C. I. BVT*) had been the original name in 44 BC when the process of turning the city into a Roman colony had been initiated by Julius Caesar (who had sought to punish the city for tax-evasion with the land confiscation that would entail). But it was completed after his death by the senate. The death of the dictator seems to have emboldened the leading landowner at Butrint, T Pomponius Atticus, to protest to Cicero who failed to stop the process but may have hampered the scale of settlement; leaving open the opportunity for the Augustan refoundation (*RPC*1, pp. 274-5; Ceka 1999, p. 15; Hansen, Hodges 2007, pp. 5-8).

CCIB and the confusion with Babba

In the revived coinage of the Claudio-Neronian period the ethnic abbreviation *CCIB* is used. Initial identification of this group assigned the 'B' not to Buthrotum but to Babba in Mauretania, and this led the pre-war excavators of Butrint into tortuous theories to explain the significant presence of such coins on their site! (*RPC*1, p. 276). In fact no such coins have been found at Babba and the mint that was located there had, in common with other provincial mints in the west, ceased production earlier in the Julio-Claudian period.

Now that the Butrint link is clear from the continuing findspot evidence, *CCIB* may be expanded (taking note of *CIL* III, 15006 which gives the name of another such 'field colony') as *Colonia Campestris Iulia Buthrotum*. It remains a tantalising possibility that that 'colonia campestris' is in reference to the development of the Vrina plain which the archaeology suggests began during the early imperial period in the traditional Roman centuriated layout (Hansen, Hodges 2007, p. 8). The reversion to the name of the original colonising authority was presumably due to the greater cachet of being a more venerable establishment than the otherwise perfectly respectable Augustan name had suggested. It doubtless occurred after the demise of the first emperor.

Coin denominations at Butrint

There seems little doubt that Butrint, as a Roman colonia, based its denominations on the base metal coinage produced at Rome. There is an *as*-size coinage of 21-25mm, which was the most favoured base metal denomination in the east (see below), and also two fractions that are close to the Roman *semis* (19-21mm) and *quadrans* (15-18mm). With the Augustan pieces the smaller denominations tend to omit reference to the emperor and, following the convention then in use at Rome, the imperial bust seems to be reserved for the *as*-sized coins (*RPC*1, p. 276).

For the revived Claudio-Neronian issues the three sizes can still be discerned (although the smallest is absent for Claudius). Again Butrint can be seen to follow the Roman convention of this later age with the imperial bust appearing on all denominations (and the loss of magistrates' names as already mentioned). Furthermore, the Neronian innovation of the radiate bust for a living emperor is also repeated at Butrint. It appears as an alternative bust on the two larger Buthrotum denominations (the lowest is always laureate). It cannot therefore be a denominational indicator, although a series indicator is suggested as a likely possibility.[10]

The importance of the old stock of Hellenistic kerma

The copper-alloy *as* and its fractions were undoubtedly the most useful small change for the local marketplace. The lack of denominations lower than the *as* in early Roman Britain demonstrates the difficulty of supplying such small value coins at a distance. The production of the *quadrans* on site at Butrint seems particularly difficult given their absence under Claudius and one of the Neronian series, and this applies to all the Buthrotum denominations during the minting hiatus under Tiberius and Caligula.

However, the city did not have to rely on its own production in the early decades of the Roman Empire. The majority of the Hellenistic bronzes found in the forum area of Butrint were probably still in circulation and lost during the early imperial period. Of the 30+ contexts with Hellenistic coins that the archaeologists have so far dated (e.g. with pottery), seven appear to be distinctly Hellenistic, while eleven seem to be from the time of the Roman Empire.[11]

RPC sees a gradual process of assimilation of the old Hellenistic bronze into the Roman system,[12] and cites a number of possibilities for assimilation.[13] Although the four-as sestertius was a common denomination and unit of account in the west, it was rare in the east during the early years of the Empire (Burnett 2005, p. 176). The Greek version of the *Res Gestae* of Augustus, for example, converted sums of *sestertii* from the Latin text into denaria (*denarii*). By tying the Greek silver drachma to the Roman silver *denarius*, bronzes could be made to fit the old Hellenistic system of 6 obols to a *drachma*. At Athens, a $^{1}/_{6}{}^{th}$ of a denarius denomination is mentioned in an inscription. This would fit neither the Roman *sestertius* at ¼ *denarius*, nor a *dupondius* at $^{1}/_{8}{}^{th}$ *denarius*. As it was only the denarius itself that moved around the empire in significant quantity, this was probably irrelevant to the user in the local marketplace. At Thessaly, epigraphy suggests eight obols to the *denarius*.[14] Thus the *as* at $^{1}/_{16}{}^{th}$ of a *denarius*, would have been recognised as a hemiobol. However, *kerma* could also be expressed in Roman denominations, particularly the *assarion*; also known as the *assarion Italikon* ('Italian *as*'). The largest inscription from Roman Ephesus, for example, mentions *assaria* throughout.[15] The unusually explicit coinage of Chios carry denomination marks that spell out *ΑΣΣΑΡΙΟΝ* as well as various multiples and fractions.[16] SE for *semis* seems to be implied on coins produced at the Roman colony of Corinth (*RPC*1, p. 245), and *colonia* in general probably used Roman denominational terms for their local coinage as an expression of Romanitas (*RPC*1, p. 33). This system seems particularly likely at the colony of Buthrotum given the affinity that the city's own coinage demonstrates to the mint at Rome.

The Hellenistic and early Roman provincial bronzes at Butrint fall into the two sizes typical for central Greece: those around 19-21mm (5-7g) and a half-unit in the 15-17mm (3-4g) range.[17]

It is plausible that the two main size groups of Hellenistic bronze coins still circulating in Roman period Butrint could easily boost the stock of *semisses* and *quadrantes* regardless of what their original arrangements had been in Hellenistic times.

Note that some coins clearly larger than the size of an *as* but with purely Hellenistic designs do appear at Butrint. These were produced at the nearby mint of Apollonia. However, it is now thought that this particular denomination was equivalent to the Roman *dupondius* and was thus probably produced in the 30s BC to match the Roman bronze denominations of the triumviral period.[18]

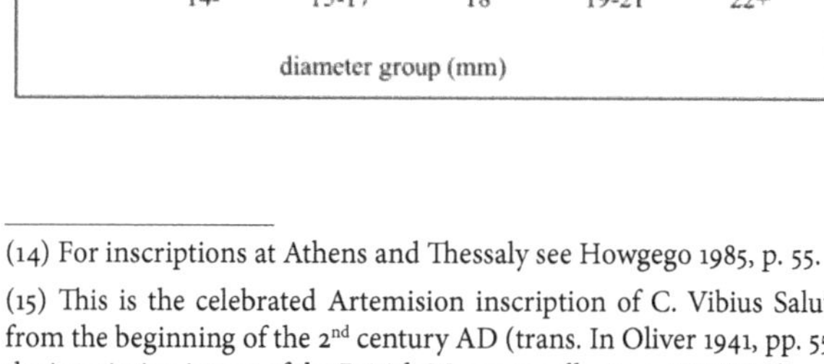

(10) *RPC*1, p. 276. A similar denominational array (but with Greek legends) is seen at Phoinike, Buthrotum's neighbouring mint city under Nero, where again two series can be discerned (see Gjongecaj 2010).

(11) I am very grateful to David Hernandez who made matrices available for comparison prior to publication. However, taking the coin evidence alone the picture is less clear with only one forum context showing mixed Hellenistic and Imperial period bronzes: Context 420 = 1x Corcyra (Philonidas); 1x Epirus Republic; 1x Corcyra uncertain; 1x Nero Buthrotum. (Note Context 423 is an example of a disturbed layer with both medieval & Hellenistic coins.)

(12) 'Roman denominations had not been suddenly imposed on newly annexed territories, but the change to using them took place only gradually, and often only in the period covered in this catalogue…' *RPC*1, p. 36.

(13) Table of kerma with marks of value *RPC*1, pp. 32-3. Corinth for instance has as, semis and quadrans, a similar situation to Butrint.

(14) For inscriptions at Athens and Thessaly see Howgego 1985, p. 55.

(15) This is the celebrated Artemision inscription of C. Vibius Salutaris from the beginning of the 2nd century AD (trans. In Oliver 1941, pp. 55-85, the inscription is part of the British Museum collection: *BMC* III (inscriptions) no. 481).

(16) *RPC*1, p. 370 and 374. There is also *ΟΒΟΛΟΣ*, possibly equivalent to a double-*assarion*. The difficulty in dating Chios coins and the possibility of changing weight standards make some relationships tentative.

(17) In order to create a clearer picture, I have found it convenient to widen these bands by 1mm over that given in *RPC*1, p. 35.

(18) Gjongecaj and Picard 2002.

The sources for the Hellenistic / Roman provincial bronze coins show the expected bias towards local sources. During the Hellenistic period this is Corcyra (Corfu) (Fig. 11) and the Epirus Republic (Fig. 12), while also nearby is Apollonia (Fig. 13; which may now count as Roman provincial but has been left in the Hellenistic section here):

Hellenistic kerma from Butrint forum found during the Butrint Foundation excavations

Corcyra (Corfu)	11
Apollonia	5
Epirus Republic	13
Dyrrachium	1
Corcyra? (or Epirus Republic?)	1
Leukas?	
Thessalian League	1
Sestos	1
Chios	1
Rhodes	1

For the Roman Provincial coinage, Butrint itself is the main supplier by a large margin, but the new great urban regional centre, the Augustan foundation of Nikopolis is also present.

Roman Provincial coins from Butrint Forum found during the Butrint Foundation excavations

Copia /Republican period	1
Pergamum / Augustus (incl. a cut half coin)	3
Thessalonica / Augustus	1
uncertain mint / Augustus	1
Buthrotum	10
Nikopolis? (Nero)	1
uncertain provincial (Nero?) (cut half)	1
Nikopolis (Hadrian)	3
Nikopolis? (Hadrian)	1
uncertain Hadrian	1
uncertain cut half (one possibly Nikopolis)	2

The story of the coin circulation in the early empire at Butrint

It is also worth looking at the Roman Imperial coinage from the same forum excavations:

Identifiable Roman Republican and Imperial coins from Butrint forum found during the Butrint Foundation excavations

Roman Republican (all 1st cent BC)	3 AR + 1 AE
Roman Imperial 27BC – AD260:	
AR:	
Otho	1
Flavian	2
Antonine	1
Severan	1
AE:	
Flavian	1
Trajannic/ Hadriannic	5
Antonine	5
post-Severan (Pupienus & Philip I)	2

(note: late Roman (AD 260-498) = 2 radiates + 31 nummi)

The impression is that Roman imperial bronze coinage had little input into the circulation before the second century AD. (With the much lower quantity of silver the pattern of loss probably better reflects the higher grade of precious metal of imperial *denarii* produced before AD 64). Amongst the bronzes there is a total lack of any pre-Flavian coinage and the solitary Flavian specimen could easily have arrived in the following century. (Presumably by the time quantities of imperial bronze coins began reaching Butrint most Flavian bronzes had long since dropped out of circulation). The production of coinage at Buthrotum was sporadic. Most of the named colleges were for the five yearly *duoviri quinquennales*. There is a hiatus between the Augustan coinage and the Claudio-Neronian. The Buthrotum series ends with Nero yet there seems to have been no ready supply of imperial bronzes during the Flavian period.

It would seem that the solution to the supply gap lay in the continued employment of the pre-Roman coinage of the area, occasionally topped up with local issues of new Buthrotum coinage. However, this situation only continued up to the reign of Nero, and it looks like it was some time after that before regular supplies of imperial bronze coinage came to Butrint. There are signs of 'stretching' the existing stock of Buthrotum coins. Most Neronian (Figs 5, 8) and occasionally some earlier coins (Fig. 10) have countermarks (*RPC*1 p. 276). The form of the countermark, *B.AV*, is less easy to understand; *Buthrotum Augusta* (Howgego 1985, p. 220) seems an odd choice for a city that had reverted to describing itself as the colonia of Julius (as noted above). As for countermarking itself, this is a well-known process of approving old stock of worn coinage for continuing circulation across the empire and although particularly prevalent for Julio-Claudian imperial coinage it survived into much later periods in the eastern provinces.[19]

The presence of halved bronze coins points to another pos-

(19) See list given on the online *Museum of Roman Countermarks*: www.romancoins.info/Countermarks.html; note that another reason for countermarking involves the validation of foreign coins in a provincial city (Howgego 1986, p. 15) but this aspect does not apply here.

sible local solution to the absence of small change. This process is well known from late Republican Italy where the halving of old Republican *asses* was carried out in the face of the disruption to bronze production caused by the prolonged civil wars (Buttrey 1972). At least one of these cut Republican *asses* reached Butrint, but where identifiable, the other cut bronzes appear to be provincial Augustan issues; wide and thin-flanned as-like coins that would be easy to cut (Fig. 14). If these coins were cut locally, they might have helped to fill the hiatus in Buthrotum coin production between Augustus and Claudius.

Conclusion – Butrint between east and west

When the colonia of Butrint was founded it began to strike its own coinage bearing designs that were important to the local community but following the conventions of the bronzes of the mint at Rome (and their immediate predecessors produced by Antony in Greece, 44-31 BC). They were sporadic issues supplementing an already strong circulation of small change predominantly composed of the surviving bronze coins of Hellenistic Epirus and Corfu. Production ceased with Nero yet the city failed to receive any significant supplies of Roman imperial coins for at least the rest of the century. The countermarking of the later Buthrotum coinage suggests the strain on the existing coinage stock. It is an interesting contrast with Butrint's neighbours Phoinike and Nikopolis; the only other cities of the region which had produced Julio-Claudian provincial coinage. Both recommenced local coinage production under Trajan after their own Neronian cessations, which is of course the obvious solution to the pressure on small change.[20]

At Butrint, the second century does look almost completely 'western' in that the bronze coins used are mostly imperial – but with small quantities of provincial coins from farther south. The third century at Butrint takes on some of the character seen more acutely further north in the Balkans. Severan and later provincial bronzes creep in to the gap left by the shortfall of supply of *sestertii* and fractions to the frontier areas. Indeed, complete harmony with the rest of the empire only fully occurs with the extinction of the entire provincial series in the third century.[21] Thus the 'imperialisation' of the empire's small change can be seen to creep in stages. The far western Mediterranean ceases to produce local small change early in the first century.[22] This extinction creeps just to the west of Italy with the Adriatic down to Butrint following suit by the AD 60s. However, Central Greece, the eastern Balkans, and the Levant only succumb by the mid-third century, with Egypt right at the end of the third century.

Burnett (2005, p. 177-8) observes that in the west those local coinages that survive longest tend to resemble the official imperial bronze coinage the most and sees the rejection of local coinage as a cultural phenomenon reflecting local aspirations within Latin-western or Greek-eastern outlooks. The Romanising outlook that seems to have doomed the western local coinages certainly applies to Buthrotum. But they must have been powerful aspirations indeed in the face of the evident strain of the small change in the city during the later first century AD - where the natural solution might have been to step up local production to eliminate the need to use the old Hellenistic coins. When one travels *East* from Corfu to Albania, the clocks are set back to western European time (GMT +1) from Greek time (GMT +2). Such modern sentiments overriding practicalities may well have had ancient precedents.

(20) For Nikopolis see Calomino in this volume. For Phoinike see Gjongecaj 2010.

(21) Moorhead *et al.* 2007 provides a full overview of the circulation character. Also for Balkan area overview see Butcher 1988, pp. 67-70.

(22) Mostly ending in the 'decade before AD 50' (Burnett 2005, p. 177).

Abbreviations

BMC III (inscriptions) (1890)= Hicks E. L. *The Collection of Ancient Greek Inscriptions in the British Museum.* Vol. III. London.

CIL III (1902)= Mommsen Th., Hirschfeld O., Domaszewski A. *Corpus Inscriptionum Latini. Inscriptionum Orientis et Illyrici Latinarum. Supplementum. Pars Posterior.* Berlin.

*RPC*1 (1992)= Burnett A. M., Amandry M., Ripollès, P. P. *Roman provincial coinage. Vol. 1, From the death of Caesar to the death of Vitellius (44 BC-AD 69).* London.

RRC (1974)= Crawford M. H. *Roman Republican Coinage.* Cambridge.

References

Burnett A. (2005). 'The Roman West and the Roman East' in Howgego, C., Heuchert, V. and Burnett, A. (eds.), *Coinage and Identity in the Roman Provinces.* Oxford.

Buttrey T. V. (1972). 'Halved Coins, the Augustan Reform, and Horace, Odes I.3', *AJA*, 76. 1 (Jan.), pp. 31-48.

Butcher K. (1988). *Roman Provincial Coins: an Introduction to the Greek Imperials.* London.

Ceka N. (1999). *Butrint, a Guide to the City and its Monuments.* London.

Ceka N. (2002). *Buthrotum, its History and Monuments.* Tirana.

Franke P. R. (1961). *Die antiken Münzen von Epirus.* Wisbaden.

Gjongecaj S., Picard O. (2002). 'Le Monnayage d'Apollonia sous l'Empire Romain' in Cabanes P. and Lamboley J.-L. (eds.) *L'Illyrie Méridionale et L'Épire dans l'Antiquité (Actes du IVe colloque international de Grenoble 10-12 octobre 2002).* Paris, pp. 135-148.

Gjongecaj S. (2010). 'Le monnayage de Phoinikè sous l'empire romain', *Revue Numismatique*, pp. 383-96.

Hansen I. L., Hodges R. (eds) (2007). *Roman Butrint, an Assessment*. Oxford.

Howgego C. J. (1985). *Greek Imperial Countermarks*. Oxford.

Moorhead S., Gjongecaj S., Abdy R. (2007). 'Coins from the Excavations at Butrint, Diaporit and the Vrina Plain' in Hansen I. L., Hodges R. (eds) 2007, pp. 78-94.

Moorhead S. (forthcoming). 'A coin struck at Butrint representing Aeneas', in S. Walker S. and Zachos K. (eds), *After Actium: new archaeological discoveries in Roman Greece*. London.

Oliver J. H. (1941). The Sacred Gerusia (*Hesperia Supplement* 6). Princeton (reprinted Amsterdam, 1975).

Ugolini L. M. (1937). *Butrinto il Mito D'Enea, gli Scavi*. Rome (reprinted Tirana 1999).

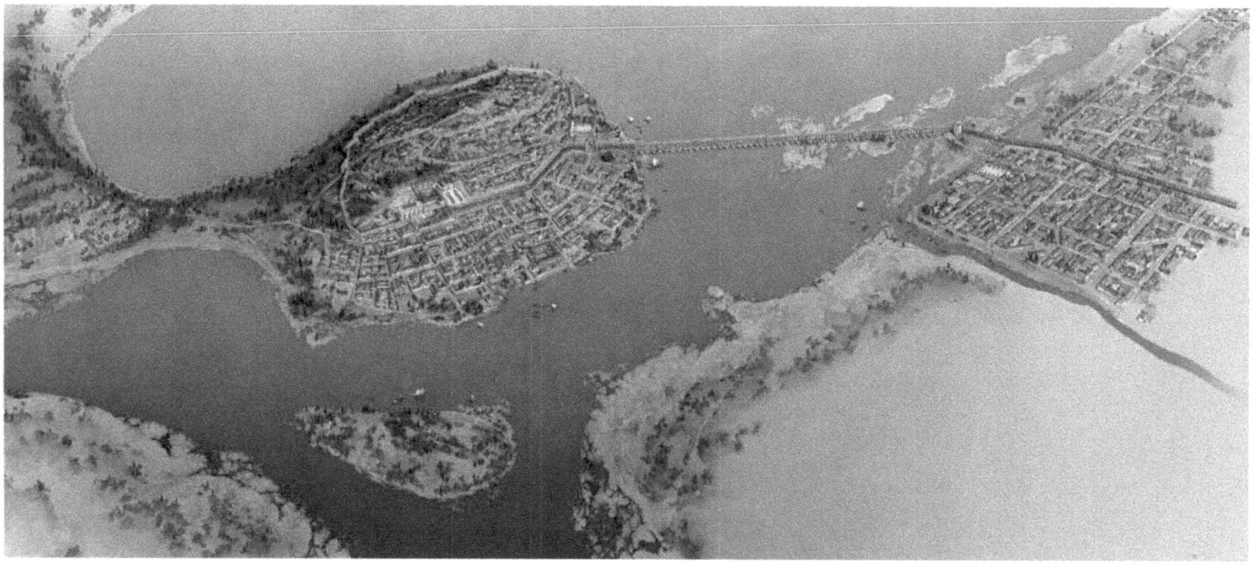

Fig. 1. Aerial view of Butrint (above) and a graphic reconstruction of the city during the 1st century AD (below) (courtesy of the Butrint Foundation; reconstruction © Studio Inklink/Butrint Foundation)

Fig. 2. Flooded floor of the forum as uncovered in summer 2007

Fig. 3. The footing of the bridge of Buthrotum as uncovered in the summer of 2007

4

5

6

7

8

Fig. 4. Bronze coin of Buthrotum, time of Claudius with unnamed duovirs (*RPC*1 1399), laureate head of Claudius (TI CLA GER CAE[S]) / swimming bull (CCIB / D D), AD 41-54, (BM 1866,1201.4068 = 18 x 20mm, 5.23g) but similar example found at Butrint, SF 501). Fig. 5. Bronze coin of Buthrotum, time of Nero (cf. *RPC*1 1400 or 1407), laureate or radiate head of Nero (NERO CLA[VDIVS CAES AVG (GERM(A))]; B.AV countermark on neck) / bridge-aqueduct ([D EX CON]SE[(N)]; [CCIB] in ex), AD 54-68 (SF 1018, ae24, 10.45g). Fig. 6. Bronze coin of Buthrotum, time of Claudius (*RPC* –), laureate head of Claudius (CLAV[...]) / uncertain multiple figs (possibly Artemis riding in chariot left with spear(?) and quiver on shoulder. Small figure above and behind (on top of arches of aqueduct?) ([...] - CCIB). AD 41-54 (SF 1005, ae23, 10.37g). Fig. 7. Bronze coin (reverse only) of Buthrotum, time of Nero (*RPC*1 1404var), radiate head of Nero, right ... O CL ...; Countermarked B.AV(ligate) / bridge-aqueduct with possible cascade feature [D] E[X C]ON [... // (C)[CIB] in ex. (SF 6543, AE 18/19, 5.66 g). Fig. 8. Bronze coin of Buthrotum, time of Nero (*RPC* –), radiate head of Nero NE[RO CL] AVDI[VS] CAES[AR] countermark B.AV (?) on neck / EXC [...] Nike-Victory (adv/stg) r, holding out wreath, AD 54-68 (SF 516, ae15, 3.26g)

Fig. 9. Graecinus inscription from Butrint and now in Butrint site museum

10

11

12

13

Fig. 10. Bronze coin of Buthrotum, time of Augustus, 31 BC – AD 14 (*RPC*1 1391 var), CAESAR AVGVSTVS in wreath (countermark CP) / GRAECINVS QVIN.TERT BVTHR lituus (countermarked AL retrograde) (SF 615, found at Diaporit, near Butrint, ae24, 6.75g). Fig. 11. Bronze coin of Corcyra (magistrate: Philonidas), Zeus / Prow (legend: ΚΟΡΚΥΡΑΙΩΝ / Φ[ΙΛΩΝ]ΙΔΑΣ) c. 229-48 BC (SF 628, ae21, 8.52g). Fig. 12. Bronze coin of the Epirus Republic, bust of Artemis with eagle to left and below, monogram (Franke 1961 Group VIII, no.629) / spear head within wreath (legend: ΑΠΕΙ / ΡΩΤΑΝ), 238-168 BC (SF 417, ae21, 6.50g). Fig. 13. Bronze coin (dupondius-sized) of Apollonia, Artemis / tripod lebes (SF496, ae25, 20.38g). Fig. 14. Halved bronze coin: SF 575, possibly an assarion-sized coin of Pergamum. [CAE]SAR [ ]; bare head (of Augustus?). Reverse is illegible, but traces of wreath visible? Cf. *RPC*1 2235. 15 x 27mm, 5.66g

Actia Nicopolis. Coinage, currency and civic identity (27 BC-AD 268)

Dario Calomino

ABSTRACT

Nicopolis of Epirus (north-western Greece), founded by Octavian to commemorate the *Actium* victory over Marc Antony and Cleopatra in 31 BC, was also known as "*Actia Nicopolis*". Ancient authors' reports suggest that the city profited from very special imperial benefits: a privileged administrative statute (as *civitas* libera and probably *foederata*), a pre-eminent political position in the Delphic Amphictiony and in the province (as capital of Epirus), a leading ethnic-cultural role in western Greece (being populated through interregional *synoecism*), a strong symbolic meaning for the Roman policy in Greece (as the only proper Greek foundation of Augustus). Due to the strategic location, the city secured military control and provided economic support to the western coast of Roman Greece and subsisted on commerce, fishing, farming and stock-raising. The coinage is still probably the best archaeological evidence of the city's economic and cultural life, spanning from Augustus to Gallien with a large production of bronze issues and exceptional silver series under the Antonines. Further special features of the mint's production are, above all, a large "pseudo-autonomous" coinage and remarkable commemorative series in memory of the founder Augustus, which continued in production during the 2nd and the 3rd centuries.

The City

The ancient city of *Nicopolis* lies towards the western coast of Epirus (north-western Greece) on the far southern tip which divides the Gulf of Ambracia from the Ionian Sea, north to Cape Actium and close to the modern harbour town of Prebeza (Fig. 1). It was founded by Octavian in order to commemorate his victory over Marc Antony and Cleopatra in the 2nd September 31 BC naval battle of Actium; becoming a model for several "cities of Victory" later founded all over the Roman world,[1] it was also known as "*Actia Nicopolis*" to be distinguished from the other ones (Tab. Peut., 6.3-4).

A memorial monument of the victory was erected on the Michalitsi hill that dominates the *Nicopolis* plain, exactly where Octavian had set his military camp, and it was decorated with the bronze *rostra* taken from the ships of Antony's fleet. According to Suetonius and Dio Cassius (Suet. *Aug.*, 18; Dio, 51.1.1-3), the monument was part of an open-air sanctuary dedicated to the gods who had granted Octavian the final victory: Mars, Neptune and Apollo. Moreover Octavian restored the IV century BC traditional sacred festivals of Acarnania, the Actian Games, and renovated the ancient sanctuary of Apollo at Cape Actium, where they used to take place.[2] People from all over the Roman world used to visit *Nicopolis* every four years to attend or simply to watch the competitions, which enjoyed a status equal to that of the Olympics (Sarikakis 1966; Lämmer 1986-1987).

The city was populated through an emblematic process of *synoikismos*, gathering inhabitants from Epirus, Acarnania and Aetolia. The whole region had suffered destruction and deportation long since the battle of Pidna (168 BC) and then again during the *Triumviri* Civil Wars that led to the defeat of Pompey at *Pharsalus* (48 BC) and of *Cassius* and *Brutus* at *Philippi* (42 BC); so the purpose of the Actian foundation was to offer many people coming from abandoned towns and villages in the surrounding areas a brand new centre of attraction and reception (Purcell 1987).

Nevertheless, far from being conceived as a mere commemorative foundation and a shelter for displaced people, *Actia Nicopolis* profited by its strategic localition which allowed it to secure military control and provide economic support to the western coast of Roman Greece. It was built on a narrow plain between the Gulf of Ambracia and the Ionian Sea; two or three harbours, one at Komaros, another probably at Vathy and a third possibly on the Eastern Mazoma Lagoon (Fig. 1), assured easy communications with the Italian peninsula, on the route from *Brundisium* and Corcyra to the major urban centres of Macedonia and Peloponnesus; the city was also linked by landlines to the

(1) The first one was *Nicopolis-Iuliopolis*, founded by Octavian in Egypt after the capture of Alexandria (30 BC); Dio, 51.18. About the cities of Victory in the Greek and Roman world, see Ellis Jones 1987, pp. 104-107.

(2) See also Strab., 7.7.6.

Via Egnatia in the north and to Patras and Corinth in the south. Commerce, fishing, farming and stock-raising contributed to the economic prosperity of the Epirotan community (Samsari 1994, pp. 45-46; Chrysostomou, Kefallonitou 2001, pp. 10-16).

Therefore Octavian secured an outstanding economic and socio-cultural role in Roman Greece for *Nicopolis*, besides a remarkable prestige and political influence in Pan-Hellenic business, through the assignation of the highest number of voting members in the Delphic Amphictiony (Paus., 10.8.3-5; Bowersock 1965, p. 98; Ellis Jones 1987, pp. 101-108; Sartre 1991, pp. 208-209). The city also enjoyed a privileged administrative status being a *civitas libera*, probably exempted from paying taxes, although Tacitus refers to the city calling it either *urbs* or *colonia* and Pliny obscurely mentions a *colonia Augusti Actium cum templo Apollinis nobili ac civitate libera Nicopolitana* (Plin. Nat., IV.5). In recent years some scholars have more carefully reconsidered literary and epigraphic sources about this problem and pointed out that Nicopolis probably was a "double" community, namely a free Greek city coupled with a settlement of Roman veterans who had taken part in the Actium battle (Purcell 1987, pp. 87-90; Ruscu 2006). This does not necessarily imply that there were two separated settlements, but two communities cohabitating under the rules of a special *foedus* ("treaty"), as Servius' commentary attests (Serv. Aen., III.50); this would make a *civitas libera* et *foederata* out of *Nicopolis*.

The city enjoyed safety and prosperity, even becoming the capital of the autonomous province of Epirus (probably under Trajan), up to the Gothic and Herulian invasions of Greece and Macedonia in AD 254-268 (Karatzeni 2001, pp. 164, 171; Chrysostomou and Kefallonitou 2001, p. 14). Despite the general economic and political decline of the Empire, earthquakes and Barbarian raids, *Nicopolis* continued to be inhabited and enjoyed further flowering under Christianity (4th-6th century), as Byzantine fortifications and six surviving basilicas testify (Chrysostomou and Kefallonitou 2001, pp. 15-16).

Modern excavations at the archaeological site (Fig. 2) have been carried out from the beginning of the 20th century, bringing to light a circuit of over 5 km city walls (including at least five main gates), the necropolis, the private residence of a rich citizen called *Manius Antoninus* and many remarkable public buildings, such as the baths, the aqueduct, the cisterns, the *nymphaeum*, the Forum and the *odeion*. Outside the urban perimeter, north to the centre, a separate district has been brought to light, the so-called *proasteion*, where the New Actian Games took place; it actually includes the main spectacle buildings, namely the *stadion*, the *gymnasion* and the theatre.[3]

During the last thirty years, further excavations and researches have been undertaken on the Michalitsi hill, where the memorial monument lies. An impressive series of sockets which pocks the façade of the upper terrace retaining wall has then been identified as the anchor-shaped cuttings to hold Antony's fleet bronze rams; several carved limestone blocks have been gathered allowing restoration of the Latin inscription that celebrated Octavian's victory; hundreds of fragments of the decorative relief celebrating the Actian triumph have also been discovered and are waiting to be entirely restored after conservation (Fig. 3).[4]

THE MINT AND THE COINAGE

The mint of *Nicopolis* of Epirus struck coins from 27 BC to AD 268; coinage spanned almost three centuries more or less regularly under every emperor, apart from a considerable period of interruption during the 1st century AD. Two important studies have been published about this coinage in the Seventies: a catalogue of specimens from the main numismatic collections by M. Oikonomidou and an accurate review by C. M. Kraay (Oikonomidou 1975; Kraay 1976). Further investigations about mint production in the Julio-Claudian Age have also been made by the authors of *Roman Provincial Coinage* (*RPC*1, nos 1363-77, pp. 272-74, pl. 69-70). The present contribution aims to present a global (and, possibly, more exhaustive) picture of the civic coinage by adding new data collected in my Ph.D. thesis to the previous researches.[5]

Little is known about the mint organisation; the excavations have not provided yet any information about the possible location of the workshop at the site. The coins themselves tell us nothing about who, among the civic authorities, was in charge of undertaking the coinage. Nevertheless the epigraphic evidence can offer some assistance, as the civic prosopography reports names and titles of the main magistrates (Samsari 1994, pp. 50-53, 149). Other provincial mints' legends sometimes indicate who was most likely to have taken care of the minting process;[6] for comparison with such cases, it is possible to search for potential moneyers in *Nicopolis* among the archon, the *grammateus thes* boules and similar members of the local government

(3) For an exhaustive picture of excavations at the site and researches over *Nicopolis* of Epirus, see: *Nicopolis* 1; *Foundation and Destruction*; Chrysostomou and Kefallonitou 2001; *Nicopolis* 2.

(4) Murray and Petsas 1989; Zachos 2003.

(5) For permission to publish the coins from collections, I should like to thank Federico Barello and Alessandra Guerrini (Medagliere dell'Armeria Reale, Turin), Maria Cristina Dossi (Museo Archeologico Nazionale, Venice), Dimitri Doukas (Athens), Paola Giovetti (Museo Civico Archeologico, Bologna), Vania Gransinigh (Musei Civici, Udine), Paola Marini (Musei Civici, Verona), Rodolfo Martini (Raccolte Artistiche e Gabinetto Numismatico - Medagliere, Milan), Dimitra Tsangari (Alpha Bank Collection, Athens). For permission to study the coin finds, I express my deepest gratitude to Despina Eugenidou (Numismatic Museum, Athens), Georgios Riginos (33rd Ephorate of Prehistoric and Classical Antiquities, Preveza) and the members of the Local Epirotan Council of Monuments, especially Konstantinos Zachos (12nd Ephorate of Prehistoric and Classical Antiquities, Ioannina).

(6) See *RPC*1, pp. 3-4, 787. However there is no certainty about the possibility that these magistrates were mentioned on coin legends because they were involved in the mint activity; as they probably were eponymous magistrates, their name could be engraved on coins just to indicate the year of minting; see Butcher 1988, pp. 25-26.

like the *agonothetes*, who superintended the Actian Games quadrennial organisation, for which many coins were actually issued. Also private citizens could have chosen to incur coinage expenses, such as eminent *amphiktiones* (the members of the *Nicopolis* delegation to the Amphictiony Council), who were frequently celebrated on inscriptions (and elsewhere also on coins) with honorific titles such as *philokaisar* and *philopatris*, that acknowledged their devotion to the emperor and the community (Calomino 2011b, pp. 32, 330).

Above all we can try to reconstruct the mint history. There are three main phases of the coinage of *Nicopolis*: Augustus to the Flavians, Trajan to Commodus and Septimius Severus to Gallienus. The first obviously coincides with the opening of the mint, which surely dates soon after 27 BC, because the obverse legend ΚΤΙΣΜΑ ΣΕΒΑΣΤΟΥ ("Augustus' foundation") reports the Greek version (*Sebastos*) of the name that was assumed by Octavian from then on. As this was probably also the date of inauguration of the new Actian Games,(7) one can likely reckon that a direct link existed between rate and scale production of the civic coinage and the quadrennial celebration of the local Festivals; in fact they surely attracted an exceptional influx of visitors and increased local market place activity, thus requiring local small-change supply.

The Augustan coinage presents quite peculiar features: style and fabric are surely local, very plain and constant; the monetary system has three denominations, but in fact the middle one, the local *assarion*, definitely dominates the whole production; it bears a fixed-reverse type, the so-called "type parlant" (i.e. the one that recalls the city name) of Nike with wreath and palm branch, combined to the legend ΙΕΡΑ ΝΙΚΟΠΟΛΙΣ, "sacred *Nicopolis*" (*RPC*1 1364; Fig. 4); nevertheless it conveys a very direct ideological message, since the legend ΚΤΙΣΜΑ ΣΕΒΑΣΤΟΥ is a *unicum* (not elsewhere attested) in the provincial repertory, which celebrates the most important Augustan foundation in Greece, surely one of the most symbolic of the whole Roman Empire.

Though the early mint output cannot be compared in scale to that of the major mints of Roman Greece, such as Corinth, Thessalonica and the Thessalian League, the Augustan *assarion* of *Nicopolis* was struck in several issues and certainly secured a satisfying supply of bronze currency to the civic and local circulation in the following decades. It is anyway surprising that the mint stopped producing new coins under the Julio-Claudian (except Nero) and the Flavian dynasty, hence this interruption was possibly caused by special Imperial measures: firstly, as Caligula forbade celebrating the Actium victory (to safeguard the memory of his ancestor Antony), the Games were likely suppressed under his reign and the mint could have already stopped striking for the same reason (Suet., Cal., XXIII. Sarikakis 1966, p. 155); and most of all, as Vespasian revoked the right to strike coins by the provincial mints of *Achaea*, *Nicopolis* could not resume the civic coinage even under Titus and Domitian (*RPC*1, p. 21; *RPC*2, pp. 1, 70).

Only under Nero we find evidence of new coinage, but it is an exceptional and very scarce copper production. Most of the Neronian issues bear the bust of the city instead of the imperial portrait and celebrate his triumphal arrival to the city with the imperial galley reverse type and the legend ΝΕΡΩΝΟΝΙΚΟΠΟΛΙΣ (*RPC*1 1368-1370; Fig. 5), which still represents the only epigraphic evidence of an actual renaming of *Nicopolis*. The aim was probably to commemorate his victory at the Actian Games (AD 66-67) by giving his own name to the most popular Augustan city of victory for self-celebration and self-legitimation. Other even rarer Neronian issues don't give the city name at all, but bear the emperor's head and the usual Nike reverse type, or the emperor's full-length portrait on the obverse and goddess *Eleutheria* (Freedom) on the reverse (*RPC*1 1371-1377); the latter category represents Nero playing lyre as Apollo *Ktistes* ("Apollo the founder", still drawing on the ideology of the Augustan foundation), or standing within a two column shrine as Patron of Greece (recalling his emphatic announcement of liberation of *Achaea* at the Isthmian Games). The attribution of these coins (previously assigned to Apollonia in Illyria) has been much debated, as Levy argued that they could have been struck by a "confederation" of Achaean mints under the supervision of *Nicopolis*, but Burnett's die study has demonstrated that they all were more likely issued by the Epirotan workshop.(8)

The second phase includes the 2nd century AD coinage. This crucial period saw the resuming of civic coinage under Trajan (AD 98-117), who likely promoted a new flowering of the city and the mint itself, since Epirus became an autonomous province and *Nicopolis* the capital; probably as sign of gratitude, many civic issues bear the obverse legend ΑΥΤ(Ο) ΤΡΑΙΑΝΟϹ ϹѠΤΗΡ (ΤΗϹ) ΠΟΛΕѠϹ, namely "emperor Trajan saviour of the city" (Calomino 2011b, nos 17-28; pp. 234-235; Figs 7, 16). *Nicopolis* also enjoyed special imperial favour by Hadrian. He visited the city at least three times during his journeys to Greece, probably in order to meet the Stoic philosopher Epictetus, who had moved there and established his own school after being banned from Rome by Domitian; the emperor made a gift of new or restored monuments (probably those depicted on his coins, i.e. a gate, a round temple and a fountain)(9) to the community and was worshipped in reward as *Zeus Olympios Dodonaios* on local inscriptions (Cabanes 1987). The scale of production definitely increased and the coins began to spread beyond the civic territory; in the Augustan age they actually circulated only in southern Epirus (mainly within the district of modern Arta, i.e. the territory of ancient Ambracia), whereas in the 2nd century AD the small bronzes of Trajan and Hadrian circulated all over

(7) Moretti 1953, pp. 205-206; Sarikakis 1966, pp. 146-156; Lämmer 1986-1987, pp. 29-30.

(8) See *RPC*1, pp. 273-74, with earlier bibliography.

(9) Calomino 2011b, nos 69-70, 72, 75, 85; 107-108; 117-129. See also Kraay 1976, p. 241.

northern Epirus, as coin finds in Dodona, *Corcyra*, *Phoinice* and Butrint (whose mint was closed after the Neronian age) attest (Calomino 2011b, pp. 312-313, 331-333).

In the age of the Antonines (AD 161-192) the coin production gradually decreased (probably also due to the earlier small change still in circulation) and one should reckon that civic issues were strictly linked to the Actian Games, as the most common and representative reverse type is a prize, the peculiar wreath of reeds, in which the legend AKTIA or simply the initial letter A is inscribed. This type also occurred on the exceptional *quinari-hemidrachmae* pure silver series struck in AD 141-144 for Antoninus Pius and Diva Faustina (*RPC*4 4177, 4184; Fig. 8); many clues suggest that their production somehow involved the mint of Rome (die-engravers or even the workshop, where the dies could have been made and then used or rather shipped to Epirus),[10] since typically Roman are style and fabric, and Roman is the imperial title in the Antoninus obverse legend, the 3rd consulship (ΥΠ[ΑΤΟC/ΑΤΕΙΑ] Γ),[11] which is here mentioned for the first and last time in the whole civic coinage (Calomino 2011b, pp. 250-251).

The last phase of the mint history includes 3rd century production. Some features indicate that a remarkable change occurred, since the mint no longer struck coins mainly (or even exclusively) in connection with the Games or with other special events (such as imperial visits to the city), but also for other needs and under more direct influence (or even control) of the central authority.

The best evidence is offered by the volume scale growth in two specific periods of this phase, under Caracalla and under Gallienus as sole emperors. During the reign of Caracalla (AD 211-217) the mint reached the highest peak of scale output ever, whereas almost all the mints of Peloponnesus (including Corinth, the capital of *Achaea* and by far the most productive workshop in Greece) definitely ceased striking bronze provincial coins (Grunauer-Von Hoerschelmann 1983, p. 46). The same occurred in the Epirotan island of Corcyra, where its local mint issued non-stop (even under Pescennius Niger) at least from Antoninus Pius to Septimius Severus (possible earlier coins lack the obverse imperial portrait).[12] Some remarkable die analogies (and type resemblances, as for large bronzes depicting two very similar Corinthian Temples)[13] suggest that Corcyra struck in close relationship with *Nicopolis* itself, probably sharing workshops and/or die-engravers at least for a short period (ca. AD 202/5-211), in the name of Septimius Caracalla, Plautilla and Geta (Figs 9-11); then, quite abruptly, it ceased any further activity.[14] It follows that *Nicopolis* became the only northern-central Greece mint still working, along with Larissa (for the Thessalian League), from Caracalla on; this probably means that it became involved in a different and wider area of coin distribution and circulation, gravitating towards Macedonia and the northern Balkans, where all major mints kept producing up to the age of Gallienus (Calomino 2011b, pp. 333-334).

A further peak of scale production is attested under Valerian and Gallienus, but the final coinage of the mint in the name of Gallienus as sole emperor and Salonina (AD 260-268) deserves special attention. It is conspicuous and very poor in fabric and die-cut, so it was likely issued in a short time because of a pressing need for further bronze supply; though the weight of both denominations is substantially equal to that of previous emperors (Philip and Trebonianus Gallus), these coins were overvalued by marks, i.e. the Greek numerals Δ (four assaria; Fig. 12) and H (8 assaria; Fig. 13).[15] A similar figure is to be recognised in the contemporary coinage of *Aegium*, Sparta, the Thessalian League and Argos, the only other mints still operating in *Achaea* (along with Athens), and in the coinage of *Thessalonica*, the most important mint of Macedonia (Johnston 2007, pp. 220-221). Since all of these urban centres were more or less directly affected by the invasion of the Goths and the Herulians between AD 250 and 268 and tried to prevent the risk of a siege by erecting new fortifications or restoring the old ones (Touratsoglou 2006, pp. 138-154), one should reckon that these were "emergency issues", probably coordinated and subsidized by the Imperial authority in order to face an imminent crisis (Calomino 2011b, pp. 282-284, 334); so these bronzes could also serve as funds for enrolling troops and providing military equipment, as stated by Kroll even for 3rd century coinage of Athens, although the mint did not mark any value on these bronzes (Kroll 1997, pp. 61-63). As a result, the marked *Nicopolis* coinage of Gallienus and Salonina was massively hoarded for its overestimated value and in fear of an sudden invasion, as the three main hoards of civic coins so far discovered clearly demonstrate.[16]

Coin Use and Circulation

No report of coin finds at the site of *Nicopolis* have so far been published, so we can offer a picture of the coin circulation based on the first systematic processing of exca-

(10) See Kraay 1976, p. 238; Walker 1977, p. 65; Butcher 1988, p. 15.

(11) As Antoninus Pius 3rd consulship spans from AD 140 to 144 and Faustina was deified after death in AD 141 (see: http://rpc.ashmus.ox.ac.uk/imperial/faustina-i/), silver issues in their honour date in AD 141-144.

(12) For the most updated catalogue of coins issued by Roman Corcyra, see Moucharte 2007.

(13) See Moucharte 2007, pp. 292-293.

(14) Calomino 2011b, pp. 270-271, 276. I suggest dating the coins of Caracalla not much later than AD 211-212, after Geta's death, since their coinages look very similar to each other for the obverse portraits style and the imperial name legends.

(15) Oikonomidou 1975, pp. 157-62, 164-66, 173-76, pl. 59-69; see also Kraay 1976, pp. 245-47.

(16) The marked bronzes make up over 30% of the contents of the hoards and represent the majority of the coins of Gallienus known at present time. Three hoards have been published so far, namely the Athens-Beyrut hoard, the Plakanida hoard and an Epirotan hoard of unknown provenance: Oikonomidou 1975, pp. 169-78, pl. 64-71, with earlier bibliography. A fourth unpublished small treasure was found in 2007 in Vathy (Preveza); it contains 31 bronze coins of *Nicopolis* dated from Septimius Severus to Trebonianus Gallus.

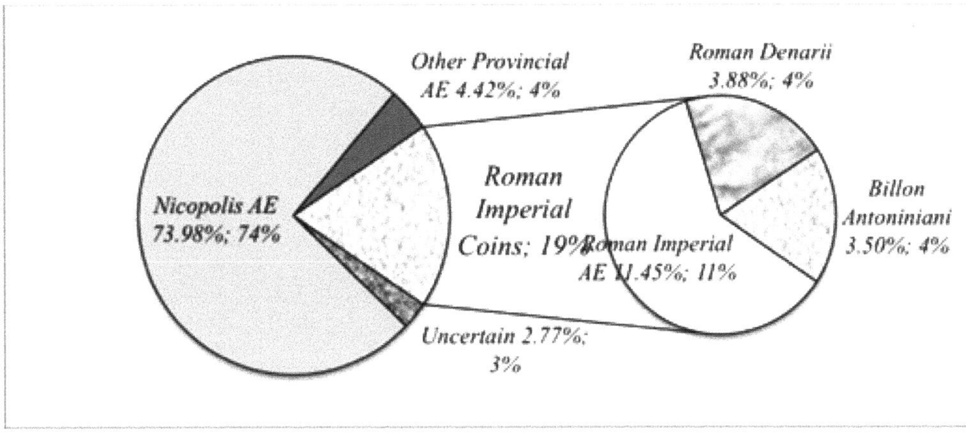

Graph 1: Coin finds of *Nicopolis* by different categories of currency

vation data, though the most part of the ancient city still waits to be brought to light and this can only be a provisional assessment.[17] From a total of 542 coins that I had the possibility to study, 401 specimens belong to the issues of the civic mint. The remaining 141 pieces consist approximately of 102 Roman imperial coins and 24 Roman provincial coins struck by other mints (besides 15 uncertain). The silver coins make up a very small part of the surviving local currency (21 *denarii* and 19 *antoniniani* of Gordian III, Trajan Decius and Gallienus), whereas the bronze coins consist of 62 imperial and 24 provincial specimens (Graph 1; Calomino 2011b, pp. 295-306).

These figures show the striking prevalence of bronze currency for everyday local transactions, in which coinage from the local mint plays a leading role, making up 74% of the total amount of finds; the Roman imperial coins account for 19% (of which 11.5% are bronzes) and provincial specimens of other mints for almost 4.5%. On the other hand, *Nicopolis* coinage is rarely found outside Epirus, as I recorded 77-79 specimens found within the provincial boundaries (besides Arta, Dodona, and Ioannina, also in Corcyra, Leukas, *Buthrotum* and *Phoinice*), but not more than 31-33 in the rest of Greece (namely in Olympia, *Pagae*, *Kabeiros*, Corinth, Patras and Athens).[18] This picture confirms the general rule of Roman provincial coin production: civic bronzes were struck almost exclusively for the local and regional circulation, whereas foreign coins had to be converted into the official currency of the community without substantially circulating within the urban centre (Burnett 1993, pp. 146-48).

Most of the coins found at the site date back either to the age of Trajan and Hadrian (more than 36% of the total) or to the age of Septimius Severus and Caracalla (about 22% of the total, but many more specimens are included in hoards). These output rates attest that the mint reached the largest volume production during the first half of the 2nd century AD and the first Severan age (thus confirming the numismatic collections data), but they also reveal two crucial periods which are hardly attested by coin finds (less than 1% of the total), the ages of Augustus and of Gallienus; such lack of evidence prompts problems of interpretation, especially because it clashes with the large number of specimens in the main numismatic collections. The rarity of Gallienus's coin finds can be explained by the intensive process of hoarding at the end of his reign, as I have already mentioned. Once again the hoards evidence attests that civic coinage was the exclusive currency circulating in the region, as only a single coin of the Thessalian League for Gallienus against 423 *Nicopolis* specimens have been found in the four roman provincial hoards so far known.[19]

It is far more surprising to find such scanty evidence of Augustan issues among the coins discovered at the site, since only four specimens (all of the Nike-type one-*assarion* denomination - *RPC1* 1364) out of the total of over 400 coming from about ten different sites of the ancient town can be catalogued. This is an extremely low percentage compared to the evidence of the numismatic collections, where more than 100 coins are known at the present time (4% of the entire coinage produced by the mint in its history) and at least 17 obverse dies and 19 reverse dies of the same unique Augustan issue can be identified, unlike any other *Nicopolis* series.

Since the mint ceased striking new coins from Augustus' death to the accession of Trajan (except for the time of Nero), the Augustan *assaria* and probably the small bronze Greek currency which survived from the Hellenistic-Republican period remained in circulation for over a century.[20] As a consequence, the very few surviving Augustan

(17) For specific reports of the coin finds of *Nicopolis*, see Calomino 2011a; 2011b, pp. 295-327.

(18) See also Oikonomidou 1975, pp. 16-17.

(19) See Kraay 1976, p. 238; Calomino 2011b, pp. 314-327. A unique Roman imperial coin hoard comes from Epirus, a small mixed *sestertii*, *denarii* and *antoniniani* treasure of Gordian III found in Anthochori (Ioannina); Touratsoglou 2006, n. 94, p. 181, with previous bibliography.

(20) See the coin finds in Epirus reported by Hammond 1967, pp. 717-25, and Rodevald 1976, p. 61, note 493; see also Abdy's contribution in this volume. On the topic of old coinage recirculation instead of new coins being supplied, see Burnett 1987, pp. 92-93 and Howgego 1990, pp. 11-15; on the survival of bronze Greek coins in Roman provincial currency, see Harl 1996, pp. 106-117.

pieces look very worn and under-weight and probably all the other specimens which one would expect to gather from excavations were withdrawn by the civic authorities after long-lasting circulation, perhaps in order to recast them and recycle the metal alloy; this could possibly have occurred when the mint resumed striking coins under Trajan. If this assumption is correct, then we should argue that most of the coins circulating within *Nicopolis* territory were called in, whereas those already taken out of the city could hardly be entirely recollected; in fact it can be observed that more Augustan coins, though still in very small quantities, come from outer archaeological sites than from *Nicopolis* itself (where the withdrawal measure might have enjoyed more efficacy), as 10 more specimens are known from excavations in the Arta and in the Ioannina Districts, especially from ancient Dodona,(21) against only 4 bronzes from the city.(22)

As I have already pointed out, the Augustan *assaria* remained in circulation for such long time because the mint was no longer allowed to strike brand new coins under the Flavians; it follows that there likely was a shortage of local small change supply during the second half of the 1st century AD and people needed to replace it with other currencies. This figure would explain the surprising high percentage of halved bronze coins found at the site. There are 29 of them (mostly very worn and not clearly identifiable), probably 22 Roman imperial and 7 Roman provincial coins; this phenomenon is actually attested by 33% of the whole bronze currency not minted by the city, whereas not one intentionally broken *Nicopolis* coin is known yet. Among the cut specimens almost exclusively Augustan and Julio-Claudian *asses* can be identified,(23) and among the Roman provincial halved specimens it is possible to recognize two Augustan bronzes, one from Thessalonica (*RPC*1, 1557-1561) and the other of the so-called CA Coinage of Asia (*RPC*1, 1138-1144), and a Claudius coin of Patras (*RPC*1, 1256; Fig. 6). Overall one can state that the halved bronze coins of the site belong mostly to the first half of the 1st century AD and that they were possibly cut soon after that date. Therefore, as well as the halved Tiberian *asses* were reutilised as small denominations along the northern Rhine border to provide new small change (and consequently Nero resumed striking *semisses*),(24) bronze coins in *Nicopolis* could be cut to produce new smaller denomination pieces (*assaria* or their fractions) and satisfy the everyday need for fractions supply. This actually looks like a local need, because it is not attested elsewhere and, for instance, in the excavations of the Roman colony of Butrint in Epirus only very few halved specimens have been recovered in a much more abundant sample of coins;(25) only further coin finds in the region could offer a clearer figure about this topic. So we can state that people in *Nicopolis* used to halve bronze coins of other mints in order to adapt them to the civic monetary system or to the local pattern of currency.

This prompts two kinds of possible conclusions: firstly, even coins of other provincial mints could be reused and spent within the city for everyday transactions in case of actual necessity;(26) secondly, as far as can be argued from the sample of finds we are able to consider, no more coins were cut in the 2nd century, so this custom was abandoned as soon as the mint restarted to strike. Further thoughts are also possible on this topic. Only bronzes not issued in *Nicopolis* were halved in order to make fresh small change out of other currencies and plug a gap in local circulation. But was such choice based only on economical or also on cultural reasons? Why were local large or medium bronzes not halved to produce new *assaria* or fractions as well? It is well-known that Greek and Asia Minor cities used to compete between each other to gain prestige through civic coinage, but recent studies have also demonstrated that in the Eastern provinces inscriptions and coin legends could refer to western Roman denominations as if they were products of a foreign power (Burnett 2005, pp. 173-78); perhaps a similar claim to cultural identity could lead people in *Nicopolis* to preserve the integrity of their own coins.

Denominations

But how much was a *Nicopolis* bronze actually worth? There is very little evidence to answer this question. Even if the city was composed of a mixed community of Greek and Roman people, the institutions and both the spoken and written official language (on inscriptions as well as on coins) were definitely Greek; it follows that the monetary and metrological system should be Greek too. This assumption would suggest to think that Greek rather than Roman denominations were used (i.e. *assaria* instead of *asses*), but does not help understand which kind of system was adopted, whether based on a division by Roman units (½=*semis*, 1=*as*, 2=*dupondius* and 4=*sestertius*) or even "ir-

(21) Two coins come from Megalo Gardiki (Ioannina), nos 28-29; I thank Georgia Pliakou for giving me this information taken from her unpublished Ph.D. thesis (University of Thessaloniki). Four more unpublished specimens are in the collections in the Archaeological Museums of Arta and Ioannina. On the other Augustan coins found in Dodona and in Arta, see Oikonomidou 1975, pp. 68-69, nos 10γ, 26δ, 27στ, 32.

(22) See Calomino 2011b, pp. 307-309. I found one from the *odeion*, one from the *stadion* and one in the old *Nicopolis* Museum exhibition; a fourth one coming from the Memorial monument of Octavian will be published by K. Zachos in the archaeological reports (I thank Yannis Stoyas - Numismatic Museum of Athens - for this information).

(23) It is possible to identify *asses* by the Augustan triumviri, Tiberius (*RIC* 81), Caligula (*RIC* 58) and Claudius.

(24) Buttrey 1972, pp. 42-47.

(25) For this information I warmly thank Richard Abdy and Sam Moorhead, who are studying and publishing the whole numismatic material found in Butrint on behalf of the British Museum and the Butrint Foundation; see again Abdy's contribution in this volume and Moorhead, Gjongecaj, Abdy 2007. Some other cases of cut bronze provincial coins in the East were reported in Leonard 1993, pp. 364-70.

(26) It follows that, even if foreign coins were supposed to be changed into the local currency, some pieces could anyway escape moneychangers' control and be currently accepted in everyday transactions. This figure was already shown by the study of countermarks on roman provincial coins, especially in Asia Minor; see Howgego 1985, pp. 32-37; Howgego 1990, p. 12.

regular" units (for instance 1 and ½, 3 or 6 *assaria*), like in other provincial mints of the Greek world.[27]

The only possible starting point on which we could base our thoughts is to be found at the very end of the civic coinage, as the marked Gallienus' issues offer a certain reference, even if too late. One should logically reckon that marks were adopted in order to change (i.e. to increase) the earlier value of the coins, otherwise such measures would not have been required;[28] so they were likely supposed to double in value the current 3rd century denominations by converting 2 and 4 *assaria* bronzes (in use at least from Septimius Severus to Valerianus and Gallienus) into 4 and 8 *assaria* pieces respectively (Figs 12-13). These already represent "anomalous" denominations, since the former correspond to the Roman *sestertius*, whereas the latter only finds reference in double *sestertii*, which were struck in Rome by Trajan Decius for a very short time and then partly resumed by Postumus and by very rare Gallienus issues.[29] The inaugural Augustan monetary system was nevertheless based on a completely different pattern, as no fewer than three denominations existed, namely the very frequent *assarion* and extremely rare fractions and multiples, possibly ½ *assarion* and 4 *assaria* (or also 1/3 *assarion* and 3 *assaria*); every possible assumption about the evolution of the system from Augustus to Gallienus is merely hypothetical.

The 2nd century AD production still included very rare multiples, but the scale of the lower denominations remarkably increased, probably in order to deal with the lack of loose change that had already caused troubles in earlier times. This figure still persisted under the Antonines, but the system became much more complex after the introduction of two more denominations, a smaller fraction and an intermediate multiple (maybe a 2 *assaria* bronze), besides the extraordinary silver issues. The evolution of the system between the end of the 2nd century and the beginning of the 3rd entailed the end of small fractions output and a remarkable decrease of the one *assarion* coinage (Calomino 2011b, pp. 288-293); this change was definitely due to inflation, that made smaller denominations valueless and forced the mint to increase the medium and large denominations supply in order to raise the actual purchasing power of local bronze currency.[30]

Coinage and Civic Identity: *Nicopolis* as a Greco-Roman community

If reconsidering literary and epigraphic sources has led scholars to give more and more credit to the theory that *Nicopolis* was a *civitas foederata* and a "double" community, new thoughts on the coinage cannot but confirm such a view. Many features actually display the growing importance not only of the Greek, but also of the Roman instances on the civic coins (Calomino 2011b, pp. 335-342).

The Hellenic nature of the coinage is surely more relevant. First and foremost, the legends are exclusively Greek, as are the great majority of the inscriptions found at the site; this obviously confirms that the ethnic core of the population was local and the synoecism process had achieved the Augustan goal.

The coin type repertory also offers one of the richest displays of Greek divinities of the whole provincial production. Not only the Olympic pantheon is fully represented (not a single god is neglected, from Zeus to Poseidon and from Dionysus to Hercules; Figs 14-15), but "minor" variants of a single cult are also attested (such as Artemis *Laphria*, *Ephesia* and probably *Kelkaia*), besides exceptional local variants of Asclepius as *Phinaios* and of Apollo as *Leukates* (Fig. 16) and *Aktios* (Oikonomidou 1975, pp. 46-50).

Greek institutions are hardly ever attested, but a single exception is really remarkable; the *Hestia Boule* type actually is a *unicum* which depicts on 3rd century coins (under Trebonianus Gallus and Valerian) the personification (a female goddess on throne, guardian of the public hearth; Fig. 17) of the local council, the logical equivalent of the Roman senate (Oikonomidou 1976).

Even more representative of the Hellenic civic identity is the personification of the city itself, which appears both on "pseudo-autonomous" (i.e. without imperial portrait, Figs 18-19) and on regular issues (Figs 24-25). The bust of *Nicopolis* is a *unicum* type as well, which originally combines the "type parlant" Nike with the traditional "town type", adding the wings to the turreted bust of Tyche. This type is equally important as it occurs on the whole three centuries production and more and more frequently in several issues and different denominations.[31]

Not surprisingly, the most frequent reverse type of "pseudo-autonomous" issues is another local patron goddess, whose origins are to be found in the IV century BC silver coins of *Anaktorion*, in Acarnania, where the original Actian Games took place (*BMC Corinth*, n. 6, tav XXXI. See also Oikonomidou 1975, pp. 26, 41). On *Nicopolis* coins she is the personification of the new games, as she sits on throne with a long sceptre and a prize-vase (Fig. 18).

The last (but not certainly least) Greek feature of the coinage lies in the most representative and frequent agonistic type, the wreath of reeds, that was awarded to the winners of the festivals competitions. The shape is really distinctive, as it cannot be confused with laurel, olive and oak wreaths, thus becoming a symbol of immediate recognition of the city (Fig. 20). Even without the inscribed letter A, it offers definite reference to *Nicopolis*, as much as it also appears very under-sized in the field of some Severan issues and

(27) See for instance *Aegium*, Thessaly, Argos and the Magnetes coinage in Roman Greece; Johnston 2007, pp. 220-221.

(28) About this topic see Johnston 2007, p. 232.

(29) See Yonge 1979, p. 50, against *RIC*5.1, pp. 35, 164, note 2.

(30) About this topic see Calomino 2008.

(31) See also Calomino 2010a.

actually works as a mint mark (Figs 11, 21); since the mark occurred when *Nicopolis* probably struck in cooperation with Corcyra, one could even argue that it was conceived in order to distinguishing each mint's issue from one another or rather to emphasise the civic pride of the Epirotan capital against its ally cum rival workshop.

On the other hand, the Roman cultural contribution to the *Nicopolis* civic identity on coins is less pre-eminent but not less significant.

Possible reference to the imperial rule and its ideological baggage are extremely rare. Military types are obviously more connected to the central mint model than the others, so marine or naval symbols such as the dolphin on trident (*RPC*1, 1367), the aplustre (*RPC*1, 1366) and the galley ram (Calomino 2011b, pp. 25, 27-28, 31, 47, 65, 79, 99, 103) obviously referred to the Actium victory and to the memorial monument on the Michalitsi hill. Echoes of imperial policy only exceptionally occur on coinage, as on the very "personalised" Neronian issues. Some Marcus Aurelius and Lucius Verus coins offer the best (and by far only) evidence of the celebration of Roman Imperial military events, apart from Actium. Very scanty, small size and poor quality bronzes actually commemorated the capture of Armenia,[32] both with legends (of which only [..]PM can be surely read) and with types (captive under trophy, Nike standing and Nike crowning a trophy; Fig. 22), which resemble the model of contemporary *denarii* struck at Rome and in Mesopotamia (*RIC*3, nos 78-86 (Marcus Aurelius) and 498-506 (Lucius Verus); *RPC*4, nos 6495, 8031, 8035, 8360), besides some *tetradrachmae* struck by Alexandria of Egypt (*RPC*4, nos 14116, 14177,14501-3, 16199).

The coin type repertory is hardly influenced by the Roman iconographic tradition. A single exception, portraying the emperor on reverse, deserves some attention; it is an "*adventus* type", depicting the emperor's triumphal arrival on horse with raised hand (Fig. 23). It occurred from the Severan to the Philip coinage (for instance, Calomino 2011b, nos 290, 338, 348, 429-431, 470, 487, 563), not very frequently but exclusively on the lower and smaller denominations (probably 3rd century one *assarion* bronzes). This figure is quite contradictory, because the introduction of such type in the mint repertory looks like a "sign of power", but relegating the emperor to the smallest fractions was not the best proof of devotion to the Roman rule. One can assume it was just a coincidence and likely served as a means of distinction among different denominations, but, recalling what was said about the possibility that Roman instances were perceived as signs of foreign power, we cannot help but think that such ambiguity reflected a mediation between opposite views.

Whether people in *Nicopolis* felt much devotion to the emperor or not, they surely worshipped the founder Augustus almost as a god. They never referred to him as a divinised emperor (and this should possibly be a Roman rather than a Greek instance), but they systematically commemorated him during the 2nd and the 3rd centuries AD on posthumous issues bearing his portrait (without radiated crown) and the legends KTICMA CEBACTOY and KTICTHC AYΓOYCTOC, again "Augustus' foundation" and "founder Augustus" (Figs 24-25).[33] This commemorative production finds no comparison in Roman Provincial coinage and represents the most original form of devotion to the official authority of the whole civic production; moreover, the Augustan posthumous portraits closely resemble those of the living emperors under which these coins were issued (Kraay 1976, p. 241), probably in order to implicitly associate them to the founder's image and legitimate their authority more as "natural heirs" than as mere successors (Calomino 2011b, pp. 339-342).

(32) See also Calomino 2010b.

(33) Kraay 1976, pp. 238-245.

Abbreviations

BMC (1989)= Head B. V. (ed.). *Catalogue of Greek Coins. The British Museum Collection. Vol. 12, Corinth, Colonies of Corinth*. London.

Foundation and Destruction (2001)= Isager J. (ed.). *Nikopolis and Northwestern Greece. The Archaeological Evidence for the City Destructions, the Foundation of Nikopolis and the Synoecism (Monographs of the Danish Institute at Athens 3)*. Athens.

Nicopolis 1 (1987)= Chrysos E. (ed.). *Proceedings of the First International Nicopolis Symposium (23-29 September 1984)*. Preveza.

Nicopolis 2 (2007)= Zachos K. L. (ed.). *Proceedings of the Second International Nicopolis Symposium (11-15 September 2002)*. Preveza.

RIC (1923-1994)= The *Roman Imperial Coinage*. Vols I-X. London.

*RPC*1 (1992)= Burnett A. M., Amandry M., Ripollès P. P. *Roman provincial coinage. Vol. 1. From the death of Caesar to the death of Vitellius (44 BC-AD 69)*. London-Paris.

*RPC*2 (1999)= Burnett A. M., *Amandry M., Carradice I. Roman provincial coinage. Vol. 2. From Vespasian to Domitian (AD 69–96)*. London-Paris.

*RPC*4 on-line= Howgego C., Heuchert V. *Roman Provincial Coinage. Vol. IV. The Antonines (AD 138-192)*. Oxford, http://rpc.ashmus.ox.ac.uk

SNG (1943)= *Sylloge Nummorum Graecorum. The Royal Collection of coins and medals. Danish National Museum, vol. III, Greece: Thessaly to Aegean islands*. Copenhagen.

References

Bowersock G. W. (1956). *Augustus and the Greek World*. Oxford.

Burnett A. (1987). *Coinage in the Roman World*. London.

Burnett A. (1993). 'Roman Provincial Coins of the Julio-Claudians', in Price M., Burnett A., Bland R. (eds), *Essays in Honour of Robert Carson and Kenneth Jenkins*. London, pp. 146-153.

Burnett A. (2005). 'The Roman West and the Roman East' in Howgego C., Heuchert V., Burnett A. (eds), *Coinage and Identity in the Roman Provinces*. Oxford, pp. 171-180.

Buttrey T. V. (1972). 'Halved Coins, the Augustan Reform, and Horace, Odes I.3', *American Journal of Archaeology*, 76.1, pp. 31-48.

Butcher K. (1988). *Roman Provincial Coins: an Introduction to the Greek Imperials*. London.

Cabanes P. (1987). 'L'Empereur Hadrien à Nicopolis', in *Nicopolis* 1, pp. 153-167.

Calomino D. (2008). 'Processi inflativi nella monetazione romano-provinciale: il caso di Nicopolis d'Epiro', in Asolati M., Gorini G. (eds), *I ritrovamenti monetali e i processi inflativi nel mondo antico e medievale, Atti del IV Congresso di Numismatica e Storia Monetaria (Padova, 12-13 ottobre 2007)*. Padova 2008, pp. 69-80.

Calomino D. (2010a). 'La civitas libera Nicopolitana nel riscontro delle fonti numismatiche: problemi di interpretazione', in *Mediterraneo antico. Economie, società, culture*, XI.1-2 (2008). Roma-Pisa, pp. 161-175.

Calomino D. (2010b). 'Some Hitherto Unidentified Roman Provincial Issues among the Coin Finds of Nicopolis', *The Numismatic Chronicle*, 170, pp. 73-84, pl. 4-5.

Calomino D. (2011a). 'Coinage and Coin Circulation in Nicopolis of Epirus. A preliminary Report', in Holmes N. (ed.), *Proceedings of the XIV International Numismatic Congress. Glasgow 31st August - 4th September 2009*. Glasgow, pp. 569-575.

Calomino D. (2011b). *Nicopolis d'Epiro. Nuovi study sulla zecc e sulla produzione monetale (BAR International Series 2214)*. Oxford.

Chrysostomou P., Kefallonitou F. (2001). *Nikopolis*. Athens.

Ellis Jones J. (1987). 'Cities of Victory. Patterns and Parallels', in *Nicopolis* 1, pp. 99-108.

Grunauer-Von Hoerschelmann S. (1983). 'The Severan Emissions of the Peloponnesus', *Israel Numismatic Journal*, 6-7, pp. 39-46.

Hammond N. G. L. (1967). *Epirus: the geography, the ancient remains, the history and the topography of Epirus and adjacent areas*. Oxford.

Harl K. W. (1996). *Coinage in the Roman Economy, 300 B.C. to A.D. 700*. Baltimore and London.

Howgego C. J. (1985). *Greek Imperial Countermarks: Studies in the Provincial Coinages of the Roman Empire (Royal Numismatic Society Special Publication 17)*. London.

Howgego C. J. (1990). 'Why did ancient states strike coins?', *The Numismatic Chronicle*, 150, pp. 2-25.

Johnston A. (2007). *Greek imperial denominations, ca 200-275: a study of the Roman provincial bronze coinages of Asia Minor*. London.

Karatzeni V. (2001). 'Epirus in the Roman Period', in *Foundation and Destruction 2001*, pp. 163-180.

Kraay C. M. (1976). 'The Coinage of Nicopolis', *The Numismatic Chronicle*, 136, pp. 235-247.

Kroll J. H. (1997). 'The Athenian imperials: results of recent study', in Nollé J., Overbeck B., Weiss P., Milano (eds), *Nomismata. Historisch-numismatische Forschungen 1, Internationales Kolloquium zur Kaiserzeitlichen Münzprägung Kleinasiens (27.-30. April 1994 in der Staatlichen Münzsammlung)*, pp. 61-73.

Lämmer M. (1986-1987). 'Die Aktischen Spiele von Nikopolis', *Stadion*, 12-13, pp. 27-38.

Leonard jr. R.D. (1993). 'Cut Bronze Coins in the Ancient Near East', in *Proceedings of the XIth International Numismatic Congress (Brussels, September 8th-13th 1991)*. Vol. 1. Louvain-la-Neuve, pp. 363-370.

Moorhead S., Gjongecaj S., Abdy R. (2007). 'Coins from the excavations at Butrint, Diaporit and the Vrina Plain', in Hansen I. L., Hodges R. (eds), *Roman Butrint. An assessment*. Oxford, pp. 78-94.

Moretti L. (1953). *Iscrizoni agonistiche greche*. Roma.

Moucharte G. (2007). 'Le monnayage de Corcyre sous les empereurs romains', in Moucharte G., Borba Florenzano M. B., De Callataÿ F., Marchetti P., Smolderen L., Yannopoulos P. (eds), *Liber Amicorum: Tony Hackens*. Louvain-la Neuve, pp. 275-329.

Murray W. R., Petsas P. (1989). *Octavian's Campsite Memorial for the Actian War*. Philadelphia.

Oikonomidou M. K. (1975). *Η Νομισματοκοπία τῆς*

Νικοπόλεως. Athens.

Oikonomidou M. K. (1976). 'ΕΣΤΙΑ ΒΟΥΛΗΣ et Nicopolis d'Epire', in Cahn H. A., Le Rider G. (eds), *Actes du 8eme congres international de numismatique. Proceedings of the 8th international congress of numismatics (New York-Washington, September 1973)*. Paris-Bâle, pp. 39-41.

Purcell N. (1987). 'The Nicopolitan Synoecism and Roman Urban Policy', in *Nicopolis 1*, pp. 71-90.

Rodewald C. (1976). *Money in the Age of Tiberius*. Manchester.

Ruscu L. (2006). 'Actia Nicopolis', *Zeitschrift für Papyrologie und Epigraphik*, 157, pp. 247-255.

Samsari D. K. (1994). *Η "Ακτια Νικοπόλη και η "Χόρα" τῆς (νοτιά Ήπειρος -Ακαρνάνια). Ιστορικογεογραφική και επιγραφική σθμβολή*. Thessalonike.

Sarikakis T. C. (1966). 'Ακτια τὰ ἐν Νικοπόλει', *Αρχαιολογικη Εφημερις*, pp. 145-162.

Sartre M. (1991). *L'Orient romain: provinces et sociétés provinciales en Méditerranée orientale d'Auguste aux Sévères (31 avant J.-C 235 après J.-C.)*. Paris.

Touratsoglou I. (2006). *Greece and the Balkans before the End of Antiquity*. Athens.

Yonge D. (1979). 'The So-Called Interregnum Coinage', *The Numismatic Chronicle*, 139, pp. 47-60.

Walker D. R. (1976). *The Metrology of the Roman Silver Coinage. Part I, from Augustus to Domitian (Series BAR 5)*. Oxford.

Zachos K. L. (2003). 'The tropaeum of the sea-battle of Actium at Nikopolis: interim report', *Journal of Roman Archaeology*, 16, pp. 65-92.

List of Figures

1.- Map of *Nicopolis* and Cape Actium (modified from Chrysostomou, Kefallonitou 2001)
2.- Plan of the site of *Nicopolis* (Zachos 2003)
3.- The Memorial Monument of Octavian on the Michalitsi Hill: reconstruction (Murray, Petsas 1989; *Nicopolis* 2)
4.- Bronze coin of *Nicopolis*, time of Augustus (*RPC*1, 1364; Calomino 2011b, n.2), bare head of Augustus r. (ΚΤΙΣΜΑ ΣΕΒΑΣΤΟΥ) / Nike advancing l. with wreath and palm branch (ΙΕΡΑ ΝΙΚΟΠΟΛΙΣ), 27 BC-AD 14, (Athens - Doukas Private Collection n. 1 ae23, 6.07g, 8h)
5.- Copper coin of *Nicopolis*, time of Nero (*RPC*1, n. 1368; Calomino 2011b, n. 6A), turreted and winged bust of *Nicopolis* r. (ΝΕΡΩΝΟΝΙΚΟΠΟΛΙΣ Η ΠΡΟΣ ΑΚΤ); / imperial galley r. (ΝΕΡΩΝΟΣ ΑΥΤΟΚΡΑ ΣΕΒΑΣΤ; above in the field ΕΠΙΦΑΝΙΑ), AD 66-68 (Milan - Raccolte Artistiche n. 1459, ae26, 10.22g, 8h)
6.- Halved copper coin of Patras, time of Claudius (*RPC*1, n. 1256), laureate head of Claudius l. ([TI CLAVDIVS CAE]SAR AVG GERM) / aquila between two standards (CO[L A A PATR X XII]), AD 41-54 (Preveza - Archaeological Museum n. 58, ae24.5, 4.29g, 7h; Calomino 2011b, p. 306, IIIQ)
7.- Bronze coin of *Nicopolis*, time of Trajan (Calomino 2011b, n. 26B), laureate head of Trajan r. (ΑΥΤΟ ΤΡΑΙΑΝΟC CѠΤΗΡ ΠΟΛΕѠC) / Nike advancing r. with wreath and palm branch (ΝΕΙΚΟΠΟΛΙC), AD 98-117 (Milan - Raccolte Artistiche n. 2322, ae19.5, 3.56g, 7h)
8.- Silver coin of *Nicopolis* (*quinarius-hemidrachma?*), time of Antoninus Pius (*RPC*4, n. 4177; Calomino 2011b, n. 150), laureate head of Antoninus Pius r. (ΑΝΤѠΝΙΝΟC CΕΒ CΕΥ ΥΠ Γ) / ΑΚΤΙΑ within wreath of reeds, AD 141-144 (Venice - Museo Archeologico Nazionale n. 4181, AR13, 1.5g, 12h)
9.- Bronze coin of *Nicopolis*, time of Septimius Severus (Calomino 2011b, n. 297), laureate and draped bust of Caracalla r. (Μ ΑΥ ΑΝΤΩΝΕΙΝΟΝ) / Zeus standing facing and looking r. with thunderbolt (ΝΕΙΚΟΠΟΛΕΩC); AD 193-211 (Bologna - Museo Civico Archeologico n. 21142, ae25, 4.74g, 3h)
10.- Bronze coin of Corcyra, time of Septimius Severus (Moucharte 2007, nos 234-238), laureate, draped, cuirassed bust of Caracalla r. ([Α Κ ΜΑ ΑΝ]ΤΩΝΕΙΝΟC), / Ares standing facing, looking r., with spear and hand on sword at hip; foot on rock or shield (ΚΟΡΚΥ[ΡΑΙΩΝ]), AD 193-211 (*SNG* Copenhagen, n. 277, pl. 6, ae22, 7.97g, 7h)
11.- Bronze coin of *Nicopolis*, time of Septimius Severus (Calomino 2011b, n. 349), laureate and draped bust of Geta r. (ΑΥ ΚΛ CΕΠΤΙ ΓΕ[ΤΑC]) / Tripod around which a snake is coiled up; in the field on the left, small wreath of reeds (ΙΕΡΑC ΝΕΙΚΟΠΟΛΕΩC); AD 193-211 (Milan - Raccolte Artistiche n. 6066, ae23, 6.24g, 3h)
12.- Bronze coin of *Nicopolis*, time of Gallienus as sole emperor (Calomino 2011b, n. 615), laureate head of Gallienus r. (ΠΟ ΛΙΚ ΓΑΛΛΙΗΝΟC CΕ) / Asclepius standing l., resting on rod, around which a snake is coiled up; in the field on the l., value mark Δ (ΙΕΡΑC ΝΙΚΟΠΟΛΙC-sic), AD 260-268 (Udine - Musei Civici n. 161-3, ae22.5, 9.69g, 1h)
13.- Bronze coin of *Nicopolis*, time of Gallienus as sole emperor, (Oikonomidou 1975, n. 41, pl. 60; Calomino 2011b, n. 611), laureate and draped bust of Gallienus r. (ΠΟΥ ΛΙΚ ΓΑΛΛΙΗΕΝΟC [ΑΥ?]) / Asclepius standing l., resting on rod, around which a snake is coiled up; in the field, value mark Η (ΙΕΡΑC ΝΙΚΟΠΟΛΙC-sic), AD 260-268 (Paris - Cabinet de Mèdailles, ae32, 18.15g, 10h)

14.- Bronze coin of *Nicopolis*, time of Septimius Severus (Oikonomidou 1975, n. 30, pl. 33; Calomino 2011b, n. 296), laureate and draped bust of Caracalla r. (M AY AN[TΩNEIN]ON) / Zeus seated l. on throne with long sceptre; before, altar (NEIKOΠOΛEΩC); AD 193-211 (Berlin - Staatliche Museen, Münzkabinett, ae25, 6.77g, 3h)
15.- Bronze coin of *Nicopolis*, time of Philip the Arab (Calomino 2011b, n. 491), radiate head of Philip r. (AYT M IOY ΦIΛIΠΠOC CEB) / helmeted Athena standing l. with spear, resting on shield (IEPAC NEIKOΠOΛEΩC), AD 244-249 (Turin - Medagliere dell'Armeria Reale n. 20701, ae25, 6.89g, 8h)
16.- Bronze coin of *Nicopolis*, time of Trajan (Oikonomidou 1975, n. 21, pl. 13; Calomino 2011b, n. 21), laureate head of Trajan r. (AYTO TPAIANOC CωTHP ΠOΛEωC) / Apollo *Leukates* standing l. with bow and arrow (AΠOΛΛωN / ΛEYKATHC), AD 98-117 (Berlin - Staatliche Museen, Münzkabinett, ae23, 7.45g, 6h)
17.- Bronze coin of *Nicopolis*, time of Trebonianus Gallus (Oikonomidou 1975, n. 13, pl. 55; Calomino 2011b, n. 550), laureate and draped bust of Volusianus r. ([AK?] BI AΦ ΓAΛΛOC BE BOΛOYC[IANOC]) / *Hestia Boule* seated facing on throne, looking r. ([ECTIA] BOYΛHC); AD 251-253 (Athens - Numismatic Museum, Plakanida Hoard n. 24, ae25, 6.60g, 3h)
18.- Bronze coin of *Nicopolis*, 2nd century AD (Calomino 2011b, n. 230A), turreted and winged bust of *Nicopolis* r. (IEPA N[IKOΠOΛIC]) / *Aktia* seated l. on throne with long sceptre and prize-vase (CEBACTOY [KTICMA]) (Venice - Museo Archeologico Nazionale n. 6134, ae25, 8.43g, 3h)
19.- Bronze coin of *Nicopolis*, 2nd century AD (Calomino 2011b, n. 122), turreted and winged bust of *Nicopolis* r. (NIKOΠOΛIC IEPA) / Tyche standing l. with rudder and cornucopia (CEBACTOY KTICMA) (Athens - Alpha Bank Collection n. 4207, ae15, 2.50g, 1h)
20.- Bronze coin of *Nicopolis*, time of Antoninus Pius (Calomino 2011b, n. 164), laureate head of Antoninus Pius r. (AIΛIOC ANTωNEINOC) / A within wreath of reeds, AD 138-161 (Turin - Medagliere dell'Armeria Reale n. 20491, ae16, 4.07g, 6h)
21.- Bronze coin of *Nicopolis*, time of Septimius Severus (Calomino 2011b, n. 246), laureate head of Septimius Severus r. ([...]) / wreath of reeds within laurel wreath (unreadable or missing), AD 193-211 (Verona - Musei Civici n. 72511, ae23, 5.64, 1h)
22.- Bronze coin of *Nicopolis*, time of Marcus Aurelius (Calomino 2011b, n. 208), laureate head of Marcus Aurelius r. (AYP[HΛ ANTωNINOC?]) / Nike standing l. and crowning a military trophy (unreadable or missing), AD 163-166 (Preveza - Archaeological Museum, *odeion* excavations n. 204, ae16, 3.79g, 12h)
23.- Bronze coin of *Nicopolis*, time of Septimius Severus (Calomino 2011b, n. 290), laureate and draped bust of Caracalla r. (A K M AY ANTωNEINOC) / emperor riding r. with raised hand (NEIKOΠOΛEωC); AD 193-211 (Venice - Museo Archeologico Nazionale n. 4446, ae22.5, 6.45g, 7h)
24.- Bronze coin of *Nicopolis*, time of Trajan (Calomino 2011b, n. 49), bare head of Augustus r. (KTICMA CEBACTOY) / turreted and winged bust of *Nicopolis* r. (IEPA NEIKOΠOΛIC), AD 98-117 (Venice - Museo Archeologico Nazionale n. 3909, ae18, 3.94g, 6h)
25.- Bronze coin of *Nicopolis*, time of Antoninus Pius (Calomino 2011b, n. 171), laureate head of Augustus r. (KTICMA CEBACTOY) / turreted and winged bust of *Nicopolis* r. (IEPA NIKOΠOΛIC), AD 138-161 (Turin - Medagliere dell'Armeria Reale n. 20433, ae26.5, g11.68, 3h)

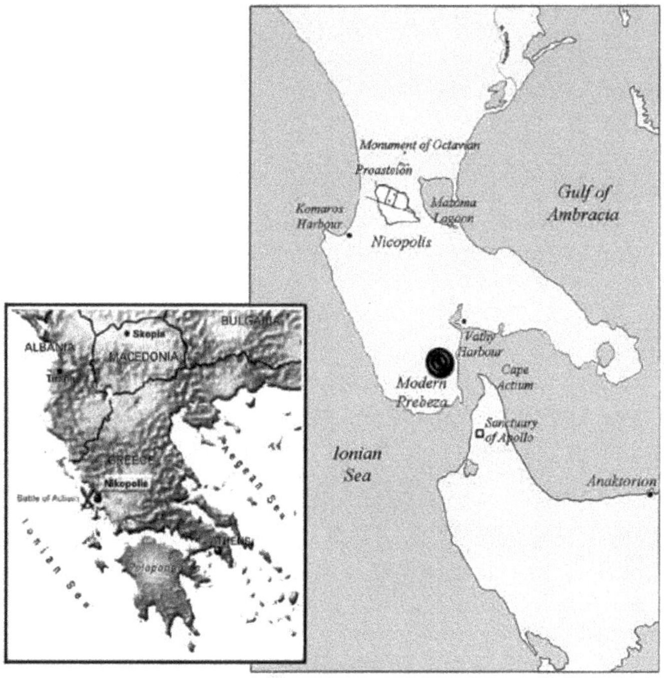
Monument of Octavian
Proasteion
Komaros Harbour
Mazoma Lagoon
Gulf of Ambracia
Nicopolis
Vathy Harbour
Modern Prebeza
Cape Actium
Sanctuary of Apollo
Ionian Sea
Anaktorion
BULGARIA
ALBANIA
MACEDONIA
Skopje
Nikopolis
Aegean Sea
Ionian Sea

1.

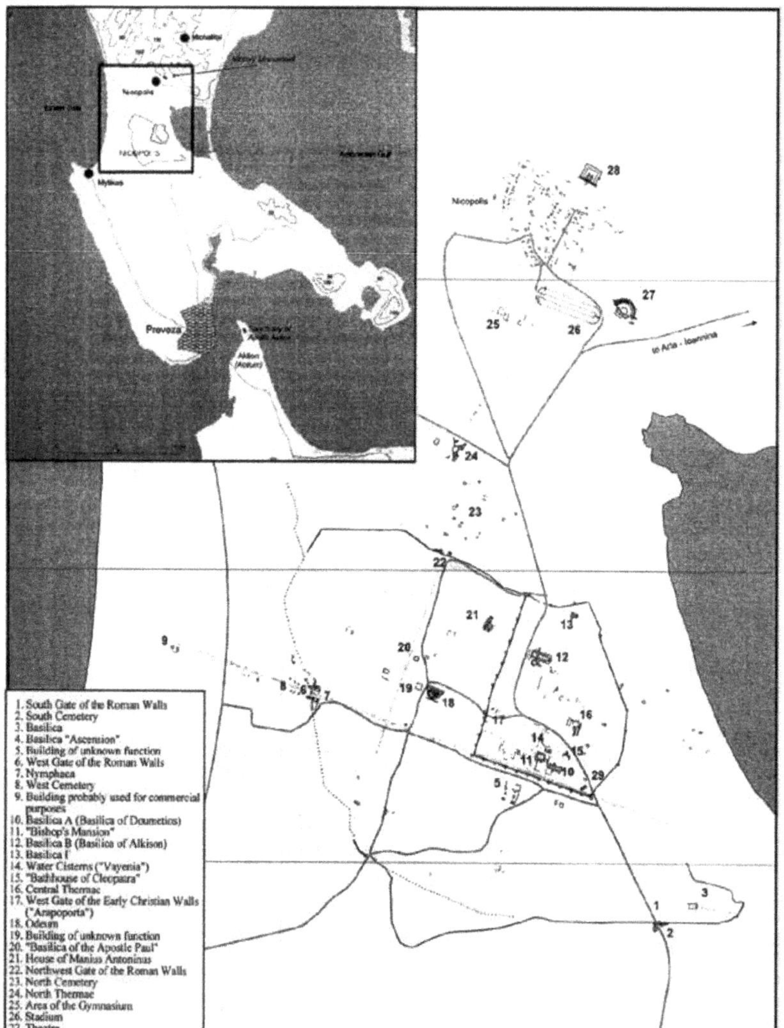
Nicopolis
Preveza
Mytikas
to Arta - Ioannina
1. South Gate of the Roman Walls
2. South Cemetery
3. Basilica
4. Basilica "Ascension"
5. Building of unknown function
6. West Gate of the Roman Walls
7. Nymphaea
8. West Cemetery
9. Building probably used for commercial purposes
10. Basilica A (Basilica of Doumetios)
11. "Bishop's Mansion"
12. Basilica B (Basilica of Alkison)
13. Basilica Γ
14. Water Cisterns ("Vayenia")
15. "Bathhouse of Cleopatra"
16. Central Thermae
17. West Gate of the Early Christian Walls ("Arapoporta")
18. Odeum
19. Building of unknown function
20. "Basilica of the Apostle Paul"
21. House of Manius Antoninus
22. Northwest Gate of the Roman Walls
23. North Cemetery
24. North Thermae
25. Area of the Gymnasium
26. Stadium
27. Theatre
28. Victory Monument
29. Museum
0 100 200 500 M

2.

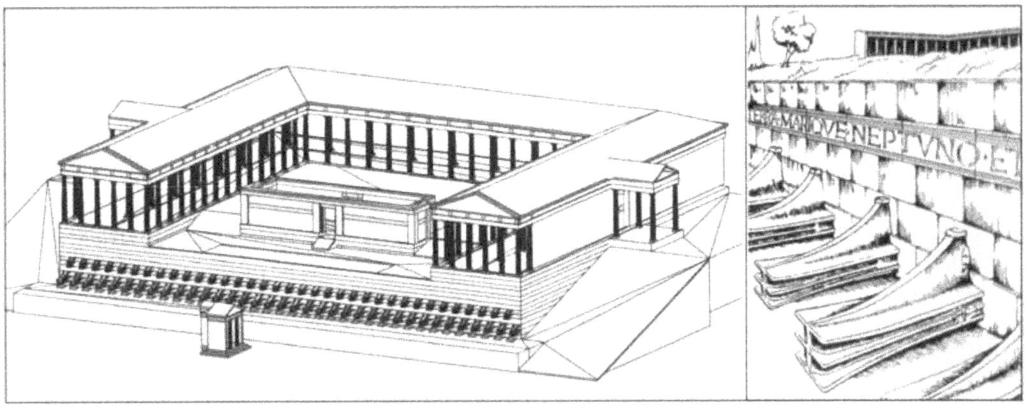

3.

4. 5. 6. 7.

8. 9. 10. 11.

12.

13

14.

15.

16.

17.

18.

19.

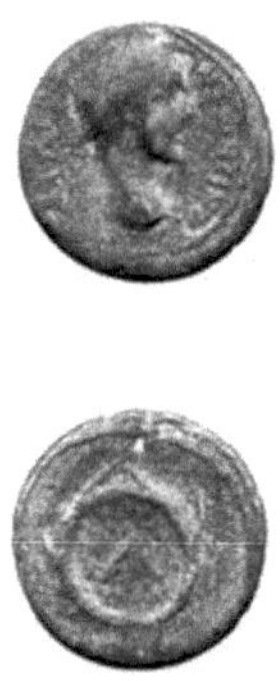

20.

21.

22.

23.

24.

25.

The Mint cities of the Kushan Empire

Robert Bracey

ABSTRACT

Cities have an allure for numismatists. The desire to associate the minting of coins with particular cities is remarkably strong, often surmounting an absence of evidence. This paper explores the evidence for the minting locations of Kushan coins. It illustrates this evidence through a series of example cities which can be connected to a greater or lesser degree with particular issues of coins.

Introduction[1]

The Kushan Empire was the dominant power of Central Asia and Northern India from the first to the fourth century AD. During that period it issued an important series of coins, including the first regular gold coinage minted in India. These coins became the model for succesive dynasties in Central Asia, Kashmir, and North India. Much remains unknown about the coins of the Kushan Emperors, in particular their relationship to the cities of the Empire. Some, one or more, of these cities must have housed the mints in which the coins were produced. A mint could of course be located anywhere as they were small affairs but minting was a political activity as much as an economic one and location in a city ensured political control. If the mints had been recorded on the coins the identification would be simpler but none of the coins have any discirnable mint name, or even the patron god or emblem of a particular city. Yet cities retain a peculiar allure and frequently the terms 'mint of Peshawar', 'product of Taxila' are encountered amongst scholars, collectors and auction catalogues. Coins must have been made somewhere and their attribution to a city, even unsupported by evidence is approached with enthusiasm. The purpose of this article is to explore what evidence is available to identify where the mints of the Kushan Empire were located. The article will proceed in two stages. In the first a cursory sketch of Kushan coin production will be made. The coins themselves provide enough evidence to permit their division into different mints. In the second stage various cities within the Empire will be examined as will the evidence that coins were minted in those locations. A comprehensive map of the Kushan mints is impossible as there are too many gaps in the evidence. However, there are some groups of gold and copper coinage which can be attributed, and at least provisionally be given the name of a city.

The Kushan Dynasty	
Kujula Kadphises	Mid. 1st Century AD
Wima Takto	Late 1st Century AD
Wima Kadphises	Early 2nd Century AD
Kanishka	AD c.127-150
Huvishka	AD 150-190
Vasudeva	AD 190-230
Kanishka II	AD 230-245
Vasishka	AD 245-260
Kanishka III	Late 3rd Century AD
Vasudeva II	
Mahi	Early 4th Century AD
Shaka	
Kipunadha	Mid 4th Century AD

Kushan Coinage

The term Kushan is essentially a modern appellation. It appears on many coins of the second to fifth centuries, perhaps as a name, a title, an ethnonym or a claim of descent. From the third century AD it is used for a geographic region in some Armenian and Coptic texts, though not one ruled by the dynasty modern historians call Kushan. For modern historians it denotes those kings for whom a solid line of succession can be established from Kujula Kadphises, as well as for their dynasty as a whole and the political entity over which they ruled. That political entity, the Kushan Empire, issued coins principally in copper and

(1) This study is based upon work undertaken as part of the Kushan Coins Project at the British Museum and would have been impossible without the generous support of all of those involved but particularly Joe Cribb and Gul Rahim Khan.

gold. The copper coinage derived from silver and copper coinages of North India, Pakistan and Afghanistan current in the first century AD. Under the first Kushan Emperors it included some silver and debased silver issues. The gold coinage was a Kushan innovation, which commenced under the third emperor Wima Kadphises. That gold coinage set a pattern which was followed for centuries in South and Central Asia (Cribb 2003; 2007).

THE STRUCTURE OF THE COPPER COINAGE

Kushan coins begin under Kujula Kadphises and the first issues consist of both silver and copper. These followed on from coinages which were already in circulation in the regions he ruled or conquered. In some parts of the Empire (the Northern regions and Sind) a silver coinage had been in use while in others silver coins had become debased and were replaced with copper before the Kushan coinages were issued. Kujula's types also followed the designs of coins already in circulation, particulary Bactrian Greek types in the north and Indo-Scythian or Indo-Parthian types in the South. These variations reflect not only a diverse prior coinage but also at least five mints.

Fig. 1.- Imperial 'Soter Megas' coinage of Wina Takto, the second Kushan Emperor (BM 1894.0506.795)

Kujula's successors made attempts to standardize the coinage, concentrating production in a smaller number of mints and using a common design. His son, Wima Takto, introduced a standard 'imperial' type (Fig. 1). This was not entirely successful and during his reign a number of distinct regional types continued to be issued or were introduced (MacDowall 1968; Sims-Williams and Cribb 1995).[2] Wima Kadphises did succeed, however, introducing a single coin type for the whole Empire. His coinage, featuring a standing king on one side, and a god with bull (resembling the Indian god Siva) on the reverse, is so homogenous as to imply a single mint. Some authors think differently. Mitchiner (1978, pp. 405-409) divides the gold coins of Wima amongst three different mints – Balkh, Taxila, and Peshawar. Most authors accept a single mint. Göbl (1984) and Perkins (2007) suggests that the small differences (which Mitchiner uses to differentiate Taxila and Peshawar) should be seen as a chronological sequence. Wima's reign appears to have marked a major reform as it was during his reign gold coins were first issued (see below).

(2) Traditional interpretations assume the coins began with many mints and these were reduced to one type during the reign but the structure may be more complex (Cribb, correspondence).

If the concentration of production under Wima Kadphises was a deliberate policy it failed or was soon reversed. His son Kanishka begins his reign with a single series continuing that of Wima Kadphises and during his reign four additional mints seem to be opened. Under Kanishka's successor, Huvishka, we continue to see several different series. Huvishka's coins can be divided easily into two phases. In the early part of his reign copper coins are struck to a standard of about 16g and this is reduced to a standard of between 7 and 11g in the latter part of the reign. Only two of the mints open at the start of the reign continue to produce coins into the second half but one new mint with a distinctive style opens and produces only coins of the reduced weight. The productions of Kanishka and Huvishka have proven quite complex but there is a curious organisation at the large scale. Both kings keep open the mint that makes Wima's coins, and which will go on to make Vasudeva I's coins later. That mint makes coins which are found throughout the Empire and even beyond the Northern borders (in Choresmia) and Southern borders (in the middle Ganges). The other mints all seem to have much more localised productions and are presumably smaller given that their coins are rarer today.

Following Huvishka, Vasudeva I certainly continued production at two mints. The main mints production was much more homogenous than those made under Kanishka and Huvishka. Distinctions are made by small control marks in the left or right field of the obverse (Image 1). The coins of Vasudeva and his successors have not been as thoroughly studied as the earlier coinage. In many early publications they could be lumped together as 'late Kushan'. Göbl (1984) made some attempts to resolve this problem. However, the problem is complicated by the issue of imitations from shortly after the reign of Vasudeva. In the reign of Vasudeva I the Sasanian Empire under Ardashir and later Shapur annexed parts of Bactria which had been under Kushan rule. The region did not pass under direct Sasanian rule and for the next century a puppet government, known as the Kushanshah, issued a coinage imitating the designs of Vasudeva. This parallel series mixes freely with official Kushan coins in hoards and both groups seem to be the subject of extensive local imitations. Fortunately since Göbl made the first attempt there have been valuable contributions by Cribb (1981;1985a; 1985b), MacDowall (2005), and Khan (2011) since.

A few general points can be made about the Kushan coinage after Huvishka. It continues to diminish in weight. In the reign of Kanishka II it drops to about 5g, and in the reign of Vasudeva II to between 3 and 4g. By the end of the Kushan dynasty under Kipunadha it has fallen as low as 2g. It also never shows as much complexity of series as the earlier coinage. No more than two mints are required to explain any of the kings' issues and in some cases a single mint would appear to be enough. The attribution of coinage becomes increasingly difficult as the edge legends disappear or vanish entirely from the coins. The last group that can be attributed with certainty are those of Vasudeva

II. These coins carry the kings name in the Indian script Brāhmī. Vasudeva II is one of the kings with two distinct types – he issues coins with both a standing and a seated king in quite large numbers. Part of the difficulty in reconstructing the structure of the mints is establishing if these distinct obverse designs represent two mints or simply two phases of a single mint. The coins presently attributed to the last Kushan Emperors, Shaka and Kipunadha, depend upon a simple co-incidence that they appear to be the coins in circulation at the same time as the kings are known to be ruling. The last of these are rough cut pieces of copper featuring a simple standing figure with a seated goddess on the reverse. Cribb (1981, p. 105) was the first to connect them with Kipunadha. As can be imagined the minting structure must remain uncertain when the attribution poses these problems. For Mahi whose reign is short-lived no coins have so far been identified, either because they are yet to be seen or because a group attributed to Vasudeva II or Shaka has been mis-attributed.

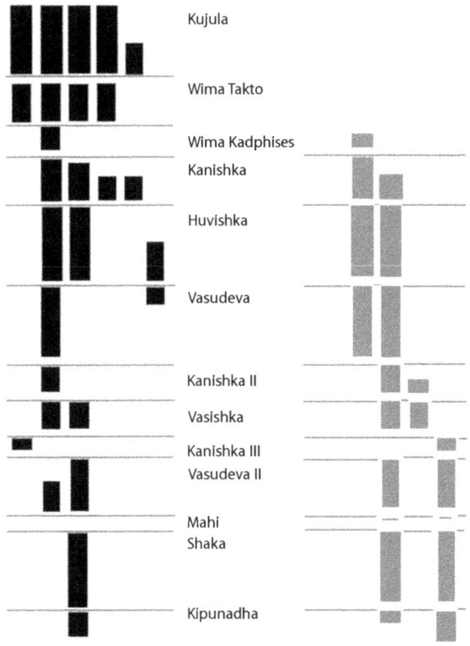

Fig. 2.- Left: structure of the copper mints. Right: Gold production

The Structure of the Gold Coinage

The diagram shows one reconstruction of the structure of the copper mints (Fig. 2) and a construction for the gold production. As can be seen at least a dozen mints need to be identified. At the start of the second century AD, when Wima Kadphises came to power, he inherited a large Empire with a centralized coinage in copper but no tradition of regular minting in gold. There were, however, clear precedents for the production of gold coinage. The Hellenistic kings of Bactria and Gandhara had issued occasional gold staters and in India the gold coins of Rome were imported and familiar to many users. A mint was established to produce gold coins some time in Wima's reign, and initially it produced only small numbers at irregular intervals. The mint increased its production, creating a large number of coins in three denominations and ultimately moved into regular production of the stater and quarter stater.(3)

So at the start of the reign of Kanishka the Kushan state had a mint, apparently distinct from its copper mints, producing gold staters influenced by Roman designs on a regular basis with occasional issues of quarter staters. Towards the end of Kanishka's reign a second mint opened and production continued at both mints into the reigns of his successors Huvishka and Vasudeva. Both mints used the same designs with only minor differences in style. It is not until the end of the reign of Vasudeva that a mark appears on the coins which distinguish the mints, with one mint using a brāhmī letter and the other mint a symbol conventionally called the nandipada. The two mints appear to have maintained the same essential relationship throughout. One, the mint founded under Wima, which used the nandipada late in the reign of Vasudeva, appears to have been the main mint, producing most of the coinage. The other, founded late in the reign of Kanishka, the subsidiary mint, producing about half as much.

At the end of Vasudeva's reign the situation becomes confused. Two series of coins appear. One uses the nandipada symbol and the name of Vasudeva. Over time the flans widen and become thinner, this scyphate shape coinage is eventually replaced by coinage issued in the name of Sasanian rulers who refer to themselves as 'king of Kushan'. Known to historians as the Kushano-Sasanians, or Kushanshah, this dynasty holds sway in the northern parts of the Kushan Empire, Bactria and sometimes Gandhara. The other series becomes thicker with increasingly corrupt Bactrian legends and an increasing number of control marks in the Indian script Brāhmī. They are issued in the names of Kanishka and Vasishka. From inscriptions we know that over a period of about 40 years following the death of Vasudeva there were three kings, Kanishka II, Vasishka and his son Kanishka III. The two series represent a divergence. One series is issued by the Sasanians or their protégés, the second series by the Kushan successors of Vasudeva II. This period begins and ends with the same essential structure to the gold coinage, a main mint and a subsidiary mint, but the picture between is less clear. Kanishka II's coins are issued from only a single mint and while Vasishka re-establishes the two mint arrangement his son issues coins from only the newly founded mint. The older mint moves directly from the production of the coins of Vasishka to those of Vasudeva II.

Vasudeva II is the first king to issue coins with his name in Brāhmī characters. By the time of Vasudeva II the volume of production had more than doubled, though the gold content was slightly debased. Vasudeva II was succeeded

(3) Or dinar, suvarna, or aureus. What to call the Kushan gold unit of about 8g is an open question. There is no evidence from the period to indicate how it is referred to and several different names are employed before and after the Kushan period for similar coins.

by Mahi, who in turn was succeeded by Shaka. Shaka's coinage marks a step change in production, being many times larger than that of any of his predecessors. This increase in production is not restricted to the Kushan state. During the reign of Shaka a previously minor dynasty in Magadha, the Gupta's had achieved hegemony over the Gangetic valley. The king responsible for the Gupta ascendency, Samudragupta, issued his own gold coinage. Based on Kushan types the scale of production was still greater than that of Shaka. The structure of this late Kushan coinage, and the question of how it was minted has been a matter of controversy for the past century. For the kings from Wima to Vasudeva die studies have elicited much about the structure. This is unlikely to yield the same results for the late Kushan kings as the sample of coins is much less complete, and the next section will explore the problem in relation to the coinage of Shaka.

NUMBERING THE MINTS

Kushan coins have no mint marks. Yet before mints can be located it is necessary to number them. The previous discussion highlighted both the areas of knowledge and ignorance regarding the structure of the Kushan mints and this will present one example of how such structures are revealed. A single example will suffice because the basic principle is always the same. A feature (weight, purity, development of design) is identified which changes over time, and then the relationship between groups is examined to establish if they are consecutive or parallel. Multiple mints reveal themselves in parallel sequences.

In the case of the last three kings of the dynasty, Mahi, Shaka, and Kipunadha, the feature which allows us to track over time is specific gravity. Specific gravity is a measure of the density of a coin and it changes according to the metal from which the coin is made. From the reign of Kanishka the gold mint seems to have adulterated the gold content of the coins, a practice which accelerated in and after the reign of Vasudeva II. This reducing gold content causes a reduction in the specific gravity which allows the coins to be ordered (Oddy, Cribb 1998b; Bracey, Oddy, 2010). From the reign of Vasudeva I the mint also began to add brāhmī letters as control marks. These marks were initially mistaken for mint towns:"The other syllables may generally be taken as initial letters of names of mint-towns and provinces. Thus 'Pa' may stand for Purusapura (ie Peshawar), 'Na' for Nagarahara (ie Jalalabad), 'Ga' for Gandhara, and 'Chu' and 'Khu' for tribes of the Chutrasa and the Kshudrakas living in the upper and the middle Indus valley." (Chattopadyay 1967, p. 100). This was clearly based upon an equation of the brahmi marks with the monograms appearing on Indo-Greek coins, still commonly treated as the designation of a mint,[4] though, such an interpretation is quite impossible. If these were mints then the number encountered would be fairly constant from reign to reign. Mahi, whose reign is quite short has just two characters 'ma' and 'pu' under his arm, while Shaka has an enormous variety and his successor Kipunadha is again restricted to just two 'bhadra' and 'bhasata'.[5] We might be tempted to see the division of Mahi and Kipunadha's coinage in two by their control marks as a division into two mints and that is precisely how it has been presented (Image 2).

<table>
<tr><th colspan="2">Mint marks (by altar/ under arm) according to Oddy and Cribb (1998b)</th></tr>
<tr><td colspan="2">-/Pa</td></tr>
<tr><td colspan="2">-/Bhr</td></tr>
<tr><td colspan="2">Vi/Bhr</td></tr>
<tr><td>Vi/Sya</td><td>Bha/Sya</td></tr>
<tr><td>Vi/Sita</td><td>Bha/Sita</td></tr>
</table>

Fig. 3

For Shaka the various marks clearly change over time so the first stage was to establish a relationship between them. Previous attempts had been made by Gobl (1984), and supplemented by Oddy and Cribb (1998b). The reconstruction given in Oddy and Cribb is shown here (Fig. 3). These reconstructions were based solely on the obverse of the coin. While the obverses have Brāhmī control marks to distinguish them the reverse consists of a single type, the goddess Ardoxsho seated upon a throne, a cornucopia resting over her left shoulder and a diadem in her extended right hand. In the top left field is a dynastic symbol known as the tamgha, and to the right a corrupt legend reduced to a decorative element which originally read ΑΡΔΟΧÞΟ in Bactrian Greek characters. The mint clearly felt no need to distinguish or mark its reverses.

As part of the ongoing Kushan Coin Project, a preliminary die study of these coins was undertaken. For earlier gold coinages of the Kushans, such as those of Wima, Kanishka, Huvishka and Vasudeva, die analysis has frequently been able to demonstrate the connections between different types. Unfortunately the sample for Shaka is far less complete,[6] probably a combination of higher original production and less modern market demand for the coins. Fortunately in the process of the die study stylistic differences were identified in the reverses.The categorisation of stylistic differences like these are subjective, and these are only temporary classifications. It is certain that as the sample of coins for Shaka increases so this division will be abandoned and replaced by a more refined understanding. For the moment, combined with the data already available from the obverse marks and gold purity (shown in Fig. 4) this gives us some sense of the structure of Shaka's minting.

(4) This is not the place but that interpretation, of Indo-Greek monograms as mints, is equally untenable. Once control marks or monograms were established as part of the coinage tradition their presence was required but their symbolism was optional. It is almost certain that different mints and periods used the marks to mean different things.

(5) Or 'bhasana'. There is some difficulty in being exact with the reading of these characters as they are deprived of any context.

(6) n=190, do=160, provisional study January 2010

Fig. 4. Obverse/Reverse Combinations in Shaka's Coinage

Brāhmī Character (by altar/under arm)			Gold Content	A	B	C	D	E	F
Mint A									
		bhr	75%			X		X	X
		vi/bha	63%			X			
		vi/sya	58%			X			
		bha/sya(dot)	55%			X			?
		vi/sina	48%		?	X	X		X
Mint B									
		pa (or ha)	76%		X				
		mi	76%		X				
		kho/mi	77%		X				?
		bha/sina(dot)	55%	X					
		je/sina		X					
		bha/sya tripartite	48%	X					

Though there is no direct linkage between the high gold content group with reverse B and the lower gold content with reverse A their combination as a single mint makes sense. The general pattern indicates two parallel series. The first with reverse types C to F predominantly (but not exclusively) uses 'vi' by the altar and when the character 'sya' is employed it is engraved in a manner that had become standard in the north-west in the second century AD. The second group with reverses A and B uses 'bha' by the altar in its later stages and when 'sya' is employed it is engraved in an archaic manner.

Candidate Cities

The data for Shaka just examined was included in the chart of mint structure. Similar analyses underpin the rest of the structure in that chart, on which basis the mints could be numbered 1,2,3... etc. Once that step is complete to move to locations a list of candidates cities must be drawn up. Where might the coins have been made? As already mentioned the mints were very small affairs. For example, at its most intense period of production Wima's mint employed only 14 people directly in the manufacture of coins.[7] However, the production was a political as much as an economic act so we would expect the mint to be located in a political centre. Map 1 shows a series of political centres, ranging from the North to the South of the Empire. This list is almost certainly not complete. Ancient texts have survived in only a patchy fashion and archaeological work is restricted. Major cities may miss our scruting entirely. These eight are eight cities which we know, for one reason or another, were politically important: **B**alkh, **Sur**kh Khotal, **Ka**pisa (Begram), **P**eshawar (Puskavalati), **T**axila, **K**anishkapura, **Sa**gala (Sialkot), **M**athura.

Balkh

Balkh, located on the Oxus river is a major citadel which is mentioned in a number of ancient texts. Archaeological explorations at the site show that it was in constant occupation from the Greco-Bactrian to the Timurid period. According to Polybius (10.49, 11.34) it was here that the Greco-Bactrian king Euthydemus was besieged by the Seleucid king Antiochus III and it was probably the capi-

(7) Bracey 2011. To these should be added those involved in providing raw materials – gold, iron, tools, fuel; and those in administrative roles. All figures we do not know.

tal of Bactria in the Greco-Bactrian period (Ball 1982, no. 99). In the third and fourth centuries Balkh was certainly employed as a mint. Coins of the Kushanshahs, a dynasty which followed the Kushans in Bactria, minted coins from the city. Unlike the Kushans the Kushanshahs sometimes included the name of the mint on their coins. Image 3 illustrates a coin of the ruler Hormizd with the name of Balkh[8] clearly visible in the right field.We know that the city was politically important, that it was the political centre for a region of significance and that coins were issued from there after it was lost to the Kushan Empire. Does this indicate it was employed as a mint by the Kushans?[9]

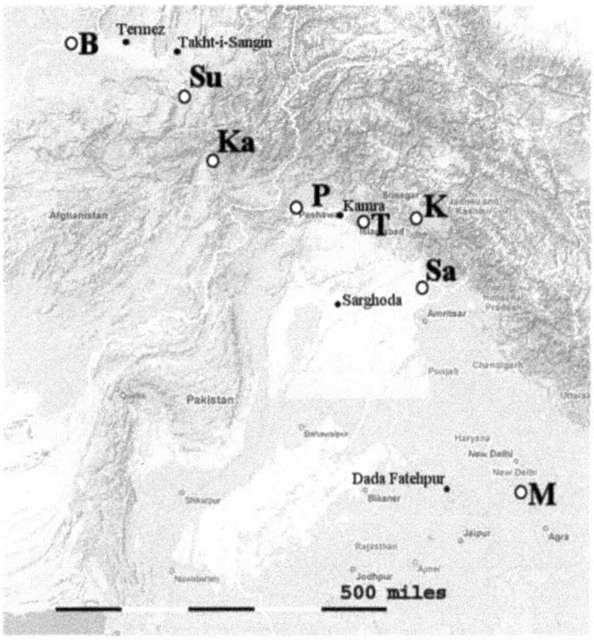

Map 1

Between the end of the reign of Vasudeva I and the coins issued by the Kushano-Sasanians there are a long series of coins issued in the name of Vasudeva. These coins gradually adopt the style and form of Kushan-Sasanain coins while retaining the Kushan Emperor's name. The transition is very subtle and is illustrated in Image 4. The type on the left corresponds to a change in control marks also seen at the subsidiary mint. Both mints introduce a nandipada symbol on the right side, apparently at the same time. So at this stage the two mints are clearly answering to the same central authority. The marks that follow -'o', dots, and parallel ribbons- are sometimes features which are unusual on Kushan coins but are encountered. The swastika mark is not encountered on Kushan coins, but it is an element on Kushanshah coins. So by the time the series has reached the type shown on the far right they are clearly not being issued by a Kushan authority. At which point does the transition of control, from Kushan to Kushanshah, take place? From the point at which the subsidiary mint introduces the nandipada there are seven obverse dies before the first issue of Kanishka II. The relationship between the main and subsidiary mints is usually that the main mint makes twice as many dies. Fourteen dies at the main mint would place the change in control after the introduction of the 'o' mark and before the introduction of the dots (subject to the usual uncertainty in estimating how representative the surviving sample of dies is).

Literary sources tell us that the Sasanian Emperor Ardashir invaded the Kushan Empire in the early third Century and that this included the city of Balkh (Basham 1968). It is the coincidence between this transitional group and the reported invasion that is useful. The coins clearly show the transition at a particular mint from one minting authority to another. The only transition known to us is the loss of Bactria to the Sasanians. This series stands before the issue of the coins of the Kushanshah, which appears to be a Sasanian creation in Bactria. The Kushanshah coins, or at least a large proportion of them, were minted at Balkh. It therefore makes sense that the Kushan mint was located in Balkh. Since there is continuity from the end of the reign of Wima Kadphises to these issues under Vasudeva I it is likely the Kushan principal mint had been located in Balkh through the second and early third century.

Surkh Khotal

Other Bactrian sites, such as Surkh Khotal, could be considered as candidates for a mint. Surkh Khotal, and the nearby site of Rabatak contain monumental temple structures associated with the dynasty of the Kushans. Surkh Khotal is built atop high ground on the edge of a valley. A monumental stair case leads from the valley to the top of the hill and it must have been a prominent site for travellers going north or south between Bactria and Gandhara (Rosenfield 1967, pp. 154-163). Both Surkh Khotal and Rabatak have yielded official inscriptions which help to identify them as 'bagolagos' (Sims-Williams and Cribb 1995; Gershevitch 1979). Known as a 'devakula' in Mathura we will return to this type of site later. This alone marks Surkh Khotal as an important political centre.

Fig. 5.- An example of Kujula Kadphises' anonymous silver coinage. British Museum 1994.0711.1

Language is one of our key clues to the minting of coins in the region represented by Balkh in the west and Surkh Khotal in the east. It is this region in which Greek was used exclusively (under the Bactrian Greeks and their imitators).

(8) Gobl 1984, p. 23, expressed some doubts about the attribution of these coins to Balkh.

(9) The argument outlined here is that of Cribb, delivered in a series of presentations in Oxford and at meetings of the Oriental Numismatic Society.

Under Kujula many of his coin types used two languages but one group, the Heraios-Sanab coinage, features only a Greek legend and it is this which is found in the Northern parts of the Empire (Cribb 1993) (Fig. 5). There is a marked preference for Greek as the Kushans consolidate their coinage. The imperial 'Soter Megas' type of Wima Takto is issued only in Greek (Fig. 1), as are the coins of Kanishka. When the use of Greek ends in the early years of Kanishka I it is replaced with Bactrian. Bactrian is employed almost exclusively in the region of Afghanistan[10] and is written in Greek script. Gandhari,[11] written in the Kharosti script, which was commonly employed in Gandhara and the mixed Sanskrit-Prakrit (sometimes known as Epigraphical Hybrid Sanskrit), written in the Brāhmī script, which had been used at Mathura and further south are not seen on the coins until the mid-third century. So language and script situate the coinage of the Kushans in the north of their Empire. As already discussed there is good reason to place at least one of the mints in this region. The city of Balkh was chosen since Al-Tabari's account of the invasion names only Balkh specifically. This is the only site that was certainly a mint later and the continued circulation of Kanishka II coins in Bactria implies the loss of control did not extend as far as Surkh Khotal and Begram.

BEGRAM (KAPISA)

The account of the Chinese monk Hsuan-Tsang's journey to India has two distinct episodes involving hostages within the Kushan Empire. In the first hostages are referred to only loosely as having been sent to the Kushan king Kanishka by various neighbours, but the second associates the tradition with Begram:"There is one Hinayanistic monastery name Sha-lo-chia. According to a tradition it has long ago been made (built) by the son of the Son of Heaven of Han when he was (living) here as a hostage." (Zurcher 1968, 383).This story is part of a description of the ancient site of Kapisa, modern Begram, which was extensively excavated by Charles Masson in the 1830s.[12] Begram was clearly of political importance but has not generally been considered as a mint site. However, there is at least one coin which indicates it may well have served as such under Wima Kadphises.

There exists in the British Museum a unique example, namely a silver coin apparently of Vima Kadphises. Mukherjee (1982, p. 49) used this and silver coins apparently struck by Wima's successors to argue that the Kushan Empire maintained a small production of silver coinage for circulation in its Indian Territories. He also suggested (1882, p.54) these might be the purana (literally 'old coins') mentioned in an inscription of Huvishka. Many of the coins (contrast Mukherjee 1982, figs 54, 56, 57 with fig. 3k in Errington 1995, p. 423) are forgeries, but general consensus (Cunningham 1892; Narain 1960) is that this silver coin is not. The silver coin was purchased by Masson, before 1840 in a town near Begram. A forgery of this quality at this time is implausible. As a precious metal coin Göbl (1984) associated this with the gold but it clearly belongs with the copper coinage. It employs a copper type on both sides and the Greek letters have tapered ends, rather than the drill holes which are normal practice on the gold. The coin is very similar in style to copper coins also found at Begram. However, there are some notable discrepancies in the legend, the term 'soter' is missing from the Greek and 'sa' is missing from 'isvarasa' on the reverse. The coin cannot have been intended to circulate and was clearly struck with a fresh die (parallel working marks are visible in the field). This leaves only the possibility that it is part of the mint's design process, this is, some sort of proof. Since a trial piece would not travel far one of the copper mints should be located in the vicinity of Begram (Bracey 2009).

Fig. 6.- Silver coin of Vima Kadphises(IOC. 273)

Which mint? The copper coins of Wima Kadphises are probably all struck from a single mint, as discussed previously. That mint remained the principle centre of production under Kanishka and his successors. So this implies most copper coinage from Wima to Kanishka II was issued from the Begram region. It seems likely since there are no dramatic breaks in the copper coinage until the time of Vasishka/Vasudeva II that Begram remained under Kushan control even after Bactria as a whole was lost to the Sasanians.

PESHAWAR (KANISHKAPURA)

"If one goes from the country of Ch'ien-t'o-wei [Gandhara] to the south for four days one reaches the country of Fu-lou-sha (Peshawar). Anciently, when the Buddh at the head of his disciples roamed through this country, he told Ānanda: 'After my Parinirvāna there will be a king named Chi-ni-chia [Kanishka] who in this spot will raise a

(10) As well as the limited number of Kushan Imperial inscriptions there are administrative documents from Afghanistan (Sims-Williams 2000) and graffiti and pot-sherds from Buddhist sites such as Kara-Tepe.

(11) Bactrian and Gandhari (unlike Kharoshti, Brahmi, Prakrit) are modern appellations with no historical basis. They are simply named after the regions, Bactria and Gandhara, from which most of our evidence of the language originates.

(12) The results of Masson's digs in the region were published by Wilson in 1841 (Masson 1971). Errington has been working on the still un-catalogued, but extensive, finds of coins from the site. For general background see Errington and Curtis (2007), for the colorful career of Charles Masson, Errington (2004).

stupa."[13] The remarkable stupa of Kanishka is often mentioned in Chinese accounts though very little survives today. Spooner undertook work at the site in 1908 digging into the foundations of the stupa and recovered a reliquary casket which was initially attributed, incorrectly, to the Kushan king Kanishka. It appears in fact to have been deposited late in the reign of Huvishka (Errington 2002) and the most recent translation of its inscription by Falk shows it was not a royal donation but a private one. He read it as follows:"In the town Kanishkapura this perfume box ... is the pious donation of the architects of the fire-hall, viz. of Mahâsena (and) Sagharaksita, in the monastery (founded by) the (Mahârâ)ja Kanishka. May it be for the welfare and happiness of all beings. In the acceptance of the teachers of the Sarvâstivâda school."

It has been extensively discussed in the past (see Errington and Cribb 1992, pp. 194-197 for previous translations). The casket indicates clearly that the town was named after the Kushan Emperor Kanishka (though it is generally referred to by its modern name to avoid confusion with Kanishkapur in Kashmir, also named after the king). This and the Chinese accounts indicate that the town had an important political role and it is sometimes referred to as the capital of the Kushan Empire. Göbl (1984) attributed the majority of Kushan coins to a mint he believed was located at Peshawar, including both Gold and Copper and the coins already suggested above as issued from Balkh. Mitchiner (1978, p. 406ff) also felt that Peshawar (Purushapura or nearby Pushkalavati) was an important mint for the Kushan Emperors. He attributed the principal part of the copper coinage from Kanishka to Vasudeva to Peshawar (and Taxila). In addition Mitchiner suggested that the Gold mints of Vasudeva were located at Peshawar and Taxila. He attributed those Vasudeva coins which would normally be seen as the production of the main (more productive) mint to Peshawar (Mitchiner 1978, pp. 446-447). This is the production which ceased operating at the end of the reign of Vasudeva and which as we saw above was probably issued from Balkh.

Sasanian penetration as far as Peshawar seems unlikely at such an early date. In the 230s Ardashir was still in power, and Kanishka II ascended to the throne at some point in this or the next decade.[14] On Ardashir's conquests Al Tabari has this to say:"Then he [Ardashir] marched back from the Sawad to Istakhr, from there first to Sagistan, then to Gurgan, then to Abrasahr, Merv, Balkh, and Khwarizm to the farthest boundaries of the provinces of Kohrasan, whereupon he returned to Merv. After he had killed many people and sent their heads to the Fire temple of Anahedh he returned from Merv to Pars and settled in Gor. Then envoys of the king of the Kusan, of the kings of Turan and Mokran came to him with declarations of their submission." (Basham 1968, appendix 1).

Burns and Mirza (1990, p. 18) also attributed a part of the Kushan production to Peshawar. In their discussion of the Topi hoard which originated from the region of Gandhara of which Peshawar was the most important centre they provide an attribution of coins. In that they presume five mints operated under Vasudeva -one at Taxila, one at Peshawar, another at Mathura, an unattributed 'Eastern-W' and a mint in Afghanistan. Much of this subdivides groups of coins actually issued at the same mint, and in general their 'Taxila' mint is the principal Kushan mint, which as already mentioned needs to be located in Bactria, while their 'Peshawar' mint represents the still unidentified subsidiary mint.

There are ten hoards (or parcels) of coins containing Vasudeva coins known. But of these only three are recorded in sufficient detail to identify dies (and thus mint of issue) and the Tehri-Gahrwal hoard contains only one Vasudeva. This leaves the Topi hoard and a Parcel of Coins recovered 'near Peshawar' and deposited in the British Museum in 1877. These two hoards both come from essentially the same area so initially appear unpromising for identifying the location of the mints. They contain a mixture of coins from both mints, as shown in Fig. 7. The Vasudeva coins are the most recent coins in both hoards, and amongst them it is notable that the most recent coins in each case are those from the main mint, not the subsidiary mint. This would suggest that though the coins of both mints reached the region between Peshawar and the Indus those from the main mint got there fastest. Since there is good reason to believe the Main Mint was located in Balkh then the Subsidiary mint would have to be located South of the Indus, not at Peshawar.

Taxila

"*Sir John Marshall has often been attacked for neglecting the scientific control of his excavations. Sometimes these attacks are absolutely justified, for when it is necessary to write in a final report that no conclusions can drawn from the stratigraphical evidence of coin finds because of their contradictory nature, without establishing reason for this position, one is entitled to doubt the entire evidence which that report contains.*" (Allchin 1968, p. 4).

The site of Taxila was excavated by Sir John Marshall as part of his work with the Archaeological Survey of India. It was a dig on a monumental scale, commencing in 1913 and completing only in 1934, and involved the excavation of three urban centres: the oldest the Bhir Mound, a Greek foundation at Sirsukh, and Sirkap which belongs to the Kushan period. There are as well a number of monastic and

(13) Biography of the Eminent Monk Fa-hsien, quoted in (Zurcher 1968, p. 374).

(14) The date at which Kanishka II assumed the throne is uncertain. Chinese records refer to a Po'tiao, which is much easier to reconcile with a name commencing in 'V' than 'K' in 230/31. Kanishka is followed by Vasishka, whose earliest inscription in the year 22 must correspond to AD 247/8. This would place Kanishka II's reign between these dates. Unfortunately establishing which dated inscriptions were issued by Kanishka II, rather than Kanishka I, remains problematic. However, Shapur I succeeded Ardashir in the period 240-242 so it seems certain that the loss of Bactria must have occurred at the end of the reign of Vasudeva or in the reign of Kanishka II.

Fig. 7.- Mint attributions of Vasudeva Coins from Hoards

	1877 Peshawar Parcel			Topi Hoard	
	Main Mint	Subsidiary Mint		Main Mint	Subsidiary Mint
Early Phase	4	2		4	3
Mid Phase	2			2	4
Late Phase				3	

religious sites around the cities (Marshall 1951). Work has not ceased at Taxila since Marshall's time (see for example Khan et al. 2002). Unfortunately the sheer volume of material, as well as some difficulties in the writing up meant that the coins have never been completely published. Recently Khan (2007; 2008) has begun to catalogue and publish the material held in the Taxila Museum but a lot of data is irretrievably lost. Taxila, like Peshawar, is a popular choice for the mints of the Kushans. Gobl assigns that coinage he doesn't assign to Peshawar to, or near, Taxila. So do we have any positive evidence that this is actually where the mint was located?

There are a few gold coins from the site of the Kushan King Vasudeva. In contrast to the two hoards already discussed north of the Indus all seven of the coins are issued from the subsidiary mint.(15) Four of these (all struck using the same obverse die) are from the middle phase and three are from the late phase. It seems likely given their similar condition that these coins were found together. This limited data is not conclusive but it suggests that the Indus marks a change in circulation. Above the Indus coins of the main mint tend to predominate but to the South those of the subsidiary mint are dominant. This would be compatible with the subsidiary mint being located at Taxila. Though it could equally be explained by a mint further south.

OTHER SITES

There are other sites that lie between the northern extremities of Surkh Khotal and Begram and the southern city of Taxila besides Peshawar. However, we rapidly hit the limit of our evidence here. Excavated sites with full catalogues of all coins (including images) are limited to the excavations (such as Butkara and Bir Kot) by Italian archaeologists in which numismatists (Göbl and MacDowall) were asked to examine and publish the coins. For some other sites we possess some details of coin finds but these are rarely complete catalogues and tend more towards brief mentions of Kushan material used to date strata. These are not sufficient to attribute the coins to particular mints and thus do not help us to relate coin distribution to the mints.

(15) Marshall 1951, p. 788 and Khan 2008, p. 40, both confirm no gold coins of Vasudeva were found between 1913 and 1934. Khan (pers. comm.) has confirmed that these coins were found in various unrecorded digs conducted after Marshall's work had been completed.

SIALKOT

The modern town of Sialkot is equated with the capital of Menander, Sagala, as mentioned in the Milindapanho. In the Milindapanho the Indo-Greek king is portrayed as the foil for a learned monk to expound on Buddhist doctrine. The text is much later than the time of Menander and the use of Menander likely reflects Sagala's importance at a later date, possibly in the Kushan period.

At some point the advance of the Kushan Shahs, or the Sasanian Emperor Shapur II, or the Kidarites, must have driven the Kushans from Taxila. Coins of the last Kushan Emperors are rare in the finds from that site. Any mint that was operating at that city must have moved and Sialkot is as good a candidate as any. As shall be discussed below the limited hoards suggest a Northern and Southern mint in the late Kushan period. If the Northern mint cannot be attributed to Taxila then it must be attributed to another site further South. Sialkot is a reasonable guess, but also reflects how little is known about administrative centres between Gandhara in the North and the region of Mathura in the South.

KANISHKAPURA AND HUVISHKAPURA

The Rajatarangini (I.168-171) mentions three kings, Hushka, Jushka, and Kanishka, and the towns they founded in Kashmir. Two sites in Kashmir have been associated with foundations by the Kushan kings. The modern town of Uskhur, on the basis of its name has been identified as Huvishkapura – a royal foundation by Huvishka (AD 150-190), and the modern town of Kanispur with Kanishkapura. Both sites have yielded Kushan material but no evidence that they were administrative centres (Mani 2004a, Mani 2004b, p. 93).

Kujula Kadphises issued a coin featuring a bull on one side and a camel on the other (Fig. 8b). These coins are a continuation of the coinage of the Indo-Scythian ruler Zeionises, which feature a bull and lion (Fig. 8a). This type was continued under the reign of Wima Takto (Cribb 1995) (Fig. 8c). It has previously been suggested that these coins are issued from the region of Kashmir. While they cannot have been issued from new foundations by Kanishka or Huvishka they could have been issued from another important centre, or a centre that was later renamed.There is very little reliable provenance information for these coins. Kushan coins have been reported from Kanishkapura and

Huvishkapura, and also from Ambaran. However, none are published in full and the earliest reported example is a Wima Takto coin of the 'Soter Megas' type. So the attribution depends upon where coins have been collected or parcels in trade are reported to come from.

a) Zeionises

b) Kujula

c) Wima

Fig. 8

Numismatic folklore is not unanimous on this point. Senior states 'In my experience, almost all Zeionises coins turn up in Kashmir, on the Indian side of the present border'. (2000: I, 96). No doubt the 'feel' of collectors is often right but it is hard to test. In this case Mitchiner (1976, 7, p. 584; 1976, 8, pp. 675-676) working no doubt on the same sort of evidence places the coins in 'South Chach' which his maps indicate is to the South and West of Taxila. Cunningham (1890, p. 125) is basing his opinion on similar grounds when he says 'I take him to have been the Satrap of Taxila, as I found one of his coins in a Stupa at Manikyala ...The coins of Jihonika are found chiefly in the north-west Punjab'. So three people experienced in collecting attribute the coins to very different locations.

Senior records only three hoards of Zeionises coins, two of which are mixed with Bull and Camel type coins of Kujula. He believes that all three originate from Kashmir, though only two are reported as coming from that region (2000: I, 193). And it is worth noting like most hoards used for evidence these are not really hoards at all but parcels of related coins that have circulated in trade.

The Bull and Camel coins are in fact found at both Taxila and at Begram, though as a small proportion of the total coins at both sites.[16] Given this it seems hard to place the Bull and Camel coins with any great certainty. They may be products of Kashmir but the attribution needs further evidence to substantiate it.

MATHURA

Mathura, located on the western bank of the Yamuna river dominates discussions of the Kushan period. In the late nineteenth and early twentieth century extensive (but careless) excavations were undertaken around the modern city. They produced statues and inscriptions in very large numbers: the remains of Kankali Tila, still the only Jain Stupa known from the period; and most important, the Bagolago at Mat. Bagolago is a Bactrian term, so not found at Mat, but the equivalent Prakrit term 'devakula' appears in the inscriptions. The Mat site is one of three certain complexes (the others at Surkh Khotal and Rabatak) which are part of the same sort of ritual activity. There may be many more similar sites. An incomplete inscription from Kamra from the third century might have been part of such a complex and the site of Kalchayan has strong similarities. In fact there are as many as eight sites across the Empire which could be part of the same pattern.

There is no way to know for certain what a Bagolago was. The sites available have several features in common. They are not public spaces (several are remote from habitations), they seem to have an association with water and they are structures within which it was deemed acceptable to erect images of both kings and gods. It is unclear if the kings attended the gods or vice-versa. Undoubtedly they served some dynastic purpose but terms such as 'dynastic shrine' or 'dynastic cult' may be too strong. They could simply be temples reflecting the beliefs of the Kushan dynasty, beliefs which were not shared by most of their subjects. However the presence of the Bagolago emphasises the importance of Mathura. Mathura was the capital of Surasena, which is the only region in the modern state of India that we can be confident the Kushans ruled.[17] There is evidence of royal patronage of Brahmanical and Buddhist worship at the site in the second century AD. It was an important political centre and therefore a likely candidate for a mint. At least from the reign of Wima Takto when the region became part of Kushan territory.

MacDowall (1968, p. 30) attributes one of the early series of Vima Takto featuring a standing Zeus to a mint located at Mathura (Image 5). His reason for doing so is that Cunningham commented 'These coins are commonly found at

(16) I am grateful to Gul Rahim Khan and John Perkins for information relating to these collections.

(17) Kushan rule in India probably included the region around Ahichchatra to the North East of Mathura, and much of Rajasthan to the west. However, the region North of Mathura (roughly modern Haryana, ancient Bahundyaka) shows few signs of Kushan rule and it seems more likely it was ruled by the Yaudheya republic. The same applies to most of the middle Ganges which is sometimes seen as Kushan territory although there is evidence of other Kingdoms (Ayodhya, Kosam, Magadha) in the region.

Mathura' (1890, p. 157) though in fact it is not clear from the context if Cunningham is referring to the particular regional variety or to the 'Soter Megas' coinage as a whole. Four hoards from Mathura have been published (Srivastava 1989), as have the coins found in excavations at Sonkh about 10 miles to the Southwest (Hartel 1993). The hoards are of limited use, two contain the same mixture of copper tetradrachms of Wima, Kanishka and Huvishka that is found throughout the Kushan Empire and beyond (most of which were minted at Begram). The second two contain late coins of Shaka or the Kushano-Sasanian Emperors, both deposited at a time when the region had passed out of Kushan control and was in the process of falling under the dominion of the Gupta Empire. They represent coins which circulated widely, crossing political boundaries easily.

The lack of Brāhmī on the coins and the general artistic style argue against production at Mathura. The dominant script of the Mathura region, as for all of Northern India, was Brāhmī. The coins, in contrast employ Bactrian -or initially Greek and Kharoshti- all scripts associated with the North of the Empire. The style of images also shows more affinity for Gandhara than it does for India. By the time the Brahmi script begins to feature prominently on the coins (under Vasudeva II) the Kushans had lost control of Mathura and no mint could be located there.

Initially the gold and copper mints must have been located further north (already in this discussion the gold has been accounted for in full by mints at Balkh and Taxila and the bulk of the copper by a mint at Begram). However additional copper mints were opened in the reigns of Kanishka and Huvishka. These mints made coins whose style differ from those of the main mint. While the main mints' coins are found throughout the Empire these other coins often have much more limited distributions. At least one type, featuring a king with somewhat enlarged head (Göbl 1984, type 8, nos. 933-945) may be associated with Mathura.

During the excavation at Sonkh four coins of this type were found (listed in Göbl 1984 and Hartel 1993). But these coins are almost impossible to place otherwise. There are 28 Huvishka and imitation Huvishka at Butkara I (Göbl 1976) but none of this type and none of these types at Taxila. There are only two amongst the material from Begram(18) out of hundreds of Kushan coins from this period. As Mathura is the only site where these coins could be considered well represented it seems likely that they originate from that region and presumably from that city.

The Missing City

Archaeological work is limited. For example the site of Kashmir Smast, a major religious site in Pakistan that commenced in the 4th century AD was completely unknown until recently (Khan, Errington, Cribb 2008). Not every city which was of political or military importance has been excavated, nor has every city which had a prominent place in the Kushan period been recorded in later literary accounts. The Sarghoda and Dada Fatehpur hoards illustrate this point. Both hoards contain coins of the Kushan king Shaka, whose mint structure was outlined earlier. At Dada Fatehpur, which lay on the southern border of the Kushan Empire the three Shaka coins are the most recent coins in the hoard. All three come from the later stages of mint A. In the hoard from Sarghoda the most recent coins are from the start of the reign of Shaka's successor, Kipunadha. One Shaka coin is from the early stages of mint A but the other 20 are from the latter stages of mint B. The two hoards are from quite distinct places, Sarghoda was likely near the northern border of the Kushan Empire, Dada Fatehpur near the southern border.

These two hoards are almost all we have but they seem to give a strong sense that we are dealing with a northern mint (A) and a southern mint (B). The northern mint could be attributed to Saketa (or, much less likely, Taxila) but the southern mint is problematic. Mathura is the only site we know to have had political importance in the South(19) but as already discussed the city had been lost, first to local control and by Kipunadha's time to the Gupta dynasty. By the time Shaka came to power there had been no Kushan rule for half a century, so where was Shaka's subsidiary mint? Somewhere in the Punjab there must have been a political centre of some importance to the late Kushan Emperors about which we presently know nothing.

Conclusion

This article began with a discussion of the allure cities have for the numismatist, particularly the desire to attribute coins and to able to say "this is the mint of..." is a powerfunl motivation. Such an allure is inevitable, it is part of the narrative of a coin, and the objects's story seems somehow incomplete without it. I went on to discuss the current understanding of the structure of Kushan coinage and the gaps, which exist in that. Only where the structure of production is understood can we begin to use the clues that might tell us where coins were minted. I have outlined some of the clues, which might help us to attribute particular coins to particular regions. Ideally this would involve a great deal of archaeological data, both site finds and hoards, to track the circulation of different coin types. The data falls somewhat short of that but some fragments do survive and it is possible to identify some of the principal minting sites of the Kushans -at Balkh, Begram and Taxila- as well as minor mints such as Mathura.

References

Allchin F. R. (1968). 'Archaeology and the Date of Kanishka: The Taxila Evidence' in, Basham A. Ll. (ed.), *Papers on the*

(18) I am grateful to Gul Rahim Khan who has examined these collections thoroughly for confirming this for me.

(19) At least the only site associated with the Kushans. Sanghol clearly had an administrative centre but coins and seals firmly associate it with the Yaudheya (Ray 2010).

Date of Kaniska. Submitted to the Conference on the Date of Kaniska, London 20-22 April 1960. Leiden, pp. 4-34.

Ball W. (1982). *Archaeological Gazetteer of Afghanistan: Catalogue des Sites Archeologiques D'Afghanisan, 2 volumes*. Paris.

Basham A. Ll. (ed.). *Papers on the Date of Kaniska. Submitted to the Conference on the Date of Kaniska, London 20-22 April 1960*. Leiden.

Bracey R. (2009). 'The Coinage of Wima Kadphises', *Gandharan Studies, 4*, pp. 25-74.

Bracey R., Oddy W. A. (2010). 'The analysis of Kushan period gold coins by Specific Gravity', *Gandharan Studies, 3*, pp. 31-39.

Cribb J. (1981). 'Gandharan Hoards of Kushano-Sasanian and Late Kushan Coppers', in *Coin Hoards. Volume 6*. London.

Cribb J. (1985a). 'Some Further Hoards of Kushano-Sasanian and Late Kushan Coppers', in *Coin Hoards. Volume 7*. London.

Cribb J. (1985b). 'Imitations of Kushan Copper Coins', in *Coin Hoards. Volume 7*. London.

Cribb J. (1993). 'The 'Heraus' coins: their attribution to the Kushan king Kujula Kadphises, c.AD 30-80', in Price M., Burnett A., Bland R. (eds), *Essays in Honour of Robert Carson and Kenneth Jenkins*. London, pp. 107-34.

Cribb J. (2003). 'The Origins of the Indian Coinage Tradition', *South Asian Studies, 19*, pp. 1-21.

Cribb J. (2007). 'Money as a marker of cultural continuity and change in Central Asia' in Cribb J., Hermann G. (eds), *After Alexander: Central Asian before Islam. Proceedings of the British Academy* 133. London, pp. 333-75.

Cunningham A. (1890). 'Coins of the Sakas', *Numismatic Chronicle, 10*, pp. 103-172.

Errington E., Cribb J. (1992). *The Crossroads of Asia. Transformation in image and symbol in the art of ancient Afghanistan and Pakistan*. Cambridge.

Errington E., Falk, H. (2002). 'Numismatic Evidence for dating the 'Kanishka' Reliquary', *Silk Road Art and Achaeology, 8*, pp. 101-120.

Errington E. (1995). 'Rediscovering the Coin Collection of General Claude-Auguste Court: A Preliminary Report', *Topoi* 5.2, pp. 409-424.

Errington E. (2004). 'Charles Masson', *Encyclopedia Iranica Online*.

Errington E., Curtis V. S. (with contributions by Cribb, J.) (2007). *From Persepolis to the Punjab: exploring ancient Iran, Afghanistan and Pakistan*. London.

Gershevitch I. (1979). 'Nokonzok's Well', *Afghan Studies, 2*, pp. 54-73.

Göbl R. (1976). *A Catalogue of Coins from Butkara I*. Swāt (Pakistan)-Rome.

Gobl R. (1984). *System und Chronologie der Münzprägung des Kušānreiches*. Wien.

Härtel H. (1993). *Excavations at Sonkh, 2500 Years of a town in Mathura district*. Berlin.

Khan M. B., Hassan M., Khan Khattak, M. H., Faiz-ur-Rehman, M., Khan, M. A. (2002). *Bhir Mound: The First City of Taxila (Excavations Report 1998-2002)*. Lahore.

Khan G. R. (2007). 'Kanishka Coins from Taxila', *Gandharan Studies, 1*, pp. 119-148.

Khan G. R. (2008). 'Gold Coins in the Cabinet of Taxila Museum, Taxila', *Gandharan Studies, 2*, pp. 39-47.

Khan, M. N., Errington E., Cribb. J. (2008). *Coins from Kashmir Smast: new numismatic evidence*. Peshawar.

Khan G. R. (2011). 'Copper Coins of Vasudeva and his Successors from Taxila', *Gandharan Studies, 4*, pp. 39-162.

MacDowall D. W. (1968). 'Soter Megas, the King of Kings, the Kushana', *Journal of the Numismatic Society of India (Varanasi), 30*.

Mani B. R. (2004a). 'Excavations at Kanispur, District Barumella' *Indian Archaeology - A Review (1998-1999), 46*, pp. 30-48.

Mani B. R. (2004b). 'Excavations at Ambaran and Akhnur Terracotta' in Sharma R. C., Ghosal P. (eds), *Buddhism and Gandhāra Art*. New Delhi.

Masson C. (1971). 'Memoir on the Buildings called Topes', in Wilson J. (ed.), *Ariana Antiqua: A Descriptive Account of the Antiquities and Coins of Afghanistan*. [First published in London 1841].

Mitchiner M. (1976). *Indo-Greek and Indo-Scythian coinage. The Decline of the Indo-Scythians [&] Contemporaries of the Indo-Scythians. Volume 7*. London.

Mitchiner M. (1976). *Indo-Greek and Indo-Scythian coinage. The Indo-Parthians. Their Kushan neighbours. Volume 8*. London.

Mitchiner M. (1978). *Oriental Coins, the Ancient and Classical World, 600 B.C.-A.D.650*. London.

Mukherjee B. N. (1982). *Kushāṇa silver coinage*. Calcutta.

Narain A. K. (1960). *The Indo-Greeks*. New Delhi. (first edition printed in Oxford, 1957).

Oddy W. A. (1998a). 'The Analysis of Coins by the Specific Gravity Method', in Oddy W. A., Cowell M. R. (eds), *Metallurgy in Numismatics. Volume 4*. London, pp. 147-158.

Oddy W. A., Gribb J. (1998b). 'Debasement and sequence of late Kushana gold coins' in Jha A. K., Garg S. (eds), *Ex Moneta, essays on numismatics history and archaeology in honour of Dr. David W. MacDowall. Volume 2*. New Delhi, pp. 275- 292.

Perkins M. J. (2007). 'Three headed Siva on the Reverse of Vima Kadphises Copper Coinage', *South Asian Studies*, 23.1, pp. 31-37.

Ray H. P. (ed.) (2010). *Sanghol and the Archaeology of Punjab*. New Delhi.

Rosenfield J. (1967). *The Dynastic Art of the Kushans*. Berkeley.

Senior R. (2000). *A Catalogue of Indo-Scythian Coins. An Analysis of the Coinage. Volume 1*. Glastonbury.

Sims-Williams N., Cribb J. (1995). 'A New Bactrian Inscription of Kanishka the Great', *Silk Road Art and Archaeology*, 4, pp. 75-143.

Srivastava A. K. (1989). 'Treasure Trove Finds from Mathurā', in Srinivasan D. M. (ed.), *Mathura: The Cultural Heritage*. Delhi.

Zürcher E. (1968). 'The Yüeh-chih and Kanishka in the Chinese sources', in Basham A. L. (ed.), *Papers on the Date of Kaniska. Submitted to the Conference on the Date of Kaniska, London 20-22 April 1960*. Leiden, pp. 346-393.

Image 1.- Various types of Vasudeva I's main mint

Image 2

A- The diadem has a series of horizontal bars, and the cornucopia has a fan like head

B- The diadem loops behind the chair leg to blend into de dress which has only three folds

C- The diadem falls straight with no bars but the girdle has a tie on it

D- Ardoxsho has long legs and her dress is depicted with slanting folds

E- Ardoxsho has long hair and her dress is depicted with 'U' shaped folds

F- The diadem falls straight with no bars and the girdle is depicted without a tie

Image 3

Image 4.- Transition from coins of Vasudeva to imitations

Late Vasudeva Coin of the Main Mint Triton Sale, XII (2008), 184; Spink 87 (1991), 87

With an 'o' mark on the altar and Wesho's triden. ANS (1944.100.63828)

Large head of the king's trident and small dots on the obverse and reverse. CNG Auction, 66 (2004) 975

Ribbons on the trident above the altar fall either side rather than to the left. Lanz, 128 (2006) 143

Swastika between the kings legs. Triton X (2007)

Image 5.- The Mathura Mint
BM Coins 1848.0803.197, 1989.0904.4033, 1850.0305.265

Les derniers monnayages d'argent de l'Antiquité tardive en Gaule du nord : les *argentei* au type à la Rome assise de moins de 0.9 g

Philippe Schiesser

ABSTRACT

Les monnayages d'argent des Ve et VIe siècles sont abondants et comportent des types nombreux et variés. Même si différents types ont été trouvés ensemble, cela ne signifie ni qu'ils furent émis à la même époque ni par la même autorité. Notre étude porte sur l'un des types d'*argentei* : ceux de moins de 0.9 g et à la Rome assise. Elle fait apparaître qu'une grande partie de ces monnaies a un poids proche de 0.26g (82,4% d'entre elles font entre 0.11g et 0.40g et 44.6% entre 0.21g et 0.30g) correspondant au quart du poids réel des dernières siliques romaines. Ces *argentei* furent principalement trouvés (76.9 % des sites et 70.6 % des monnaies) entre la Somme, la Loire, La Meuse et la Manche, soit le « royaume » de Syagrius avant sa conquête par Clovis en 486 et dans des sites d'implantation franque postérieurs. Ce groupe d'*argentei*, dont le poids se situe autour de 0.26 g., correspond à des légendes (volontairement ?) inintelligibles, pouvant correspondre à la période postérieure à 476, où il n'y avait plus d'empereurs en Occident. Ces nano-monnaies montrent la nécessité de petits divisionnaires dans la vie quotidienne et la continuité de la monétarisation de l'économie au Ve siècle.

Introduction : le monnayage d'argent des Ve et VIe siècles

Le monnayage d'argent des Ve et VIe siècles est un vaste sujet qui a été abordé et débattu depuis longtemps (Prou 1891 qu'il reprend mot pour mot l'année suivante, Lafaurie 1964, *MEC*, Lafaurie 1990, Bompaire 1993, Arslan 1998, etc.). Il ne s'agit pas ici de traiter de toutes les émissions d'argent de cette époque, car elles sont bien trop nombreuses et variées. Les *argentei* à la victoire à gauche reprennent le type des demi siliques, ceux à la croix ancrée sont une déformation des légendes de Vœux (Lafaurie 1987, p. 297), certains portent une croix latine dans une couronne de feuilles (Cahiers Ernest-Babelon n° : 12.220.2.1 et 2), d'autres une victoire de face tenant une couronne et une palme (Cahiers Ernest-Babelon n° : 44.143.1), un monogramme NS (Cahiers Ernest-Babelon n° : 58.39.1.4) ou l'empereur debout tenant une haste et une couronne (Cahiers Ernest-Babelon n° : 59.313.1).

La Provence et le couloir Rhodanien jusqu'à Lyon connurent, dans la mouvance méditerranéenne, des frappes variées en or, argent et bronze, dont certaines étaient des *argentei* qui connaissaient également une circulation en Gaule septentrionale (Foucray 2004). Certains de ces *argentei* figurent un chrisme (Cahiers Ernest-Babelon n° : 13.55.6.10), d'autres une croix accostée de A et R entourée d'une couronne (Cahiers Ernest-Babelon n° : 70.279.1 et Fig. 1) ou bien un monogramme royal : celui d'Odoacre, roi des Ostrogoths 476-493 (Foucray 2004, n°2), ceux des rois des Burgondes Gondebaud 473-516 (Foucray 2004 n° 1), Sigismond 516-524 (Lafaurie 1987, n° 26 p. 11 et pl. 1) et Gondemar 524-534 (Cahiers Ernest-Babelon n° : 69.123.3.3), ou ceux des rois des Francs Théodobert 534-548 (Cahiers Ernest-Babelon n° : 13.100.1.16), ou encore le nom du roi des Francs écrit sur plusieurs lignes : Childebert I 534-558 (Cahiers Ernest-Babelon n° : 13.98.1.2) ou Gontran 561-592 (Cahiers Ernest-Babelon n° : 13.98.1.3), etc.

Certains types d'*argentei* sont des imitations des monnaies d'or. Le type d'Ouerre, un personnage debout de face tenant une croix de la main droite, et une crosse de la main gauche (Lafaurie 1964 Ouerre et Cahiers Ernest-Babelon n° : 14.623.1.2) (Fig. 2), semble imiter des *solidi* de Justinien. Ceux à la victoire allant à droite (Fig. 3) ou tenant une grande croix (Fig. 4) sont des imitations des tremisses (l'*argenteus* au nom de Valentinien III présenté à la Fig. 5, fut trouvé en Charente-Maritime et semble être le premier attribuable aux Visigoths). Et l'énumération présentée rapidement ici n'est pas exhaustive.

Nous ne nous intéresserons pas ici à tous ces types, car même si différents types ont été trouvés ensemble (à Arcy-Sainte-Restitue, Eprave ou Fel par exemple), cela ne signifie ni qu'ils furent émis à la même époque, ni qu'ils le furent par la même autorité. C. Van Hoof donne de nombreux exemples de trouvailles funéraires qui regroupent des monnaies beaucoup plus anciennes (celtiques, du haut ou bas Empire) trouvées dans des tombes franques et des monnaies contemporaines de l'inhumation franque. Le plus célèbre trésor est celui trouvé dans la sépulture de Childéric, le père de Clovis, mort en 481, et qui comprenait pas moins de 100 *solidi* et de 200 monnaies d'argent romaines (dont au moins 42 deniers du haut empire et une silique). Des trésors regroupant des monnaies franques, ostrogothes et de Justin I existent aussi (Mitard 1978, p. 127-128= Cahiers Ernest-Babelon n° 55.285.2).

Certains types semblent plus tardifs et portent un nom de lieu de frappe. Il s'agit des *argentei* de Strasbourg datés d'après 496 (Lafaurie 1988e), de Worms vers 500-530 (Lafaurie 1988), de Paris (Cahiers Ernest-Babelon n° :14.341.1, Dhénin 1993, p. 834), qui portent au droit un buste de face avec un casque sommé d'une croix, et au revers un monogramme en forme de dôme sommé d'une croix. Il est possible de lire clairement PARISIVS sur certaines d'entre elles. Dhénin les date des années 575-600) et de Metz (Cahiers Ernest-Babelon n° : 57.134.2 Fig. 6).

Dans une société où la majorité de la population est analphabète, la légende importe peu et il est légitime de se demander comment les contemporains interprétaient ces monnaies. La confiance que l'on avait dans une monnaie était-elle basée sur le monnayage d'or, c'est-à-dire sur la garantie de la présence de métal précieux (le CONOB présent sur certaines monnaies d'argent pourrait ainsi s'expliquer aisément, voir Fig. 7, Guillaume 1988 ; Cahiers Ernest-Babelon n° : 55.1.1.1), ou reposait-elle tout simplement sur la présence d'un portrait impérial (*imago* impérial) ? Cela expliquerait la présence jusqu'au VIIIe siècle d'un portrait imité de ceux figurés sur les frappes impériales byzantines sur presque toutes les monnaies mérovingiennes d'or et d'argent.

Nous ne nous intéresserons ici qu'aux monnaies présentant le type (*imago*) de la monnaie romaine d'argent, celle de la silique à la Rome assise (à gauche, à droite ou de face) sur un trône.

J. Lafaurie a magistralement, et à plusieurs reprises, présenté les frappes d'*argentei* de Trèves (Lafaurie 1987) qu'il attribue à Aetius (Lafaurie 1987, p. 315) frappées entre 445 et 455 (Lafaurie 1987, p. 314) et qui pèsent « autour d'un gramme » (Lafaurie 1987, p. 300). Les monnaies d'un moindre poids sont généralement décrites comme étant des imitations de ces *argentei* (Mitard 1978, pp. 127-128; Dhénin 1980, p. 202; Lafaurie 1987, p. 303; Blackburn 1988, p. 171 par exemple) et bien peu parmi elles portent une marque d'atelier. C'est à ces monnaies de moins de 0.9g (voir l'introduction au catalogue) au type à la Rome assise que nous consacrons cette étude.

L'étude statistique permettra d'établir si une cohérence pondérale existe, puis si l'aire de répartition de ce type peut être définie. Finalement nous tenterons d'établir quelle fut l'autorité émettrice.

Le poids

La répartition du poids des monnaies à la Rome assise de moins de 0.9g (voir tableau 1 et graphique 1) montre clairement une concentration d'exemplaires dont le poids varie entre 0.11g et 0.40g (82.4% des monnaies) et plus précisément entre 0.21g et 0.30g (44.6% des monnaies). En revanche il n'y a pratiquement pas de monnaies dont le poids se situe entre 0.41g et 0.9g (16% des monnaies) ce qui serait très étonnant si ces monnaies n'étaient que des imitations des *argentei* de Trêves qui pèsent « autour d'un gramme ».

Le poids moyen des ces monnaies de moins de 0.41g est de 0.2629g, ce qui les situe entre une silique-poids romaine (1/1728e de la livre romaine de 326 g [Bompaire 1993, p. 108] soit environ 0.188g) et 2 siliques-poids (0.377g).

poids (g)	nombre
0.1	1
0.11 à 0.15	5
0.16 à 0.2	7
0.21 à 0.25	16
0.26 à 0.3	17
0.31 à 0.35	9
0.36 à 0.4	7
0.41 à 0.45	2
0.46 à 0.5	2
0.51 à 0.55	1
0.56 à 0.6	3
0.61 à 0.65	1
0.66 à 0.7	2
0.71 à 0.75	0
0.76 à 0.8	1
0.81 à 0.85	0
0.86 à 0.9	0
Total	**74**

Tableau 1 : répartition de monnaies par poids

Une classification fine de centième de gramme en centième de gramme (voir graphique 2) ne permet pas de préciser le poids exact de ces monnaies, mais montre qu'il s'agit bien là d'un ensemble de monnaies taillées sur la même base. L'oxydation des monnaies et le fait que certaines soient ébréchées ne semble pas pouvoir expliquer une aussi grande différence (30%) entre une moyenne de 0.2629g et le poids romain qui serait de 2 siliques-poids (0.377g). On peut se demander si c'est cette mesure romaine qui a été utilisée, ou si le poids n'a pas été étalonné sur celui des monnaies romaines d'argent encore en circulation. L'usurpateur Constantin III (407-411) est le dernier à frapper en grande quantité des siliques à la Rome assise. La moyenne des poids de celles-ci est de 1.54g, alors que pour Jovin (411-413) elle n'est plus que de 1.43g (*RIC* X, p. 16) mais l'usurpateur Maximus (410-411) frappe sur une base encore plus légère de 1.16g (*RIC* X, p. 150) ou peut être même de 1.12g (King 1987 p. 49). Les *argentei* de Trêves d'Aetius font « autour d'un gramme » (Lafaurie 1987, p. 300). J. Lafaurie écrit même « une taille originelle de...1.12g » (Lafaurie 1978, p. 423). Elles seraient alors des siliques très légères, comme le pensent les auteurs du *MEC* (p. 45) et du *RIC* X (p. 171 et pp. 374-375). Mais que peuvent être les monnaies étudiées ici qui font 0.2629g en moyenne ? Elles correspondent à peu près au quart du poids des siliques contemporaines (de 1.05g ?). Il conviendrait donc de limiter le terme d'*argentei* à ces monnaies que les auteurs du *MEC* appellent *minuti argentei* (pp. 111-112).

Pour mémoire, le centime d'euro pèse 2.3g, soit presque 9 fois plus (Fig. 8), et le penny 3.56g, soit presque 14 fois plus... Nous suivons Prou (p C-CI) dans son raisonnement pour affirmer qu'il s'agit ici aussi de monnaies, malgré l'écart considérable de poids existant entre ces exempaires et les siliques romaines. La seule de ces monnaies analysées (Envermeu 76.235.2.1) contenait 82.86% d'argent fin, mais ces types sont effectivement souvent de teneur élevée en argent, comme semble l'indiquer la couleur du métal et leur résistance, étant donné leur extrême finesse (ces monnaies font généralement moins de 0.5 mm d'épaisseur, parfois 0.1 mm, et bien moins encore entre les deux champs). Si l'on se base sur une moyenne de 0.2629g x 80% d'argent (?), la teneur en argent fin serait de 0.21 g. On est alors presque exactement avec la même valeur en argent fin que les monnaies de billon, tels les *aureliani* taillés à 1/84e de livre (environ 3.88g) à 5% d'argent, soit 0.194g d'argent fin, auquel il faut rajouter la valeur du cuivre valant environ 120 fois moins. Ainsi, les 3.686 g de cuivre restant équivalent à 0.03g d'argent fin, soit une monnaie équivalant au total à 0.225g d'argent fin (Lafaurie 1990, p. 214). Ces monnaies d'aspect bien peu romain présentaient donc une valeur intrinsèque équivalente à celle d'un *aurelianus,* ou de 25 g de bronze.

La répartition

La carte de répartition des *argentei* à la Rome assise diffère sensiblement de celle du type à la croix ancrée - voir supra pour la typologie - (Lafaurie 1987, p. 298), qui est plus au nord, et correspond à des territoires contrôlés tôt au Ve par les Francs. La majorité des sites (14 des 26 sites soit 53.8%) ayant fourni des monnaies à la Rome assise de moins de 0.9 g se trouve dans un espace situé entre la Somme, la Seine, la Meuse, et la Manche (voir carte de répartition). Cette zone regroupe une grande partie des monnaies de ce type (33 monnaies sur 68 soit 48.5%).

Néanmoins, si l'on inclut Soligny, les étangs à 10 km au sud de la Seine, Vron, à 15 km au nord de la Somme, et Eprave, à 20 km à l'est de la Meuse, ces chiffres montent à 65.4 % des sites et à 60.3% des monnaies. Vron présente la particularité d'être aussi une nécropole saxonne (Soulat 2009, p. 28 ; Lebecq 1990, p. 33).

Si l'on inclut la zone situé entre Seine et Loire, 76.9 % des sites et 70.6 % des monnaies à ce type s'y concentrent. C'est précisément dans cet espace que l'on situe la dernière autorité romaine en Gaule, le maître de la milice Aegidius, puis son fils Syagrius, « roi des romains» d'après Grégoire de Tours, avant sa conquête par Clovis en 486.

Les principaux sites hors de cet espace sont tous francs et plus tardifs (de la fin Ve siècle et VIe siècle). Les sites Rhénans semblent former un ensemble à part : 3 des 4 sites contiennent des monnaies de Strasbourg et de Worms, alors que 2 autres sites seulement en ont fourni. Ces monnaies sont datées plus tardivement par J. Lafaurie : après 496 pour Strasbourg (Lafaurie 1988e, p. 383) et vers 500-530 pour celles de Worms (Lafaurie 1988, p. 541), même si nous sommes réservés concernant l'identification de ce dernier atelier. Elles représentent la moitié des monnaies retrouvées dans les sites rhénans, et 71.4 % des monnaies de ces 2 ateliers ont été trouvés dans cette zone. Il semble donc que ces 2 types de monnaies ne soient qu'une variante locale marquant l'atelier d'un type plus général sans nom. À moins que d'autres circulations régionales ne nous échappent du fait de la non signature du, ou des atelier(s), émetteur(s).

Le site de Courbillac, au lieu dit Herpes, est celui qui a fourni le plus grand nombre de monnaies à la Rome assise de moins de 0.9 g, et le cas de ce site semble être unique. Ce site funéraire est exceptionnel à la fois par les monnaies et par les perles qui y ont été déterrées. Courbillac fait part de ce qu'on appelle « l'isolat de Charente » car son *facies* archéologique ressemble de très près à celui des sites du nord de la Loire (Rajade 2009, p. 30). S. Lebecq a pu ainsi lier les trouvailles découvertes à Courbillac-Herpes à des groupes de guerriers francs venus du nord de la Loire pour occuper l'Aquitaine (Lebecq 1990, p. 69).

Un problème s'est posé lors de la rédaction du corpus des monnaies à la Rome assise de moins de 0.9 g. La liste des monnaies que nous avons dû exclure par manque de fiabilité des informations (types ou poids inconnus) est plus importante (82 monnaies, voir annexe 1) que celle des monnaies que nous avons pu inclure dans le corpus (68 monnaies). 3 ont été exclues, car le poids connu correspondait à celui des « siliques légères » (plus de 0.9g, voir introduction).

Le groupe exclu le plus important est celui de Bâle-Kleinhüningen (14 *Argentei*), dont le poids est absent de la publication concernant ce type (Geiger 1979, pp. 106-107, Lafaurie 1987, pp. 319-320), et qui pourrait modifier sensiblement la carte de répartition. Néanmoins, Lafaurie le considère comme une frappe « officielle » de Trèves des années 443/444-455 (Lafaurie 1987) et il est donc probable que le poids de ces *argentei* soit supérieur à 0.9 g et ne rentre pas dans le cadre de cette étude. De plus, comme à Courbillac, au lieu dit Herpes, il est probable qu'il s'agisse ici aussi d'une implantation militaire franque (Lebecq 1990, p. 69).

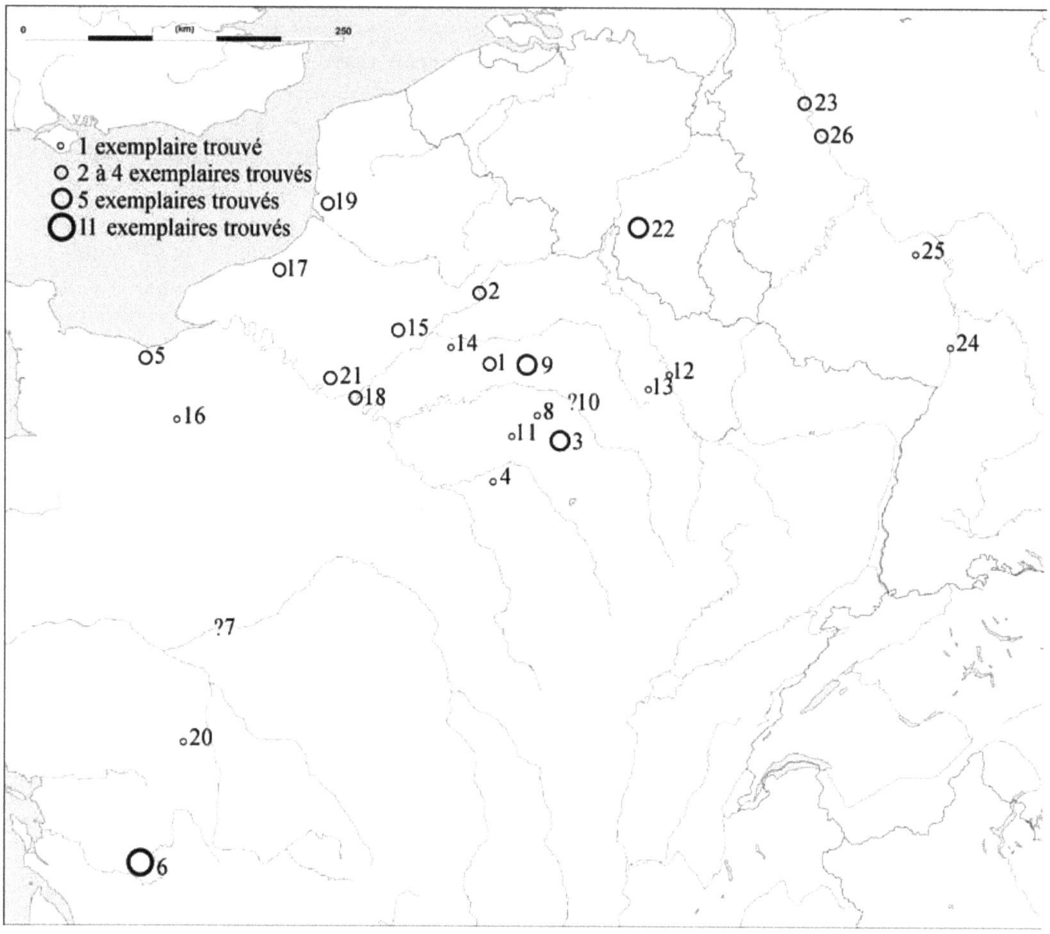

Carte de repartition

Légende de la carte

France

1.- Arcy-Sainte-Restitue (02130) : 2 exemplaires trouvés.
2.- Mayot (02800) : 2 exemplaires trouvés.
3.- Mailly-Le-Camp (10230) : 5 exemplaires trouvés.
4.- Soligny les étangs (10400) : 1 exemplaire trouvé.
5.- Environs de Caen : 3 exemplaires trouvés, 1 exemplaire à Fleury-sur-Orne (14123) à 5 km au sud de Caen, 1 exemplaire à Saint-Martin-De –Fontenay (14320) à 9 km au sud de Caen et 1 exemplaire à Sannerville (14940) à 12 km à l'est de Caen.
6.- Courbillac lieu dit Herpes (16200) : 11 exemplaires trouvés.
7.- Touraine (37 ?) : 1 exemplaire trouvé. Il provient probablement d'une trouvaille locale.
8.- Bergères-Les-Vertus (51130) : 1 exemplaire trouvé.
9.- Ville-Dommange (51390) : 5 exemplaires trouvés.
10.- environs de Châlons-en-Champagne (51 ?) : 1 exemplaire trouvé.
11.- environs de Sézanne (51) : 1 exemplaire trouvé.
12.- Dugny-sur-Meuse (55100) : 1 exemplaire trouvé.
13.- Lavoye-Autrecourt (55120) : 1 exemplaire trouvé.
14.- Chelles (60350) : 1 exemplaire trouvé.
15.- Noroy (60130) : 3 exemplaires trouvés.
16.- Fel (61160) : 1 exemplaire trouvé.
17.- Envermeu (76630) : 3 exemplaires trouvés.
18.- Andrésy (78570) : 3 exemplaires trouvés.
19.- Vron (80120) : 2 exemplaires trouvés.
20.- Poitiers (86000) : 1 exemplaire trouvé.
21.- Genainville (95420) : 4 exemplaires trouvés.

Belgique

22.- Eprave (55380) : 5 exemplaires trouvés; 3 exemplaires trouvés au cimetière sur le mont; 1 exemplaire trouvé au cimetière de la Croix-Rouge et 1 exemplaire trouvé à Ave-et-Auffe (55380), à 800 m d'Eprave.

Allemagne

23.- Cologne (Köln) : 4 exemplaires trouvés.
24.- « Rheinhessen » (Jugenheim in Rheinhessen 55270 ?) : 1 exemplaire trouvé.
25.- Rheinsheim (76661) : 1 exemplaire trouvé.
26.- Schwarzrheindorf (Bonn- Schawarzrheindorf en Nord-Westphalie) : 4 exemplaires trouvés.

Datation et attribution

Le tableau de répartition par poids en fonction des empereurs (voir tableau 2), fait apparaître que les monnaies qui portent un nom d'empereur intelligible sont celles qui ont

	Honorius	Théodose II	Valentinien III	Avitus	Anthemius	Julius Nepos	Empereur incertain	Anastase	Strasbourg	Worm
gr.	(393-423)	(402-450)	(425-455)	(455-456)	(467-472)	(474-475)		(491-518)		
0.1							1			
0.11-0.15							3			3
0.16-0.2		1					6			
0.21-0.25			1				13		1	
0.26-0.3			1	2		1	12		1	
0.31-0.35			3				5	1		
0.36-0.4	1		3				1	1	1	
0.41-0.45	1	1						1		
0.46-0.5	1				1					
0.51-0.55			1							
0.56-0.6		1	1							
0.61-0.65			1							
0.66-0.7	1	1	1							
0.71-0.75										
0.76-0.8			1							
0.81-0.85										
0.86-0.9										
Total	**4**	**4**	**13**	**2**	**1**	**1**	**41**	**3**	**1**	

Tableau 2. Répartition des *argentei* par poids et en function des empereurs et des ateliers

le poids le plus important. Ces deux facteurs ont été déterminants dans le choix préférentiel que l'on a eu pour ces monnaies par rapport à d'autres aux légendes inintelligibles et au poids plus léger dans la constitution des collections publiques. Généralement, ce sont ces seules frappes qui ont connu une publication.

Il est généralement admis que les *argentei* ont été frappés durant le règne de l'empereur dont ils portent le nom mais nous avons malheureusement un contre exemple contemporain avec les siliques de Rechiarius, roi des Suèves de 448 à 456, qui portent le portrait et la titulature d'Honorius (395-423) qui lui est antérieur de 25 ans. (Fig. 9).

La reprise postérieure, pour des raisons politiques, du nom d'Honorius, pourrait expliquer le hiatus chronologique jusqu'au deuxième tiers du Ve siècle, moment où Trèves reprend les frappes au nom de Théodose II et Valentinien III (445-455 pour J. Lafaurie 1987, p. 397, mais 425-430 pour Grierson et May, p. 69, cité par Arslan 1998, note 62 pp. 396-97). Pour nos monnaies « légères » de moins de 0.9g, celles au nom de ces deux empereurs pourraient être, en partie, des imitations ou des hémi-siliques, car les poids sont majoritairement répartis de 0.31 à 0.8g.

Pour les empereurs postérieurs : Avitus (455-456), Anthémius (467-472), Julius Nepos (474-475) et Anastase (491-518), les frappes semblent plus légères que celles au nom de Théodose II et Valentinien III. Néanmoins, le faible nombre d'exemplaires connus pour chacun des empereurs ne permet pas d'en être totalement certain.

Aucun exemplaire dont l'empereur ne peut être déterminé n'a un poids supérieur à 0.4g, et 61 %. Ce type de monnaies est situé dans la fourchette comprise entre 0.21 et 0.30 g. Ces monnaies sont donc beaucoup plus légères. Les exemplaires de Strasbourg ont sensiblement le même poids, mais celles de Worms sont encore plus légères. Ce groupe pondéral apparaît donc aussi comme un groupe typologique.

Il serait tentant de supposer à une baisse progressive du poids, que ces monnaies inintelligibles sont postérieures à 476 et qu'elles appartiennent à une époque où il n'y a plus d'empereur romain d'Occident au nom duquel on pouvait frapper. La carte de répartition semble le confirmer par une implantation similaire à celle des nouvelles conquêtes de Clovis : le « Royaume » de Syagrius après 486, et les implantations militaires au sud de la Loire après 507. Mais qui peut avoir été l'initiateur de ces frappes ? Syagrius qui aurait ainsi continué les frappes de Trèves et dont les troupes de Clovis auraient diffusé le monnayage ? Ou le roi des Francs lui-même qui aurait aussi pu frapper au nom d'Anastase, après son élévation en 508 au consulat honoraire ? L'argent que Clovis jeta au peuple en cette occasion (Grégoire de Tours *H. F.* 2.38) pourrait-il être ces *argentei* ? Une chose apparaît néanmoins clairement : elles furent utilisées par les troupes franques installées dans les nouvelles conquêtes.

Conclusion

Des *argentei* visigoths, ostrogoths et burgondes existent aussi, mais il semble qu'ils furent frappés avec d'autres types que celui à la Rome assise.

Une grande partie des *argentei* à la Rome assise a un poids proche de 0.26g, correspondant au quart du poids réel des dernières siliques romaines. Ces monnaies furent principalement trouvées dans une zone située entre la Somme, la Loire, La Meuse et la Manche, soit le « royaume » de Syagrius avant sa conquête par Clovis en 486, et dans des sites d'implantation franque postérieurs.

Le groupe d'*argentei* dont le poids se situe autour de 0.26 g correspond à des légendes (volontairement ?) inintelligibles, pouvant correspondre à la période après 476, et durant laquelle il n'y a plus d'empereurs d'Occident au nom de qui frapper. Les frappes plus lourdes au nom d'Anastase (le dernier empereur au nom duquel on a battu ce type) peuvent être liées, de son côté, au consulat honoraire dont il gratifia Clovis.

Ces nano-monnaies montrent la nécessité de petits divisionnaires dans la vie quotidienne et la continuité de la monétarisation de l'économie, bien éloignée du monométalliste longtemps proclamé. Des monnaies d'argent très légères continuèrent par la suite à être frappées (voir introduction et les 1/8e de siliques de Maurice Tibère et leurs imitations lombardes de 0.12g; Arslan 2004, p. 120). On peut même se demander si, dans le futur, des divisionnaires de bronze ne pourront pas être découverts dans le nord de la Gaule comme ce fut le cas récemment pour l'Espagne visigothique.

Introduction au catalogue

Ne seront citées que les références consultées, celles-ci pouvant renvoyer à des ouvrages plus anciens.

« La chevelure dressée sur le diadème » parfois décrite, qui apparaît comme un trait partant d'un croissant posé dans les cheveux doit être comprise comme étant une main tenant une couronne. Cette couronne représente une légitimation de l'Auguste. Elle nous renseigne sur le besoin d'avoir un appui dans sa légitimation impériale et sur les faiblesses de cet Auguste qui a besoin d'un appui militaire pour légitimer son autorité impériale et avoir des frappes à son nom.

Par exemple, les *solidi* "à la couronne" d'Arles furent frappés dès 439 par les Visigoths pour reconnaître Valentinien III en tant qu'empereur. Après la régence de Galla Placidia, Valentinien III revint d'Orient et devint empereur d'Occident à la suite de son mariage avec la fille de Théodose II (439). La couronne visigothique de 439 signifie donc la reconnaissance du nouvel Auguste par le roi de Toulouse. Elle nous renseigne aussi sur la faiblesse fondamentale de Valentinien III en 439 (López Sánchez 2011).

Incertain : la titulature impériale nous semble trop incertaine pour pouvoir être reprise dans les statistiques, la description et l'interprétation qui suivent sont celles de la bibliographie citée.
Les A sont barrés ou non, les N et S peuvent être rétrogrades ou non.
Les D initiaux ne sont pratiquement jamais fermés et sont presque toujours rétrogrades sous forme de C.
tn. = tenant
d. = droite
g. =gauche
dr. = drapé(e)
à l'ex = à l'exergue
[?] la légende nous est inconnue

Corpus dont le type est assuré et le poids connu
Argenteus, (demi-*Argenteus*) de Trèves de 443/444-455 au nom de Théodose II
A) DN THEODO/ [SIVS PF AVG] b d. dr. sous une main divine tenant une couronne
R) VRTVS RO/[MANORVM] Rome assise à g. sur un trône, étoile dans le champ à g.
Fragment de 0.33g (0.43 g. à l'origine ?)
Cahiers Ernest-Babelon n° : 2.22.1.17, Lafaurie 1964b n°2, pp. 197-198; Lafaurie 1987 n°17, p. 318, Arcy-Sainte-Restitue (02130)

Argenteus, (demi *argenteus* ou imitation ?) de Trèves de 443/444-455 au nom de Valentinien III (425-455)
A) DN VALENTINI/ANVS PF AVG b d. dr. sous une main divine tenant une couronne
R) VRTVS RO/MANORVM Rome assise à g. sur un trône, étoile dans le champ à g., TRPS à l'ex
0.70g (avec la bélière et le rivet qui la tient)
Cahiers Ernest-Babelon n° : 2.22.1.19, Lafaurie 1964b n°2.5, p. 197 et Fig. 9 p. 218, Lafaurie 1987 n°19. p. 318 et Pl. 26 Arcy-Sainte-Restitue (02130)

Argenteus
A) *ONI/TIII b. à d.
R) VIC... Rome assise de face
0.30g
Cahiers Ernest-Babelon n° : 2.473.2, Lafaurie 1964b n°24.a, p. 203 et photo 27 p. 219, Mayot (02800)

Argenteus
A) DVOII IOII b. à d
R) IIIA TORV Rome assise de face, ONO à l'ex
0.10g
Cahiers Ernest-Babelon n° : 2.473.3, Lafaurie 1964b n°24.b, p. 203 et photo 26 p. 219, Mayot (02800)

Argenteus de Strasbourg après 496
A) C ARCE/NTO VSIC b d. dr. main divine tenant une couronne
R)OI / trait ondé en guise de légende, Rome assise à g. sur un trône tn. une grande croix et un globe, trait ondé à l'ex
0.37g
Cahiers Ernest-Babelon n° : 10.216.1.1, Lafaurie 1988 n° 1, p. 380, Mailly-Le-Camp (10230)

Incertain, imitation d'*argenteus* au nom de Valentinien III (425-455) du début du VIe.
A) sans légende ; b d. dr.
R) L[ ] [Rome assise]. sur un trône, trait ondé, une perle dans les creux à l'ex
0.20g (erreur de frappe p. 380, p. 379 de « 0.18g à 0.37g »)
Cahiers Ernest-Babelon n° : 10.216.1.2, Lafaurie 1988 n° 2, p. 380, Mailly-Le-Camp (10230)

Incertain, imitation d'*argenteus* au nom de Valentinien III (425-455)
A) [ ]CISSNOS b d. dr. Chevelure dressée sur le diadème
R) [ ] Rome assise à d. sur un trône, étoile à d, trait ondé à l'ex
0.18g fortement ébréché (0.22g à l'origine ?)
Cahiers Ernest-Babelon n° : 10.216.1.3, Lafaurie 1988 n° 3, p. 380, Mailly-Le-Camp (10230)

Incertain, imitation d'*argenteus* au nom de Valentinien III (425-455)
A) DN[ ] b d. dr.
R) DN AV[ ]AS Rome assise de face sur un trône
0.23g légèrement ébréché (0.25g à l'origine ?)
Cahiers Ernest-Babelon n° : 10.216.1.5, Lafaurie 1988 n° 5, p. 380, Mailly-Le-Camp (10230)

Incertain, imitation d'*argenteus* au nom de Valentinien III (425-455)
A) [ ] /NIIIII (pseudo légende) b d. dr.
R) pseudo légende, Rome assise de face sur un trône tête à d, série de points à l'ex
0.30g fortement ébréché (0.33g à l'origine ?)
Cahiers Ernest-Babelon n° : 10.216.1.6, Lafaurie 1988 n° 6, p. 380, Mailly-Le-Camp (10230)

Imitation d'*argenteus* au nom de Valentinien III (425-455)
A) DNIVAL/(E ?)NT[I ?]NV b d. dr., main tn. une couronne
R) VH[ ]/ VNNAI Rome assise à g. sur un trône tn. une victoire, étoile à g, trait ondé à l'ex
0.34g, 16 mm., épaisseur 0.4 mm
Inédit, provient de Soligny les étangs (10400)
Photo 10

Argenteus, fin Ve
A) []L[]V[] b. d. dr.
R) IN[] Rome assise de face sur un trône, 5 points à l'ex.
0.13g fourré, ébréché, cassé et recollé (0.16g à l'origine ?), 13 mm
Cahiers Ernest-Babelon n°: 14.271.1., Lafaurie 1964b n° 14, p. 201 et photo 1 p. 217, Fleury-sur-Orne (14123) à 5 km au sud de Caen
Photo 11

Argenteus, au nom d'Anastase
A) ANASTA SVS b d. dr.
R) VICTOR AVG Rome assise à g. sur un trône tn. une haste et une victoire, étoile à g, COND ou CONB à l'ex
0.32g, 14 mm
Cahiers Ernest-Babelon n° : 14.623.1.1 et photo p. 95, Saint-Martin-De -Fontenay (14320) à 9 km au sud de Caen

Argenteus,
A) [ ] CTV b d. dr.
R) légende déformée Rome assise à g. sur un trône
0.24g
Cahiers Ernest-Babelon n° : 14.666.1.1 Sannerville (14940), lieu-dit Lirose, sépulture 11, à 12 km à l'est de Caen

Argenteus,
A)IIIIIIIII/IIIIIIII pseudo légende b. d. dr.
R) OIIIIIII/IIIIIIII pseudo légende Rome assise de face sur un trône
0.30g, 13 mm.
Cahiers Ernest-Babelon n° : 16.109.4, Lafaurie 1964b n° 11, p. 200 et photo 23 p. 219, Prou n°28, Prou 1891 n° 12 pl. V, Belfort 5008, Courbillac lieu dit Herpes (16200)
Photo 12

Argenteus,
A) IIIII/NIIII pseudo légende b. d. dr.
R) NIII/IINII pseudo légende Rome assise de face sur un trône, [CO]NOB à l'ex
0.39g, 14 mm
Cahiers Ernest-Babelon n° : 16.109.4, Lafaurie 1964b n° 11, p. 200 et photo 22 p. 219, Prou n°29, Prou 1891 n°14, Belfort 5010, Courbillac lieu dit Herpes (16200)
Photo 13

Argenteus,
A) IIII[ ]IIII pseudo légende b. d. dr.
R) [ ]IIIIII Rome assise de face sur un trône
Cahiers Ernest-Babelon n° : 16.109.4, Prou 1891 n°13 pl. V, Belfort 5009, Courbillac lieu dit Herpes (16200)

Argenteus, après 491 d'après Prou, car les bustes ornés d'une croix apparaissent sous Anastase (Prou 1891, p. 141). Néanmoins, l'une des monnaies trouvées lors des fouilles de Chatham Lines dans le Kent est au nom de Valentinien III et semble porter cette croix (Blackburn 1988, p. 170).
A) IIII/ .III pseudo légende b. d. dr. avec le buste orné d'une croix
R) IIIIII/IIII pseudo légende Rome assise de face sur un trône
Cahiers Ernest-Babelon n° : 16.109.4, Prou 1891 n°15 pl. V Belfort 5011, Courbillac lieu dit Herpes (16200)

7 autres *Argentei* « de même type » (que les 2 décrits précédemment)
A) pseudo légende b. d. dr.
R) pseudo légende Rome assise de face sur un trône
0.28g, 0.27g, 0.26g, 0.25g, 0.23g, 0.21g, 0.2g et 0.2g (Prou 1891 p 135)-l'un des poids correspond à l'un des 2 *argentei* décrit précédemment.
Cahiers Ernest-Babelon n° : 16.109.4, Lafaurie 1964b n° 11, p. 200, Prou 1891, Courbillac lieu dit Herpes (16200)

Argenteus,
A) [ ]/IIIAVC b. d. dr.
R) [CRO]R [/T] AAOC Rome assise à g, tn. une victoire, [C]ONO(B ?) à l'ex
0.40g, 14 mm, 0.4 mm d'épaisseur.
Inédite, ancienne collection privée de Touraine, provient probablement d'une trouvaille locale (d'Indre et Loire ?)
Photo 14

Argenteus, au nom de Julius Nepos (474-475)
A) DNIV NIE/POS [ ]AVC b.d. dr
R) GLORIA RO/MANO [RVM] Rome assise de face, COMOB à l'ex
0.27g
Cahiers Ernest-Babelon n° : 51.49.1, Bel 5007, Lafaurie 1964b n°4, p. 198 et photo 12 p. 218, Bergères-Les-Vertus (51130)

Argenteus, au nom de Valentinien III (425-455)
A) [ ]AVNT / IANVC b d. dr., main tn. une couronne
R) VII [ ]/ ITVN Rome assise à g. sur un trône tn. une victoire, étoile à g, trait ondé à l'ex
0.33g (0.35g à l'origine ?), 15 mm., 0.1 mm. d'épaisseur.
Inédit, Collection privée, provient des environs de Sézanne (51)
Photo 15

Argenteus, de Trèves de 443/444-455 au nom de Théodose II
A) DR TNEODO/SIVS PF AVG b d. dr. sous une main divine tenant une couronne.
R) VRTVSR/NANORVM Rome assise à g. sur un trône, tn. une haste et une victoire, étoile à g. TRPS à l'ex
0.69g, axe des coins 6-7h, 16 mm.
Médaillé de Lyon Inv. No 1998-3, ancienne collection de Marcel PESC. Elle provenait d'une vieille collection de Châlons-en-Champagne (51 ?) et elle a été trouvée probablement aux environs. Nos statistiques étant terminées nous n'avons pu l'inclure dans l'étude des poids. Planet sous presse.
Photo 16

Argenteus,
A) [ ]INIAVS PIC b. d. dr.
R) [ ]VIA PF AVG Rome assise à g, tn. une victoire, étoile à g
0.35g
Cahiers Ernest-Babelon n° : 51.622.1, Lafaurie 1964b n°37, p. 206, Prou 1891 2 pl. V, Bel 5012, Ville-Dommange (51390)
Photo 17

Argenteus,
A) DNNOT/IVTVII b. d. dr., main divine tenant une couronne ?
R) VA[ ]//III Rome assise à g, tn. une victoire, étoile à g.
0.32g
Cahiers Ernest-Babelon n° : 51.622.1, Lafaurie 1964b n°37, p. 206; Prou 1891, 4 pl. V, Bel 5014, Ville-Dommange (51390)
Photo 18

Argenteus,
A) DNAT/OAVE b. d. dr. ., main divine tenant une couronne ?
R) VA/VO Rome assise à g, tn. une victoire, étoile à g, ligne courbe à l'ex
0.35g
Cahiers Ernest-Babelon n° : 51.622.1, Lafaurie 1964b n°37, p. 206 et photo 19 p. 219, Prou 1891, 5 pl. V, Bel 5015, Ville-Dommange (51390)
Photo 19

Argenteus, au nom de Valentinien III (425-455)
A) AI VAI /LNII b. d. dr. ., main divine tenant une couronne ?
R) [ ]VAI/[ ]VIVI Rome assise à g. tn. une victoire, étoile à g
0.25g
Cahiers Ernest-Babelon n° : 51.622.1, Lafaurie 1964b n°37, p. 206; Prou 1891 6 pl. V, Bel 5016, Ville-Dommange (51390)

Argenteus,
A) [ ] /NCIO b. d. dr.
R) V [ ]/VI Rome assise à g. tn. un globe crucigère
0.22g, (0.25g à l'origine ?),
Cahiers Ernest-Babelon n° : 51.622.1, Lafaurie 1964b n°37, p. 206 et photo 20 p. 219, Prou 1891 7 pl. V; Prou 27, Bel 5017, Ville-Dommange (51390)
Photo 20

Argenteus (franc de Soissons d'après Cahiers Ernest-Babelon p 219)
A) DADV []NC b. d. dr. croisette devant l'effigie
R) Ligne sinueuse en guise de légende, Rome assise à gauche tn. une petite croix de la m d. et une grande croix de la m g, CON[OB] à l'exergue
0.23g avec la réparation plastique
Cahiers Ernest-Babelon n° : 55.166.2 Dugny-sur-Meuse (55100)

Argenteus, de Trèves de 443/444-455 au nom de Valentinien III (425-455)
A) DN VALENTINIANVS PF AVG b d. dr.
R) VRTVS RO/MANORVM Rome assise à g. sur un trône, étoile dans le champ à g. TRPS à l'ex
0.50g ébréché (0.55g à l'origine ?), 16 mm
Cahiers Ernest-Babelon n° : 55.285.2, Lafaurie 1964b n°21, p. 202; Lafaurie 1987 p. 322 et 10 Pl. 25, Lavoye-Autrecourt (55120) sépulture 194

Argenteus, au nom d'Avitus (455-456)
A) SVANIVIT AVG ou VANIVIT AVG b. dr.
R) IN-IN Rome assise à d. tn. une croix et une victoire.
0.30g, 20 mm.
Cahiers Ernest-Babelon n° : 60.145.2, Lafaurie 1964b n°10, p. 200 (sic Rome assise à g), Chelles (60350)

Argenteus, de Strasbourg après 496
A) CARCE NTIS ? b dr.
R) OI[ ] Rome assise de face sur un trône ?

0.23g, 13 mm.
Cahiers Ernest-Babelon n° : 60.466.1, Lafaurie 1964b n°29g, p. 204; Lafaurie 1988, p. 383 « de même coin que celui de Mailly », Noroy (60130)

Argenteus,
A) IIVA b dr.
R) IIII III Rome assise de face sur un trône
0.24g, 13 mm.
Cahiers Ernest-Babelon n° : 60.466.1, Lafaurie 1964b n°29h, p. 204, Noroy (60130)

Argenteus,
A) AIVI N IVI b dr.
R) ITV ITV Rome assise à g. sur un trône
0.31g, 13 mm.
Cahiers Ernest-Babelon n° : 60.466.1, Lafaurie 1964b n°29i, p. 204, Noroy (60130)

Argenteus, de Trèves de 443/444-455 au nom de Valentinien III (425-455)
A) DN VAL[ENTINI ANVS] PF AVG b d. dr. sous une main divine tenant une couronne
R) [VIR]TVS [RO M]ANORVM Rome assise à g. sur un trône
0.65g (0.78 au départ ?), 16,5 mm.
Cahiers Ernest-Babelon n° : 61.161.1 Lafaurie 1964b n°14, p. 201; Lafaurie 1987, p. 322 n°11 Pl.25, Fel (61160)

Incertain, imitation d'*argenteus* au nom de Valentinien III (425-455) frappé à Trèves
A) +VA<IV/M AVIV (légende commençant à 12h) b. d. dr.
R) [ ]VOMFI Rome assise à g. sur un trône, étoile à g
0.19g (poids originel)
Cahiers Ernest-Babelon n° : 76.235.1.1, Lafaurie 1964b 13.1, p. 200 (erreur victoire à d, étoile devant), Envermeu (76630)

Argenteus de Théodose II (402-450)
A) DIITEOD[ ]b. d. dr
R) MVANANI ? Rome assise de face sur un trône, ONOC rétrograde à l'exergue
0.16g (poids originel) (82,86 % d'argent, 17,14% de cuivre)
Cahiers Ernest-Babelon n° : 76.235.2.1, Lafaurie 1964b 13.2.c p 200, Envermeu (76630)

Argenteus
A) MONASH ? b. d. dr. très déformé
R) [ ] Rome assise à d. une étoile à d
0.16g (poids originel)
Cahiers Ernest-Babelon n° : 76.235.2.2., Lafaurie 1964b 13.2.b, p. 201, Envermeu (76630)

Argenteus
A) NS[]AVSLAVC b. d. dr
R) ONVICTOPIAAVG Rome assise de face NOB à l'exergue
0.32g
Cahiers Ernest-Babelon n° : 78.15.1.1, Lafaurie 1964b 1.1, p. 197, Andrésy (78570)

Argenteus
A) :CICVI b. d. dr
R) Rome assise à g
0.29g
Cahiers Ernest-Babelon n° : 78.15.1.2, Lafaurie 1964b 1.3, p. 197, Andrésy (78570)

Argenteus
A) légende formée d'un trait b. d. dr
R) Pseudo légende Rome assise de face
0.27g
Cahiers Ernest-Babelon n° : 78.15.1.3, Lafaurie 1964b 1.2, p. 197, Andrésy (78570)

Demi-*Argenteus*, de Trèves de 443/444-455 au nom de Valentinien III (425-455)
A) DN VALENTINI/ANVS PF AVG b. d. dr. sous une main divine tn. une couronne.
R) VIRTVS RO/MANORVM Rome assise à g. tn. un globe nicéphore et une haste croisetée, dans le champ à gauche une étoile TRPS à l'exergue
0.57g, 15 mm.
Cahiers Ernest-Babelon n° : 80.815.1.1 Dhénin 1980, p. 202, pl. XIX A; Lafaurie 1987, p. 323 et Pl. 25 Vron (80120) sépulture 140 A

Argenteus incertain, Justin ou Justinien pour J. Lafaurie mais imitation au nom de Théodose II (402-450) (rétrograde) pour M. Dhénin (Dhénin 1980, p. 203)
A) [ ]IVSVSIAAVC b. d. dr
R) [ ]ISVTIV (VIRTVS ROMANORVM rétrograde ?) Rome assise à d. tn. un globe et une haste, une étoile à d, SVII à l'exergue
0.20g très ébréché (poids originel 0.30g ?)
Cahiers Ernest-Babelon n° : 80.815.1.2, Dhénin 1980, p. 203, pl. XIX B, Vron (80120) sépulture 63A

Imitation d'*argenteus* au nom d'Anthémius (467-472)
A) DN ANTHE/MIVS PF AVG b. d. dr.
R) SALVS REI/[PVBLI]CAE Rome assise de face tn. une longue croix et une haste CONOB à l'exergue
0.48g
Cahiers Ernest-Babelon n° : 86.194.1, Lafaurie 1964b n° 30, p. 205 et photo 11 p. 218, Poitiers (86000)

Argenteus, de Trèves de 443/444-455 au nom de Valentinien III (425-455) (imitation possible)
A) DN VALENTINI/ANVS PF AVG b. d. dr, (sous une main divine tenant une couronne ?)
R) VRTVS RO/HANORVM Rome assise à g. tn. un globe nicéphore et une croix une étoile à g, TRPS à l'exergue
0.40g, 16 mm.
Cahiers Ernest-Babelon n° : 95.270.1.1, Mitard 1978 n°1, p. 119 et photo 1 et 1a pl. XVII, Lafaurie 1987, p. 323 et Pl.25 Genainville (95420)

Argenteus, au nom de Valentinien III (425-455)
A) [DN VALENTINI]ANNV[S] AVC b. d. dr
R) []NO[] Rome assise à g.
0.39g fragment (restitué 0.55g/0.60g) ,14 mm.
Cahiers Ernest-Babelon n° : 95.270.1.2, Mitard 1978 n°2, p. 119 et photo 2 et 2a pl. XVII, Genainville (95420)

Argenteus incertain, Justinien I pour Lafaurie et Valentinien III (425-455) pour P.-H. Mitard
A) [ ]IN[IA]N[VS] b. d. dr
R) [ ]T.IIO[ ] Rome assise à d. tn. une croix à d, [CO] NO[B] à l'ex
0.21g, 13 mm.
Cahiers Ernest-Babelon n° : 95.270.1.4, Mitard 1978 n°4, p. 220 et photo 4 pl. XVII et 4a pl. XVIII, Genainville (95420)

Argenteus, incertain
A) [D]NA[VITV ou STA]SIIIS b. d. dr
R) incertain Rome assise de face P.-H. Mitard ([]IIIII Rome assise à d. tn. une croix pour Lafaurie)
0.29g, 13 mm.
Cahiers Ernest-Babelon n° : 95.270.1.5, Mitard 1978 n°5, p. 121 et photo 5 pl. XVII et 5a pl. XVIII, Genainville (95420)

Belgique

Argenteus incertain, (« imitation franque de la 2e moitié Ve s. - 1e moitié VIe s de Valentinien III. » pour C. Van Hoof)
A) IIIC/IAN b d. dr.
R) INI/ IIN Rome assise de face sur un trône
0.24g, 14 mm
Lafaurie 1964b n°41, p. 208 et photo 25 p. 219, Ave-et-Auffe (55380) à 800 m d'Eprave.

Argenteus, au nom d'Avitus (455-456) (au nom de Valentinien III (425-455) pour J. Lafaurie et imitations franques d'Avitus de la 2e moitié Ve s. - 1e moitié VIe s pour C. Van Hoof)
A) DVAN IV/ITAVC b d. dr.
R) AV/IAVI Rome assise à g. sur un trône, étoile à g, trait ondé à l'ex
0.285g, 15 mm
Lafaurie 1964b n°42.1 p. 208 et photo 24 p. 219 ; G. Cumont 1890 gravure p. 213; Belfort 4999, Eprave (55380) au cimetière de la Croix-Rouge

Imitation d'*argenteus* de Trèves de 443/444-455 au nom de Valentinien III (425-455)
A) DNS VALEN/[TI]NIANVS b d. dr. main divine tenant une couronne ?
R) VRTV/NVTON Rome assise à g. sur un trône, étoile dans le champ à g., TR[ ] à l'ex
0.40g (0.40g G. Cumont 1890, pp. 214-215 mais 0.31g G. Cumont 1890, p. 256 et Lafaurie 1987, p. 323), 14 mm
Lafaurie 1964b n°42.2, p. 208; G. Cumont 1890 gravure p. 214, Belfort 5000, et Pl. 25, Eprave (55380) au cimetière sur le mont

Argenteus, au nom de Valentinien III (425-455)
A) DAVNT/IANVC b d. dr. d. main divine tenant une couronne ?
R) VIN/TVN Rome assise à g. sur un trône, étoile dans le champ à g., trait ondé à l'ex
0.313g, 14 mm
Lafaurie 1964b n°42.2, p. 208; G. Cumont 1890 gravure, p. 217; Belfort 5001, Eprave (55380) au cimetière sur le mont

Argenteus, au nom de Valentinien III (425-455)
A)[ ] AVI/NNNIS b d. dr. main divine tenant une couronne ?
R) VAN/[ ] NIN, Rome assise de face sur un trône, NII à l'ex
0.28g, 12 mm. (pesait 0.30g ?)
Lafaurie 1964b n°42.4, p. 208; G. Cumont 1893 gravure p. 427, Eprave (55380) au cimetière sur le mont

Allemagne

3 *Argentei*, de Worms vers 500-530
A) [?] b d. dr.
R) [?] Rome assise à g. sur un trône tn. une haste et une victoire, étoile dans le champ à g.
0.102g (arrondi à 0.11g) et 0.128g, le troisième est brisé
Lafaurie 1964b n°52.2, p. 213; Lafaurie 1988e, p. 420; Cologne (Köln), dans une tombe d'enfant de la cathédrale

Argenteus,
A) [?] b d. dr.
R) [VIRTVS ROMAN]ORV[M] Rome assise à g. sur un trône tn. une haste et une victoire
0.118g
Lafaurie 1964b n°52.2, p. 213; Cologne (Köln), dans une tombe d'enfant de la cathédrale

Argenteus, au nom d'Anastase
A) [D] N AN [ASTASIVS] b d. dr.
R) [?]/ AVA Rome assise à g. sur un trône tn. une haste et une victoire, étoile dans le champ à g., TRPS à l'ex
0.37g
Lafaurie 1964b n°53, p. 213 et photo 18 p. 219, « Rheinhessen » (Jugenheim in Rheinhessen 55270 ?)

Argenteus, de Worms vers 500-530
A) [?] b d. dr.
R) [?] Rome assise à g. sur un trône tn. une haste et une victoire
0.14g
Lafaurie 1964b n°54, p. 214 et photo 31 p. 220; Lafaurie 1988e, p. 420, Rheinsheim (76661)

3 *Argentei* incertains, au nom de Valentinien III (425-455)
A) [?] b d. dr.
R) [?] Rome assise à g. sur un trône tn. une haste et une victoire
0.21g, 0.23g et 0.25g
Lafaurie 1964b n°56.a, p. 214, Schwarzrheindorf (Bonn-Schwarzrheindorf en Nord-Westphalie)

Argenteus, de Strasbourg après 496
A) [C ARCE/NTO VSIC] effigie remplacé par un double arc surmonté d'une flèche.
R) [OI / trait ondé en guise de légende ?], Rome assise à g. sur un trône tn. une grande croix et un globe (trait ondé à l'ex ?)
0.26g
Lafaurie 1988, p. 383, Bonn- Schwarzrheindorf en Nord-Westphalie (Lafaurie 1964b n°56.b, p. 214, Schwarzrheindorf)

Lieu de trouvaille inconnu

Argenteus,
A) [ ]A/O[ ]VI b. d. dr
R) [ ]/ V.IIOoI, Rome assise de face, [C]ON[O]à l'ex.
0.30g, 13 mm.
Collection de la Monnaie de Paris n°2, p. 25, lieu de trouvaille inconnu.
Photo Jean-Jacques Castaing, Monnaie de Paris
Photo 21

Argenteus,
A) [ ]AVN/[ ] b. d. dr.
R) OLINIII[ ]OSC, Rome assise de face, AONO à l'ex.
0.27g, 13 mm.
Collection de la Monnaie de Paris n°3, p. 25, lieu de trouvaille inconnu.
Photo Jean-Jacques Castaing, Monnaie de Paris
Photo 22

Argenteus,
A) [ ] A/ [ ] ANI b. d. dr.
R) [ ]/ANI, Rome assise de face
0.25g, 13 mm.
Collection de la Monnaie de Paris n°4, p. 25, lieu de trouvaille inconnu.
Photo Jean-Jacques Castaing, Monnaie de Paris
Photo 23

Argenteus, au nom d'Honorius (393-423), Visigoths ?
A) DII IIOIIOII/VS PF AVG b. d. diad. dr et cuir.
R) VICTOII/A AVGGG, Rome assise de face tenant une croix chrismée
0.42g, 12 mm, 0,6 mm d'épaisseur
Comptoir Général Financier, Monnaies 38, 20 avril 2009, lot 1358 (*RIC* X, n° 3709, p. 452)
Nos statistiques de poids étant terminées nous n'avons pu l'inclure.
Photo 24

Argenteus, au nom d'Anastase (491-518)
A) DN ANAST.ASIVS PAC b d. dr.
R) VICT/O/RIAVCC Rome assise à g. sur un trône, tn. une haste et une victoire
0.45g, 15 mm.
Lafaurie 1964b n°40, p. 207 et photo 17 p. 219, Lieu de trouvaille inconnu Don Fillon, Prou 1891 8 pl. V
Photo 25

Argenteus, au nom d'Honorius (393-423), Visigoths ?
A) DN HONORI/VS PF AVG b. d. dr
R) GLORIA RO/MANORVM, Rome assise de face, RVPS à l'ex
0.67g
Gemini CCC, auction 4, 8 janvier 2008, n°523
Photo 26

Argenteus, au nom d'Honorius (393-423), Visigoths ?
A) DN HONORI/VS PF AVG b. d. dr
R) [GL]ORIA NO/MANORV, Rome assise de face, RVPS à l'ex
0.40g
Prou 1891, p. 137, G. Cumont 1890 gravure p. 237, Belfort 5006, lieu de trouvaille inconnu, « conservée au cabinet des médailles de Marseille »

Argenteus, de Trèves au nom de Valentinien III de 443/444-455
A) DN VALENTINI/ANNS PF AVG b d. dr. main divine tenant une couronne ?
R) VRTVSRO/MANORVN Rome assise à g. sur un trône, étoile dans le champ à g., TRPS à l'ex
0.648g
G. Cumont 1890 gravure p. 232, lieu de trouvaille inconnu, Belfort 5002, « pièce du British Museum »

Argenteus, de Trèves de 443/444-455 au nom de Théodose II
A) DN THEODO/SIVS PF AVG b d. dr. main divine tenant une couronne ?
R) VRTVSRO/MANORVM Rome assise à g. sur un trône, tn. une haste et une victoire, étoile à g. TRPS à l'ex
0.60g
G. Cumont 1890 gravure p. 234, Belfort 5004, lieu de trouvaille inconnu, «pièce de la Bibliothèque Nationale»

Argenteus, au nom d'Honorius (393-423), Visigoths ?
A) DN HONORI/VS PF AVG b. d. dr
R) VICTORI/A AVGGG, Rome assise de face (tenant une croix chrismée ?), RVPS à l'ex
0.46g
RIC X, n° 3709, p. 452

Annexe 1

82 monnaies ont été exclues du corpus, car le type ou le poids était trop incertain ou parce qu'elles étaient d'un poids supérieur à 0,9g. Certaines pourraient appartenir au type étudié ici.

France
-Bourg-en-Bresse, Cahiers Ernest-Babelon n° : 1.53.1 *Argenteus*, Arcadius, 383-408 de Milan, type ?
-Vireux-Molhain, Cahiers Ernest-Babelon n° : 8.486.3.1 Lafaurie 1987b, pp. 321-322 sépulture 23, type ?
-Mayot, Cahiers Ernest-Babelon n° : 2.473.3, Lafaurie 1964b n°24, p. 203 (les 3 *Argentei* en débris), poids ?

-Monceau-le-neuf, Cahiers Ernest-Babelon n° :2.491.2, Lafaurie 1964b n°26, p. 203, 2 *Argentei*, type ?
-Vermand sépulture 71, Cahiers Ernest-Babelon n° :2.785.2.1 et n : 2.785.2.2, poids ?
-Vermand sépulture 397, Cahiers Ernest-Babelon n° :2.785.3.1 et n : 2.785.3.2, poids ?
-Vireux-Molhain Cahiers Ernest-Babelon n° : 8.486.2, Lafaurie 1987b, pp. 321-322 sépulture 14, 0,92g
-Mailly-Le-Camp Cahiers Ernest-Babelon n° : 10.216.1.7, Lafaurie 1988 n° 7, p. 380 (2 fragments), poids ?
-Chatelaillon-Plage, Cahiers Ernest-Babelon n° :17.94.2, Lafaurie 1980b, 3 fragments, RVP(S) à l'exergue, poids ?
-Saintes, Cahiers Ernest-Babelon n° : 17.415.3, poids ?
-Bretenière, Cahiers Ernest-Babelon n° : 21.106.1, type ?
-Ile-de-Bréhat, Cahiers Ernest-Babelon n° : 22.16.1, poids ?
-Sauveterre, Cahiers Ernest-Babelon n° : 30.312.1, poids ?
-Soulac-sur-Mer, Cahiers Ernest-Babelon n° : 33.514.1, poids ?
-Sceau du Gâtinais, Cahiers Ernest-Babelon n° : 45.303.3, type et poids ?
-Ville-Dommange, Cahiers Ernest-Babelon n° : 51.622.1, Lafaurie 1964b n°37, p. 206, Prou 1891, 3 pl. V, Bel 5013, poids ?
-Cutry, Cahiers Ernest-Babelon n° : 54.151.1 (2 *argentei*), poids ?
-Abainville Cahiers Ernest-Babelon n° : 55.1.1.2 et 55.1.1.3, poids ?
-Koenigsmacker, Cahiers Ernest-Babelon n° : 57.370.1 et 3, Lafaurie 1964b n°20, p. 202, type et poids ?
-Delincourt, Cahiers Ernest-Babelon n° : 60.195.2, type et poids ?
-Le Mans, Cahiers Ernest-Babelon n° : 72.181.1, poids ?
-Blangy-sur-Bresle, Cahiers Ernest-Babelon n° : 76.101.1, type ?
-Andrésy, Cahiers Ernest-Babelon n° : 78.15.1.4 Lafaurie 1964b 1.4 ?, p. 197 sic monnaie de bronze, type et poids ?
-Templeux-la-Fosse, monnaie visigotiques Cahiers Ernest-Babelon n° : 80.747.1.3, type et poids ?
-Vron sépulture 129 A Cahiers Ernest-Babelon n° : 80.815.3, Dhénin 1980, p. 204, pl. XIX C, type ?

Royaume Uni
-Chatham Lines, (Kent), 3 *argentei* au nom de Valentinien II (425-455) et Anthémius (467-72) sans poids, Blackburn 1988.

Belgique
-Ave-et-Auffe, Un fragment d'*argenteus* de Worms Lafaurie 1988e, p. 421, type et poids ?
-Eprave « DIM » t 55, C. Van Hoof 1991, p. 114, «imitation franque d'Honorius», type et poids ?
-Eprave au cimetière sur le mont, Lafaurie 1964b n°42.2, p. 208, Brisée en plusieurs fragments, type et poids ?
-Hantes-Wiheries, C. Van Hoof, p 114, «imitation franque indéterminée détruite de la 2e moitié Ve s. – 1e moitié VIe s. », type et poids ?
-Harmignies, Lafaurie 1964b n°43 p 209, G. Cumont 1890 note 2, pp. 219-220, type ?
-Tournai « StB » t 10, C. Van Hoof, p 113, « 3 imitations franques d'Honorius de la 2e moitié Ve s. – 1e moitié VIe s. », type et poids ?
-Vieuxville, 3 *Argentei* de Trèves de 443/444-455 au nom de Théodose II ou Valentinien III : 0,98g et 2 non pesés, Lafaurie 1987, pp. 312-323

Suisse
-Bâle-Kleinhüningen : 14 *Argentei* de Trèves de 443/444-455 au nom de Théodose II ou Valentinien III sans les poids Lafaurie 1964b n°48, p. 210, Lafaurie 1987, pp. 319-320.

Allemagne
-Andernach, Lafaurie 1964b n°51 p 213, 2 *Argentei* Type Belfort 5000/5001, poids ?
-Bonn-Schwarzrheindorf en Nord-Westphalie : Lafaurie 1988e, p. 420, 3 *Argentei*, de Worms (Lafaurie 1964b, n°56.b p. 214, Schwarzrheindorf), type et poids ?
-Fridingen an der Donau en Bade-Wurtemberg, Lafaurie 1988, p. 383, *Argenteus* au nom de Valentinien III de Strasbourg (ARGENTO CIVIS après 496), type et poids ?
-Trèves, fouilles de Saint Maximin, Lafaurie 1988, p. 383, type et poids ?
-Trèves, liebfrauenstrasse, 6 *Argentei* de Trèves de 443/444-455 au nom de Valentinien III sans les poids (Lafaurie 1987, p. 321)
-Rittersdorf tombe 89 et tombe 95, Lafaurie 1964b n°55, p. 214, poids ?
-Rheinsheim tombe 227, Lafaurie 1964b n°54, p. 213; Lafaurie 1988, p. 382, poids ?
-Rubenach, Lafaurie 1988, p. 383, type et poids ?
Wattenheim, Lafaurie 1988, p. 383 et Lafaurie 1964b n°57, p. 214, de Worms Lafaurie 1988e, p. 420, poids ?
-Waldwisse, Lafaurie 1988, p. 383 de Worms Lafaurie 1988e, p. 420, poids ?
Douvrend, Lafaurie 1980e, type et poids ?

Collections et catalogues
« Pièce du British Museum », G. Cumont 1890 gravure p. 233, Belfort 5003, 0,907g
Belfort 5005, poids ?
Dumbarton Oaks collection, Grierson 1983, poids ? et p 217 1 g au départ (0.7g actuellement)
Lafaurie 1964b, photo 21, p. 219 perles à l'ex.

Nous remercions tous ceux qui, par leur patience, leur relecture, ou les informations transmises, nous ont soutenus pour la rédaction de cet article et particulièrement : Jean-Jacques Castaing, Jean-Luc Desnier et Sylvie Juvénal de la Monnaie de Paris; © Eric Gaba (http://commons.wikimedia.org/wiki/User:Sting) auteur de la carte, licence « Creative Commons Attribution ShareAlike 3.0 unported (http://creativecommons.org/licenses/by-sa/3.0/); François Planet ; le Comptoir Général Financier et Gemini CCC.

Abréviations

Cahiers Ernest-Babelon n° 8 (2003)= Lafaurie J., Pilet-Lemiere J. *Monnaies du Haut-Moyen Age découvertes en Fran-*

ce (Ve-VIIIe siècle). Paris.

Collection de la Monnaie de Paris (1987)= Belaubre J. *Les Collections monétaires, monnaies médiévales. Tome I. L'époque du denier.* Paris.

Lafaurie/Ouerre (1964)= Lafaurie J. Monnaies franques en argent trouvées à Ouerre, *Bulletin de la Société Archéologique D'Eure-et-Loir, n°20, 1er trimestre 1966 (Chroniques 2)*, pp. 49-54.

MEC (1986)= Philip G., Blackburn M. A. S. *Medieval European Coinage, I. The Early Middle Ages, 5 th-10 th. Centuries.* Cambridge.

RIC X (1994)= Kent J. P. C. *The Roman Imperial Coinage. Volume X. The divided Empire and the fall of the Western parts (395-491).* Londres.

Références

Arslan E. A. (1998). 'Mutamenti di funzione e di struttura degli stock monetari in Europa tra V e VIII secolo', in *Morfologie sociali e culturali in Europa fra tarda antichità e alto medioevo, Settimane di studio del Centro Italiano Studi Alto Medioevo di Spoleto, 3-9 aprile 1997, 45.* Spoleto, pp. 379-461 (http://www.ermannoarslan.eu/Contributi/index.php).

Arslan E. A. (2004). 'Le monete della necropoli di Campochiaro e la monetazione anonima beneventana del VII secolo', in *Atti del Convegno "I Beni Culturali nel Molise", (Campobasso 18-20.11.1999).* Campobasso. pp. 87-131, 387-391 (http://www.ermannoarslan.eu/Contributi/index.php)

De Belfort A. (1892-95). *Description générale des monnaies mérovingiennes par ordre alphabétique des ateliers (publiée d'après les notes manuscrites de M. Ponton d'Amécourt).* 5 volumes. Paris.

Blackburn M. (1988). 'Three silvers coins in the name of Valentinian III (425-455) and Anthémius (467-472) from Chatham lines, Kent', *The Numismatic Chronicle*, 148, pp. 169-174.

Bompaire M. (1993). 'Du solidus d'or au denier d'argent : genèse de la monnaie médiévale', in Contamine P. (ed.), *L'économie médiévale.* Paris, pp. 103-134.

Cumont G. (1890). 'Monnaies franques découvertes dans les cimetières francs d'Eprave (province de Namur)', *Revue Belge de Numismatique*, 46, pp. 212-269.

Cumont G. (1893). 'Monnaies découvertes dans les cimetières francs de Corbois, près de Rochefort et sur le Mont à Eprave', *Revue Belge de Numismatique*, pp. 425-430.

Dhénin M. (1980). 'Monnaies des Ve -VIe siècle des nécropoles de Vron (Somme) et de Hordain (Nord)', in Bastien P. (ed.), *Mélanges de numismatique d'archéologie et d'histoire offerts à Jean Lafaurie.* Paris, pp. 201-207 et pl. XIX-XX.

Dhénin M. (1993). 'L' or, l'argent, le bronze, métaux monétaires', dans *Mercati e mercanti nell'alto medievo: l'area euroasiatica e l'area mediterranea (23-29 aprile 1992) (Settimane di studio del centre italiano di studi sull'alto medievo 40).* Spoleto, pp. 827-846.

Foucray B. (2004). 'Deux *argentei* d'Odoacre et Gondebaud provenant de Caulaincourt (Aisne)', *Cahiers Numismatiques*, 162, décembre, pp. 43-47.

Geiger H.-U. (1979). 'Die merowingischen Münze in der Schweiz' *Schweizerische Numismatische Rundschau (Revue Suisse de Numismatique)*, 58, pp. 83-178.

Grierson (1983). 'A rediscovered siliqua of Valentinian III (425-455)', *The Numismatic Chronicle*, 143, pp. 217-218 et pl. 43.

Guillaume J. (1988). 'La nécropole d'Abainville (Meuse)', in *Actes des Xe journées internationales d'Archéologie mérovingienne (Metz 20-23 octobre 1988)*, pp. 97-102.

King C. E. (1987). *Roman silver coins V, Carausius to Romulus Augustus.* London (reprint 2004).

Lafaurie J. (1964). 'Monnaie en argent trouvée à Fleury-sur-Orne. Essaie sur le monnayage d'argent franc des Ve et VIe siècles', *Annales de Normandie*, 14e année, n°2/6, pp. 197-216.

Lafaurie J. (1978). 'Monnaies d'argent franques trouvées à Envermeu (Seine-Maritime) (Ve siècle)', in *Actes du colloque internationale d'archéologie, Rouen, 3, 4, 5 juillet 1975. Centenaire de l'abbé Cochet 1975.* Rouen, pp. 421-428.

Lafaurie J. (1980). 'Trouvailles de monnaies franques et mérovingiennes en Seine-Maritime. Histoire et numismatique en Normandie', *Cahiers des Annales de Normandie*, n°12 A, pp. 95-107.

Lafaurie J. (1987). 'Les dernières émissions impériales de Trèves au Ve siècle', in Huvelin H., Christol M., Gautier G. (eds), *Mélanges de numismatiques offerts à Pierre Bastien à l'occasion de son 75e anniversaire.* Wetteren, pp. 297-323 et Pl. 23-26.

Lafaurie J. (1988). '*Argentei* francs attribuables à Worms', *Bulletin de la Société Française de Numismatique*, 7, pp. 419-421.

Lafaurie J. (1988e). 'Monnaies trouvées dans la tombe 22 de la nécropole de Mailly-le-Camp (Aube) (résumé)', *Bulletin de la Société Française de Numismatique*, 6, pp. 379-384.

Lafaurie J. (1990). 'Communication du 23 mai sur « les émissions de monnaies en argent, en Gaule, au VIe siècle » (résumé)', *Bulletin de la Société Nationale des Antiquaires de*

France, pp. 202-217.

Lafaurie J. (1996). 'Monnaies mérovingiennes du musée des beaux-arts de Lyon', *Bulletin des musées et monuments lyonnais*, supplément 1-2.

Lebecq S. (1990). *Les origines franques, Ve-IXe siècle, nouvelle histoire de la France médiévale. Tome 1*. Seuil.

López Sánchez F. (2011). 'Suevic Coins and Suevic Kings', in Curta F. (ed.), *Neglected Barbarians. Studies in the Early Middle Ages (SEM)* 32, pp. 503-536.

Mitard P.-H. (1978). Monnaies des Ve/VIe siècle découvertes à Genainville (Val-d'Oise), *Revue Numismatique*, VIe Série, 20, pp. 117-130 et pl. XVII-XVIII.

Perin P. (2008). 'Les Francs et Rome', dans *Rome et les Barbares : la naissance d'un nouveau monde. Catalogue de l'exposition au palazzo Grassi. Venice, 26 janvier-20 juillet 2008*. Venice, pp. 342- 345.

Planet F. (2009). 'From Aetius to Clovis. An unpublished *argenteus* struck at Trier at the end of the 5th century', in Woloszyn M. (ed.), *Byzantine Coins in Central Europe between the 5th and 10th Century. Moravia Magna. Vol. V (Actes du colloque organisé par l'Académie des Sciences et Arts de Pologne et Université de Rzeszów tenu à Cracovie les 23-26 avril 2007)*. Craków, pp. 35-36.

Prou M. (1891). 'Monnaies barbares d'argent trouvées dans le cimetière mérovingien d'Herpes', *Revue Numismatique*, VIe Série, 9, pp. 134-145 et pl. V.

Prou M. (1892). *Catalogue des monnaies françaises de la Bibliothèque nationale. Les monnaies mérovingiennes*. Paris.

Rajade A. (2009). 'Fonction des « grosses perles de ceinture » éléments de parure ou objets fonctionnels ? (durant l'Antiquité Tardive et le Haut Moyen Age en France)', in *Revue Archéologique de Picardie, 1-2 (L' actualité de l'archéologie du haut Moyen Âge en Picardie. Les apports de l' expérimentation à l' archéologie mérovingienne. Actes des XXIXe Journées internationales d' archéologie mérovingienne. Musée des Temps Barbares, Marle (Aisne) 26-28 septembre 2008)*, pp. 77-86.

Soulat J. (2009). 'Dynamique de peuplement dans le nord, l'implantation saxonne et anglo-saxonne dans le Ponthieu entre le fin du IVe et le milieu du VIe siècle', in *Revue Archéologique de Picardie, 1-2 (L' actualité de l'archéologie du haut Moyen Âge en Picardie. Les apports de l' expérimentation à l' archéologie mérovingienne. Actes des XXIXe Journées internationales d' archéologie mérovingienne. Musée des Temps Barbares, Marle (Aisne) 26-28 septembre 2008)*, pp. 27-35.

Van Hoof C. (1991). 'Un aspect du rituel funéraire dans les tombes franques et mérovingiennes en Belgique, la présence des monnaies', *Acta Archeologica Lovaniensia*, 30, pp. 95-115.

Liste de Figures

1.- Théodebert Ier (533-548), BN 56a 23-6-81 Z 2733, Cahiers Ernest-Babelon n°: 70.279.1, 0.45g, 11 mm.
2.- Ouerre 1, Cahiers Ernest-Babelon n°: 14.623.1.2, 0.185g, 10 mm.
3.- Ville-Dommange n°16, 0.3g, 14 mm.
4.- Majorien 457 – 461, Numismatica Ars classica, Action 40, lot 911, 0.44 g, 11 mm.
5.- Trouvé en Charente maritime, 0.19g, 13 mm.
6.- Metz, 0.21g, 11 mm.
7.- Abainville (Meuse), poids et diametre non précisés.
8.- Comparaison entre une pièce de 1 centime d'euro et un argenteus.
9.- Siliques de Rechiarius (448-456 apr. J.-C) au portrait et légende d'Honorius (395-423 apr. J.C.), 19 mm.
10.- Soligny Les Etangs, 0.34 gr, 16 mm, épaisseur 0,4 mm.
11.- Fleury sur Orne, Bnf 1971-444, 0.16g à l'origine ?,13 mm.
12.- Courbillac lieu dit Herpes A 12 pl. V, 0.30g, 13 mm.
13.- Courbillac lieu dit Herpes A 14 pl. V, 0.39g, 14 mm.
14.- 14 mm, 0,4 mm d'épaisseur.
15.- 0.33g (0.35g à l'origine ?), 15 mm, 0,1 mm d'épaisseur.
16.- Planet, photo A. Basset, Médaillier de Lyon, Inv. No 1998-3, 0.69g, 16 mm.
17.- Ville-Dommange 2 pl. V, 0.35g, 14 mm.
18.- Ville-Dommange 4 pl. V, 0.32g, 15 mm.
19.- Ville-Dommange 5 pl. V, 0.35g, 15 mm.
20.- Ville-Dommange 7 pl. V, 0.22g, (0.25g à l'origine ?), 14 mm.
21.- Collection de la Monnaie de Paris n°2, photo Jean-Jacques Castaing, 0.30g, 13 mm.
22.- Collection de la Monnaie de Paris n°3, photo Jean-Jacques Castaing, 0.27g, 13 mm.
23.- Collection de la Monnaie de Paris n°4, photo Jean-Jacques Castaing, 0.25g, 13 mm.
24.- Comptoir Général Financier, Monnaies 38, 20 avril 2009, lot 1358, 0,42g, 12 mm, 0,6 mm d'épaisseur.
25.- Don Fillon, Bnf, 0.45g, 15 mm.
26.- Vente Gemini CCC 4, 8 janvier 2008, n°523, 0.67g

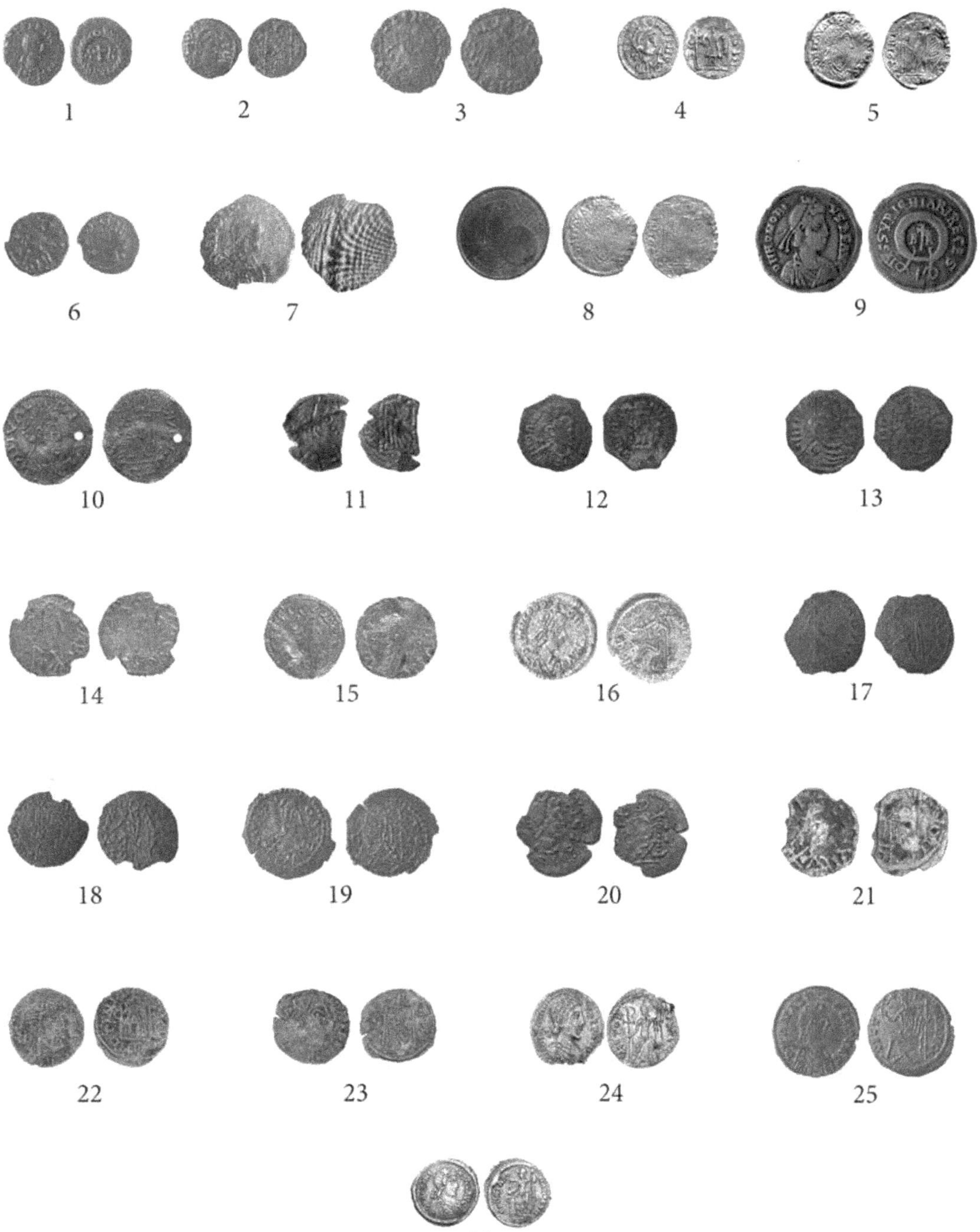
1
2
3
4
5
6
7
8
9
10
11
12
13
14
15
16
17
18
19
20
21
22
23
24
25
26

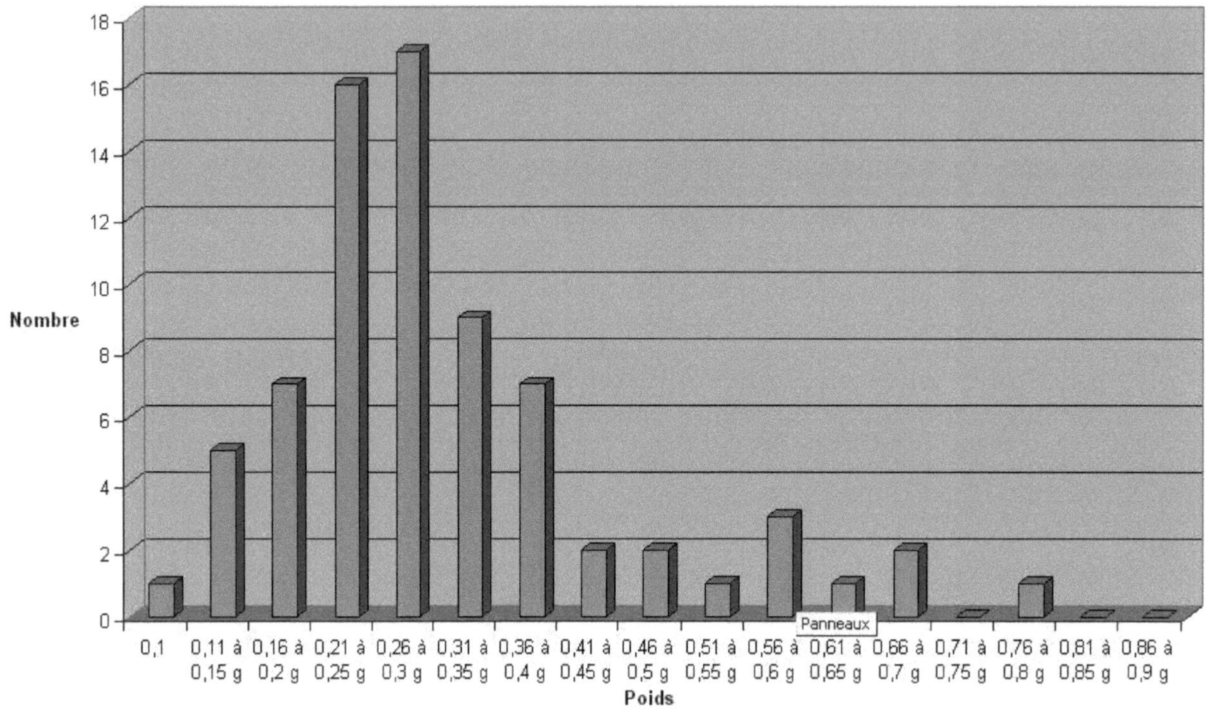

Graphique 1.- Répartition des monnaies par poids

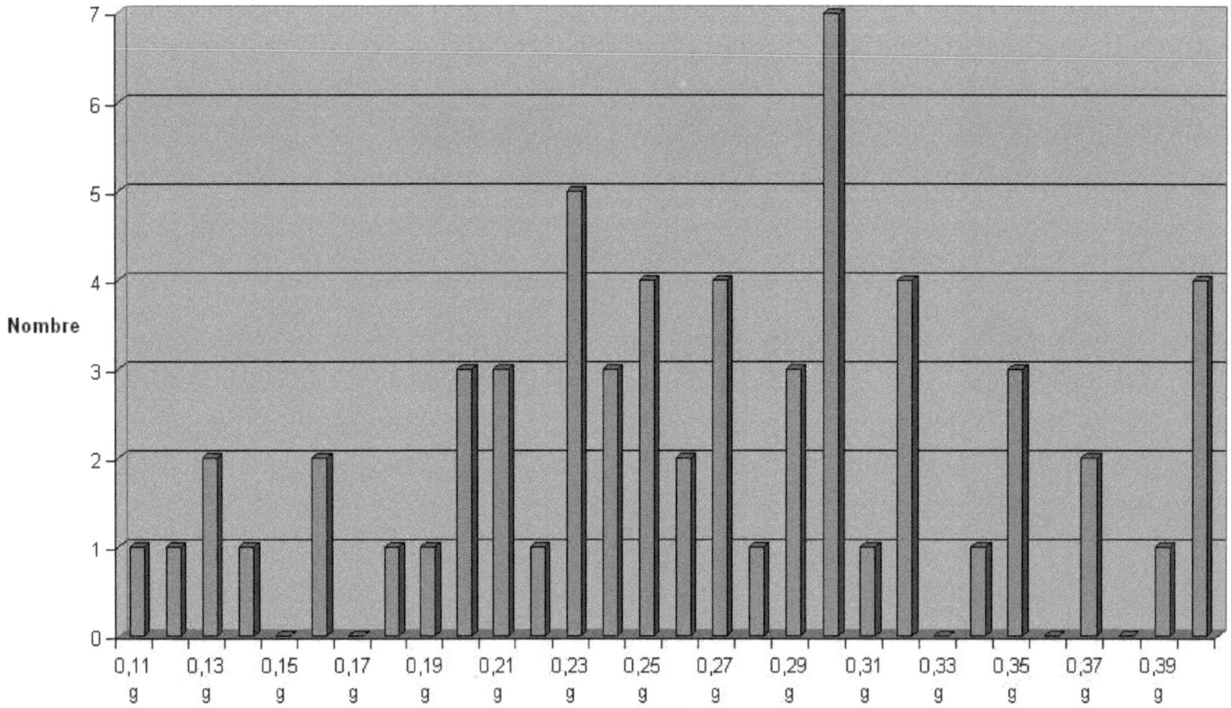

Graphique 2.- Répartition fine des monnaies par poids de 0.10g à 0.40g

Towns and minting in norhern Europe in the early Middle Ages

Gareth Williams

ABSTRACT

This paper considers links between towns and minting in northern Europe in the period from the fifth to the eleventh centuries AD. Since both coinage and towns in early medieval Europe can be traced back to the late Roman period, the paper considers three areas with different relationships with the Roman Empire: the Frankish kingdom(s), which succeeded directly to the later Roman Empire, with elements of continuity in both urban occupation and the use of coinage; Anglo-Saxon England, which had formerly been part of the Roman Empire but saw significant discontinuity in both urban occupation and coin use following the collapse of direct Roman rule there in the early fifth century; and Scandinavia, which had never formed part of the Roman Empire, although some coin use is recorded in the late Roman period. The paper concludes, perhaps unsurprisingly, that in the early period links between towns and minting are strongest and most explicit in the Frankish coinage, but that similar links are observable in Anglo-Saxon England, with the development of a national network of mints issuing coinage under royal authority from the tenth century, possibly in part as a result of Frankish influence. Scandinavia was slower to develop both coins and towns, but gradually developed both, probably as a result of both Frankish and Anglo-Saxon influence. In all three cases, the association between coins and towns appears to relate in part to the economic role of towns as centres of production and exchange, and in part to the role of towns as local/regional centres for royal authority and administration.

Introduction

The minting of coinage in early medieval Europe had two main functions. On the one hand, it served an economic function, facilitating trade and exchange both on a local level and over longer distances. On the other, coins provided a medium for the expression of the authority of the issuer, and of a range of political, cultural and religious identities. The balance between the two varied between different currencies: the largely inscriptionless English coinage of the seventh and eighth centuries, although rich in Christian iconography, did little to promote clear identities for the authorities or even the kingdoms by and in which they were issued, but circulated in large quantities and in some cases point to the existence of extensive trading networks around the North Sea (Metcalf 1998; Gannon 2003). By contrast, the earliest Norwegian coinage from the 990s to the 1020s was minted in such small quantities that it can hardly have had an effective monetary function, and seems to have been designed solely to express the identity of the issuing kings as Christian rulers of the newly unified Norway within a wider pattern of Romanised Christian kingship (Williams 2007a, pp. 190-192).

The more developed coinages, such as those of the Carolingian empire and the English kingdom of the tenth and eleventh centuries had a third function, which was to support and extend the authority of the ruler more directly, through the regulation not only of the circulating coinage itself, but through the coinage of prices and values for trade, fines and taxation. A carefully managed coinage could generate revenue directly for the king, either through the premiums charged on frequent re-coinage, as seen in the *renovatio monetae* of the late Anglo-Saxon system,[1] or through taxes such as the Norman *monetagium*, which the dukes of Normandy received from their subjects in exchange for not altering or renewing the coinage (Bisson 1978, pp.14-28; Moesgaard 2009a).

These different functions reflected in many ways the multiple functions of early medieval towns. A classic definition of the town was provided by Martin Biddle (1976, p.100) in a survey article on Anglo-Saxon towns. He argued that, in a period of developing urbanisation, a minimum definition of an early medieval town was that it should show at least three or four of the following characteristics: defences; a planned street-system; a market(s); a mint; legal autonomy; a role as a central place; a relatively large and dense population; a diversified economic base; plots and houses of 'urban' type; social differentiation; complex religious organisation; a judicial centre. Obviously not all towns pos-

(1) Grierson 1985; Metcalf 1987; Allen forthcoming.

sessed every one of these features, but core groupings of functions relating to economic activity, the visible expression of authority and identity, and the practical application and extension of that authority closely reflect the core functions of coinage, although as with coinage the balance between those functions could vary. Thus, for example, recent thinking on the Anglo-Saxon burghal system introduced by Alfred of Wessex and his successors in the late ninth and tenth centuries suggests that economic activity was in many cases a later development, and secondary to the core functions of defence and the extension of royal authority (Hall 2011; Williams forthcoming a). Nevertheless, given the similarities in the range of functions represented by both coins and towns, it is hardly surprising that, while the circulation of coinage was by no means limited to towns, there is a broad pattern of association between minting and towns or other pre-urban settlements. This is visible across the coin-using areas of northern Europe, and this paper will consider the different manifestations of this association in the Frankish kingdoms of the 7th to 9th centuries, the Anglo-Saxon kingdoms of the 7th-11th centuries, and the Scandinavian kingdoms of the 8th-11th centuries. Since, as I have argued more fully elsewhere, the issuing of coinage in this period appears to correlate with the adoption of a concept of Romanised Christian kingship (Williams 2006; 2007a), in which the issuing of coin (literate or otherwise) was a symbol that the ruler identified himself within that particular tradition of kingship, it is interesting to compare these three areas as representing respectively an area within the former Roman empire with a considerable degree of continuity after the fall of Rome; an area within the former empire in which both Roman authority and urbanism largely collapsed and had to be reinvented; and an area which had always lain beyond the bounds of the Roman empire.

The Frankish kingdoms

Of the three areas in question, the Frankish kingdoms show the greatest continuity from Rome, even though some parts of these kingdoms went through intermediate stages of Visigothic or Burgundian rule. Without going into the detail of the similarities and differences of Roman and Frankish rule, two points are of importance here. The first is that the extensive network of towns and cities established in Roman Gaul largely survived under the Franks. Few of these had been mints in Roman times, but their role as regional centres of both secular and ecclesiastical authority continued and developed, with counts and bishops emerging as the main tier of authority below the Merovingian kings and their mayors of the palace.

The second point is that there seems to have been little or no break in coin use, although the scale of coin-use gradually diminished, and the Roman tri-metallic currency system had by the late sixth century been replaced by a system limited almost exclusively to gold. Following the fall of Rome, the gap was filled initially by imported Byzantine imperial coins and anonymous pseudo-Imperial imitations produced by the Franks themselves, together with the Burgundians, Visigoths and the Patricians of Provence. During this transitional period, while some lower-denomination coins carried the names of local rulers, the issue of gold coinage still seems to have been regarded to some extent as an imperial prerogative, and the pseudo-imperial gold coins directly imitated those of the reigning Byzantine emperor of the time. The first departure from this was the coinage of Theodebert I, king of the Franks (534-48) who issued coins in his own name, although continuing to copy Byzantine designs (Grierson, Blackburn 1986, pp. 5, 111, 115-117).

Regal coinage continued throughout the Merovingian period, although it only ever made up a small proportion of the Frankish coinage. Up to *c.* 580, the majority continued to be anonymous pseudo-imperial issues. Since these directly copied Byzantine designs, most did not carry specific mint-names, although some began to show letters in the reverse field indicating the mint, continuing from late Roman practice (Grierson, Blackburn 1986, p.113).

From *c.* AD 580, although specifically regal coins continued on a small scale, pseudo-Imperial issues were largely replaced by coins of the 'mint-and-moneyer' series. As the name implies, these coins carried on one side the name of the issuing moneyer, and on the other the name of the town or city in which the moneyer was based. These coins reveal an extensive network of at least 800 mints, including every known major Frankish town or city, and many more less important ones, some of which cannot be identified today on the basis of the Latin names which appear on the coins.(2) The mint names appear with varying degrees of qualification. Some are accompanied by the word *civitas*, meaning city, and all of these can be identified as former Roman cities, which remained as major urban centres and episcopal sees under the Franks. These are typically the major mints, accounting for a significant proportion of the coinage overall, and pointing to a degree of direct continuity of authority from the Roman period, although not all of these had been Roman mints. Other names are qualified by the term *vicus*. This could indicate a town or trading centre of some importance, but without the full range of rights and functions as a *civitas*, and the term was used of major ports such as Dorestad and Quentovic. However, *vicus* could also indicate a much smaller settlement, including small towns/trading centres, districts within larger settlements, and perhaps also both secular and ecclesiastical estate centres. Other names had no qualification at all, and again probably included smaller settlements as well as towns. In addition to mint names in the inscription, pairs or groups of letters began to appear as part of the designs, e.g. MA for Marseilles (*Massilia*), CA for Chalons-sur-Sâone (*Cabilonnum*), LV for Lyons (*Lugdunum*), LEMO for Limoges (*Lemovicus*) all of which were major towns. However, these then also began to be imitated along with

(2) For catalogues with varying readings and attributions, see Prou 1892; Belfort, 1892-1895; Depeyrot 1998.

the rest of the design on coins produced by minor mints, especially the CA of Chalons-sur-Sâone.[3]

Minting thus had an urban focus, with the major mints focused in towns and cities, but with minor mints in a variety of lesser settlements. However, it is now recognised that a wide variety of sites across early medieval Europe acted as centres of production, exchange and authority, even if many of these lacked a full range of what might be considered urban functions. Some of these may be considered proto-urban or pre-urban. This is too large a subject to consider here in any detail, and has an extensive literature of its own. An influential hierarchical and chronological model of trading centres by Richard Hodges (1982) is still much cited, although with increasing qualification and dissent.[4]

Thus, while Frankish kings reserved the right to issue coins in their own names, and others were struck in the (itinerant) royal palace or by bishops and monasteries, the bulk of the coinage represents a system whereby minting authority was devolved to individual moneyers based at specified centres across the Frankish kingdoms. These centres were typically towns, or settlements with some urban characteristics. The small size of the regal coinage, the large number of mints, and the absence of any specific reservation of royal authority over minting and coinage in early Frankish law-codes (in contrast to the Visigoths and Burgundians) has led to the argument that there was little royal authority over the Merovingian coinage (Grierson, Blackburn 1986, 90-91). However, although designs varied from mint to mint, and there was also a degree of variation at any given point in both weight and metal content, coins seem to have circulated on a national basis, with broadly shared standards, rather than each town or city representing a separate currency zone, and this suggests that individual mints may not have been quite so independent.

Throughout the lifetime of the mint-and-moneyer coinage, there was a gradual decline in gold content, and gold tremisses were replaced *c.* 670 by silver deniers, or pennies. Some of these carried literate inscriptions, but many are anonymous, or carry only the moneyer's name, and can only be assigned to specific mints on the basis of continuity of design from the gold phase, or of the distribution of finds. Nevertheless, it is clear that a wide variety of types were issued from a large number of mints distributed across the Merovingian kingdoms, although the total number of mints may well have contracted, especially in the south and south-west. Since the late 7th and early 8th centuries saw the expansion of trade, and the apparent development of an increasing number of centres with some urban characteristics, there is no reason to assume that the association of minting with towns and related sites ceased during this period, even if the identity of individual mints is often unclear. The same is true of the coinage of Pepin the Short (752-68), the first king of the Carolingian dynasty. Pepin restored an inscribed coinage as part of his revitalisation of Frankish kingship and royal authority, but the mints are still often invisible, although sometimes indicated by letters, inscriptions or monograms.[5]

Coinage with explicit reference to towns was restored under Pepin's son Charles (768-814), better known as Charlemagne, who ruled first as king of the Franks before being crowned emperor in Rome in 800. In a series of reforms, he introduced a series of coin types, each of which combined the name CARLUS (REX), and sometimes also a monogram KAROLUS, with the name of the town in which the coin was minted, while the names of the moneyers disappeared. Charlemagne extended his kingdom over much of western Europe, including modern France, Belgium, the Netherlands, Switzerland, much of Germany, and northern Italy, and mint-signed coins were produced across his kingdom. After his first issue, which shows a greater degree of variation, the coins were produced to more or less standard designs across the whole kingdom, although a small number of mints had special issues towards the end of his reign with designs which in some way reflected their character. Thus the major mint of Melle in Aquitaine, which was also the source of much of the silver for the Carolingian coinage had a design of a hammer and pick, reflecting silver mining, while the northern port towns of Quentovic and Dorestad had ship designs. However, these were the exceptions, and the general pattern of standardisation reinforced the role of towns as foci for government and royal authority within the Carolingian empire. As in the earlier Merovingian coinage, many but not all of these were former Roman towns and cities, and in most cases the Carolingian mints were also known in the Merovingian mint-and-moneyer coinage, although the total number of mints was much smaller under Charlemagne than in the Merovingian period, despite the greater size of his kingdom.[6] This may reflect wider changes in the organisation of the Carolingian state, with fewer urban centres acting as foci for larger individual territories, territories which were to become the counties and duchies of the later Middle Ages. Nevertheless, the fact that many of the same mints are visible under Charlemagne as in the earlier mint-and-moneyer coinage reinforces the possibility that minting remained predominantly urban throughout the intervening period, although the mints are not mentioned on the coins during that period.

The Carolingian Empire remained united under Charlemagne's son Louis the Pious (814-840) but fragmented permanently under their successors. However, with the exception of a few issues such as the *Christiana religio* type of Louis the Pious (which combined the emperor's name and title with a statement of Christian identity), the coins of the later Carolingians indicate the names of the mints in

(3) Stahı 1976; Grierson, Blackburn 1986, pp. 117-121.

(4) For a sense of the gradual change in attitudes, see Hodges, Hobley 1988; Clarke 1998; Anderton 1999; Pestell, Ulmschneider 2003; Pestell 2011.

(5) Grierson, Blackburn 1986, pp. 138-140, 204; Depeyrot 2001, pp. 11-16; 2008, pp. 30-32.

(6) Grierson, Blackburn 1986, pp. 204-210; Depeyrot 2008, pp. 19-20, 33-38.

which they were issued, whether these were situated in the kingdoms that developed into France and Germany, or the short-lived Middle Kingdom in between, which developed into a series of semi-independent states from the Netherlands down to northern Italy. The specified mints were all towns, typically those which had been important under Charlemagne, and the overall number of mint towns was normally fairly small, although there were occasional exceptions, such as the wider network of mint-towns required by Charles the Bald following the introduction of his *Gratia D-I Rex* coinage in 864.[7] Frankish coinage, and that of the successor kingdoms of France and Germany, thus continued to provide a model of coinage with specific urban associations throughout the 9th and 10th centuries, which could be observed by other northern European neighbours.

England

The Anglo-Saxon settlement took place against the background of the decline and/or collapse of Roman authority in Britain. Opinion remains divided between those who see a decline under way in the fourth century, including a re-focus from urban to rural settlement, those who favour a dramatic change following the cessation of regular payments from the Roman authorities to Roman troops in Britain in the early fifth century, and those who favour a greater degree of continuity into the mid-fifth century or beyond. Historical sources are too scanty to provide a definitive interpretation, while archaeological interpretations are generally bedevilled by the circularity of arguments around the dating of particular types of objects and sites. With reference to this study, however, two patterns become clear. Firstly, towns and cities were largely abandoned, and did not provide a focus for the organisation of the early Anglo-Saxon kingdoms. Secondly, while there now seems to be consensus that there was some continued use of the existing coin stock into the fifth century, and while there is unambiguous evidence for continued importation of foreign coin on a limited scale throughout the fifth and sixth centuries, there is no evidence to suggest minting in the emerging Anglo-Saxon settlements and kingdoms before the end of the sixth century (Williams 2006; 2010a).

I have already alluded to an apparent link in post-Roman Europe between conversion to a Romanised form of Christianity and the introduction of minting, and the early development of the early Anglo-Saxon coinage provides a good example of this. Since almost none of this coinage carries the name of the issuing ruler, it is difficult to date coin types within the Anglo-Saxon gold series precisely, but an apparent decline in the gold content throughout this period, mirroring to some extent a more dateable decline in the Merovingian coinage, provides some evidence for dating which, together with the few legible inscriptions and the distribution of individual types, allows us to map the spread of minting across England in the seventh century and this appears (although with a danger of circular argument) to correspond broadly with the spread of Christianity, with minting beginning in Kent at the time of Augustine's mission, and spreading to the East Saxons and Deira with Mellitus and Paulinus respectively, and subsequently to the East Angles and other kingdoms, with gold coinage circulating in increasingly debased form from c. 600 to c. 675, after which a silver coinage developed in its place.[8]

This period does not seem to have seen the introduction of urbanisation in any meaningful sense, but Christianisation does seem to have created a revived focus on former Roman cities (and to some extent lesser settlements) as centres of power and administration, and it is probably primarily in this sense that the Latin word *civitas* should be understood in Anglo-Saxon texts before the ninth century. The Kentish bishopric was established at Canterbury, the East Saxon at London, the Northumbrian at York, and so on. Although Lichfield as the Mercian bishopric seems at first sight to be an exception, the first element of the name includes the name *Letocetum*, belonging to the neighbouring Roman settlement at Wall, and I have argued elsewhere that the two should be seen as effectively a single settlement within this period (Williams forthcoming c). Just as few rulers can be identified with certainty on this coinage, the lack of inscriptions on many types, and the blundered inscriptions on others, makes attributions to individual mints problematic. Only two can be identified with any certainty, although the existence of imitative types means that not all issues which apparently carry a mint name can necessarily be attributed to that mint.

By far the most common mint name to appear on the gold coinage is that of London. A rare type, which uniquely shows a bare-headed facing bust rather than a Roman or Merovingian profile bust, carries a reasonably literate reverse inscription of LONDVNIV. On account of the distinctive bust, it has been suggested that this is a royal rather than an ecclesiastical issue, and that it should be attributed to Bishop Mellitus (604-616/618).[9] The approximate dating suggested by the gold analysis supports this, although the dating is not sufficiently accurate to provide firm proof (Hook, Williams forthcoming). Various blundered reverse inscriptions, coupled with an obverse inscription AVDVARLĐ REGES (taken to refer to Eadbald of Kent, 616-40), seem to indicate a moneyer's name ending in -bald, combined with an inscription LONDENVS for London.[10] The suggestion of a London mint signature is interesting if the attribution to Eadbald is correct, since the (admittedly scanty) historical narrative of the period provided by Bede suggests that London was under East Saxon control throughout this period. Whoever was in control, however, there is no evidence to suggest that London was a commercial centre at this time, and the link between the minting of both these types and London probably reflects its symbolic

(7) Grierson, Blackburn 1986, p. 233; Depeyrot 2008, pp. 38-62.

(8) Sutherland 1948; Metcalf 1993-1994, vol. 1; Williams 2006; forthcoming c, e and f.

(9) Sutherland 1948, pp. 41-45; Gannon 2003, p. 25.

(10) Blackburn 1998a; Williams 1998; for an alternative reading of the obverse see Shaw 2008.

link with Roman authority, whether that link was now being exploited by kings or bishops or both.

A type closely related to the AVDVARLĐ REGES issue carries what is probably a Canterbury mint signature, perhaps indicating that Canterbury and London were seen as having similar roles (Blackburn 2006). Otherwise Canterbury is only known in this phase of the coinage from a rare type with the reverse inscription DOROVERNIS CIVITAS (Sutherland 1948, no. 2). This type is closely related to Merovingian mint-and-moneyer issues, but it is uncertain whether this indicates an attempt to develop a Frankish-style *civitas* at Canterbury, or simply a moneyer/die cutter (who may himself have been Frankish) copying a familiar Frankish model, since until at least the mid-seventh century, imported Merovingian tremisses seem to have remained rather more common in England than locally minted issues (Abdy, Williams 2006; Williams 2010a). Either way, the fact that most early Anglo-Saxon issues, including those that can be attributed to Kent on the basis of distribution, lacked any meaningful inscription suggests that Frankish influence at this time was relatively limited. Other types may well also have been minted in former Roman cities, but the numbers available for distribution studies are currently insufficient to provide clear evidence of individual mints rather than kingdoms. Probably the most convincing attribution is the series of related types which can be attributed with some certainty to the kingdom of Northumbria, or perhaps to its constituent kingdom of Deira. This has until recently been referred to universally as the 'York' type/group, despite the lack of a literate inscription, on the basis that early examples – possibly representing a dispersed hoard –were all found in York. However, recent finds show a broader distribution in Yorkshire and north Lincolnshire, probably reflecting the documented temporary Northumbrian dominance of the kingdom of Lindsey, and prompting a more cautious 'Northumbrian' attribution (Williams 2007b; forthcoming f). Nevertheless, given the emergence of the bishopric of York at this time, and York's later role as the sole mint north of the Humber (see below), it is likely that these coins were minted in York. Other types late in the gold series can also be attributed with some certainty to the kingdom of East Anglia, but the distribution does not permit the attribution to any particular mint (Williams forthcoming e and f).

The next phase of the coinage is particularly difficult to interpret. The early silver pennies, sometimes also referred to as sceattas, were minted in large numbers, and in a large variety of types, but again largely lack literate inscriptions, with London once again the only mint explicitly named on the coinage. In part, the variety in types reflects chronological developments across the 80 years or so that this coinage was struck, but in part it represents the fact that from the early 8th century, minting was increasingly widely distributed with a number of different regional types. Some types had comparatively limited circulation and can thus be attributed with reasonable certainty to specific regions and even in some cases to specific settlements. Others show a much broader distribution and are correspondingly difficult to attribute. This is not a period in which true urban settlements are visible either historically or archaeologically, but one which saw the emergence of a number of centres with some urban characteristics. This type of settlement, known as *wic* in Old English (from Latin *vicus*) was typically a trading emporium, with some specialised production, but without the range of non-economic functions included in Biddle's definition of towns, and observable in Frankish towns of the period. However, the *wics* probably provided the main focus for coin-based exchange, and in some cases particular types can be attributed to individual *wics* on the basis of distribution, such as the coins of series H attributed to Hamwic (Southampton).[11] Other types can be attributed to regions, some of which can be identified with named kingdoms or sub-kingdoms, but not necessarily to individual *wics*.

Furthermore, it is uncertain whether all of the coins were necessarily minted in *wics*. John Blair (2005, pp. 246-290) has argued that many sites which show evidence of production and exchange should be interpreted instead as minsters, monastic centres with the wealth to engage in trade on their own account, without the need for secular emporia. The coin designs of this period have been interpreted by Anna Gannon (2003) as representing a wide range of Christian iconography, and in the absence of literate inscriptions may well be attributable in some cases to minsters rather than *wics*, especially as the few literate Latin inscriptions, with the exception of DE LVNDONIA, appear to point to ecclesiastical associations (Naismith forthcoming). One may also note that this period also apparently saw the growth of pseudo-monasteries, which called themselves monasteries to attract the grants of lands and privileges associated with the Church, but without recognisably following a monastic rule. It is possible that such false minsters may also in some cases have been responsible for minting coins.

Matters become somewhat clearer from the mid-8th century with the emergence of literate inscriptions naming the issuing authority and the moneyer, although rarely the mint. Regal coinage can be observed in Mercia, East Anglia, Kent and Northumbria. Within Kent, minting can probably be assigned with some confidence to Canterbury since in addition to coins in the names of Kentish kings or Mercian over-kings, there are issues in the names of archbishops of Canterbury, both as sole issues and joint issues with kings. Under Offa of Mercia (757-96), Mercian authority extended over East Anglia and Kent as well as Mercia, and coins of individual moneyers can be assigned on stylistic grounds to groups relating to each of the three kingdoms. As mentioned, there is good reason to assume that Canterbury was the major, if not the only, mint in Kent. Another episcopal coinage can be linked with London, and it is generally accepted that Offa's 'Mercian' issues were all minted in London, while the East Anglian issues have been

(11) Metcalf 1993-1994, passim for the overall development, p. 321 for the attribution of Series H.

attributed to Ipswich,[12] which points to a growing link between coins and towns if these attributions are correct. In this context, one should note that archaeological evidence appears to support the development of a number of towns in the western part of Offa's kingdom of Mercia (Bassett 2007; 2008), and it has been suggested that these represent a structured network of towns which prefigures the burghal network established by Alfred the Great in Wessex a century later (see below). At the time of writing, rather more evidence would be required in other parts of Offa's kingdom to make a structured network of towns a convincing proposition, but the apparent development of towns within Offa's west Mercian heartland warn against the rigid acceptance of the current attributions to Canterbury, London and Ipswich. A concentration of finds in south-eastern Mercia, together with London's certain role as a mint both before and after make it a likely candidate for the main, if not necessarily the only, mint within Mercia itself, but finds within East Anglia are rather too widely dispersed to have confidence in Ipswich as the sole mint there. The Kentish, Mercian and East Anglian groups within Offa's coinage are recognisable groups, but these groups tell us more about die-cutting than necessarily about minting, and a greater number of mints is a possibility.

The possible disjunction between die-cutting styles and minting becomes clearer under Offa's successor Coenwulf (796-821), who also ruled Kent and East Anglia in addition to Mercia. Again, the moneyers (some of whom continued from Offa's reign) can be divided into Kentish, East Anglian and Mercian groups, although the Kentish group can now be seen to include Rochester as well as Canterbury, since mint-signed coins exist from both (Naismith 2011, pp.10-46; 2012, pp.128-132), prompting the question of whether coins may also have been minted in Rochester in the previous phase without mint signatures However, there is one coin which raises particular problems. This is a unique gold coin of Coenwulf, which bears the reverse inscription DE VICO LVNDONIAE (from the *wic* of London), but the style of both obverse and reverse designs as well as the inscriptions shows strong similarities with silver pennies assigned to Canterbury rather than London (Williams, Cowell 2009). If one thinks purely in terms of mints and moneyers, this becomes a problem: why should a Canterbury moneyer strike coins for London, when London had moneyers of its own? If we think in terms of die-cutting, however, the matter becomes simpler: a die-cutter (who could have been based anywhere) who normally supplied dies to Kentish moneyers was also commissioned to cut dies for the special gold coinage, which was to some extent a special issue, aimed at international as well as internal circulation.

The DE VICO LVNDONIAE inscription is also interesting because for the first time in the Anglo-Saxon coinage it tells us something about the relationship between town and coinage. As in the Frankish kingdoms, there are several terms which could be used to describe towns, including Latin *civitas*, *urbs* and *vicus*, and Old English *burh* and *wic* (Yorke forthcoming). These terms are not always used consistently, and different terms are in some cases used to describe the same settlement in different contexts. Broadly speaking, it would appear that *vicus/wic* was used primarily of commercial centres, whereas *civitas* implies a centre of authority and administration, *urbs* usually a defended settlement and *burh* serving as a translation of either of these, although these are not hard and fast distinctions. Although archaeologists have tended to draw a distinction at London between *Lundenwic*, a trading centre outside the Roman walls in the area of Aldwych and The Strand, and *Lundenburh*, referring only to the former Roman city (e.g. Hobley 1988), this distinction does not fit particularly well with the historical references, and it seems more likely that the term *vicus/wic* was used when describing London in a commercial context, and *civitas/burh* in other contexts. Both the design and inscription of the coin reflect the gold coin of Charlemagne from the important trading centre of Dorestad (see above), which carries the inscription VICO DVRISTAD, reflecting Dorestad's status as probably the most important of the Carolingian *wics* facing onto the North Sea. Coenwulf's decision to issue a gold coin with such a clear visual relationship to this one was probably designed to suggest that he saw both himself as the equal of Charlemagne, and London as the equal of Dorestad (Williams 2010b).

This stands in contrast to the next reference to London on a coin, a few years after Coenwulf's death. It appears as LVNDONIA CIVIT[AS] on a silver penny of Ecgberht of Wessex of c. 829, following his conquest of Mercia. Here Ecgberht, who styles himself REX M[ERCIORUM], is celebrating his assumption of authority over both Mercia and its traditional capital, so London's status as a centre of authority is stressed by the use of Civitas (Williams 2010b).

Mint names largely disappeared thereafter until the final decades of the 9th century, with a pattern across all the Anglo-Saxon kingdoms of combining the ruler's name on one side with the issuing moneyer on the other, although it appears that Northumbrian coins continued to be issued at York, and Mercian coins continued to be issued at London and, on stylistic grounds, a second mint in south-west Mercia, while West Saxon coins were apparently struck at Canterbury, London, Winchester and elsewhere, with the attribution of different groups to particular mints again primarily on stylistic grounds.[13] However, all but the West Saxon coinages were extinguished in the 860s and 870s with the conquest of Northumbria, East Anglia and part of Mercia, leaving Alfred the Great (871-99) as ruler both of Wessex (which had already expanded to included Kent and Sussex) and from c. 879-80 also of southern Mercia.

Although a small number of towns conforming to Biddle's criteria now existed in England, these were divided between areas under Anglo-Saxon and Viking control, and it was the latter part of Alfred's reign through to the late

(12) Stewart 1986; Chick 1997; Naismith 2012, pp. 128-132.

(13) Blackburn 1998b; 2003; Blackburn, Keynes 1998; Naismith 2011.

tenth century that saw a major development towards urbanisation both in Anglo-Saxon and Anglo-Viking areas. Alfred established a network of fortified towns, or *burhs*, to defend Wessex against further attacks, and this network was gradually extended by his successors as they brought Mercia, East Anglia and eventually Northumbria under West Saxon authority. In addition to their military function, these *burhs* functioned as centres for royal administration and authority, and increasingly also as centres of production and trade. These were matched by the development of Viking towns, which also combined military and economic functions, although it is less certain that these had the same sort of administrative role as the Alfredian *burhs* (Hall 2011; Williams forthcoming a and d). Like Ecgberht, Alfred celebrated his assumption of authority over both Mercia and London with a coinage which explicitly highlighted his control of London from *c.* 879-80 with the use of a monogram of LVNDONIA as the main reverse design, while another extensive coinage from *c.*880 to the end of his reign indicates his control of Canterbury, including the mint name in the inscription ÆLFRED REX DORO[VERNIS] (Blackburn 1998b; 2003). However, rare issues from late in the reign also include mint signatures for Exeter, Winchester, Gloucester and Oxford. Their rarity suggests that these issues never circulated widely, and they may have been special issues to celebrate the completion of burghal defences in each of the towns, rather than a wider burghal issue, although the Exeter and Winchester types share a common design (Archibald 1991, 287), and these were joined by a very similar issue from Bath, dating from early in the reign of Alfred's successor Edward the Elder (Lyon 2001, 75). Minting probably likewise took place in this period across a number of Anglo-Viking towns, definitely including Lincoln, York, Leicester, Norwich and 'RORIVACASTR' (possibly Rocester in Staffordshire), and perhaps others, although as in the contemporary Anglo-Saxon issues, many of the coins carry only moneyers' names rather than mint names (Williams forthcoming d).

The majority of Alfred's later coins, however, carry no mint signature on the reverse, but rather the name of the moneyer divided into two lines, and the same is true of all of Edward's coins except for the rare Bath issue already mentioned. In both cases, however, regional variations suggest that minting took place at several different centres, and given the increasing prominence of the *burhs*, it seems very likely that coins were issued from a number of different *burhs* in both reigns, although this is inferred rather than established fact.[14]

Matters become clearer in the reign of Edward's son Athelstan (924/5-39), since not only do mint names become standard on coins in the latter part of his reign, but for the first time we have explicit reference to minting in an Anglo-Saxon law code. Two types, giving Athelstan the title REX TO[TIUS] BRIT[ANNIAE] include a range of *burhs* which between them cover most of England, which was unified by Athelstan for the first time in 927. The identification of individual moneyers with specific mints can also be projected back into Athelstan's earlier types, and forms the basis for the attribution of those moneyers to the same mints in the coinage of Edward the Elder (Lyon 2001, pp. 71-72). Not only are most of the places named on the coins identified as *burhs* in written sources of the period, but the point is reinforced in many of the inscriptions by referring to many of the places as either *civitas* or *urbs* in the mint inscriptions on the coins (Blunt 1974, p. 45).

The law-code known as the Grately code was enacted somewhere in the period AD 926-30, and contains a group of six chapters on trade and commerce, including a chapter on minting. It has been suggested that this group of chapters was inserted *en bloc* from another source, and may therefore be earlier.[15] This would make sense since the chapter on minting includes a list of *burhs*, specifying the number of moneyers permitted in each, with a general catch-all of 'otherwise in the other boroughs one' (II Athelstan, 14.2). All of those mentioned by name are in the south, suggesting that this section may have been drafted before the conquest of northern Mercia and Northumbria in the latter part of Edward's reign and in the reign of Athelstan. The code also specifies that 'no one is to mint money except in a town', and goes on to specify the number of moneyers permitted in different *burhs*, where this was two or more. The term *port* or porte is used in the first reference, but burg in the second, and it is clear from the context that the two are perceived as equivalent. The linkage with burghal status is made even clearer by the insertion of a clause on the maintenance of fortifications between related sections on trade and minting (II Athelstan 12-14).

From this point onwards, there can be no doubt of a fixed relationship between minting and the Anglo-Saxon *burh*, although mint names appear inconsistently on the coins of Athelstan's immediate successors. However, a permanent and explicit relationship was established in the late Anglo-Saxon coinage, following the introduction of a national coinage towards the end of the reign of Edgar (959-75). Within this coinage, although the precise detail of design changed over successive types, the king's name and title was combined with a royal bust on the obverse, with the name of the mint and moneyer around a cross on the reverse. The named mints had a national distribution, so that nowhere in England south of the Humber was more than a day's travel from the nearest mint. Distribution was somewhat uneven, with several relatively small mints in the south-west, York as the only mint north of the Humber and Lincoln and Stamford (after a short period of experimentation in other minor mints) as the only mints in the large shire of Lincolnshire. This perhaps reflects the imposition of a basically West Saxon model over other former Anglo-Saxon kingdoms following the unification of England under the West Saxon dynasty, with *burhs* (and therefore mints)

(14) Blackburn 1996, pp. 163; 2003, pp. 207-208; Lyon 2001, pp 72-77; Williams forthcoming a.

(15) Blunt 1974, pp. 40-41; Blackburn 1996, p. 167; Lyon 2001, p. 72; Screen 2007, pp. 154-5.

less densely distributed in the Midlands and Northumbria (Williams forthcoming a).

The size of individual mints varied; from major mints such as London, York and Lincoln which each had several moneyers operating at a time, down to single-moneyer mints which only appear to have operated intermittently, subject to demand. The network developed over time, with some mints acting as short-term emergency replacements for others during Viking raids in the reign of Æthelred II (978-1016). There is also a general trend which sees a more limited network at the time of Edgar's reform growing to a peak late in the reign of Æthelred II through to the reign of Cnut and diminishing towards the end of the Anglo-Saxon period in 1066 (Allen 2012). However, the evidence may be influenced by the concentration of large hoards in Denmark and Sweden from the reigns of Æthelred II and Cnut, with fewer and smaller hoards from Edgar's reform through to the early part of Æthelred's reign, so the total body of available evidence is smaller, and minor mints are perhaps under-represented in the surviving record.

Scandinavia

Coinage was known in Scandinavia from Roman times, although even southern Scandinavia always lay beyond the borders of the Roman Empire. Especially in the late Roman period the dual need to recruit Germanic mercenaries and to avoid Germanic invasions caused an outflow of coinage from the Empire to northern Germany and Denmark, and this is reflected in both hoards and single finds, as well as in the coin-inspired pendants known as bracteates (Horsnæs 2009; 2010; Axboe 2007). However, this did not lead to the development of local currency, and there was almost a complete gap in coin use from the late 6th to the mid-8th century. Coinage was then reintroduced on a very limited scale and in a very limited area. The trading centre of Ribe on the west coast of Denmark was the eastern end of a trade route across the North Sea, which also included the *wics* of Frisia and Anglo-Saxon England. This North Sea trade resulted in the influx of some of the anonymous silver pennies (sceattas) discussed above, predominantly coins of Series E, minted in Frisia. This led in turn to the minting of a local type minted in Ribe, Series X. For a long time it was debated whether this was minted locally or in Frisia, but recent work has demonstrated beyond reasonable doubt that it was minted in Ribe, and that its use there continued up to the end of the 8th century and even into the early 9th. However, although Series X pennies are found in both England and Frisia, they did not circulate in Scandinavia beyond Ribe and the immediate hinterland (Feveile 2008). This earliest Scandinavian coinage thus relates directly to the pre-urban settlement of Ribe, although we have no idea of the identity of the local ruler responsible for its issue. The coinage also shows a direct relationship with both coinage and pre-urban trading centres around the North Sea.

The same is true of the next phase of Scandinavian coinage in the early 9th century. This saw the minting of broader, flatter pennies, of around the same diameter as Carolingian pennies, but with a weight around that of the Carolingian obol or half-penny. These were minted in two centres, with distinct, but overlapping designs, and also with distinct areas of circulation. One group was minted in and distributed around Ribe, and the main designs were based around the obverse and reverse designs of the earlier Series X. The other group was minted in and distributed around Hedeby, a trading centre on the River Schlei established by Godred, king of the Danes, in 808, following the forcible transfer of traders from the rival trading centre of Reric. The main designs here were based on Carolingian deniers, including a type with the name CARLVS and the name of the mint and trading centre of DORESTAT, and another type from Dorestad showing a ship. Both groups of coins are normally said to have begun *c.*825, and to have ceased shortly after the middle of the 9th century.[16] This coincides with a historically documented Christian mission, and would thus be consistent with the broader correlation with Christianity suggested above. However, the Carolingian prototypes were long obsolete, having been replaced by coins of the *Christiana Religio* type of Louis the Pious, which is known to have circulated in Denmark, and which would have been more appropriate for a coinage directly associated with a Christian mission (Moesgaard 2004; Coupland 2011). It therefore seems more likely that these coinages were introduced around the beginning of the 9th century. Here it is interesting to note the links with Dorestad, which by this time was emerging as one of the most important trading centres in northern Europe, so like the previous phase of coinage from Ribe, the minting of these coins is connected with an international network of urban or pre-urban trading centres, even if we do not know the religious/political background of their circulation (Williams 2010b; 2011). Both probably also connected into a wider trade network of lesser settlements in southern Scandinavia (Sindbæk 2010), but this trade was primarily driven by the use of imported coin and by bullion, and to some extent by the quasi monetary use of commodities to provide both a measure of value and a means of exchange.[17]

Both Hedeby and Ribe continued to develop into full-fledged towns, although minting seems to have ceased at both in the mid-9th century. It was, however, revived *c.* 900 in Hedeby alone, with an increasingly abstract version of the earlier Hedeby design based on a CAROLVS/DORESTAT prototype, although once again the poltical/religious background is unrecorded (Wiechmann 2007; Hilberg 2011). A larger coinage developed in Denmark during the reign of Harald Bluetooth (958-85/6). This coinage has also traditionally been linked with Hedeby, but recent studies suggest that minting may have been more widespread, with different types within the series perhaps minted in different places. By the middle of the tenth century both Hedeby and Ribe are mentioned in historical sources as both towns and Episcopal sees, along with

(16) Malmer 1966; 2007; Wiechmann 2007; Hilberg 2011.

(17) Gullbekk 2011; Skre 2011; Williams 2011.

Århus, and it is possible that some of the coin types of this phase were minted in Århus. Harald's reign also saw the development of a series of planned geometrical fortifications, known as Trelleborg forts after one of the first to be excavated. Together with Hedeby, Århus and Ribe, and a royal enclosure at Jelling in eastern Jutland, they formed a network of setttlements across the whole kingdom, and excavations suggest that they may have had a wider range of functions than purely military. This raises the possibility that they may have been intended as equivalents to the late Anglo-Saxon *burh*, in which case minting may also have taken place at these sites, although this cannot at this point be stated conclusively.[18]

The Trelleborg forts were in any case short-lived, and seem to represent a failed experiment, but it is notable that in most cases they were replaced by permanent towns in the 11th century. Minting continued in Denmark with an explicitly regal coinage in the name of Svein Forkbeard (*c.* 986-1014), copying the CRVX type of Æthelred II of England from the mid to late 990s. Minting was initially concentrated in the town of Lund (now in southern Sweden), but under Svein's son Cnut spread around a wider group of towns, named on the coins, and spread around the whole Danish kingdom (Andrén 1983). Although the Danish coinage was less regulated than that of late Anglo-Saxon England, the fact that Cnut was ruler of both kingdoms leaves little doubt that the Danish system was intended to emulate the Anglo-Saxon system (Williams 2007a, pp. 194-195).

Around the same time as Svein's Danish national coinage, similar coinages were introduced in Norway and Sweden, reflecting in all three cases the broader link with Romanised Christian kingship discussed above (Williams 2007a). In the latter case, this coincided with the establishment of a planned town under royal authority at Sigtuna in Sweden, and in the early 11th century there seems to have been tight control over both coinage and a weight-based bullion economy in Sigtuna, which remained the only real town in Sweden at this period. The coinage was substantial but comparatively short-lived, as minting was abandoned when Sweden reverted to paganism on the death of the second Christian ruler, Anund Jacob (1022-*c.*1050) (Malmer 1995). By contrast the first Norwegian coinage was on a tiny scale, and initially appears to have been more of a symbolic than an economically functional coinage. However, after a false start, a coinage became permanently established from the middle of the 11th century in the emerging town of Trondheim, and once again it is possible to observe a correlation between urbanisation, coinage and Christianisation in Norway in the late 11th and 12th centuries, although from this period it also had a clearly economic function.[19]

(18) von Hejne 2004, pp.80-81; Moesgaard 2009b; Hilberg 2011; Williams 2011; forthcoming a.

(19) Skaare 1976; Risvaag, Christophersen 2004; Williams 2007a, pp. 192-193.

Conclusion

The development of coinage in northern Europe was influenced by a variety of factors, most of which it has not been possible to discuss in any detail here. These include economic factors as well as the use of coinage as a symbolic expression of authority and of political and religious identity. This symbolic use of coinage has its origins in the late Roman Empire, and reflects identities and an approach to kingship which were directly transmitted to a number of successor kingdoms in western Europe, including the kingdom of the Franks. Continuity in the Frankish kingdom also extended to the survival of towns and, to a great extent, urban economy, and it is unsurprising that Frankish minting was focused on urban centres, although it temporarily became more widespread before returning to a more narrowly urban focus. In Anglo-Saxon England, links with Roman practice were largely broken, but never forgotten, and something akin to the Frankish system gradually developed, probably as a result of Frankish influence, and again a clear pattern of urban minting was established by the end of the Anglo-Saxon period. Scandinavia was even more remote from direct Roman influence, but Frankish and Anglo-Saxon influence in turn spread to Scandinavia, and although the emerging Scandinavian kingdoms of the late 10th and 11th centuries lacked the full structures of the Carolingian and late Anglo-Saxon states, they demonstrated the same general trends, not least of which was a firm link between towns and minting.

References

Abdy R. A., Williams G. (2006). 'A catalogue of hoards and single finds from the British Isles, *c.* AD 410-680', in Cook B. J., Williams G. (eds), *Coinage and history in the North Sea World, c. 500-1200. Essays in Honour of Marion Archibald.* Leiden-Boston, pp. 11-74.

Allen M. (2012). *Mints and Money in Medieval England.* Cambridge.

Allen M. (forthcoming). 'Mints and Money in Norman England', *Anglo-Norman Studies*, 34.

Anderton M. (1999). *Anglo-Saxon Trading Centres: Beyond the Emporia.* Glasgow.

Andrén, A. (1983). 'Städer och kungamakt – en studie i Danmarks politiska geografi fore 1230', *Scandia*, 49, pp. 31–76.

Axboe M. (2007). *Brakteatstudier.* Copenhaguen.

Bassett S. (2007). 'Divide and rule? The military infrastructure of eighth- and ninth-century Mercia', *Early Medieval Europe*, 15, pp. 53–85.

Bassett S. (2008). *The middle and late Anglo-Saxon defences of western Mercian towns (Anglo-Saxon Studies in Archae-*

ology and History, 15), pp. 180–239.

Belfort. A. de (1892-1895). *Description générale des monnaies mérovingiennes*, 5 vols. Paris.

Biddle M. (1976). 'Towns', in Wilson D. M. (ed.) *The Archaeology of Anglo-Saxon England*. Cambridge, pp. 99–150.

Bisson T. N. (1978). *Conservation of Coinage. Monetary Exploitation and its Restraint in France, Catalonia and Aragon (c. A.D. 1000-c.1225)*. Oxford.

Blackburn M. A. S. (1996). 'Mints, *burhs* and the Grately code, cap. 14.2', in Hill D., Rumble A. R. (eds), *The Defence of Wessex, The Burghal Hidage and Anglo-Saxon Fortifications*. Manchester, pp. 160-175.

Blackburn M.A.S. (1998a). 'A new coin of King Eadbald of Kent (616–40)', *Chris Rudd List*, 34, pp. 2-4.

Blackburn M. A. S. (1998b). 'The London mint in the reign of Alfred', in Blackburn M. A. S., Dumville D. N. (eds), *Kings, Currency and Alliances*. Woodbridge, pp. 105-123.

Blackburn M. A. S. (2003). 'Alfred's coinage reforms in context', in Reuter T. (ed), *Alfred the Great. Papers from the Eleventh-Centenary Conferences*. Aldershot, pp. 199-218.

Blackburn M. A. S. (2006). 'Two new types of Anglo-Saxon gold shillings', in Cook B., Williams G. (eds), *Coinage and History in the North Sea World (c. 500–1250). Essays in Honour of Marion Archibald*. Leiden-New York, pp. 127-140.

Blackburn M. A. S., Keynes S. D. (1998). 'A corpus of the Cross and Lozenge and related coinages of Alfred, Ceolwulf II and Archbishop Æthelred', in Blackburn M. A. S., Dumville D. N. (eds), *Kings, Currency and Alliances*. Woodbridge, pp. 125-151.

Blair J. (2005). *The Church in Anglo-Saxon Society*. Oxford.

Blunt C. E. (1974). 'The Coinage of Æthelstan, King of England 924–39', *British Numismatic Journal*, 42, pp. 35–160.

Chick, D. (1997) 'Towards a Chronology for Offa's Coinage: An Interim Study', in Backburn M. A. S., Naismith R. (eds), *The Coinage of Offa and his Contemporaries*. London, pp. 1-16.

Clarke H. B. (1998). 'Proto-towns and towns in Ireland and Britain', in Clarke H. B., Mhaonaigh M. Ní., Floinn R. Ó. (eds), *Ireland and Scandinavia in the Early Viking Age*. Dublin, pp. 331–380.

Coupland S. (2011). 'Raiders, Traders, Worshippers and Settlers: The Continental Perspective', in Graham-Campbell, J., Sindbæk S., Williams G. (eds), *Silver Economies, Monetisation and Society in Scandinavia AD 800-1100*. Århus, pp.113-132.

Depeyrot G. (1998). *Le numéraire mérovingien, l'âge de l'or, 4 vols (Collection Moneta 10-11, 13-14)*. Wetteren.

Depeyrot G. (2001). *Le numéraire mérovingien, l'âge du denier (Collection Moneta 22)*. Wetteren.

Depeyrot G. (2008). *Le numéraire carolingien, corpus des monnaies: Troisième édition augmentée (Collection Moneta 77)*. Wetteren.

Feveile C. (2008). 'Series X and Coin Circulation in Ribe', in Abramson T. (ed.), *Two Decades of Discovery (Studies in Early Medieval Coinage 1)*. Woodbridge, pp. 53–67.

Gannon A. (2003). *The Iconography of early Anglo-Saxon Coinage - Sixth to Eighth Centuries*. Oxford.

Grierson P. (1985). 'Domesday Book, the geld de moneta and monetagium: a forgotten minting reform', *British Numismatic Journal*, 55, pp. 84-94.

Grierson P., Blackburn M. A. S. (1986). *Medieval European Coinage 1, The Early Middle Ages, 5th–10th centuries*. Cambridge.

Gullbekk S. H. (2011). 'Norway: Commodity Money, Silver and Coins', in Graham-Campbell J., Sindbæk S., Williams G. (eds), *Silver Economies, Monetisation and Society in Scandinavia AD 800-1100*. Århus, pp. 93–112.

Hall R. A. (2011). 'Burhs and boroughs: Defended places, trade and towns. Plans defences, civic features', in Hamerow D., Hinton D. A., Crawford S. (eds), *The Oxford Handbook of Anglo-Saxon Archaeology*. Oxford, pp. 600–621.

Hilberg V. (2011). 'Silver Economies of the Ninth and Tenth Centuries AD in Hedeby', in Graham-Campbell J., Sindbæk S., Williams G. (eds), *Silver Economies, Monetisation and Society in Scandinavia AD 800-1100*. Århus, pp. 203–226.

Hobley B. (1988). 'Saxon London: Lundenwic and Lundenburh: two cities rediscovered', in Hodges R., Hobley B. (eds), *The rebirth of towns in the West, AD 700-1050 (CBA Research Report 68)*. London, pp. 69-82.

Hodges R. (1982). *Dark Age Economics: the origins of towns and trade in the West AD 600–1000*. London.

Hodges R., Hobley B. (eds) (1988). *The rebirth of towns in the West, AD 700-1050 (CBA Research Report 68)*. London.

Hook D., Williams G. (forthcoming). 'Analysis of gold content and its implications for the chronology of the early Anglo-Saxon coinage', in Gannon A. (with contributions by Archibald, M. M., Hook D., Williams G.), *Sylloge of Coins of the British Isles, 63. British Museum. Anglo-Saxon Coins. Part I. Early Anglo-Saxon Coins and Continental Silver Coins of the North Sea, c.600-760*. London.

Horsnæs H. W. (2009). 'Late Roman and Byzantine Coins found in Denmark', in Woloszyn M. (ed.), *Byzantine Coins in Central Europe between the 5th and 10th Century, Moravia Magna, Seria Polona, vol. III.* Kraków, pp. 231-70.

Horsnæs H. W. (2010). *Crossing Boundaries. An Analysis of Roman Coins in Danish contexts. Vol. 1. Finds from Sealand, Funen and Jutland.* Copenhagen.

Lyon C. S. S. (2001). 'The coinage of Edward the Elder', in Higham N. J., Hill D. H. (eds), *Edward the Elder, 899-924.* London, pp. 67-78.

Malmer B. (1966). *Nordiska mynt före år 1000 (Acta Archaeologica Lundensia. Series in 8°, 4).* Lund.

Malmer B. (1995). 'Från Olof till Anund. Ur sigtunamyntingens historia', in Jonsson K., Nordlind U., Wiséhn I. (eds), *Myntingen i Sverige, 995-1995.* Stockholm, pp. 9-26.

Malmer B. (2007). 'South Scandinavian Coinage in the Ninth Century', in Graham-Campbell J., Williams G. (eds), *Silver Economy in the Viking Age. Publications of the Institute of Archaeology University College London.* Walnut Creek, pp. 13-27.

Metcalf D. M. (1987). 'The taxation of moneyers under Edward the Confessor and in 1086', in Holt J. C. (ed.), *Domesday Studies. Papers read at the Novocentenary Conference of the Royal Historical Society and the Institute of British Geographers, Winchester, 1986.* Woodbridge, pp. 279-293.

Metcalf D. M. (1993-1994). *Thrymsas and sceattas in the Ashmolean Museum Oxford, 3 vols (Royal Numismatic Society. Special Publication).* London-Oxford.

Metcalf D. M. (1998). *An Atlas of Anglo-Saxon and Norman Coin Finds: 973-1086 (Royal Numismatic Society. Special Publication, 32).* London.

Moesgaard J. C. (2004). 'Christiana Religio', *Skalk*, 6, pp. 12-17.

Moesgaard J. C. (2009a). 'La monnaie au temps de Guillaume le Conquérant' in Lemagnen S. (ed), *La tapisserie de Bayeux, une chronique des temps Vikings.* Bayeux-Rouen, pp. 88-99.

Moesgaard J. C. (2009b). 'Harald Blåtands "Jellingemønter" cirka 975-985', *Nordisk Numismatisk Unions Medlemsblad*, 2, pp. 43-46.

Naismith R. (2011). *The Coinage of Southern England, 796-865.* London.

Naismith R. (2012). *Money and Power in Anglo-Saxon England. The Southern English Kingdoms, 757-865.* Cambridge.

Naismith R. (forthcoming). 'Money of the Saints. Church and Coinage in Early Anglo-Saxon England', in Abramson T., Williams G. (eds), *Studies in Early Medieval Coinage 3.* Woodbridge.

Pestell T. (2011). 'Markets, emporia, wics, and 'productive' sites: pre-Viking trade centres in Anglo-Saxon England', in Hamerow D., Hinton D. A., Crawford, S. (eds), *The Oxford Handbook of Anglo-Saxon Archaeology.* Oxford, pp. 556–579.

Pestell T., Ulmschneider K. (eds) (2003), *Markets in Early Medieval Europe: trading and 'productive' sites, 650–850.* Bollington.

Prou M. (1892). *Les monnaies mérovingiennes (Catalogue des monnaies françaises de la Bibliothèque Nationale).* Paris.

Risvaag J. A., Christophersen A. (2004). 'Early Medieval Coinage and Urban Development: A Norwegian Experience', in Hines J., Lane A., Redknap M. (eds), *Land, Sea and Home, Settlement in the Viking Period. (Society for Medieval Archaeology Monograph 20).* Leeds, pp.75-91.

Screen E. (2007). 'Anglo-Saxon law and numismatics: A reassessment in the light of Patrick Wormald's The making of English law', *British Numismatic Journal*, 77, pp. 150-72.

Shaw P. (2008). 'Orthographic standardisation and seventh- and eighth-century coin inscriptions', in Abramson T. (ed.), *Two Decades of Discovery. Studies in Early Medieval Coinage 1.* Woodbridge, pp. 97–112.

Sindbæk S. M. (2010). Close ties and long-range relations: the emporia network in early Viking-Age exchange, in Sheehan J., Corráin D. Ó. (eds), *The Viking Age. Ireland and the West.* Dublin, pp. 430-440.

Skaare K. (1976). *Coins and coinage in Viking-age Norway: the establishment of a national coinage in Norway in the XI century, with a survey of the preceding currency history.* Oslo.

Skre D. (2011) 'Commodity Money, Silver and Coinage in Scandinavia', in Graham-Campbell J., Sindbæk S., Williams G. (eds), *Silver Economies, Monetisation and Society in Scandinavia AD 800-1100.* Århus, pp. 67–92.

Stahl A. (1976). 'The Merovingian CA coinage of Austrasia', *Museum Notes*, 21, pp. 129-151.

Stewart I. (1986). 'The London mint and the coinage of Offa', in Blackburn M. A. S. (ed.), *Anglo-Saxon Monetary History. Essays in Memory of Michael Dolley.* Leicester, pp. 27–43.

Sutherland C. H. V. (1948). *Anglo-Saxon Gold Coinage in the Light of the Crondall Hoard.* Oxford.

Von Hejne C. (2004). *Särpräglat. Vikingatida och medeltida myntfynd från Danmark, Skåne, Halland och Blekinge (ca 800-1130) (Stockholm Studies in Archaeology 31)*. Stockholm.

Wiechmann R. (2007). 'Hedeby and its Hinterland: A Local Numismatic Region', in Graham-Campbell J., Williams G. (eds), *Silver Economy in the Viking Age*. Walnut Springs, pp. 29-48.

Williams G. (1998). 'The gold coinage of Eadbald, king of Kent, AD 616-40', *British Numismatic Journal*, 68, pp. 137-140.

Williams G. (2006). 'Monetary circulation in England in the Age of Conversion, c. AD 580-680', in Cook B. J., Williams G. (eds), *Coinage and history in the North Sea World, c. 500-1200. Essays in Honour of Marion Archibald*. Leiden-Boston, pp. 145-192.

Williams G. (2007a). 'Kingship, Christianity and Coinage: Monetary and political perspectives on silver economy in the Viking Age', in Graham-Campbell J., Williams G. (eds), *Silver Economy in the Viking Age*. Walnut Springs, pp. 177-214.

Williams G. (2007b). 'The Gold Coinage of Seventh-Century Northumbria Revisited', *Numismatic Circular*, 115/1, pp. 6-8.

Williams G. (2010a). 'Anglo-Saxon Gold Coinage: Part 1. The Transition from Roman to Anglo-Saxon Coinage', *British Numismatic Journal*, 80, pp. 50-74.

Williams G. (2010b). 'The Influence of Dorestad Coinage on Coin Design in England and Scandinavia', in Willemsen A., Kik H. (eds), *Dorestad in an international Framework. New Research into Trade Centres in Carolingian Times*. Turnhout, pp. 105-111.

Williams G. (2011). 'Silver Economies, Monetisation and Society: an Overview', in Graham-Campbell J., Sindbæk S., Williams G. (eds), *Silver Economies, Monetisation and Society in Scandinavia AD 800-1100*. Århus, pp. 337-372.

Williams G. (forthcoming a). 'Civil defence or royal powerbase? Military and non-military functions of the late Anglo-Saxon burh', in Baker J., Brookes S., Parsons D., Reynolds A. (eds), *Landscapes of Defence in the Viking Age: Anglo-Saxon England and comparative perspectives*. Turnhout.

Williams G. (forthcoming b). 'Hack-silver and precious metal economies: a view from the Viking Age' in Hunter F., Painter K. (eds), *The Traprain Law Hoard (Society of Antiquaries of Scotland Monograph Series)*.

Williams G. (forthcoming c). 'Why were there no coins in the Staffordshire hoard?', in Abramson T., Williams G. (eds), *Studies in Early Medieval Coinage, 3*. Woodbridge.

Williams G. (forthcoming d). 'Towns in the Danelaw: cultural, regional and political identities', in Hadley D. M., Ten Harkel L. (eds), *Everyday Life in Viking Towns: Social Approaches to Viking Age Towns in Ireland and England c. 850-1100*. Oxford.

Williams G. (forthcoming e). 'The circulation, minting and use of coins', in Bates D., Liddiard R., Marten L. (ed), *East Anglia, c. AD 580–675', East Anglia and Its North Sea World*. Woodbridge.

Williams G. (forthcoming f). 'Anglo-Saxon Gold Coinage. Part 2: Corpus, chronology and attribution of Anglo-Saxon gold coinage', *British Numismatic Journal*, 83.

Williams G., Cowell M. R. (2009). 'Analysis of a gold mancus of Coenwulf of Mercia (AD 796-821) and other comparable material in the BM collection', *British Museum Technical Research Bulletin*, 3, pp. 31-36.

Yorke B. (forthcoming). 'West Saxon fortifications in the ninth century: The perspective from the written sources', in Baker J., Brookes S., Parsons D., Reynolds A. (eds), *Landscapes of Defence in the Viking Age: Anglo-Saxon England and comparative perspectives*. Turnhout.

www.ingramcontent.com/pod-product-compliance
Lightning Source LLC
LaVergne TN
LVHW071213210926
848482LV00015B/798